The Adventures of the REAL Tom Sawyer

A Memoir

The Story of a Very Fortunate Life

By
Tom Sawyer
**Novelist, Playwright, Illustrator,
Screenwriter, Filmmaker,
Head Writer/Showrunner
of *Murder, She Wrote***

BearManor
Media

Albany, Georgia

Published in the USA by
BearManor Media
P.O. Box 71426
Albany, GA 31708
www.BearManorMedia.com

Hardcover Edition
ISBN-10: 1-62933-105-8
ISBN-13: 978-1-62933-105-8

Printed in the United States of America

With Love and Gratitude
to my wonderful children,
grandchildren, my truly remarkable friends,
and to my incredible Holly who, displaying her
customary brilliance, came up with the title
for this memoir (mine wasn't even close).

Table of Contents

ONE
A Day in TV Land

"Look, Tom, we really do appreciate what you've done this season – and – well – we're counting on you to be a team player."

Suppressing my rage for the moment, I smiled and managed a barely convincing: "I – I certainly want to be..."

Peter nodded and, with David, exited my office and closed the door. It required a *major* effort for me to contain it for that long.

Team fucking player? I'd <u>saved</u> their goddam series – and I'm supposed to take a pay-cut?

I lunged at my phone and dialed my agent, Barry Perelman. Before he finished his hello, my words – mostly invective – spewed, as I described what had just taken place: I had been visited by Angela Lansbury's husband/ manager, elegant Brit Peter Shaw and his son/assistant, David. We were coming up on contract renewal time – in this case, the end of Season 8 of the top-ten hit CBS TV series, *Murder, She Wrote*.

With the show in dire ratings-trouble several weeks into that year's run, and amid large-scale angst, I had been hired as Showrunner/Head Writer. My assignment: rescue the series.

I did. For the upcoming season Barry had requested for me a substantial – and *much* deserved – pay-bump.

In effect, they had just delivered their response – to my face. Their argument: belt-tightening. Everyone, Peter assured me, was taking a cut. The rumored reason: Angela would be getting a budget-straining three hundred K raise, per episode. Not unjustified, given her popularity and status.

But at *my* expense? No way, thankyouverymuch.

When I finished my rant, Barry finally spoke: "Tommy, look – I gave it my best shot – but they absolutely won't budge... I – I've gotta say, I think you should take it. I mean – we're still talking high six-figures..."

I didn't need the reminder. He waited for me to speak.

When I did not, he added: "So...?" Another count or two before I spoke: "I'll call you." I rang off and sat back, trying to clear my head, to calm my churning anger to a level that would permit me to think rationally – if not objectively. To try reviewing what had happened – and my options, if any.

I had begun writing for *Murder, She Wrote* before it went on the air, in 1984. I *had* been busy indeed over its initial seven seasons. In addition to selling and writing series pilots and films, I had written and produced other series. I had been Showrunner for the Jerry Orbach-starring *MSW* spinoff, *The Law & Harry McGraw*. That one, regrettably, lasted only one season. But during much of that time I'd been primarily involved with *Murder, She Wrote*, contributing to its style as, on-and-off the staff, I wrote more than a dozen episodes for the series.

Essentially, along with a *very* few other writers, I *knew* the show.

Then, before the beginning of Season 8, Angela Lansbury became Executive Producer, replacing series creator Peter S. Fischer, who had decided to exit the show. She also replaced his staff with, among others, her brother, experienced series Writer/Producer Bruce Lansbury, her husband and his son. Further, out of a certain level of accumulated pique toward Fischer, she no longer wished to use *any* of the four or five key writers who had created most of the scripts for the preceding 154 episodes. Including me.

Which, because I continued to have more work than I could handle, was not a problem for me. Moreover, having been an intimate part of the scene, working with the talented but often irritatingly autocratic Fischer, I quite understood where she was coming from.

The problem for Angela and the series, however, became evident within the first installments of Season 8. The writers she and her family hired, while experienced, respected professionals, had not a clue about how to write for this rather singular show.

Thus, ignoring the "cozy," no-action-and-no-violence flavor expected by its audience, these guys were writing car-chases and men running around in jumpsuits and ski-masks, engaged in automatic-weapons shootouts. The result: hundreds of thousands of viewers were turned off. That in turn was discouraging advertisers. Bigtime. Understandably, CBS and Universal Studios, both of which had been very hands-off for the previous years, went into panic-mode.

Out of their desperation, and the fact that I was the only available writer from the old regime, they asked me to come on board.

Flattered by their confidence-vote, I happily signed on. Within a few weeks I had turned things around, restoring the show's traditional qualities – and its audience.

Sitting there, finishing my mental review, I reached a decision. To do a bit of dice-rolling – instead of angrily blowing them off, which I *really* wanted to do.

Before thinking it through again – and possibly reconsidering – I rose from my desk, inhaled deeply, and quickly left my office. I walked the few yards down the corridor of Universal Studios' Producer's Building, to Peter Shaw's suite. Entering, I nodded at his secretary and crossed to his open office door. Inside, I saw that he and David were talking. I knocked. They welcomed me expectantly.

With a pleasant face, I went into my number: "Listen, guys, I've been thinking about what you said, and – well, I know you're being straight, that if you had the money, you'd pay what my agent's asking…" I paused, punching up my sincerity. "But – you don't, so…" In fact, despite being more massively pissed off than I could remember, I meant what I said next: "…I just want you and Angie to know how honored I've been to work with her, and I truly wish you – and her – and the show – years and years of continuing success."

I shook their hands. Neither Peter nor David spoke. Sneakily, I hoped I understood why.

I solemnly exited their office, and returned to mine. I closed the door and sat at my desk, reflecting with some surprise, actually, on my calmness, my non-angst.

Less than three minutes later, my assistant, Janice, spoke on the intercom: "It's Barry, on line one."

I reached for the phone, raised it to my ear. "Yeah…?"

My agent's words instantly burned into my memory: "Tommy, what the *fuck* did you say to them?"

"They---?"

"Yep. They *caved*! Everything we asked for."

I smiled. Beamed really, as I explained to Barry: the gamble had been – *would* they be astute enough to face up to the obvious (to me, anyway) reality that they could *not* do the show without me?

It was, and remains, one of *the* most satisfying moments in my life. Especially, the Hollywood part.

A life *filled* with satisfactions.

And yeah, some struggle…

Oh – and of course there was something key that I did *not* admit to Peter, David, Barry, or *any*one except my amazing mate, Holly, and a few very close friends. The work I was doing was such *total, flat-out <u>fun</u>* that I would have paid *them* for the privilege.

TWO
Destiny

You're fourteen years-old, male, skinny, horny, and you're in your swim-trunks, standing thigh-deep in the Beverly Hills backyard swimming pool of major movie star William Powell.

You are trying, not very successfully, to maintain your composure. Because what you're staring at, a few feet away, are his gorgeous, sexy wife's bare, very serious Hollywood tits.

You're an only-child, middle-class, and for the last seven years you've spent most of your Saturday and Sunday afternoons sitting in movie theaters. There, your life and values were being shaped in ways you could not then imagine, by Hollywood's largely Jewish Moguls in their attempt to portray – create, really – the W.A.S.P.y America of their fantasies. Though you've glimpsed a few nude photos of women, they were, along with profanity and "dirty" language, *never* a part of the prudishly-censored films of that era. Nor had you ever encountered nudity in real-life – until that afternoon.

You live with parents Ed and Dorothy in Chicago, where you have twenty-four first cousins. One on your father's side, and the rest, products of your mother's eight siblings.

All of them, as well as your eighteen aunts and uncles, are (forgive the pun) relatively conventional.

Read: in your then barely teenaged eyes, massively uninteresting-to-boring.

Except for one cousin. And her father.

Uncle Milt's an affable ne'er-do-well who seems to enjoy life more than any of his straight arrow, white-collar siblings. Or your necktied, go-to-an-office-every-day Dad.

Way more. Milt drinks, laughs, and spends a lot of time at racetracks and – in what passes for a "job" – he manages his daughter's career.

The daughter – *she's* your icon. A singer/dancer/actress. A movie star. B-pictures, but a star. Oaters mostly, for Republic and Monogram, but a few first-rate comedies as well. Formerly Ruthie Mae McMahon from Benton Harbor, Michigan, Ruth Terry is talented, beautiful, glamorous, sexy, witty, and your only human connection with the gods and goddesses up there on the screen – with Hollywood.

That summer, your parents have brought you west to visit Tinseltown – and Ruthie.

It's your first day out there, and you eagerly say yes when Ruth asks if you'd care to go swimming, figuring wow, *not* crummy old Lake Michigan. The Pacific Ocean at *last*.

But instead, minutes later Ruthie had pulled her Cadillac into a residential driveway a few blocks from her home and announced that we'd arrived at our destination. Through the adjacent hedge, a swimming pool was visible. Your disappointment was brief, vanishing entirely when, as you climbed out of her car, she explained whose pool it was.

After changing in the pool house, and swimming a few laps, you're now standing in the shallow end.

Seated a few feet away, chatting with your cousin at the patio table, is her best-friend from Benton Harbor, Powell's wife. You're staring because Ms. Powell's halter-top has just accidentally fallen to her waist, displaying the aforementioned movie actress tits.

But – unlike what you'd expect, she – Diana Lewis, AKA Mousie Powell – *doesn't* frantically try to cover them up!

Instead, she performs an act of so-total Cool that – even all these decades later – it continues to represent for me the *essence* of hip sophistication, one that – were it onscreen – could *not* have been more effectively written or directed.

She sooo casually glances downward at her bare breasts, follows it with a smile at you, presumably amused by the incident and by your predictable reaction. Then, she nonchalantly resumes her conversation with Ruthie as, a perfectly-timed moment later, she unhurriedly hikes-up her top.

Not a bad Day One.

On the second day, you're taken to a soundstage at Warner Brothers where, between takes of the movie they're shooting, you *meet* and shake hands with – actually *touch* – major bigtime film stars Errol Flynn and Ann Sheridan! Both of whom seem, and still do in your memory, about eleven feet tall.

While those incidents could hardly be topped, the following evening comes damned close.

Your mother's cousin, Mary King Patterson, invites you, your parents, Ruthie and her Mom and Dad to dinner at the Bel Air Hotel. Mary happens to be in town from her home in New York., where her husband is Publisher/ Owner/Editor-in-Chief of the huge-circulation tabloid Daily News.

You've just been seated when Mary looks up from her menu. A man and woman have entered the room. The gentleman, dapper, dark-haired, pencil-mustached, in a perfectly-tailored double-breasted blazer. On his arm, a drop-dead gorgeous blonde.

Mary waves to him: "Oh, Howard – won't you join us?" As the couple approaches, even you recognize the man you're about to meet.

Howard Hughes.

After that trip to California, for the rest of your life, you are *never* the same.

It isn't that you died and went to heaven. It's better.

Your fate, though you won't come to realize it for another twenty-some years, has been decided.

You *will* end up in Hollywood.

But first…

THREE
The Adventure Begins

I EMERGED FROM GRAND CENTRAL STATION, and suddenly, magically, *all* of the invisible baggage I'd schlepped from my hometown was trumped. Standing there on 42nd Street, I literally inhaled the excitement, the mid-morning energy of the place, the *thrill* of being there.

Manhattan!

The place that – since my first visit at age eight – I had *known* – with *absolute* certainty – I truly *belonged*. From that moment, it had represented for me *Escape*!

From Chicago.

From my parents. From my childhood.

I was barely twenty years-old. By then I'd learned that New York City was also the *Gateway*. To the career on which I'd been focused for years. Then the *only* place where I could "break-in," practice it and hope to succeed. Symbolic of my liberation, still clutched in my fist were the few dollars of just-refunded money from the return-half of the round-trip ticket my mother had insisted I purchase, despite my insistence that I intended to stay in New York, no matter what.

Her demand, I see now, might well have been that it afforded a reduced fare compared to buying two one-way tickets. But being who I was then, I chose to read it as representative of my parents' expectation that I would fail. Yet another no-confidence vote.

Thus, cashing in that ticket was a definite nose-thumber. There was *no* goddam way I was going back. Not until I could do it *my* way, on *my* terms. *Showing* them that they were *wrong*.

It would take far longer to rid myself of guilt about once again disappointing/pissing-off my father. To prove to him – *and* to myself, actually – that I wouldn't turn out to be – as he feared, and had made *very* clear to me – a loser.

Nobody told me back then that, given my German-and-Polish Jew/Irish Catholic background, Guilt-with-a-capital-G was an integral part of my genetics. But hey, knowing it probably wouldn't have helped. To say that I was hauling other baggage does not come close.

I was born Thomas Benjamin Scheuer, named Tom because my father's last name, when pronounced properly (Shawyer), sounded like Sawyer. Benjamin was the first name of my already deceased grandfather. For years, upon verbal mention of my name, I heard endlessly-repeated jokes: "How's Becky?" – "Where's Huck?" – "Painted any fences lately?" and so on. But when read aloud, it was nearly always mispronounced, in variations from "Shoo-er" to "Sheener" to "Sheever" and more. Tedious. By the time I'd reached my teens I resolved to someday change it.

Moreover, I was a misfit – a pain-in-the-ass. Bored by school almost from the get-go, from fifth-grade onward I was essentially a dropout. Uninterested in, and unchallenged by what they were teaching.

What *did* fascinate and test me was drawing.

That had grabbed me when I was first able to hold a pencil. Even before kindergarten – I had become hooked by newspaper comic strips. Particularly those, numerous at that moment, that were realistically drawn. Not yet into the TV Era, newspapers all over America featured syndicated comic strips. The non-cartoon, more literal of them were known as "story-strips." The better of these, via interesting characters and believable dialogue, told ongoing dramas in serial form, cinematically illustrated, with a new installment every day. Their purpose: to sell newspapers; each of these brief chapters, consisting of three or four panels, ended in a suspenseful punchline designed to hopefully leave the reader no choice but to buy tomorrow's edition in order to find out what would happen next. I eagerly listened and followed the pictures as my mother or my father read them aloud for me.

Further, as soon as I learned to read and write, I was excitedly composing dialogue for the figures I drew, lettering it in comic strip-style balloons over their heads. This then-common form had so consumed me that I had almost no interest in painting, or working in any medium other than black & white line-drawing.

To my parents' great credit, during those early times they generously indulged and encouraged me. At age seven they enrolled me in Saturday classes at the Art Institute of Chicago.

That experience, incidentally, provided me with one of the earliest clues in my own journey to self-knowledge: in what would become a familiar pattern in my regular schooling, I was already too advanced for the curriculum – and thus bored. I gave up on the Art Institute class after a few weeks.

By age twelve, I was fixated on my goal: to become the next Milton Caniff.

Caniff was my hero, a writer/illustrator who drew and wrote my runaway favorite realistic strip: *Terry and the Pirates.*

My mother and father stepped in, and I began attending Saturday morning cartooning classes at the Chicago Academy of Fine Art. These proved to be excellent, taught by Martin Garrity, a charming guy who drew gag-cartoons for *The Saturday Evening Post* and other major national magazines. Though Garrity was able to successfully operate out of Chicago, he made it clear from the start to those of us with comic-strip ambitions that we would eventually need to relocate to New York City.

This had been reconfirmed during my more recent full-time stint at CAFA. New York was where aspiring comic-strip artists, or those who wished to become magazine or advertising illustrators, *had* to go. Because that was *the* marketplace. Book and magazine publishing, newspaper syndicates, advertising agencies – Manhattan was home to *all* of them. Everyplace else was Out-of-Town. Moreover, we were told, entry to the commercial art World was via freelance illustrating of the many comic-books being published, *all* of them headquartered there. All, incidentally, then priced at ten cents. That I regarded the artwork in most of the comic-books as mediocre made that path feel even more accessible.

Sure, if you were Norman Rockwell you might not have to make such a move. But the rest of us…

Additionally, as mentioned, I *relished* the prospect. A few weeks before heading for Manhattan, with the advice of my instructors at CAFA, I eagerly prepared what I hoped would be appropriate samples of my drawing skills.

Though not voiced by either parent on the occasion of my departure, their doubts about my possible success were implicit, drummed repeatedly over the years. From admonitions about bad school-grades, to my attitude, to the most frequent – and indelible: "Tommy, you're *not* living up to your potential."

Excessive, but not, from their frustrated perspective, unwarranted. Grade-wise, I finished 425th in my high school class of almost 500. Then, despite my poor academic scores, my father borrowed on the clout of a business acquaintance, a Purdue University alumnus-and-former-football star, and managed to somehow finagle for himself and me an on-campus audience with the then-President of Purdue, Frederick L. Hovde. Eliciting my solemn – though hardly enthusiastic – promise that I would "apply" myself, Mr. Hovde granted me admission as a freshman in their Engineering School.

An area of study for which had zero interest and about the same level of talent.

I dropped out after a desultory year and one half, likely about ten minutes before I would have been thrown out; I'd received failing grades in all but 3 of the final 22 credit-hours for which I was enrolled. Those were tech-courses. My single passing grade, a B+ in *Essays – From Montaigne to Goldsmith.*

That disappointment to my parents I then compounded by quitting art school less than halfway through the two-year course in which they had grudgingly enrolled me, conditional on my promise to complete it.

They were quite understandably fed up. But so was I, knowing that I was way ready to get started with the life I'd chosen.

Sadly, the years of conflict between us resulted in my despising both of them. Reflecting, having fathered four relatively problem-free children, I have no trouble imagining what a difficult son I was to my parents.

I'm sure they "meant well." In many ways, their actions had proven it – not least indulging me in art schooling. But overall, the effect on my feelings toward them was negative.

The good news about all that – instead of defeating me, it made me tougher. More rebellious.

Before departing Chicago I had been less than direct with my fiancé, Leona. The "plan:" she would continue her art school studies, joining me once I got settled in New York. I estimated that that might take six months or longer. Our parting was hardly dramatic. Or emotional. In fact, with the exception of a few laughs, the same was mostly true of our entire time together.

My initial attraction to Lee had been largely nostalgic. Physically, she resembled my high school steady, Naomi, who was two years younger than me. That relationship had begun to dissolve when, in my senior year in high school, her father moved his family to a distant, upscale western suburb of Chicago. Saddening for me, it ended completely when I went off to Purdue.

15

While Lee and I did have some fun times together, and shared dreams of "making it" as artists, true passion for each other was never part of it. I now realize that my becoming engaged to Lee had resulted from a combination of my going along with her needs and, undoubtedly, some of my own.

Moreover, in the Midwest of that time, young couples did *not* live together. They got married. Essentially, we were subscribers to what we later referred to as "*The Andy Hardy School of Romance.*" It was an ethos laid out – and hammered repeatedly – in films of that era, particularly in a series of MGM movies. These, built around the above-referenced Mogul-inspired moralistic fantasies of a White-Bread America, starred Mickey Rooney. Their essential message: if you held a girl's hand you were obligated to take care of her for the rest of your lives.

Thus left unsaid along with so much else on the eve of my journey to New York was my hope that time and distance would effectively dissolve our far-from-deep relationship.

Now, on that exhilarating first morning in Manhattan, I knew there would be a lot more shit for me to get past. But *all* of that was for the moment entirely drowned by the sheer *freedom* I felt. The *tingle* at the back of my neck as I melded into the crowd of self-involved, rapid walkers and honking drivers at the bottom of that incredible Midtown canyon. As I began absorbing their energy – the thrill of it still resonates for me.

I was *finally* On My Way.

To adventures – and *pleasures* – and a level of near-magical good luck – I could *never* have imagined.

FOUR
Acquiring My Suit
of Armor

It was a true Life-Changer.

I have come to regard it as one of the *single* most important moments in my experience. Painful it was. For a few *very* final-seeming minutes.

First, a bit more context.

By age eight, I had begun to sense that few of my contemporaries were ever looking at the page I was seeing.

Similarly, I was already realizing that the same was true of most of my adult relatives, and my parents' grownup friends. I remember, at family dinners, their conversations mostly boring the hell out of me. Thus my consciously, sometimes mischievously manipulating their conversation-topics to areas more interesting to me.

I was also becoming aware that in order to survive in that little world, I frequently had no choice but to dumb myself down. Additionally, that aspect of my misfit-ness awakened even then the realization that I was different. Lonely. Thankfully, as an adult I would find that there were many others like me – people with whom I *could* have stimulating, challenging conversations.

Further, by age eleven, I was already being paid for my drawings. Some were poster-advertisements for neighborhood Southside shopkeepers who placed them in their windows. My gag cartoons were being published in a Baking Industry trade magazine – work I obtained through an introduction by one of my father's friends. For each of those drawings I earned five dollars. I earned additional "spending money" by hanging around outside the local grocery store with my pull-wagon, hauling bags of groceries for local housewives. Later, during high school, I clerked part-time in a phonograph record store.

But my scholastic problems continued. Intensified, really. Judged to be a "disruptive influence" by my eighth grade teacher, Ms. Horrigan, for my final half-year of elementary school she did not allow me to enter her classroom. Instead, I was exiled to a bench at the end of the school's long, broad, empty top-floor corridor, where the classroom work was delivered to me – and my assignments picked up – by a delegated fellow-student.

In truth it was definitely preferable to listening to our teacher. In retrospect, I still find it incredible that she *kept* that name. Ms. – as she was almost inevitably, laughably known to us – "Whore-again."

Except for my social-life, my high school years were a continuation of the mostly dismal blur of boredom, alleviated slightly by one or two classes I found interesting – one of them: Print Shop. Plus, continuing pursuit of my drawing skills. That was highlighted by writing and illustrating, for the school's weekly newspaper, a *Tom Sawyer*-ish comic strip, titled *Rusty Riley*.

Those times were also brightened by my personal, non-school-approved reading: immersion in the likes of Steinbeck, O'Hara, Fitzgerald, Hammett, Chandler, Hemingway, Twain, Conan Doyle, Sandburg and others. These, in contrast to the curriculum-dictated study of such pathetically inept crap as *Silas Marner*.

Among my few memories of that period: my – way more than once – looking around at my classmates and wondering if I was the only one who *got* whatever the actual "it" of the moment happened to be.

But for my father, my scholastic shortcomings were only part of the problem. There were my overall "attitudes." More currently, these would be referred to as "issues."

Which I acted out on often, via what he regarded as my social gaffes. Some were cases of "bad manners." Stuff he and my mother took *very* seriously. In truth, it was via some of these admonitions that I did learn a lot of necessary social-behavior conventions.

Anyway, berating me about them from as far back as I can recall, as I got older, I found his lectures more and more tedious, essentially tuning him out.

Then, when I was not quite sixteen, came the afternoon that I shall *always* remember. The one I tried-to-but-couldn't ignore.

That defining, nothing-would-ever-be-the-same-from-then-on incident.

The one in which he finally "got through to me." As you will see, I mean "finally" in two ways.

I have zero memory of the offense for which my father was ripping me a new one that day. Though probably it involved my being thrown out of school again for some version of my by-then routine contempt for authority and rules. Likely further complicated by yet another of my typical, generic violations of his and my mother's "civilized-behavior" code. In any case, judged from his level of anger and frustration, it was – in his mind anyway – at least an eight or nine.

I'm certain that I am hardly the only person who, when special experiences are recalled, can *see* the whole scene in detail, all the way to the smells, the light in the room. Even in situations from that far back. Other than a few of my father's words, my recollections are mostly visual.

The afternoon sunlight, filtered through the slatted Venetian blinds of my bedroom, reflected off the opposite yellow-brick façade of the courtyard-style three-story apartment building in which we lived. We stood, my father's face maybe sixteen inches from mine, my back to the nearby row of closet-doors. My bunk-bed behind him. My drawing table under the window to my right. To its left, my desk. Overhead, his particular decorative touch: the shiny brass nautical lantern suspended from the ceiling by a length of thick ship's-rope.

Most of his rant, delivered as usual without even a hint of empathy – only with disgust – was typical and unmemorable.

But for a sentence or two. A bottom-line warning, really, which I had not heard before: "…Son, if you continue to behave this way, you are going to have *no* friends. I mean *nobody* will want to have a goddam thing to do with you!"

In other words, I would become a total outcast, a person so antisocial, so loathsome, that – well...

I had looked him in the eye for the whole time, stifling one or two reflexive/contemptuous laugh-urges, listening-but-not-listening to stuff I'd heard before.

But this *was* new. Its effect was startling.

Atypically, his statement was *getting* to me.

For some reason that I have never understood, I was in that instant truly vulnerable.

Try as I did to as usual let his words sort of breeze past me, those quoted above were – unexpectedly – *really* bringing me down.

This blunt, freshly-for-him phrased accusation that I was *so* fucked socially that *nobody* could like me.

He glared at me for a few sink-in moments. Then, with *very* obvious contempt, he turned and strode out of the room.

Seconds later, I heard the front door slam shut. I was alone in the apartment. I remained where I'd stood when he departed. Then, slowly, I moved toward my drawing table, confused, trying to sort out my thoughts. I slumped into my chair and, as minutes passed, I felt lower and lower, more and more devastated. More than I *ever* had before.

I leaned forward, arms and head on the table.

I *knew* that my father was right.

Worthless. Completely, *irrevocably* worthless. I was a piece of shit that nobody could possibly like or want to be with.

Nobody.

My spirits hit a depth that I'd never before come close to experiencing. Nor have I since.

For the first – and what would be the *only* – time in my life, I thought about ending it.

I mean, what the hell? I was unredeemable on such a level that there was just about *no* point in going on. I briefly considered methods. The big bottle of aspirin in the bathroom? My mother's kitchen knives…? No, the aspirin would probably…

Then – an image. A face – and a name…

John O'Gara.

My closest buddy.

John liked me.

And – and wait a minute – so did my other best-friend, Milton Danner.

And Billy Bridge.

They were my *friends*. Had been since early grade school.

I began to think about others. Merle Rosenberg, Diane Goodrich, Norman Kaye, Myra Dreyfus, Teddy Chanock, Myron Wolens, June Daly…

I slowly raised my head, my eyes still turned inward.

They *all* liked me. Or at least accepted me. They did not – *any* of them – *ever* show or say *any*thing that indicated they regarded me as a terrible person.

I mean – okay – so I wasn't "perfect."

So what…?

My world began to – to brighten a little. A weight – an almost palpable mass – started to lift. I sat upright. Looking at – nothing. Then…

I *decided.*

Though I could not have known, it would turn out to be one of *the* most significant, far-reaching choices of my entire life.

Because in that moment, I resolved that I would never, *never* again permit *any*one to get to me as my father had.

Not him, not 'them.' No matter who 'they' might turn out to be.

No one.

Ever.

From that afternoon onward, I was not the same person. I knew – *knew* – from then on, with not a smidgen of doubt – that my father, *and* his values, were *totally*, irredeemably full of shit. I regarded him, and them, that way for the rest of his life.

I do not remember anything of that evening, after my parents returned. But next morning, walking the corridors of my high school, I carried myself differently – as I never had before. I regarded *every*one I passed – the hundreds with whom I didn't have a personal bond – with "hard eyes" and body-language to match. A look, a demeanor that *dared* them to diss me, to criticize or reject me.

A kind of in-advance, just in case, unspoken "Fuck you!"

I recall that at first it was as if, not unlike a new garment, I was trying it on.

It turned out to be an excellent fit, needing very little alteration.

Did my armor-plate have a downside? Almost none.

Oh, some years later I discovered one: the statement that my attitude put forth to others: "I am totally self-sufficient. I don't need you." That would not always work to my benefit, in that there have been a few times when I'd have appreciated some unasked-for offers of help.

Fortunately, such needs have been minimal.

Another that might have been a truly destructive aspect – had I not eventually learned to understand and overcome it – was that it delayed my development as an artist: for years it resulted in denial of much of that most essential part of any creative person, my *own* emotions. To the point of blocking my awareness of what I was *feeling*. Though my ongoing resentments toward my parents continued, a number of my other relationships suffered. I had become, like so many of my contemporaries, too damned civilized for my own good.

This by the way, in my years of teaching writing, is a phenomenon I've encountered repeatedly among students. For the older ones especially, it is reflected in their arm's-length approach to their characters' feelings. A result of the "boys don't cry"/"don't show anger toward a parent or sibling" credos and, reaching adulthood, years of having swallowed such normal responses in order to "get along." Until it has become a way of life. All of which runs 100% counter to the *need*, in drama or comedy, to keep the audience entertained by having our characters in constant conflict. The very reason people are drawn to such entertainments: to enjoy – vicariously – other people actually acting out on their emotions.

Happily, with the help of a wonderful shrink, I eventually got past that.

All else about those moments following my father's exit that afternoon has been and continues to be a singular *major* mitzvah.

In the bargain, another *so valuable* lesson not fully comprehended by me for a long time: he had cured me forever of *any* level of automatic respect for authority-figures. They've had to earn it.

Few have done so.

But *most* importantly, and it would be decades before I came to fully understand and appreciate it, and a few years before I even knew, their endless criticism had inadvertently given me a truly *great* gift: a *Bulletproof Ego*.

Without any of us realizing it, they had made me *invulnerable to rejection*.

If you're looking for irony, it's damned near impossible to top that.

FIVE
Some Self-Discovery

My mother's brother, Bill McMahon and his pretty wife, Rose, lived on 225ᵗʰ Street in Marble Hill, just across the Harlem River from the northern tip of Manhattan Island. They had generously offered to house me in their one-bedroom apartment during my first few weeks in New York, bunking on their living room sofa.

Childless, Aunt Rose had been a frequent visitor to Chicago and for years personified for me New York style, glamour and sophistication. She carried the additional cachet of having once served as private secretary to famed composer Irving Berlin. Yes, as a young teenager I'd had the hots for her. Uncle Bill was a good-natured, easygoing non-achiever who, while earning a modest living as a salesman – I was never quite sure of what – had long been pursuing various get-rich ventures that never seemed to happen. The one he was promoting at that moment, incidentally: *Guava Jelly*. Bill had convinced himself that it was about to become a national craze – the next Peanut Butter.

Moreover, since Rose and Bill, plus my mother's more distant, lofty, and reserved-for-later connection with the owner-publisher of *The New York Daily News*, were my *only* contacts in the East – I knew that getting started careerwise was totally up to me.

I *liked* it that way.

So, with advice gleaned from my instructors at CAFA, before leaving Chicago, I'd prepared some drawing-samples – a portfolio of sorts. Also, examining comic books at newsstands, plus a few that I had purchased, I'd compiled a list of publishing-house names. With the help of Rose and Bill's copy of the Manhattan telephone directory, I quickly found their addresses. Back in art school, I had learned via scuttlebutt as well as from faculty that the business was fairly casual; no neckties (whew!), no appointments necessary. One simply showed up, told the receptionist your name and purpose, and then took a seat in the waiting-room while your samples were handed off for perusal, presumably by a nameless editor. Thus, I eagerly, excitedly began making the rounds of the comic-book houses.

Within a few days I discovered several important things.

One was the, to me, stunning phenomenon known as *The New York Times*! It was instantly obvious that this publication was a delight like no other, and remains just as impressive even now. Better, it was available *every* day, even the most minor items beautifully written! Plus, its coverage/critiques of the arts – movies and theatre – were/are awesome. Moreover, I quickly came to appreciate what was, and continues to be for me, of major value: the book reviews. In addition to alerting me to the books that I wanted to read, they gave me familiarizing summaries of all those hundreds that I knew I would never open. Overall, for me, the incredible quality and value of *The Times* has never, *ever* waivered. Once I became a writer, it became and continues to be a steady source of story ideas.

But without question the most vital early-on knowledge I acquired was about myself: as my samples were handed back to me by an editor whom I'd managed to meet face-to-face, I received my *first* outright rejection: "Kid, your stuff isn't very good. You really oughta think about goin' back to Chicago."

The lesson: somewhat to my surprise, instead of feeling discouraged, my instant, fully automatic, no-processing-required reaction: *This guy has gotta be out of his fucking mind.*

I thanked him and left, slightly dismayed by my imperviousness – but *only* for a moment or two. By the time I was on the sidewalk, I was smiling. I recognized that I'd just experienced – and benefited in a *new* way – from that immunity with which I had cloaked myself back in my bedroom five years earlier. *Another* so-valuable asset my over-the-top father had inadvertently bestowed on me that day.

Oh, sure – the rejection brought me down. But only the tiniest notch.

Far more time would pass before I came to *fully* appreciate how uniquely well-equipped I was to face life and such challenges. As, for instance, when it eventually dawned on me that most *other* people were extremely sensitive to such put-downs.

Not incidentally, I've never had a problem accepting *constructive* criticism – especially from qualified individuals. Ergo, I didn't discount the *possible* validity of at least *some* of that comic-book editor's negative reaction to my artwork.

Among the other stuff I took from that that meeting: As the editor examined my samples, I glanced around at the numerous comic-books and the several pages of original art in his office. It hit me: *that* was what was expected. My samples needed to *look* like comic-book pages. *Not* the assortment of individual drawings and one or two examples of daily comic strips I'd produced before leaving Chicago. Rather, I would have to come up with artwork that walked-the-walk and, in this case importantly, talked-the-talk. *Comic-book pages.* With balloons containing dialogue! Samples that *looked* more like what the editors were buying.

So that afternoon, after purchasing drawing paper and other supplies, I eagerly boarded the subway train bound for Marble Hill. With Aunt Rose and Uncle Bill's permission, by nightfall I had converted their small dining room/foyer into a *sort-of* studio. There, in an attempt to demonstrate my range, I quickly created several pages covering the few popular genres for which I felt qualified. Those to which I could relate.

Which, even then, did *not* involve fantasy.

One, a mystery/spooky page, based on remembered shots from John Huston's movie version of *The Maltese Falcon*. Another contained an action sequence, and finally a Western page, again recreating remembered images from favorite films.

Two days later I was back in midtown, armed with the identities of a few editors, acquired simply by phoning and asking for their names. That way, when I approached the receptionist, I could ask to see this-or-that person – thus hopefully making me seem a tiny-touch less like a newbie.

Damned if I wasn't already sensing the "con" aspects of the game.

Way better prepared for – and on the *verge* of – my *first* New York breakthrough!

SIX
The Comic Books—
and Some of the Characters

THAT REMARKABLE MORNING, I was in the offices of Avon Comics, feeling pleased with myself. My instincts and research were already paying off. I'd just been told by the receptionist that if I didn't mind waiting, I would be able to present my samples to the Editor himself, Sol Cohen. Clearly because I'd asked for him by name. But that, I would learn, was the exception; at most comic-book houses, unless you were an established cartoonist, you handed your samples to the receptionist, who took them inside – to the editor – or someone.

Anyway, as I sat, leafing a magazine, another artist entered, checked in with the receptionist, and seated himself across from me. His acceptably scruffy, casually clad self – sweater and wrinkled cotton slacks – plus his scuffed two-foot by three-foot zippered, suitcase-handled leather portfolio identified him as a professional comic-book artist.

Pleasant, lanky – skinny really – mid-30ish, with short, thinning curly reddish-blond hair, his enormous ears projected at right angles from too far back along each side of his head. His long-legged, skeletal frame didn't come close to containment in the chair he occupied.

He looked up as I was still eyeballing him. "You new in town?"

Not a difficult deduction: my samples were in a large manila envelope. I had already priced portfolios like his, and had resolved to purchase such a badge with the proceeds from my first assignment.

"Yeah."

"Can I see your stuff?"

I was a bit surprised – put off, actually – by his request, as well as curious about why another artist would want to look at my drawings. I had no interest in seeing his – though – hey – it flashed past me that maybe it was a local custom nobody had told me about.

I shrugged. "Sure…" Reaching into my envelope, I withdrew my just-finished pages and passed them to him.

He examined my work briefly. Then, throwing me a little further off-balance with his lack of any discernible reaction, he handed it back. "You interested in picking up some background work?"

'*Background*?' I didn't know what the hell he meant. But, reluctant to seem too green, I guardedly faked it: "Yeah. I might."

"Y'heard of Leonard Starr?"

"Nope."

His brief eye-movement, I would realize later, was saying something on the order of *Geez, is this kid out of it.* "Draws a lotta comic-books."

He explained that he had been assisting Starr, who could use more help. It sort of registered for me that the term 'background' almost had to mean just that: cars, buildings, furnishings – while this Starr fellow, whoever he was, would draw the human figures. He jotted something on a scrap of paper, passed it to me: "I'm Tex Blaisdell. C'mon by the studio…"

Just then, the inner door was opened, and he was beckoned inside. I read the note he'd given me.

144 West 57th Street – 4th floor – rear.

Newcomer and non-fan of comic-books that I was, I would learn within a few days that I may have been the only person in the vicinity who didn't know of Leonard Starr's status. He was in fact one of the most prolific, respected and gifted people working in a business where, at that time, except to insiders and aficionados, artists were largely anonymous. Starr was among the few whose signature on their work actually sold magazines.

A note here about how the business worked at that time, and in many ways still does. Some of the artists were pencilers, some were inkers, and some – like Starr – did both, which was my aim. Some did lettering only, while others just did backgrounds, though many of those were newcomers like myself. Coloring was almost exclusively handled by the publishing house. The writing of story and dialogue, which was presented in more-or-less screenplay-form, was rarely done by the illustrator. About the only exceptions to that occurred in the related medium of syndicated newspaper comic strips.

My meeting a short time later that morning with Avon Comics editor, Sol Cohen, gave me a further lift. It confirmed that creating new samples had definitely been the right move. Enthusiastic about my work, he promised me an assignment, penciling and inking, within the next few weeks.

Not a major victory, but it sure beat the hell out of being told I should return to Chicago. To say I was elated doesn't come close.

Sol, incidentally, was a pleasant, Groucho-mustached guy, late 30ish, a WWII veteran whose most notable characteristic was the consistency of his costume. *Every* time I met with him, no matter the season, he wore the same increasingly tattered, moth-eaten wool olive-drab GI sweater.

The following morning, with no little trepidation, both work-and-people-wise, I showed up at the smoke-filled studio on West 57th Street. Tex rose as I entered, welcomed me and introduced his busy, mostly steadily chattering work-mates, all of whom remained seated.

Ben Oda, the quiet one, nodded, smiled, returned his attention to the dialogue balloons he was lettering. I was impressed to learn from Tex that Ben did the lettering for several major comic strips, including my favorite, *Terry and the Pirates*.

Punching the keys of his typewriter, gray-haired John Augustin was the old man of the group. He was – memorably for me – in mid-conversation with the artist across the room: "…Hey, they could write, they wouldn't be doing this crap---" He continued typing as he squinted briefly at me through smoke from the cigarette clamped between his lips: "Yo."

Carl Anderson, about my age, looked up. "Hey." Then, waving at the penciled comic-page he was inking, he resumed his dialogue with Augustin: "…I mean – if I see another goddam character saying *'what the…?'* I'm gonna puke."

A sentiment, not incidentally, that I share to this day, along with the seemingly required use at least once in every TV episode, of "With all due respect…"

John continued tapping keys, squinting. "Hey, don't fucking blame me."

Tex rolled his eyes as he explained that John was a comic-book scriptwriter, formerly Washington, D.C.-based, where he'd written for *The Voice of America*, the government-funded radio propaganda outfit.

Then, jerking a thumb at an unoccupied chair behind a drawing table adjacent to Carl's, Tex indicated that I should sit. I deposited myself a bit uneasily, not knowing what to expect.

I found out in a hurry when he shoved several half-sheets of three-ply kid-finish Strathmore drawing paper in front of me. Each was an original-art comic-book page containing six or seven panels of already-inked borders, dialogue, *and* my first viewing of Leonard Starr's penciled-and-inked figures.

Dazzling, they blew me away.

Ultra-realistically drawn and astonishingly rendered by a guy I'd never heard of until yesterday, almost vibrating with energy and appeal, they actually *topped* the work of Milton Caniff!

"Whoa. The guy's *really* good!"

"No shit." Carl laughed. "Yeah."

Instantly excited by the entirely unanticipated prospect of how much I could learn from Starr, I had to force my thoughts back to Topic A: the space around the figures in each panel was either blank or bore sketchily penciled indications of key interior or exterior objects. The story Starr had illustrated was a Western, and on the second page, one of his figures in particular, a kneeling young gunslinger, really wowed me. "He works from photographs, right?"

"Sometimes…" Tex shrugged, waved at the tools on the adjacent tabouret – India ink, pencils, pens and erasers – and at the nearby filing cabinet. "Scrap – just about anything you'll need…"

'Scrap,' was a term I hadn't learned in art school. But I correctly surmised that it meant visual reference material; photos or artwork clipped from magazines, mostly. Of everything from automobiles to guns, railroad trains, trees and so on. A lot of it, one would likely not know how to draw from memory.

"…Seven bucks a page. The deal is – unless it's in the figure's hand – youknow – like a gun or a phone, it's background. You draw it. So – go ahead. Start." He handed me several finished, fully-inked pages as a guide to how the end-product should look.

"Nice. These your backgrounds?"

Tex nodded. His work was impressive, too.

"Really nice."

He thanked me, and a minute later I was eagerly though not entirely confidently working around Leonard's figures. My insecurities notwithstanding, enjoying the hell out of it! Penciling lamps, furniture, crockery or whatever else was needed to fill up the empty space. The purpose: to add atmosphere and otherwise help tell the story. In those frames containing no humans or animals, a challenge: to draw appropriate scenery, from foliage to rock-formations to town-or-cityscapes. The latter, with dialogue balloons coming out of windows, I quickly learned, were jokingly described as 'talking buildings.' I was less sure of myself when it came to the nature stuff. That was more than a bit intimidating, especially on viewing Tex's finished work, wherein such scenery had a loose, expressive but still authentic flavor.

Concentrating as I had since early childhood on the challenge of drawing the human figure, I had virtually avoided trying to portray nature. *That*, I knew, was going to require some practice. When Tex left the room, I somewhat tentatively shared that thought with Carl.

"Hey, no sweat..." He rose, gesturing for me to join him. Together, we crossed to the file cabinets, where he dug out several bulging folders, one labeled *TREES*, the others *MOUNTAINS*, and *SHRUBBERY*. He passed them to me. "...Lotsa trees and shit..."

He was right. So, relaxing a bit, while sorting through the files I took a few moments to glance around at my surroundings, and was further impressed – and diminished – by the pair of framed paintings on the nearest wall. Expertly done, both, I noted, were by Starr. One, a nude, the other a landscape. The guy worked in color, too? Wow! As with the nature-stuff, given that my focus was to become another Milton Caniff, I had found black-and-white line drawing to be difficult enough. In fact, ever since that had become my goal I'd not even had the urge to work in color.

Happily, the smile-generating, easy banter from the others quickly distracted me from my thankfully momentary feelings of inadequacy. Anecdotes about this or that oddball they'd encountered on the subway, or baseball or political comments. Or a movie they'd just seen. All of it with attitude, and wit. If I'd had had any doubts that I was in The *Real New York*, this particular Alternate World would have instantly chased them off. *These were people I could talk to.* People whose common bond, I would gradually come to understand, was that they lived outside the mainstream. Doing – daily – what they *wanted* to be doing.

The walls of the studio's small kitchen and two main rooms were, except for the paintings, relatively bare. But the place seemed to my eyes fully furnished, containing as it did four or five drawing tables, tabourets, chairs, and Augustin's small typing desk.

Capping its specialness, its *atmosphere*, the apartment looked out on the backside of legendary Carnegie Hall and its rehearsal facilities. From there, with the windows open, one could hear practicing: violinists, cellists, horn and woodwind players, both jazz and classical, plus opera singers, the whole shot. Also visible beyond the maze of ducts on the rooftop of the adjacent Little Carnegie Movie Theater were windows into several dance studios where ballet was being taught or rehearsed. Thrilling then, thrilling now.

An hour later, I rather tentatively showed my first penciled page to Tex, who grinned: "Yeah. Nice. Go ahead – ink it."

Damn! I was *into* it!

In the East for a week, there *I* was, the kid from Chicago, laughing and telling jokes with colorful, working *professionals*. But mostly, I was listening and learning.

Earning my *first* few grown-up dollars!

I should have been better prepared for what came next, but in my elated state, I was not.

SEVEN
Complications—
and a Distraction

Still heady about having gotten started, and by the expectation of working with Starr, on my return to Rose and Bill's apartment that evening, a letter awaited me. Not unlike being electrically jolted back to reality, it was from Lee, informing me that she had decided to leave art school, and Chicago – and join me in New York.

She would be arriving, she said, in "ten days or so." Brief, cursory other than mentioning that she was excited by the prospect, and the words "Love you," above her signature, she offered no further details. Oddly, no return address.

It was truly an *Oh shit* moment, raising a *lot* of uncomfortable questions.

Where would she live?

Did she think we would marry anytime soon?

What would she do for income?

Plus – topping *all* of them: did I *really* want this – *us* – to continue?

Oy.

Following that was an awkward dinner, during which my aunt and uncle picked up on my obvious mood-change. I managed to finesse it, certainly not wanting to go there with them. Immediately afterward, I faked a need to make a drugstore purchase, and, at a nearby phone booth, called Lee. My urgent hope: to convince her to reconsider. Or at least postpone the move until my career was more solidly established.

But her number had already been disconnected. Bummer.

Next, I phoned her parents' home in Rockford, Illinois. Her mother informed me that they had not seen nor heard from her recently. Nor did I sense any knowledge of Lee's relocation plans. Maddeningly frustrated, I pleaded with her mother to get in touch with Lee and tell her it was urgent and important that I speak to her.

I did not get much sleep that night. As evidence of the depth of our attachment, until receiving her letter – well, she'd pretty much vanished from my radar. We had not been in touch since I'd departed Chicago.

In truth, I had liked it that way.

I resolved to settle it with her. If unable to reach her first, I would break it off immediately on her arrival. Wishing like hell that I'd spoken up before I'd departed Chicago, I was kicking myself for somehow having hoped she'd read my mind. Her coming all the way to the East was, I *knew*, going to make the whole damned business a *lot* more difficult.

It was still weighing on me as I boarded the subway the following morning. But what happened a few hours later at the 57th Street studio was, happily, more than enough to distract me from all that. Temporarily, anyway.

I met Leonard Starr.

My eagerness to do so was further whetted, leading up to his arrival, by the intriguing buildup from my new workmates. Almost as if they felt the need to prepare me for something special. Starting with Tex's nickname for him: '*Glamorous-and-Unpredictable*,' which, as I got to know Leonard, seemed more and more appropriate.

Further piquing my expectations were various overheard snippets and throwaways, mostly between Tex and John, about Starr's opinions of people, restaurants, and other matters. They obviously regarded him with respect.

Leonard, I'd been told the previous day, did most of his artwork at his home on Long Island, coming into town only one or two days each week.

When he appeared shortly before noon, his presence did *not* disappoint. Handsome, tall, blonde, self-assured, witty and, true to Tex's billing, striking in a star-quality way.

Far better than that, Leonard and I seemed to immediately, effortlessly connect.

I could not have known – nor imagined – that it was the beginning of what would evolve into the single most enduring friendship I would *ever* have. The kind where, even after weeks or months without contact, our wide-ranging conversations would resume as if there had been no interruption, endlessly stimulating as always. The topics, almost invariably flavored with humor: books, art, movies, theatre and music.

At the beginning, of course, our relationship was mentor/apprentice. Starr was only five years older than me, but he had been a working, very successful professional cartoonist-illustrator since age sixteen. Polished, erudite, cultured, extremely literate and well-read – though totally unpretentious – there was not a hint that he'd grown up on Manhattan's notoriously slummy, hoodlum-y Lower East Side. His formal education, beyond high school, had consisted of a year of art studies at the famed Pratt Institute. I later learned that he'd been a first-generation kid who had completely transformed himself.

But of those initial exciting moments, among the best of all was the fact that Leonard liked my work. The following week, he showed up with a script for an eight-page comic-book story which he thrust at me: "So – kid – how'd you like to do the breakdowns on this one?"

I was knocked out by the compliment – by his confidence in me.

Another new piece of terminology, 'breakdowns' consisted of reading the script and then laying out the pages, deciding on panel-size, shape and composition, deciding on poses for, and rough-penciling the figures, plus arranging and loosely lettering dialogue balloons so that the lettering-man had sufficient space. Basically, he was trusting *me* to figure out how to visually *tell* the story!

Oh, and dominating Leonard's one or two day per week work sessions at the studio, another unexpected bonus: my introduction to classical music. Opera, mostly. Played at loud volume on his professional-grade equipment. Best of all, made truly thrilling and educational, thanks to his knowledgeable narration and explanation of the subtleties and nuances of compositions and their performances.

Man, was I having fun!

Things quickly got even better. Further – happily – distracting me from obsessing over Lee's imminent arrival.

Leonard, it turned out, read books. Lots of them. We talked about them in detail and on levels that I had *never* experienced with another individual. Authors such as Maugham, Hammett, O'Hara, Chandler. Amazingly stimulating discussions, where for the first time in my life I found myself verbalizing thoughts, attitudes and insights I'd never before had the opportunity to express with another person. It turned out that our tastes were similar, though Leonard had read far more of the "classics" than me. Which resulted in my turning to such reading as well.

Another delightful side of my relationship with Leonard, and with the others, was our conversations about movies. Discussing them in ways that I had also never done, coming at them, arguing and critiquing their direction, screenplays, cinematography and even cutting. Truly mind-expanding for me, and in a real way, surprisingly liberating: almost invariably, when alluding to a film he didn't like, Leonard would start the discussion with: "I hated it."

I suppose partly because of my Midwest upbringing, I had literally *never* heard anyone express their dislike for a movie or book in terms that strong, that flat-out absolute. No grays. Which turned out to be another excellent fit for my approach to ideas, premises and the like: once I've reached a thought-through position, I'm done.

"Next…?"

EIGHT
Another Keeper—
and *Reality-Time*—
Or What Passes for It...

AMONG THE BENEFITS WHILE CRANKING OUT breakdowns and backgrounds for Leonard, was learning insider-jargon of the business. A memorable example: the caped, tights-clad action characters that had started with *Superman*, *Batman*, *Captain Marvel* and a few others – and were at that point beginning to proliferate – were not yet known as "Superheroes." Rather, they were collectively and somewhat derisively regarded by artists and writers as "Underwear Characters."

Another almost daily part of the studio repartee became a serious contribution to my ongoing education; though I would not come to appreciate its enormous value for more than twenty years.

Nearly every morning, one or more of the group would, almost as soon they entered, tell a joke – a gag – he'd just heard. What followed the punchline-delivery I still find remarkable. After the laughs, if any, came a period that would sometimes continue for an hour or more, during which the gag was verbally de-constructed – played-with, actually. This came in the form of such comments/suggestions as: "Wait. What if the word '_____' came *after* '_____'?'"

These exchanges would usually – and quickly – turn funny/argumentative:

"Nah! It should be '_____' and *then* '_____'!'"

"C'mon! That's about as funny as death. Y'start the whole thing with '_____.' And then, suppose you don't let on about '_____' till youknow just before the end?"

"Nonono. The setup-line shouldn't even be there. Instead you just begin with '_____.'"

Almost invariably, by the end of these entertaining sessions, the original gag had been punched-up and rearranged to the point where it was way better-told and *far* funnier than the original version.

In the bargain, without having a clue that it was happening, I was learning truly valuable lessons about *storytelling*. Including the fact that effective joke-construction was and is the basis for longer forms, such as novels and screenplays, whether comedy or drama. Techniques and sensibilities that were to prove *vitally* valuable to me once I moved on to Hollywood. On a number of levels.

On the professional cartooning side, there was ample opportunity for me to ask questions and absorb insights about that business, as well as seek advice.

One of their suggestions in particular hit me as especially valuable, and also confirmed my own instincts, helping me to hone my strategy. It was about the wisdom of waiting before I solicited work from the biggies, such as DC Comics and Marvel, until I had a few comic-book pencil-and-inking jobs under my belt from smaller publishing houses. It made sense to me that by doing so I would more readily be regarded as a professional. But as of then,

I still had not even received the call from Sol Cohen at Avon Comics, with that first, promised assignment.

However, a few days later Tex alerted me about Ziff-Davis. An old-line magazine publishing company, Tex explained, they had recently decided to try becoming a force in the increasingly-hot comic-book biz. As a path to 'buying their way in,' they had placed under contract as Editor-in-Chief, for the rumored, then-huge salary of $100,000 per year, the legendary co-creator of *Superman*, Jerry Siegel. And, Tex added, word was out that they were looking at new artists. In no small part because so many of the more experienced guys were already busily working for other publishers.

So, next morning, I presented my samples to the receptionist in Ziff-Davis's offices at 292 Madison Avenue. Their editor being the near-celebrity that he was, I didn't even bother to ask for an audience. Alone in the waiting-room, I seated myself and began paging through a magazine.

I could not have imagined anything close to what happened about four minutes later.

I heard the door to the inner offices open, and looked up to see a nondescript, sort of frumpy little guy clutching my samples. "Are-are y-you T-T-Tom?"

Figuring, not entirely unexpectedly, that he was an office assistant, I nodded and concealed my disappointment with a smile as I rose to retrieve my pages. "Yeah. I'm Tom."

"H-hi. I 1-1-love your d-d-drawings…" He extended his hand, grinned and continued stuttering. "M-m-my name is J-J-Jerry Siegel."

Holy shit!

Close to speechless, I managed: "Hi, Jerry. Great to meet you. I---"

He shook my hand and waved for me to follow. "C-c'mon in."

Seconds later, in his office cubicle, he presented me with the script for a new, two-page monthly 'filler' titled *Little Al of the FBI!* Even better, if that was possible; its small number of pages notwithstanding, it was to be a *regular* monthly feature. I had already learned from Tex and the others that being assigned to draw a recurring series was *way* more of a confidence vote than a one-shot story. Not, of course, on a level with drawing the title-character of a comic-book, but still, no small matter.

As I emerged onto Madison Avenue, it began to hit me: this pleasant fellow with the stutter, in whose presence I'd just been, was not only a genuine *Comics Immortal* – he *dug* my artwork – and had given me my *first*, drawn-by-me, gonna-be-published, New York gig!

Hot damn!

Given how/why I had come to that office, that morning, *what* a comment – I realize now – it made about the value of that which would someday be called "*Networking*."

As I headed uptown, my feet barely felt the pavement.

In truth, my drawing ability at that point wasn't terrific – certainly not by Caniff or Starr standards. But it *was* improving, coming closer in reality to my ahead-of-my-own-curve confidence level. I realized a few years down the line that during that period, and for some time after, there was always this gap; at any given moment I *believed* my work was better than it actually was. But hey, that belief did the job for me. *And* – my samples had convinced Jerry Siegel!

After thanking Tex for his brilliant advice and heads-up about Siegel & Co., and receiving his and the others' congratulations, I immersed myself in the backgrounds I'd been drawing for Leonard. Still elated by the Ziff-Davis assignment, the day raced by. The others departed for the evening, and I was alone at the studio when the phone rang.

"Hi! I'm here. At LaGuardia. Plane just got in…" I heard the excitement in Lee's voice. I sagged.

To describe my thoughts as 'churning,' doesn't cut it. Grinding says it better. If her words or tone indicated affection, I would have been incapable of recognizing it at that moment. Following the relatively momentary upset after receipt of her note, I had avoided thinking about this whole tedious mess I'd gotten myself into. Now it was about to be *in* my face.

I managed: "Great!" Followed by, I suppose, a reasonably convincing: "I can hardly wait to see you…" I gave her the address. The call ended, I tried to remain cool, returning to the room-furnishings I was inking around Leonard's figures.

But I was unable to concentrate. My head was filled with rehearsing – and revising – my lines. With far-from-enthusiastic anticipation. As the sky darkened and lights came on in the Carnegie Hall rehearsal studios, there was this growing knot in my stomach, the feeling as I saw the minutes pass on the clock, of oppressive pressure – of – what *was* it…?

The regret, dammit, that I had ever allowed myself to become involved with her. That it was coming to this.

This in-the-next-half-hour confrontation – in which I was determined to be blunt. To end it before it went any further. When guilt reared its head I was ready for it: hell, it wasn't *my* fault that she had suddenly chosen to come to New York without even running it past me – without---

The buzzer interrupted my grim thoughts. I breathed deeply, rose and crossed, determined that *no matter what*, I was about to clean up this mistake so that, unburdened by such stuff, I could continue this exhilaratingly free start to my life in New York.

I opened the door.

Lee's smile was radiant – as was all 5'8" of her. Gorgeous. "Hi. I'm here."

We hugged, kissed. I took her bags, and guided her inside the dimly lit studio. Almost wordless, we embraced again.

Within about three minutes – there being no sofa – we were on the floor, making love.

Twenty year-old Lust – 10.

Resolve – 0.

NINE
Some Short-Form,
A Complication or Two,
and—Bingo!

A FEW MONTHS LATER, LEE AND I WERE MARRIED.

Her parents were happier about it than mine. A relationship doomed from the start, we didn't fight. We went through what passed for "the motions." We rented an apartment in Chelsea, on the lower West Side of Manhattan. She found employment, and I continued working. Oh, we had some laughs, socialized, and so on. The details are hardly worth reciting, and certainly don't justify being read about.

On the plus-side, my career continued to progress. As did the fun I had wrestling with the challenges. I had scored with Jerry Siegel, who was giving me repeat assignments. Sol Cohen at Avon and a few others had come through with comic-book pencil-and-inking assignments, including one or two that included script-writing.

Along the way, I was absorbing life-and-writing-and-drawing lessons, some of them throwaway lines, gems, really, that would stay with me forever. Like the take-it-to-the-bank forehead-slapper from a crusty editor, gesturing at the penciled pages I'd presented for his okay to go ahead and ink them: "Thing you gotta remember, kid – even yer bad guys hafta be attractive."

During those days, through Leonard, John, and Tex, I began to meet and hang out with other artists. Some dropped by the studio, and with them we'd lunch or have drinks. There were parties. Warren King, the editorial cartoonist for the *New York Daily News* – and former assistant to the legendary Rube Goldberg – was a particularly witty, garrulous fellow. Another was Dan Barry, who was then doing the *Flash Gordon* comic strip for King Features Syndicate. Stan Drake was outgoing and charming. Not yet doing his memorable strip, *The Heart of Juliet Jones*, Stan was drawing comic books and some advertising illustration. Several would become longtime friends, meaningful players in my life for years to come.

Some of the all-guy conversations tended to be raunchy in the extreme. In one very singular area they surpassed *any* I encountered before or since, covering a certain truly unique – and tasteless – discussion-topic. One that made me singularly uneasy even as I was (occasionally) laughing, these conversations remain – in my experience – totally peculiar to this tiny subculture.

While neither Leonard Starr, Ben Oda or Carl Anderson – nor I – *ever* participated (read: shared), we would listen as Tex Blaisdell, John Augustin, Warren and occasionally one or two others routinely described, in humorous, crudely intimate detail, the sex they'd had the previous night with wife, girlfriend or, sometimes, other men's wives.

When it was spousal, especially, their depictions of their mates' quirks and the like would stick in my mind, causing me to view these women differently – and often uncomfortably – when I next encountered them in social situations. Weird indeed.

From my then-limited, sheltered perspective, I felt as if I'd been dropped into a fount of *true* sophistication. The reality-check came when I'd mention this to outsiders, as for instance my Aunt Rose and Uncle Bill. Their without-hesitation reaction: I was hanging out with a bunch of Philistines.

During that period, I experienced another of those Moments – the 'remembering the light in the room' kind.

In that instance, along with the surprising, intense sadness I felt, what I learned lowered my level of trust, my belief in the truth of history-as-written in a way that would stay with me for the remainder of my life. It would affect my basic thinking, and my art.

Later I would come to understand it on other deeper levels, as a process that in effect had given me a set of filters through which I would process almost everything. History, politics, my world-view. Arguably, it was a rite of damned near anyone's passage, though I now understand mine with far greater clarity. Conditioned as I was by my father, and the resultant near-forever doubts about and disdain for authority – and its purveyors – had virtually dictated how I would react to the news that day.

I was alone in the 57th Street studio, looking out at the Carnegie Hall Rehearsal Studio as I tried to digest it. That morning it had been revealed that the U.S. Military had, early in December ten years earlier, intercepted and decoded the Japanese messages confirming their intention to attack Pearl Harbor the following Sunday.

It was a shocker. From my childhood I so-vividly remembered that morning, and how we had been 'sold' the premise that it was this totally unexpected 'sneak' raid. How, from December 7, 1941, across America, even 'little old ladies' were so enraged that they seemed ready to pick up weapons and kill 'Japs.' Hell, even as kids, that day my male pals and I were already playing pretend war-games.

I stood at the studio window, staring out across the rooftops, attempting to process this instance of history being rewritten. Of truths revealed. Perceptions changed. I had my very first inklings of something that would take months – years really to fully comprehend: I began to understand how easily great masses of people can be misled.

Manipulated.

Deceived.

And not *always* for entirely wrong reasons. In that case, President Franklin Roosevelt had promised British PM Churchill that we would join the U.K. in the war against Germany. But, despite the War News, and German U-boats repeatedly attacking and sinking U.S. ships in the Atlantic Ocean, the American public's enthusiasm for such a venture was exceedingly low. As a result, we eventually learned, FDR realized that it would require something dramatic to get us into the war. So, shrewdly, and unreported in the news, he gave Japan an ultimatum.

He warned the Japanese that unless they *promptly* withdrew from certain Far East areas they had conquered, The U.S. would go to war against them. A clear provocation – brilliant, really – and it worked. It would also be revealed – much later – that the only American warships destroyed in Pearl Harbor that day were obsolete, ready for the scrap-heap. Our few modern vessels – including an aircraft carrier – were conveniently elsewhere in the Pacific.

But – the '*Sneak Attack*' had been etched into the pages of History, where for most people it remains today. That news about the codes being broken? Forgotten. Ignored, really – and almost never mentioned to succeeding generations. Lest, I suppose, it disturb that comfort-requirement.

The march of our world since then has for me provided numerous similar examples, and further confirmation of the phenomenon.

But as evidenced by subsequent events such as the JFK Assassination, 9/11, the Vietnam and Korean wars, and others, as well as the justification of our participation in such earlier fiascoes as the first World War: once history has been written, it becomes part of the public's comfort-zone. Thus *not* to be questioned or reexamined. Put another way, when large numbers of people die for a 'noble' cause, or as innocents, they must *forever* be regarded as Heroes, or Victims of Bad Guys. Ergo, we – the masses – must *never* entertain the possibility that they may have died for other, shallower reasons. Such as simply aiding our economy by perpetuating the Military/Industrial/Congressional Complex.

It may well be that in order for a society – *any* society – to survive, it *must* buy into such mythology. Certainly, our species' willing, eager really, worldwide embrace of magic – aka religion – confirms this.

As you'll see, my emotional/intellectual filters have made me, almost invariably, a questioner of such things.

Several months after Lee's and my wedding, I was ironically rescued from our marriage – I suppose we both were – by my being drafted into the Army. I certainly didn't view my recruitment that way at the time. Quite the opposite.

It felt to me as if I'd been sentenced to prison.

Conscription was a possibility that had been hanging over me for some time. It had reached near certainty as America's anti-Communist hysteria grew. Famously fed by the despicable Senator Joseph McCarthy, our attendant involvement in the ridiculous Korean War continued to escalate.

The marketing of that type of venture, incidentally, had become *so* much easier following August 10, 1949. On that day, one of America's oldest government institutions was renamed: the War Department, so labeled in 1778, became the Defense Department.

Think about that one…

I had done my best to ignore the war news, and also kept hoping that if it came to my being drafted, I might not pass the physical requirements. I still clung to that outside chance as, early on a foggy morning, Lee and I said our virtually emotionless goodbyes and I departed our 23rd Street apartment, headed for the Federal Courthouse in lower Manhattan.

But – no such luck. The "physical" was a joke, consisting of hundreds of us standing naked in a long snaking line, passing the doctor several times. Clearly bored and disinterested, he asked each young man the usual "Say 'ahh,'" listened briefly with a stethoscope, finishing with a rubber-gloved finger-jab to the groin, accompanied by the order to cough. I also observed that since I had entered the room, the guy *never* changed to a clean rubber glove, a stack of which were visible on the small table at his side. As it got closer to being my turn, I had found it disgusting. Angering. I mean, who knew what kind of germs or diseases or just plain filth these bozos were carrying on their balls?

So, not exactly out of character for me, when he finished doing his number on the guy just ahead of me, and beckoned me to step forward, I held back, shaking my head. "Not until you change to a clean glove."

He growled impatiently. "C'mon – c'mon!"

"Uh-uh."

Silence. He glared, thinking about it for a moment. I was aware that our little disagreement had drawn the attention of nearby recruits, as well as the approaching uniformed MP. Then, grudgingly and a touch ceremoniously the physician removed his glove, dropped it on the floor, and pulled a clean one onto his hand.

My first, but *far* from my last nose-thumbing of – and acting-out-on my contempt for – the two years of bullshit I was facing. A tiny-but gratifying win, I felt a small confidence gain in that area.

As we were bussed that afternoon to Fort Dix in New Jersey, I reflected on a few things, starting with Lee. It was far easier to leave her that morning than it had been to say goodbye to my new artist-friends. I was mightily pissed off to be torn away from them, and my work. Worse, I fucking *despised* the prospect of the whole military thing. Uniforms, discipline, being hovered over and told what to do and when to do it, and most of all, about being trained to kill people.

My aversion to all of that had manifested itself – since it had loomed as a possibility more than a year earlier – in my conscious refusal to wear anything brown-colored.

But even more distasteful than *any* of the above, I hated being forced to take part in that first of America's endless series of post-WWII wars-to-keep-the-country-prosperous. Of course *that* historical aspect of it wasn't then apparent to me, but the part about it being pointless was quite plain to see. Plain enough in fact that there was *no* way I was going to risk losing my life over the so-obviously-concocted "Commie Threat."

Moreover, before being sworn in, I had decided on a mindset for survival. I would, to whatever extent possible, game the system. That's pretty much how I survived the next almost-two years. In fact, by risking prison, I actually managed to enjoy some of it.

The manipulating approach began for me on my first day in uniform. Based on an intelligence test we'd been required to take, I was offered – sold, really – the "opportunity" to go directly to Officer Training School. Instantly skeptical, I asked questions. I was hardly surprised when told that there were catches. One was minor, confirming what I had read somewhere about officers having to purchase their uniforms. Another piece of advice I acquired from an active-duty corporal I met that first day didn't take on meaning or value for me until some months later: he confided that commissioned officers' orders came from the Pentagon. Ergo, officers had virtually zero influence over where they'd be sent for their next assignment.

But – for enlisted men, those decisions were made *at* the camp where you were located, in an office titled *Classification & Assignment*. The potential advantage: it was staffed – at all but the top levels – by fellow enlisted men who, the chances were excellent, you knew personally. Guys who were in a position – if they were willing – to "tinker" with things like the wording of orders before they were officially issued.

But for me the no-brain deal-breaker was that if I became an officer, I would be required to sign on for four years, rather than the two for which I'd been drafted.

Relieved that I had a choice, I instantly flat-out passed on officer-training.

A few days later, I began to learn – in *very* satisfying ways – how fortuitous that decision had been. Shipped to Aberdeen, Maryland for eight weeks of Basic Training, I met several soldiers who, having just completed the previous training cycle, had not yet shipped out. They willingly shared key advice on how to make things easy for myself during the ensuing two months.

First, that it was essential that I become a Squad Leader. The reason: those guys *never* had to "pull shit-duty," such as KP or cleaning toilets. Rather, the Squad Leader was the guy who chose men for those tasks from among his dozen or so charges.

How to achieve this status? I was told that I had an advantage because as a *Boy Scout* I'd become acquainted military-style marching-drill and commands ("right-face," "left-face," etc.), thus understanding what the uninitiated would over the first days have to learn. So, rather than try to remain as invisible as possible, at each order to "fall in" (aka line up for drill), make sure I was the *first* in line at the far right. Why? Because that was the Squad Leader's position. It would send a message to the NCO's who were training us, that you were sharp, needed less training, behaved like a leader, and *wanted* the job.

In less than a week, Squad Leaders were appointed. I was one of them. It was sweet indeed, making the eight weeks of Basic Training – while tedious – a relative breeze.

Another useful and memorable piece of advice came from a corporal who had recently returned from Korea. I had instant respect for him when he told me how he had gotten himself out of danger. During a snowstorm near the Yalu River, in the face of advancing Chinese troops, he had intentionally shot himself in the foot.

The wisdom he confided: "Listen – every time you meet a new officer, check his fingers. If he's wearing a West Point ring, stay as far away from him as you can, 'cuz he's probably an asshole." While my take wasn't necessarily as blunt as his, I recognized the truth-part: those officers were obviously the ones who took soldiering most seriously. That one served me *very* well over the course of my time in the Army.

None of this knowledge ever caused me to hate the Army *any* less than I did. But these and other insights definitely helped to make the experience more bearable.

The most immediate dividend from my system-gaming: because I'd become a Squad Leader, unlike my squad-members, even during Basic Training I had an automatic "weekend pass." Starting Friday evening and ending early Monday morning, before roll-call, my weekends were free of military bullshit.

Usually, I went back to Manhattan to be with Lee, go to parties, hang with my friends and earn a few extra dollars on quicky comic-book jobs or assisting Leonard. But things with Lee were getting dicier. We were becoming more and more distant.

Further anxieties were preoccupying me as the end of Basic Training loomed. I was already plotting ways to avoid being sent directly to Korea and getting my ass shot off. The alternative seemed at the time to get myself – if I could so manipulate it – sent to Germany. Hardly appealing, but certainly less risky than the other. Fortunately, I was able to temporarily at least lay those concerns aside; I was ordered into six additional weeks of preparatory training. To become an Ordnance Storage Specialist. Army-speak for, basically, a parts-clerk in a guns-and-ammunition warehouse.

Yawn.

But theoretically, a job-description that would keep me out of combat.

Still, I was *in* the fucking Army. Which continued to feel like a prison-sentence. I was aware as never before of my ongoing anger and frustration, reawakened daily by the constant, tedious supervision, the petty regulations, and demand for conformity to this or that bullshit regulation. It reminded me of the high school need for a "Hall Pass," multiplied by the hundreds. Near the top, contempt-wise, the requirement that I pretend to respect people I regarded as fools and schmucks, the experience was relentlessly annoying, all-the-way-to infuriating. Fortunately, for a few months anyway, I was able to conceal/suppress my attitude sufficiently to keep myself out of Army-trouble.

But, there was the gnawing, growing anger at myself for having allowed Lee and me to happen.

The Army experience was, however, not without its fascinating observations and revelations, some of them slow to gel. Finding myself feeling more isolated than ever by being thrust for the first, and really the only time in my life, into a true cross-section of society – into the midst of people from *everywhere*, from every level of society, had heightened my awareness of how few there were to whom I could personally relate on an intellectual or social level.

Along with that, a few discoveries. Surprises, really. Being essentially a middle-class city kid, I had never knowingly encountered grown-ups who were literally illiterate. Among the draftees, there was an astonishing number of them. These soldiers – many of them a few years older than me – were actually, as part of their training, being *taught* by the Army to read and write.

But the most startling part, in interacting with those least educated, was how often I saw that a few were – in terms of practical, day-to-day-existing/getting-along abilities – actually *smarter* than many of their far more schooled and academically credentialed fellow draftees. *Way* smarter. It gave a whole new meaning to "native intelligence."

During that period, Lee and I finally, officially broke up.

After that, when in New York I bunked at the 57ᵗʰ Street studio. By then, she had found employment as an airline reservations person, so she had a modest income. The biggest problem she and I faced – though not immediate or particularly pressing – was how to sever our marriage legally. This was exacerbated by the fact that as long as we were husband-and-wife she automatically received half of my pathetically meager Army pay. Further, at that time, in New York, the only grounds for divorce were adultery or desertion. While divorces were easily obtainable in Mexico or, following six weeks of residency, in Nevada, neither of those options were a workable financial fit for us. Worse, the Mexican decrees were proving in court to be of questionable value. The expense and logistics rendered the Nevada option not do-able.

A few weekends later, during one of my Manhattan visits, my crusty pal, John Augustin, solved our dilemma. Brilliantly. Economically. And totally off-the-wall. Over drinks one evening, listening to my lament, he brightened: "Wait a minute. Lee was raised Catholic, right?"

"Yeah. But she doesn't actually practice---"

"Doesn't matter. All you guys hafta do is be willing – along with me – to lie under oath." Off my acquiescent but questioning nod, he continued. "You get her to claim to a Judge that she married you on the condition that you turn Catholic. You admit you promised her. And I swear I heard you say so…"

Not quite following him, I spoke. "Yeah. And…?"

"And then, you lying fuck, you went and broke your promise." He grinned, waved a hand. "They grant you an annulment – and you're done. No alimony, no lawyers – nothing."

Damned if John hadn't nailed it! Less than a month later, our marriage was decreed to have never happened. Total cost. $130 for fees and Court costs. Plus a gift-bottle of Johnnie Walker Black Label for Augustin.

TEN
Turning Shit Into Gold—
and Acquiring
(Inadvertent) Wisdom

As MY STORAGE CLASS COURSE RAN its boring course, and preparing for the worst – that is: being sent overseas – I began making a fantasy plan.

At the time, while the war in Korea continued, peace talks had begun. Interestingly to me, no photographers were allowed. So a few major magazines had artists assigned to sit in, to illustrate their written reportage. The national exposure of such artwork was huge. It occurred to me that if I were to be shipped overseas, I would – through my contacts in *Classification & Assignment* – make sure I was sent to the Far East. Importantly, I had learned a piece of good news: personnel being transferred from the U. S. were sent to Japan, to a 'Replacement Depot' outside of Tokyo, known as Camp Drake. Once there, they received orders to wherever they would be assigned. Thus, on my arrival, I would somehow finagle my way into getting assigned as staff artist to *Pacific Stars & Stripes*, the GI daily newspaper which, I had learned, was officed in Tokyo. Once there, I'd convince them to let me cover the proceedings. The beauty part: if I could do so, I would come out of the service with a national reputation as an illustrator.

I mean – what would be wrong with that?

However, on completion of *Ordnance Storage Specialist* training, I was rescued from such concerns. I got lucky. Or – so I thought. Also, relieved. I did not get sent – anywhere.

Instead, without any manipulation on my part, rather than being shipped out, I was assigned to what was known as "Permanent Party." I was to be stationed at Aberdeen, actually working as an *Ordnance Storage* clerk.

Hardly a party in any literal sense, I had luckily gotten off the hook in terms of any risk of war-participation. Or of needing to game the system in order to avoid it.

Based at Aberdeen, presumably for the remaining year-and-a-half of my term, I had no trouble spending every weekend in New York with my friends. Another privilege: I was allowed to have my car on-base, and thus could make the relatively easy drive, instead of riding a train or bus. It was – bearable. Made more so by the fact that, being a kind of insider, there was tacit understanding that I did not need to be present for Saturday morning roll-call – that I would be automatically, routinely recorded as being present. Thus, my weekends and those of my fellow cadre-members, began at 6PM Friday. At that time I routinely departed for Manhattan, sometimes not returning until early Monday morning, sometimes minutes before roll-call.

Ironically, when my penchant for getting into rule-bending trouble next reared its head, it was *not* the result of rebellion, but rather, of accepted practice. Or so I thought. I mention this incident because – painful though some of it was – it became the door-opener to one more unanticipated highlight of my very fortunate life.

Including another revelation about the benefits of gaming the System, instead of fighting it.

Among cadre members at the base, it was understood that weekend morning roll-call was a kind of look-the-other-way affair – if you were absent, nobody cared and it didn't get reported.

Ergo, since I had some furlough-time coming, and I owed my parents a visit – I hadn't been back to Chicago since moving to New York – I did what my barracks-mates had been doing without any problems. I arranged for my one-week leave to begin on a Monday morning, and end on Friday night. Add the two weekends, and I'd get nine days out of it, while only using up five of those fourteen per-year to which I was entitled. So, with my furlough orders duly issued, early on a Friday evening I piled into my car and headed west. Driving all night, I wearily arrived at my mom and dad's Chicago apartment about 10 AM Saturday morning. I was greeted with unanticipated warmth by both, made especially pleasant because of their enthusiastic approval of Lee's and my breakup. After brief catch-up, I quickly crashed into a deep sleep.

I was awakened three hours later by my intensely not-happy father: there was a phone call for me – from a serious-sounding Major at Aberdeen. I listened groggily:

"Private, I am calling to inform you that as of this morning you are absent-without-leave, and officially under arrest. You will voluntarily return to base in time for Monday morning roll-call, or you *will* be transported back here by Military Police. Do you understand?"

"Yessir. But I – I only did what---"The disconnecting click interrupted my somewhat punchy attempt to explain. I hung up the phone, my rage quickly overcoming my drowsiness. Some shitheel had reported me absent from that morning's lineup. It *had* to have been malicious, but I couldn't imagine who, or why.

My father made no effort to conceal his total disgust. "I'm going back with you." It was understandably motivated by his and my mother's concern for my safety, given my brief sleep and the long drive I was facing. But as I hastily dressed, I protested emphatically, dreading the hours of sitting beside him in the car, being forced to absorb his disapproval and listen to what I knew would be endless recriminations and – as was his style – the dredging up of previous offenses.

I tried to explain my take on what had happened, that I wasn't defying authority, but rather had simply played it the way everyone else did.

"Whatever. I'm riding with you, and that's that."

The prospect was more than I could handle. "No, dammit. You're *not*! Look, I promise, I'll check into a motel tonight. And I'll phone you."

Less than an hour later, with my father simmering for the whole time, I was back on the road to Maryland. Alone.

My rage at being reported AWOL continued to fuel my edgy alertness for the entire 700 mile return trip. Along with that, I was savoring the prospect of finding the individual who had reported me absent – and beating the shit out of him.

Monday morning following roll-call, I duly reported to my commanding officer, who greeted me from behind his desk with predictably chilliness. As I stood at attention, he read aloud in a *very* serious voice an Article from the Uniform Code of Military Justice, one which I would come to know *very* well, memorized actually, since it was recited to me so often from that point until I received my discharge. It was the Army equivalent of the civilian notice that I was indeed under arrest and anything I said could and would be used against me.

Which was more than enough to convince me that it would be pointless, if not risky, to try explaining that I had only done what everyone else did.

He added that while it had been decided I would not be court-martialed, I had been docked my furlough time, and sentenced to 'Company Punishment,' which consisted of confinement for the next three weeks to the barracks, or at my job and, at mealtimes, the mess hall. Moreover, I was stripped of my weekend pass privileges indefinitely.

That ripped it. Even as the officer curtly dismissed me, I was doing an internal balancing act, struggling to control my anger while rapidly processing my next moves. For the first few minutes none were instantly clear, save for a single certainty: between the weekend's debacle and the accumulated pile of other military nonsense, I was finished with Aberdeen – *and* with stateside duty.

The rest of it quickly fell into place.

First off, I discarded my plan to find and get even with the guy who'd reported me. While still almost irresistibly tempting, doing so would undoubtedly be reported, compounding my troubles.

What I did, though way *less* rational, was decide to act on a plan I'd been thinking about well before the long drive to Chicago-and-back: my previously laid-aside fantasy. My far-out gamble, but one that, if I could pull it off, might just make the then-ten-percent of my life I was having to piss away in the Army worthwhile. I would indeed contrive to wangle myself onto the staff of *Pacific Stars & Stripes*. From there, I'd finagle my way into that Peace Tent in Panmunjom, Korea – get my drawings published all over America – and become an overnight Star.

Besides, what the hell? If it didn't work out, at least it would expose me to some new, way less-predictable experiences – *and* get me out of my current shithole.

So, exiting the Company Commander's office, I went directly to *Classification & Assignment* where – thankful for the early advice I'd received about why not to become an officer – I sought out an enlisted-man from our company and told him to put me on orders to the Far East, ASAP.

I knew it was a really farfetched dice-roll. Not least because there was no guarantee that I wouldn't just be sent on to Korea, handed a rifle, and ordered into combat.

To cover that possibility, I made a no-contest pact with myself: in that worst-case event, I would hand the weapon back to them and refuse.

I figured a court-martial, plus spending a year or so in the stockade and coming home alive made a *lot* more sense than possibly dying or being maimed in a war they'd failed, despite their endless, ludicrous succession of sales-pitches, to convince me was worthwhile.

In *any* way.

Especially not because of the then-near-hysterical, Joe McCarthy-fed fear and hatred of '*The Godless Commies*.'

Fortunately, it never came to that. As things turned out, I enjoyed one helluvva year on another planet – the one known as Tokyo. No small part of that fun would be the result of a totally out-of-my-league adventure in law-breaking which – if I hadn't seen so many movies – would almost certainly have gotten me sent to prison – and dishonorably discharged.

ELEVEN
Another World

THE TROOPSHIP VOYAGE FROM SAN FRANCISCO was a forgettable, boring, endless two-weeks of cramped quarters, stinking disgusting toilet facilities, vile food and close-packed sleeping arrangements. The bunks, five-deep, were so close vertically that if you laid on your side, your shoulder touched the canvas bottom of the one above. The only relief from the unvented stench and/or stale air was to grab as much time as possible on the open upper deck. About the only good news: unlike many of my less fortunate fellow GI's, I did not suffer sea-sickness. It was not enough of a plus, however, to prevent my resolving that when it came time to return to the U.S., there would be no *way* it was going to be on a troopship.

But finally, one morning, there we were, pulling into busy Yokohama harbor. Its look, feel and smell – plus the sight and voice-sounds of the active, animated Japanese crew-members on ships we slowly passed, and Japanese longshoremen loading and off-loading cargo, instantly made me feel as if I was landing in a different Universe. A feeling, by the way, that I was immediately relishing, and which would continue for my most of my time in Japan.

By that evening, we'd arrived at Camp Drake. Already briefed that we would likely be at that location no more than 48 hours before being shipped elsewhere (meaning: Korea), I knew I'd have to work quickly.

So, my first urgent order of business before climbing into my bunk that night was to learn the phone number of *Pacific Stars & Stripes*, and to get my hands on a copy of that day's edition. After locating the number in a local sergeant's phone directory, I borrowed his copy of the tabloid. I was instantly impressed by the quality of the writing, plus its look, layout, photography, artwork and general professionalism. I quickly found the masthead, and was relieved to find the name of the commanding officer. So, following a somewhat restless night, and breakfast the next morning, I stalled impatiently near a phone until 9:30 AM. Presuming that by then, the newspaper's office-day had begun, I grabbed it and, after mentally running a final quick rehearsal, I dialed.

After two rings, a male voice: "Pacific Stars and Stripes…"

I tried my best to not sound like my life was depending on this call. Or that I was a 21 year-old bullshitter. As businesslike as I could muster, I gave him my name, then: "I need to speak to Major Morgan."

"About what?"

"There's been this screw-up. I'm a prominent, very successful illustrator from New York, and they're shipping to Korea, instead of---"

My immediate, gut-impression of the *click* I heard was a serious *oh shit* feeling. But then!

"Major Morgan here…"

I quickly inhaled, and repeated my act, adding some made-up credits as an artist – stuff one could *maybe* get away with in that distant, pre-internet time – finishing with: "…and Major Morgan, I really believe I can be of far more value to the Army by working for your newspaper."

Very businesslike – but encouraging – he requested my Army ID number, and my MOS number. The latter, *Military Occupational Specialty*, had me classified as the Ordnance Storage guy.

Major Morgan continued: "Hmm. We'd have to get that changed…"

His conclusion was disappointingly noncommittal. "I'll see what I can do, Private."

Two suspenseful days later, I learned that I'd been assigned to the Tokyo Ordnance Depot, and told to phone Major Morgan, who confided that I had called him just in time. I'd been scheduled to be shipped to Korea the following day, but he'd managed to have me pulled off those orders.

Whew!

My new assignment, he assured me, was temporary. I would be transferred to *Stars & Stripes* as soon as my MOS number was changed to Artist, a bureaucratic procedure that would require a hearing, paperwork, etc.

Oy… But hey – my cockamamie plan was working! I'd gamed the goddam system that far, anyway. My job at the Ordnance Depot, which sprawled over many acres on the north side of the city: Inspector, along with a few other GI's and several very interesting Japanese civilian employees, of various rebuilt or newly manufactured parts for tanks and other combat vehicles damaged in Korea. Along with that, though I was assigned a bunk in the barracks, my freedom at the end of the workday was complete. No roll-call, no lining up in the morning, and I was free to exit the base after work, and to not return until next morning. Amazing!

A few weeks – and some noodging on my part – later, I made it to *S&S*.

But before that, on my new, plentiful free-time, and to my great surprise, I was falling in love with Tokyo!

It was my first visit to a foreign country – and this one was *truly* foreign. As much as I did not want to be there, nor in the Army, I was astonished by my fascination with the experience. Really, by my eager enjoyment of it. The often picture-book visual – women walking along on sandals, wearing colorful kimonos, many carrying parasols – and the extraordinary, routine, so-civilized courtesies of merchants and other strangers – to each other and to me. *Plus* the characters I was meeting. Happily, and far from incidentally, most of the younger ones spoke English. The result of the Japanese educational system's pragmatic response to the war's end, and subsequent occupation by Americans; all students, at least in large metropolitan areas, were required to learn our language.

Of course there was my relative freedom, over the bounds of which I was all too quickly overstepping. Within a week, I was already in trouble with my superiors, for ignoring various nitpicky military bullshit – from not properly maintaining my bunk-and-locker area, to carelessness about my uniform and other horseshit. I tried – sort of – to mend my ways, figuring I definitely did not want to jeopardize my chance to get transferred, but there were a lot of temptations. One of them was a pretty young woman named Kiyoko Takagi (pronounced Ta-kahng-yi), whom I met in a downtown saloon, where she was serving drinks. We would play key roles in each other's life during that year.

At the time that I found myself in Tokyo, the place was still recovering from the devastation of WWII, and the years of endless bombing raids by the USAF. The pace of traffic, of people on the streets, and traveling on the modern, very efficient subway lines displayed an energy not unlike that of New York City. There, somewhat oddly and surprisingly, I became aware of another telling phenomenon: virtually *all* of the "car cards," the advertisements just above the windows in their curved holders, were – unlike those in the US – aesthetically pleasing, beautifully designed, lovely to look at. An indicator, if you will, of a kind of ethnic, national appreciation for beauty. Which was of course reflected elsewhere, in gardens, architecture, bonsai, home interiors and the like. In a very real way, they seemed to try to surround themselves with beauty.

But while there were few remaining obviously visible signs of the war, major commerce had yet to fully recover. Some of the newer office buildings in the downtown area were as high as ten or fifteen stories, but that was about it. Japan was still a few years shy of achieving its world-class status in automobile production and electronic innovation. The then-relatively few cars manufactured in Japan were regarded by the citizens as unreliable and of low-quality. In fact about the only area in which they were making an international impression – and it *was* impressive – was in 35mm photography. Canon and Nikon were at that time beginning to give the revered German brands, such as Zeiss and Leica, some serious challenges. But automobiles, while being produced on a small scale, were still years away from becoming a major industry.

Besides the unique look of the place, and the special music of public spaces where the language was overheard, there were the smells. For instance, I was quickly – if somewhat condescendingly – informed by native-born acquaintances that if a neighborhood projected the odor of garlic, it was probably Korean.

But unquestionably one of the most striking, emotionally affecting parts of being there was to actually associate with people who had lived through those unspeakable bombardments – to hear about their experiences firsthand. Almost none were self-pitying or judgmental, and as I got to know more of them, and listened to their descriptions of what it had been like for them, I found myself deeply touched and sympathetic. It was difficult to imagine the near-nightly explosions, the fires, and especially the horror of injuries suffered or seen, and the personal tragedies. As I heard and observed those I did not know – strangers, individuals, the crowds in public areas who had survived it, who I knew carried those memories – I came to view all of them with a whole different sensibility.

The Ordnance Depot held special interest, historic in fact, in a unique way: I learned that it had been a primary target of Col. Jimmy Doolittle's famous, daring 1942 first ever U.S. air raid on Tokyo. In fact, still standing were several of the long, warehouse-type building-shells, sans roofs and large wall-chunks burned away by the bombs.

Also as touched on above, some of my Japanese civilian workmates were intriguing indeed, one of them in his special relationship to that place and to that air raid. Binichi Doi was a bright, handsome, unusually tall, slender fellow about my age, who had grown up a few blocks from our workplace. Not quite twelve years-old at the time of the raid, Binichi told me of how, one day in his classroom, he, his fellow students and their teacher were startled by the sound of nearby low-flying airplanes. They looked out the window, and as they passed, less than a mile distant, Binichi instantly identified them, even as they were dumping their bombs on the place where he and I were sitting, as American B-25 bombers. It turned out that he and his pals, as were similar-age boys in America, immersed in learning to identify aircraft silhouettes. These side and bottom views of the warplanes operated by Germany, England, Japan and America had been all too familiar to me and to most of my friends, and it was startling – though it made perfect sense – to learn that Japanese kids were into it as well.

Another, a somewhat older fellow in our office, had been a mounted police officer in Hiroshima. He walked with a limp, the result of a broken hip suffered when the nuclear bomb struck. Not far, according to him, from Ground Zero, both he and his horse had been blown over by the blast. The animal fell on him, causing the painful fracture, but ironically enabling his survival by shielding him from the intense heat and radiation. The entire exposed side of the horse had been incinerated.

My "gateway" to *Stars & Stripes* came about three weeks after my arrival at the Ordnance Depot. It was in the form of an audience with an officer, wherein I was asked to state my case for having been given an inappropriate MOS number. When I was notified of the meeting, I took satisfaction in the assumption that it been instigated at the request of Major Morgan – in response to that phone call I'd made from Camp Drake.

While admittedly not as much was riding on the outcome as there had been on my arrival in Japan, given my having been effectively removed from the combat pipeline, it was for me still damned important. And a bit nervous-making, aware that I was taking a gamble by exaggerating – to the point of outright bullshitting about – my professional-artist credits.

But, I asked myself, what're they gonna do if they find me out? Have me taken out and shot?

It turned out *very* satisfyingly, relying as I had since childhood on one of my father's *most* useful, memorable, though unintentional lessons. I can still hear him reciting it, as he did so often: "Tommy, you can *always* tell if someone's lying. Because when they are, they can't look you in the eye."

Talk about a kid's take-it-to-the-bank lesson in everyday survival! Maybe the most easily-acquired skill-set in my bag. I quickly rose to that challenge, and became *very* adept, successfully testing myself over and over on – who else? My father.

But it still carried that edge, that tightrope-quality, which I actually enjoyed. The really cool part: no guilt.

Well-l-l – maybe sometimes, a touch…

TWELVE
My Life in Crime—
The Beginnings

MEANWHILE, I WAS ALREADY FEELING an increasingly acute itch. A financial one. To cover the expense of enjoying myself in Tokyo – of availing myself of the dining, the entertainments – as well as satisfying my curiosity and desire to visit other parts of this remarkable, scenic, tiny country. Plus – Kiyoko's and my more and more urgent desire to live together.

Not *any* of it even close to accomplishable on my buck-private's pay.

The beginning of my solution to that presented itself a few weeks before my transfer to *Stars & Stripes* came through, at a restaurant in a part of Tokyo not frequented by many GI's.

It came, following some thought and a lot of questions about risk, rewards and the like, in the form of my introduction, via Kiyoko, to Mr. Hoshino.

Scary. A dark, short, somber, guarded, trench-coat collar turned up, almost type-cast-sinister underworld figure, well-dressed, of few words, his main transport was a German-built motorcycle. I really didn't want to know how my girlfriend had connected with him. Hoshino, whose name, she told me, meant "star-shine," was a very successful operator in what I soon learned had become a major subculture of postwar Japan.

He was a Black-Marketeer. Of everything from American cigarettes and imported liquor to high-end Swiss watches, to German cameras and even used American automobiles. Those were shipped in from Hong Kong. All the rest? Purchasable by American Military Personnel, at Army Post Exchanges. At prices *way* lower than retail, even back in the U.S.

I was aware – because the Army made a serious point, repeatedly warning us – that the penalties for a GI being caught participating in this "business" were serious: up to a year in military prison, plus dishonorable discharge, for being apprehended selling even a single carton of cigarettes. The discharge thing could haunt you in civilian life for years.

But I had also been informed by several GI's I knew who were active in the trade that the Japanese Police pretty much looked the other way, and a surprising number of my fellow soldiers had ventured into it without being apprehended. Almost unanimously, they assured me that there was little danger, that virtually nobody got caught.

So, still with misgivings, I decided to work with Mr. Hoshino. Early on, it was a confidence-building experience for both of us. His, in me. Mine, trust in him, and seeing if I could pull it off. The way it worked: he provided me with cash. Several hundred dollars, with which for starters I was to purchase American cigarettes.

Unless one was apprehended while actually in the *act* of reselling them to people who didn't have "*PX* privileges," cigarettes presented the least chance of trouble: along with groceries, candy, toothpaste and other everyday items, we weren't required to sign a pledge to not resell them to a Japanese citizen.

That detail I would encounter later, when I moved upmarket, to wristwatches, cameras, TV's and the like.

The brand most favored by Japanese, I was told by Mr. Hoshino – with Kiyoko translating as usual – was Phillip Morris. The reason: advertisements, glimpsed by Japanese in American publications, which often carried images of U.S. Military Officers smoking them. The brand was thus was perceived to be the most prestigious, and as such commanded a higher price. Lucky Strikes, Camels and others were acceptable, but Phillip Morris was to constitute at least half of my purchases. Go figure.

So, excited but a bit tentative at the start, during lunch-hours, and early evenings, I began visiting various Tokyo *PX*'s, mostly accessible via subway, buying no more than four or five cartons at each – at one dollar per carton. I'd store them each day in my foot-locker, and at the end of the week, I delivered them – fifty-to-seventy or more cartons, to Mr. Hoshino, who paid me, on the spot. Essentially, an average commission of more than one hundred percent! It was his money in the first place. Not bad…

Further – it was a welcome and unfamiliar rush: for the first time in my life I was knowingly, consciously, *breaking the law*! Living on an edge I'd never gone to before.

But way better than that, for the only time since I'd landed in Japan – hell, really since I'd been dragged into the army – I had cash in my pocket. *Spending money*. With the promise – along with the unaccustomed, spicy flavor of danger – of more to come! It was a *genuine* thrill. One that heightened as business – and my other already good fortunes – quickly got even better.

My Black Market *PX* purchases graduated to a whole new, higher-end level: Rolex watches and Leica Cameras. Those, too, at a 100% markup to me, on delivery to Mr. Hoshino. More income for me, but, I was aware, at a markedly increased risk. Unlike cigarettes, each such transaction required my signed pledge on the earlier-mentioned little rectangular form, in triplicate, that I wouldn't resell the item to anyone who did not have *PX* privileges. I was thus leaving a record of my purchases.

Hey, what the hell…

I also learned that sort of merchandise involved an additional degree of intrigue: Hoshino and his fellow traders were paying Japanese who were employed as *PX* clerks, on the side, to notify them whenever a new shipment of such highly desirable merchandize arrived. Then, GI's like myself were immediately dispatched, armed with plenty of cash, to the various Exchanges to buy up as much of their stock as we could before it was even put on display for general sales.

In fact, the riskiest, and only nervous-making part was working for myself, independent of Mr. Hoshino, delivering liquor to the bars and downtown nightclubs. Most of these establishments had no back doors, no alley-access. I'd arrive, always after dark, with one, two, or sometimes three taxicabs filled with cases of booze, acquired from GI's who, late each month, nearing payday and running out of cash, were happy to receive the $10 I offered for them to buy – with my money – the single case of whiskey they were allotted. I would unload the cases onto the curb, from which, carton-by-carton, employees moved them inside. Fortunately, no MP cars or Tokyo Police ever drove past, but had they done so, I was prepared to claim that I was simply a pedestrian happening by.

The headiness, along with the ease of transfer, and on-the-spot receipt of payment, enabled me to *almost* forget about possible consequences.

Moreover, it led to another problem-solver for Kiyoko and me, and as it turned out, for Mr. Hoshino. Over drinks one evening, through Kiyoko, I pointed out to him that these new shipments were distributed to all of the *PX*'s in Japan. Thus, if I could get to, say, any of the numerous *PX*'s in and around Yokohama, the major seaport some miles south of Tokyo, I'd be able to increase his volume. But without convenient transportation, that was impossible. I suggested that if I had an automobile at my disposal, I could greatly increase his inventory of saleable goods. It was an idea that yielded *way*-more-than-expected results.

Hoshino asked how much longer I would be in Tokyo. I said I had about nine months until I'd be shipped home. His face lit up. It turned out that he badly wanted to own a particular British sports car. The very-popular-at-the-time MG TD Roadster. A new one. The problem: in order to stimulate domestic car manufacturing by discouraging the importation of new foreign cars, the Japanese Government had imposed on its own people a *very* stiff, 100% tax on such purchases. Thus, whatever the cost of your new, imported British, German or American car, if you were a Japanese citizen, the price was *doubled*.

But the same automobile in used-condition was *free* of such taxes. Anyway, being a member of the conquering U.S. Army, I was not liable for sales taxes of any kind.

Less than a week later, thanks to Mr. Hoshino and the sack-full of yen he gave me – each one-thousand-yen note being worth roughly $3, I had to wait while they were hand-counted by the dealer – I became the owner of a brand new, pale yellow MG with a tan canvas top and green leather upholstery. Mine until I "sold" it to Mr. Hoshino before departing Tokyo. Interestingly, there was nothing in writing between us – no document promising that I would do so. My presumption that Kiyoko and/or her family might suffer physical harm if I reneged, she privately, somewhat reticently, confirmed just prior to my taking possession of the car. Which, in a real way, added to my already surreal sense of living out a movie-like fantasy.

My new, extra income, was affording Kiyoko and me numerous pleasurable luxuries, such as staying in pleasant, though not deluxe hotels, dining in higher-end restaurants and indulging ourselves in nice clothing. But one of the best parts was for me a feel-good experience, one that was making me a kind of hero to Kiyoko and her family. Her younger, very pretty sister, age sixteen, was also gifted, with dreams of becoming a performer in Japan's leading dance company. At Kiyoko's request, I agreed to pay her tuition at one of the top dance-schools, the training-ground for much of the big company's talent. Seeing her impressive dancing, it was a genuine pleasure to be contributing to her future.

Happily, Kiyoko and I quickly found and moved into a charming, cozy apartment – the top floor of a two-story private home, actually – in Shibuya Prefecture, on the west side of Tokyo. Where, I soon discovered, I was the only non-Asian in the neighborhood. Our rooms were lovely, classic Japanese-style, with straw tatami-matted floors and sparse-but-adequate, tasteful furnishings. Kiyoko and I quickly settled in, our only furniture-addition: a *"Stateside"* bed. Meaning, to the Japanese – and to GI's – with legs, mattress and box-spring, rather than the native, rollup floor-pad.

It was an easy subway ride, or fifteen minute drive, from downtown, where I was that same week, *at last*, posted to *Pacific Stars & Stripes* as a Staff Artist!

THIRTEEN
The Army—*My* Way.
Well-1-1—Close Enough...

WITHIN MINUTES OF MY ARRIVAL at the *Stars & Stripes* offices, I had my first actual meeting with the welcoming, very pleasant Major Morgan. After thanking him for his efforts in arranging my transfer, I pitched my by-then several months-old plan, volunteering to go to Panmunjom, Korea to draw sketches of the Peace Talks. He seemed genuinely intrigued, explaining however that it might take several weeks to arrange. The Major then introduced me to several staffers, who greeted me warmly, and they in turn presented me to others.

My initial – and *not* unpleasant – surprise: most wore very casual civilian clothes – and those in uniforms of any kind were strikingly non-regulation, unlike anything I'd seen since being drafted: shirttails out, unbuttoned, untucked t-shirts and the like. In fact, we were *only* required to wear a uniform *once* a month! On payday – and even then, fatigues were acceptable!

For those and many other reasons, *Stars & Stripes* (known to the Japanese as "*Seijoki Shimbun,*" meaning: "Flag Newspaper"), with its daily circulation of 150,000, would turn out to be the near-perfect posting for someone with my below-zero-level appreciation of/tolerance for standard Army life.

The staff living quarters were in a building several blocks from our offices, on the west side of Hibiya Park. It was, especially for those who chose to *not* live there, like having a civilian job. Sure, we were still in effect prisoners of the Military, and thus could not quit if we were dissatisfied. But that was about it.

I was further delighted to discover that my fellow *Stars & Stripes* staffers were generally bright, creative, witty and very sociable – a great, diverse, bunch of guys, many of them quite colorful, a few of whom would become close, longtime friends. All seemed to love the gig. Several of them had real, professional credits, working in newspaper, radio and magazines. One of them, John Sack, had written for *The New Yorker*. Some were novices, and not a few were 'exaggerators' like myself. Including, amusingly, one fellow who avoided me for months. His reason, I eventually learned, was that some of the 'creds' he'd made up in order to get transferred to *S&S* overlapped mine in ways that made him fear, if we'd compared notes, being found out. When we were finally able to open up to each other about our mutually enhanced background-stories, it proved that his worries were groundless, and afforded us some laughs.

One of the more colorful of my co-staffers, Korea Bureau correspondent Dick Brooks, would become a lifelong buddy, both of us eventually migrating to Hollywood. Garrulous, funny, with a wry New Yorker's-take on the world, my earliest recollection of Dick was his gleeful reading aloud, to anyone who'd listen, from that day's just-received copy of the *New York Daily News*, mailed to him religiously by his mother. It never dampened Dick's excitement or the anchorman-urgency of his delivery, that these accounts, the 'latest' on this or that scandal or sporting event, were by then at least 30 days-old because his mom sent the tabloid via the cheapest-possible method, boat-mail.

Pleasurably, *S&S*'s singularly non-deluxe, but very professional-feeling offices were on the third (top) floor of *The Nippon Times* building. One of Tokyo's major daily newspapers, it was located in the heart of downtown, about two blocks from one of the world's great architectural masterpieces, Frank Lloyd Wright's thrillingly gorgeous Imperial Hotel. Another block further, among the central business buildings was the Ernie Pyle Theater, the primary movie house/dining hangout for GI's, where all of the first-run Hollywood movies were shown at nominal admission cost.

Additionally, to my very pleasant surprise one day in the Ernie Pyle complex, I found myself face-to-face with an acquaintance from New York, fellow cartoonist Carl Anderson. A very talented artist, Carl, it turned out, was stationed a few blocks away, designing and illustrating propaganda leaflets and other materials in the *Psychological Warfare* section. Though our paths had crossed only intermittently after those first weeks on West 57th Street, over the coming months Carl and I spent a lot of time together, forming a warm, caring, lasting friendship. Kiyoko and I enjoyed frequent double-dating with Carl and Miyako, his charming girlfriend, as well as their numerous visits to our apartment. While Carl envied the extra cash I was earning in the black market, his assessment, amusing and likely true: "Hey, if *I* tried it – I'd get caught for sure."

At *S&S*, our small, cramped, partitioned Art Department was located in a single- windowed corner of the large, noisy main room. It contained two drawing tables in very close proximity. One was occupied by Carl Methfessel, a talented, humorous-sarcastic young guy about my age. Carl's specialty: 'funny' cartoon drawing. On that first day, I was immediately put to work creating small "spot" illustrations for a feature story scheduled to appear in the next day's edition.

It was a hoot, and *not* just because I had managed to game the system. After more than a year in the Army, the experience itself was for the first time, *fun*! My weekends were free. I was in a fascinating city, with a fascinating culture, living with a bright, charming, lovely young woman with similar tastes, and doing work that challenged and entertained me!

In another eight months, I'd be back – unscathed – in New York.

My efforts to go to Korea as an artist/correspondent got as far as requisitioning proper uniforms and cold-weather gear, and then quickly fizzled. Major Morgan informed me that there just wasn't sufficient money in the budget for such a venture. But by then I was so savoring Japan, my new friends and my work at *S&S* where, in addition to illustrating feature stories, I drew occasional gag cartoons, that I wasn't all that disappointed.

The pointless war dragged on, my sole contact with it happily distant, occurring via a few early evening telephone conversations with people at our bureau in Seoul, during which I'd hear the background whump-whump of the nightly bombing runs by the "*Bedtime Charlies*." These nuisance raids were carried out via ancient, two seat, open cockpit biplanes, their concussion bombs hand-dropped by the rear seat passenger.

I continued to be enthralled by Tokyo, its nightlife and bustle. With Kiyoko, I enjoyed lovely, memorable side trips to places such as the ancient, gorgeously ornamented shrines at Nikko, high in the heavily wooded Japanese Alps. We loved exploring the countryside with its tiny, primitive, medieval, walled farming villages and other little towns connected by a single narrow gravel road, paved for only the hundred or two hundred-yard lengths of their commercial areas.

Kiyoko, her friends, and other natives I came to know were, incidentally, the first civilians I ever met who had lived through actual warfare, exposed to the ugliness of it, its surviving victims. In Kiyoko's case, she and her family had been firebombed out of three homes. Her, and their personal accounts of what it was like made profound, lasting impressions on me.

A singularly moving such moment took place one evening at the movies. Kiyoko and I were sitting in the dark at the Ernie Pyle Theater when the newsreel preceding the feature film displayed some footage of WWII B-29 Bombers. These were the airplanes that had so devastated Japan late in the war with round-the-clock high altitude incendiary raids, as well as, finally – shamefully and unnecessarily – dropping the two nuclear bombs on Hiroshima and Nagasaki. As the camera pushed into a close shot of one, on the ground, with the crew beside it, I leaned close to Kiyoko and whispered that it was a B-29. Her surprised reaction was unforgettable: "*Honto?* ["Really?"] So *big?*"

In that instant I had a startling insight into what it must have been like to have been in their target-zone. The B-29's she and her countrymen had seen daily, as moving dots in the skies over Tokyo, had been five-to-ten miles up.

Beyond my sympathy for the difficult-to-imagine horrors these innocents suffered, not least, such stories reinforced then, and now, the truth that aerial bombing attacks on noncombatants – while even today embraced by our government and others who choose to ignore/deny history – succeed *only* in hardening the resolve of those being thus assaulted, and are therefore strategically counterproductive.

On the other hand, happily for our military/industrial-supported economy, they *do* effectively prolong wars and use up even more materiel which then must be profitably replaced.

Sigh…

An amusing, understandable social pattern was the ease with which young Japanese men and women could identify which American GI's lived with Japanese girls. Whenever a member of that large group of us spoke Japanese, he was unknowingly employing the feminine idiom, because that was who we'd learned the language from. Being an overtly "polite" society, whatever disdain or contempt natives might have felt, it was, beyond occasional knowing grins or condescension, rarely expressed or revealed.

On the downside, for Kiyoko and me, I sensed a growing, uncomfortable complication. Though not yet expressed by Kiyoko in literal terms, she was giving me increasing hints that she wanted – expected, really – for us to marry. While I was genuinely fond of her, that was for me simply not an option. Yet, selfishly – hell, cruelly, I knew – out of fear that she would leave, I'd avoided spelling it out. I knew that I was not the first GI with whom she'd been involved, and that even if I'd been the only one, per the postwar cultural climate of that era, because of her having crossed that line, no Japanese male would consider marrying her. Added to that, being a few years older than me, she quite understandably felt that her time was running out – and that I was looking more and more like her final hope.

Not a role I relished, I did my best to avoid thinking about it, and attempted to divert both of us. That we did by maintaining a social life: evenings with Carl Anderson and his girlfriend, with other couples we'd come to know, and my increasingly prosperous pursuit of Black Market dollars. Aside from the MG Roadster giving greater mobility and range of *PX*'s I could visit, and having expanded my operation to include cases of Scotch and American hard liquor, which I supplied to downtown Ginza bars and nightclubs, I began helping meet the native demand for large American used-cars. A somewhat irrational phenomenon, given the narrowness of most streets and roads, big Buicks were the most popular, and I'd begun importing a few from Hong Kong. My income – again, all of it in cash – had for the six months or so in which I'd been trafficking, already exceeded $20,000, which at that rate and time was considered in the U.S. to be mid-to-upper level executive pay. It certainly served its purpose for Kiyoko and me. We took weekend trips, dined at the best restaurants, bought her some nice clothes – and me, too – and generally enjoyed a very entertaining, diverting lifestyle.

Until that day…

FOURTEEN
Another Example of Life—Mine, Anyway —Imitating the Movies

My criminal career had gone remarkably smoothly.

Until one morning when things changed abruptly   and scarily – as I arrived at *Stars & Stripes*.

En route to my cubicle I was promptly intercepted by Major Morgan, who gravely announced that he'd taken a phone call for me a few minutes earlier. "Tom, they want to see you down at *CID* – immediately. You're supposed to report to this guy." He handed me a note with the name of the Master Sergeant who had called. One of the most disorienting, thought-rush-provoking, *truly* oh-shit moments of my life: the letters '*CID*' stood for *Criminal Investigation Division.*

The Major did not ask me what it was about. Though I was hardly curious at the time, I suspect that his reading of my face was answering any questions he might have had. He turned and crossed to his office.

The chill, the dread, the aloneness I felt as I descended the stairs a few minutes later was only the beginning.

Mygod – I was facing – *prison…?*

Exiting our building, I crossed to my car – an additional reminder of the fix I'd gotten myself into. It occurred to me that it might be unwise to arrive in it – that they might ask how I acquired it – but that, I realized was easily explainable: my father paid for it. I climbed in and began the several mile drive to *CID* headquarters, to which a fellow staff-member had provided me with directions.

The mental processing and sorting I went through along the way as I considered the various possibilities yielded an unexpected anomaly. A question, really

Its effect – just the asking of it – was unexpectedly calming.

Backing up a bit: obviously, this was about my black market activities.

Okay. Then – *why* hadn't they simply come to arrest me, and taken me away in handcuffs? Why was I being told to come to *them?*

The answer was even more stress-relieving, though admittedly its source, its logic, were hardly intellectual.

It was all those cop-and-gangster movies I'd grown up on, and some novels I'd read: the longer I pondered, and the closer I got to the *CID* offices, the more I found myself thinking of, and *like*, characters I'd watched in such films – those who'd been in similar situations – the common cliché being that they'd been "called in for questioning."

The equally hackneyed – but probably valid in my case, too – reason: the cops didn't "have enough on them" to actually arrest them!

The situation and classic response that leapt immediately to mind was from *The Maltese Falcon*, hardly surprising, given the movie and book's effect on my life before and since. In a similar fix, PI hero Sam Spade's line when the official who'd summoned him asked for Sam's supposition on the matter at hand was: "Mrs. Spade didn't raise any children dippy enough to make guesses in front of a District Attorney."

And, damned if *other* movie-lines didn't begin popping into my consciousness. On the order of: "C'mon, you're fishing. You don't have anything on me."

That, I began to toy with, was very likely the truth in this unreal-yet-real-life instance: the goddam *CID* people probably *didn't* have the kind of proof for which they could actually nail me.

As outrageous as my arrival at that seems at this distance – I was twenty-two years-old, and my entire education on the subject had been from all those Saturday Matinees, and a few novels – it worked for me, made *total* sense. Thus, as I pulled into the parking lot adjacent to their offices, I was beginning to feel – if not confident and unafraid – at least a bit more cool.

To hopefully avoid questions about my transportation, I parked in a distant corner, a large truck between my MG and the factory-like structure on the flatland adjacent to Tokyo Bay.

I reported to the uniformed Corporal near the door, who grabbed his phone, dialed an extension, and announced that I had arrived. A few seconds later, a stocky, civilian-clothed fellow descended the stairs, crossed, and with his face expressionless beneath his buzz-cut, receding hair and with no wasted words, introduced himself as the Sergeant who had summoned me. A fortyish career-soldier-type, what we draftees referred to as "RA" (Regular Army), it was obvious that he took his role quite seriously – almost comically so. He was dressed in civilian clothes, wearing a tie around his bull-neck, and a sport jacket of a size to accommodate, but not hide the presence of the cannon-like .45 caliber Colt automatic in his shoulder holster.

Immediately following identifying himself, with a thumb-jerk he added: "Follow me, soldier."

Before I could even say "Sure," he'd done an about-face and headed for the stairway. I fell in behind him, his appearance and demeanor already causing me to feel a touch more confident – more like I was participating – performing, really – in a movie-scene. As we reached the second-floor, I observed that he wasn't alone in costuming or demeanor, noting several of his fellow, similarly dressed central-casting-type "detectives," none of whom seemed to be into more reasonably-sized weapons or, for that matter, into subtleties in general. They, along with the atmosphere of the place, were totally, near-laughably consistent with the B-movie metaphor.

The Sergeant led me into his small office, dead-pan silently indicated the guest-chair and shut the door before seating himself opposite me at his desk. I watched while he gravely, ceremoniously reached into a drawer and withdrew a rubber band-bound three-inch stack of postcard-size papers which he wordlessly placed on the desktop between us.

Instantly I knew that they were copies of the pledge-slips I'd signed with each *PX* purchase. After studying my face with a suitably menacing – in his mind, at least – look on his: "And – what's your monthly pay?"

Which caused a bit more of the weight to lift off me. I *had* guessed correctly – it was indeed the old-film routine. Presumably he'd seen the same ones I remembered, and we were playing it together – fellow actors.

Remembering as I had so many times before, my Dad's lie-detection tutoring, I looked him in the eye, put blinking on "hold," and shrugged. "I guess – what is it – around 90 dollars a month…" Actually it was only half of that, because, out of sympathy for Lee being alone on her own in Manhattan, following our annulment, I'd not reported my change in marital status to the Army. Thus she continued to receive the other 50%.

My co-star leaned in and addressed me in this almost comically-bad, over-the-top, smug, 'gotcha' tone: "So – tell me, soldier, on 3 dollars a day, how d'you explain these..?" He gestured at the stack of slips. "Your *PX* purchases – over the last two months, more than four thousand bucks worth…"

Mentally thumbing *my* script, I could see – as if on a teleprompter – the words: *Circumstantial Evidence.*

Yeah! *All* this bozo had were the goddam slips.

Which *were* a lot, but…

I improvised, determinedly without "uh," or any other outward betrayal of my uncertainty: "That was all stuff I bought for other GI's. Because I've got a lot of free time, they tell me what they want and give me the money and I---"

He jumped in. "Okay..." Still nailing me with his eyes, he grabbed a pencil, held it poised over a notepad. "You wanta give me names of the guys you've been doin' this for?"

The 'game,' as they say, was afoot. Not without some surprise – I felt a small confidence-boost. Not exactly a surge, but I sensed that I might have *some* control. I waved dismissively. "Y'know – I would. If I could remember. Thing is, they're not my friends. Just guys I meet, they're about to be sent back to the U.S., they ask me to you know buy stuff for 'em..." I recalled – with some relief – that my most recent purchase had been more than a week earlier. "...The last one I did it for, he shipped out a few days ago."

That the Sergeant didn't believe me was immaterial. Mentally paging through my movie-acquired criminal law knowledge, as far as I could imagine, anyway, short of my giving him a name – which I could not because there were none – and then his trying to contact this person thousands of miles away, for a statement – there was *no* way he could disprove or even contradict what I'd said.

He hesitated for a moment, which made him seem further put off that this wasn't in his copy of the script. "You're aware of the penalties – dishonorable discharge – prison...? I mean we got guys doin' a year hard labor for coupla cartons of cigarettes. An' here..." He made another over-acted ominous gesture at the bundle of pledges. "...We got stuff a *lot* more serious."

I held onto our eye-contact. "Hey, yeah. I mean that's why I never got into it."

Then, predictably, he played the D.A.'s card from the old screenplay: "Okay. Would you be willing to take a lie-detector test?"

Damn! Again, I recalled – hell, I *recited* – the scene I'd watched *so* many times. "I don't think so. I understand that they're unreliable, and I'm not about to take a chance on incriminating myself."

"That's bullshit. They're *very* reliable."

"That's not what I've heard."

He stared at me. I stared back, and felt a tiny sense of elation.

The sergeant gripped the stack with both hands, tapped it against the desktop in an evening-the-edges motion. Then he spoke his first unexpected words. "When're you scheduled to go home, soldier?"

"Three months. A little over…" I could hardly wait, though with the money I had earned from my nefarious activities I'd been considering taking my discharge in Japan and touring the Orient for a while. That fantasy, I discarded on the spot. "Early September."

He returned the bundle to his drawer, slid it shut with finality, leaned on his elbows, eyed me for a beat, and in a deadly-level voice delivered his threatening clincher. One that – if I had been the film's director, I'd have been thrilled with. "You're never gonna make it."

Then, silence, his eyes never moving nor blinking, staring into mine.

I was back to the chills.

A few long seconds later, I managed a lame, more-or-less innocent shrug. "So – are – we done?"

"Yeah."

I stood, turned and, with the assumption that he was watching, did my best to appear relaxed as I left his cubicle, crossed to the stairwell, descended to street level, and exited. My movements must have been wooden; I barely breathed until I'd reached the corner of the parking lot where I'd deposited my car. I climbed in – and sat there, both hands gripping the wheel, exhausted, unable to move – beyond my trembling – for almost ten minutes.

I'd won. But had I…?

Again, straight out of the movies, and no better written, the button to the scene we'd just played had unexpectedly gotten to me – in no small measure because I – not an actor on a screen – had been on the receiving end of the cliché.

But it wasn't an ending. More like a twist, really. Because over my remaining few months several things changed.

The first began immediately. Continuing the scenario, the following morning I pulled the MG out of the parking space beside my apartment, and as I turned onto the street and headed for the *Stars & Stripes* offices, I glanced at the mirror – and then looked again. A black late-model Ford sedan had pulled away from the curb and slipped into traffic behind the vehicle directly behind me. My first thought was that my paranoia was at work. But the damned Ford followed me all the way to the office. For the rest of that morning at my desk, I thought about it, telling myself that A.) I was imagining it, or B.), it was a joke.

Or – C.)...

Sure enough, when I left to go to lunch with a pair of the guys, there was the Ford – or one exactly like it, parked across the street, a fellow wearing civilian clothes and a GI haircut behind the wheel, making a too-obvious point of not looking at me.

Which for me revived and amplified the almost cartoonish movie-satire unreality of it. Once more I was feeling relieved, this time less to my surprise. They were so eminently visible that all I had to do was avoid my suddenly-former M.O.

For my remaining time in Japan, their singularly obvious surveillance continued, though it did seem to taper off toward the end. Exiting the office during the day, wherever I went, whether on foot or in my car, as well as when I drove home, or if Kiyoko and I went out to dinner or a nightclub or a movie, there they were.

I could only assume that the people in the *CID* didn't have a lot going on in their lives. Because these plain-clothes 'operatives' were so ludicrously obvious, all of them wearing those truly awful oversized sport jackets, I'd occasionally approach one in a bar or restaurant and chidingly ask him to light my cigarette, once or twice even tauntingly joking – again a la the movies – with a smartass line such as: "So, how's business?"

Its humorous aspects notwithstanding, my "*Most Wanted*" status did force me to greatly curtail my black market activities, which of course, dramatically diminished my income. Fortunately however, I was helped by several

Japanese nationals employed by *PX*'s in the area, to whose earnings I'd earlier contributed in exchange for their putting certain merchandise aside for me. They aided me in reverting to dealing in the one commodity that posed the least risk – cartons of cigarettes. Via mostly clandestine, late-night deliveries to, and sales out of my apartment, with only a minimum of angst I was able to maintain the best of my lifestyle until it was time for me to leave the Far East.

FIFTEEN
A (Sad) Bump or Two—
and a Parting
(Satisfying) Nose-Thumb

As my time in the Orient wound down, a few weeks before I was to be shipped home, I encountered – sigh – another complication. One that, had I been dealing with the issue rather than ignoring it, might have been avoided. Or at least prevented from coming to quite such a ghastly head: Kiyoko announced – matter-of-factly and without theatrics – that if I did not marry her, she would kill herself.

Moreover, she insisted, our wedding would *have* to take place *before* I left. Because, as had happened with too many of her girlfriends, GI's who promised to come back and marry *never* did so. Her plan: she would then accompany me when I returned to the States, or follow me shortly thereafter.

Shit!

While I cared about Kiyoko, and wished her no harm or unhappiness, *there was no way I was going to marry her.*

But – how the *hell* was I going to have a life if I had this young woman's suicide on my conscience?

So, I made a cold-blooded-but-pragmatic decision. A Plan. A gamble, but one that was necessary.

One that did not make me feel good about myself.

First, I lied. I promised we'd marry.

I then set about attempting to convince a skeptical Kiyoko that first I had to go back to the States to put certain affairs in order, to make sure my previous marriage had indeed been dissolved, and so forth, *and* that I *was* the exception. I *would* return. I traded on the good will I'd already sown with her and her family by having paid her younger sister's tuition to train with the dance troupe.

We made a for-me-far-less-than-comfortable visit to her family's home, where I met and was welcomed by Kiyoko's parents and siblings. Over a *very* long, awkward evening we dined and attempted small-talk. While I had for much of my life lied with relative ease whenever I felt it necessary, for gain or self-preservation, it was also with an inner understanding that doing so was unlikely to cause serious harm.

But this was different – both painful and, guilt-inducing.

Finally, having more-or-less sold her – and them, I departed for the US, hoping that my gamble would work: that time, distance, her family and friends would, once it became clear that I wasn't coming back, prevail on her to change her mind.

Hoping also – but truly not all that worried – that my outlaw past wouldn't catch up with me before I was safely discharged and out of the Army's reach.

One last note about manipulating the military system. The year-earlier troopship ride from San Francisco to Yokohama had been indelibly, memorably, rough, grungy and interminable. As earlier cited, I so hated it that I'd resolved that, during my stay in Tokyo, I'd somehow, somewhere, learn what it would take to get myself flown back to the States – a journey at that pre-jet time of 40 hours, versus another wretched 11 or 12 days aboard a filthy, smelly, cramped, pitching, rolling boat.

It turned out that I was not alone. One morning at *Stars & Stripes*, about six weeks before the end of my tour, I heard that the editor had decided to do a feature story about the medical cadre at Camp Drake, the earlier-referenced replacement depot through which all troops, coming and going, were processed. I quickly cornered the writer who was going to be doing the story, shared my feelings about boat-travel and my desire to avoid it, and found a kindred spirit. He agreed to make a point of inquiring about what the people at *Camp Drake* needed that would justify their ordering us to be flown home.

Lo, that evening all of us at *Stars & Stripes* had our answer – one that turned out to be a lot easier than anticipated. The drill, from the horse's mouth, was that each of us should report to "Sick Call" the first morning at the camp. There, we were to claim to be sufferers of severe "*motion*-sickness" (as opposed to less official-sounding "sea-sickness"). So acute in fact that en route to Japan, unable to digest *any* food, we were bedridden in sick-bay, being fed intravenously for nearly the entire voyage.

Now, the almost freakish beauty-part of all this was that since no shipboard health records were shared with the Army in Japan, there was no way they could refute this outrageous story! So all you had to do was look the medic in the eye and, working from the script, deliver your lines in a convincing manner. The quid pro quo for this gem: the *S&S* reporter had promised our Camp Drake "insider" that he'd be the primary focus – the "star" if you will – of the feature story, which would then be sent on to the fellow's hometown newspaper.

So, after "selling" my MG to Mr. Hoshino, saying "so longs" to my friends at *S&S*, and others, I provided Kiyoko with the few hundred dollars I still had. Then, helping her clean out our apartment, I offered her appropriately solemn goodbyes – and assurances – and departed for Camp Drake.

Along with, as it happened, two other *Stars & Stripes* guys, all of us intent on avoiding that damned boat-ride.

The obvious problem: each man reciting our motion-sickness tale almost word-for-word, consecutively – or even at intervals – to the same medic would *certainly* draw suspicion, if not outright rejection. So, before lights-out that evening, we anxiously huddled with our inside man. He calmly advised us to relax: there were always four or five medics listening to health complaints. We should simply line up one-after-the-other and make sure each was interviewed by a different medic.

First thing next morning, there we were in the "Sick Call" line. And – *Bingo* – each of us told our *identical* stories to separate medics who, with no questions or hesitation of any kind, filled out the appropriate "buck-slip" on the spot, exempting us from boat-travel.

That night, my last in Japan, was memorable in an odd way. Having finished packing, and excited by the prospect of flying home, I was on my bunk, trying to relax by finishing a novel I'd been reading. It was Graham Greene's *The End of the Affair*. I had been, for the several years since I had read and been hooked by his first novel, *Brighton Rock*, not so much a fan as – in a way – a fascinated student of the man's mind. Because, beginning with that book I had been privately – until I shared and discussed it with Leonard Starr – fascinated by a tortured theme which seemed to affect most of his stories: his own battle, as a converted Catholic, between his obviously powerful intellect – and his belief in the mysticism of the Church. I'm not sure I understood then, or now, why – as someone with no religious beliefs of my own – it even caught my interest. Possibly it was because of a kind of curiosity about which side was going to win. But in some way it did add a dimension to my general enjoyment of his writing. I was rooting for his *mind*.

Especially so as I neared the final pages of *The End of the Affair*. In it, he had set up rather suspensefully, so that it might really go either way, a female protagonist, dead before the end of the story, who might or might not perform miracles.

Given that overtly religious flavor, the only reasons I stayed with it were: One, disbelief that a man with Greene's chops would actually with a straight face try to sell me such bullshit. Two, my growingly fervent hope that he would *not*.

But – damned if he didn't. I reached the last page, still hoping – *hoping* – he'd retract it. But no. His heroine, Sarah *was* performing miracles.

I was pissed. Bigtime. It was just before lights-out. I did something I'd never done before, nor have I since. I angrily hurled the book across the room, where it smashed noisily against a wall, then clunked to the floor.

Years passed before I could bring myself to read Graham Greene again.

On a cheerier, *very* gratifying, system-beating note, early the following morning we were bussed to the airfield, where we boarded a Pan American Airlines charter – complete with attractive stewardesses – and took off for California, with refueling stops at Wake Island and Honolulu. From there I was flown to New Jersey for my discharge.

Within a week, I was back in New York City. In my own life. Along with the continuing hope that Kiyoko would get over it.

Did I feel guilt? Of course, but bottom-line, that one had been *all* about self-preservation.

What a trip the Army had been! Not least, the amazing life-lessons I absorbed, and – exceeding what I'd thought possible – the extent to which I had been able to manage my fate.

Plus the confidence it gave me that I could continue along that route.

Altogether, one helluvva two years. The second one, anyway...

SIXTEEN
Some Focus Shifts and Image Moves—at Least One of Them Problematic

Upon my re-entry into the Real World, the first items on my agenda involved some long-considered goal-adjustments and serious, urgent self image-tweaks.

These, however, required some immediate modifications when I was confronted with several significant changes that had occurred among my friends during my time in Japan.

The workspace on West 57th was no more. Leonard Starr had broken up with his wife, sold the Long Island house, and moved into Manhattan. He'd leased a studio on West 69th Street, in the same building that housed his old friends, and by then ours mutually; editorial cartoonist Warren King, and his beautiful wife, Nadine.

Which motivated me to apartment-hunt in that neighborhood. I quickly found what I needed a block away, on West 70th Street, a few doors from Central Park. The space was nice, and while the air-shaft view was less than thrilling, it was consistent with my limited budget. It certainly did not diminish my excitement to be settling in and resuming my dream-pursuit. I eagerly began furnishing the place and preparing new samples with, thanks to Starr, some unexpectedly fresh intentions.

Professionally over the past year, Leonard had moved on, and markedly upward. Though his goal – like me – of writing and drawing a syndicated "story-strip" remained the same, he had transitioned professionally to something far more lucrative and attractive than grinding out comic-books: he was drawing advertising art in comic-strip form.

Ubiquitous at that time, such ads appeared in the Sunday four-color-comics sections of newspapers all over America. The bulk of them were produced for major ad agencies through an art service located on Lexington Avenue, just north of 58th Street, Johnstone & Cushing. Most were half-or-one-third page affairs, promoting national brands: everything from breakfast cereals to detergents, toothpaste, automobiles and cigarettes. Some were realistically drawn, others in cartoon style.

But – what particularly caught my attention: they paid roughly *ten* times the going rate for ordinary comic-book pages.

I immediately asked Leonard what particular skills were required to obtain such assignments. Obviously, being able to draw well was number-one. He succinctly confided the specific area I would need to hone: "The key with these – you've gotta be able to draw pretty girls and handsome guys."

An area in which I clearly understood my then-weaknesses, it provided me with a new – and specific – professional goal. An intermediate strategy on my continuing journey toward that end-frame – my own strip.

Similarly exciting – my friendship with Leonard was beginning to provide me with unanticipated access to a whole new, exciting group of creative people. Along with his dramatic change in occupational status, he had also moved up socially. He'd become a member of the prestigious Society of Illustrators, hanging out with – and introducing me to – a whole new, much tonier set. Most were painters, bigtime magazine and/or advertising illustrators, the work of several achieving true artistic value. They were the superstars, really, of the business.

Thanks to Leonard, attending their parties, and joining him and others for drinks at the club, I quickly got to know a number of the members. In fact, I was awed by several that I met, whose work I'd been clipping out of magazines since I was a kid. In a very real way it was, without realizing it, upwardly-mobile "networking." That so valuable phenomenon would play a startlingly vital role during my later transition to Hollywood.

Among the more flamboyant and entertaining of the illustrators was Len Steckler, an extremely talented artist with whom I enjoyed instant rapport. Already prominent in that field, Len would later have an extraordinary career as a photographer and TV commercial director. Between marriages, Len shared an apartment with Carl Sandburg, most famously photographing a visit from one of Carl's admirers, Marilyn Monroe.

Meanwhile, there were those personal adjustments. The *image* stuff.

Almost from the day I had initially touched down in Manhattan, and reinforced in a way by the Army experience, I'd been struck by the observation that nearly *everyone* in that city seemed to wear a uniform. Still the era of more formal business attire, and few women in executive positions, most of course were male. With their rank as clear and obvious as if there were bars or eagles pinned to shirt-collar or shoulder-epaulets, or chevrons stitched onto their sleeves.

These costumes that city residents and suburban commuters got into every morning were sometimes *too* on-the-nose symbolic of their professions, their levels of success. But in another way I perceived it as a measure of how they regarded *themselves*. As what and with whom they wished to be identified.

There were the solid, and stolid, management-types – bankers, lawyers, investment, advertising and book-publishing execs, their status telegraphed by their three-piece suits and neckties. Just below, the slightly-looser group – self-employed, successful professionals. Doctors, or those in "creative" fields

– who, along with their "regulation" shirts-and-ties, wore suits without vests, or slacks and nicely-cut sport jackets. Plus, the fairly obvious young wannabes for both groups.

Then there were the others: secretaries, clerks, bus drivers, maintenance people, menials, and beggars.

And – *sigh* – the comic-book artists.

Entirely consistent with *their* chosen costumes, I had judgmentally concluded, that group of way-too casual-to-outright-shabby dressers was, almost universally underpaid. Worse, they seemed to be meekly accepting of whatever paltry fees were offered.

I mean, there *had* to be a connection.

It was almost as if they were making a statement: "I don't deserve better…"

If proof was needed – and that sure as hell was not a necessity for me – one had to look no further than the vivid contrasts of Leonard Starr, Stan Drake, Warren King and the other better-dressed-and-paid exceptions among my acquaintances. Of course, those bigtime magazine and advertising illustrators, some of whose pay – per drawing/painting – was as much as *one hundred* times that of the comic book guys! Sure, this elite group was perhaps more talented, their work better-drawn and/or more polished.

But still…

Okay, call me mercenary. I was at that time, still focused, as I had been for almost as long as I could remember, on *Success*, measured in *Dollars* – on my compulsive *need* to prove – nose-thumbingly – to my father – and admittedly, to myself – that I was *not* a loser. That he was *wrong*. Now, following those two years of Army bullshit, and even though I would have to restart my career by drawing comic-books, I had become *driven* to disassociate myself from that crowd.

To approach my profession as a *business*.

ASAP!

So for starters, following my deeply mature, 22 year-old reasoning, I purchased two gray Brooks Brothers three-piece flannel suits, one of them with a faint pin-stripe, plus some silk neckties, several white Oxford-cloth shirts with French cuffs, and elegant, polished wing-tip shoes.

The new, post-Tokyo me was at least going to *appear* to be a player.

To see if I could fool 'em.

To help with that part of the game, my new comic-book samples, though a few were "action" pages, focused mostly on – you guessed it – pretty girls and handsome men. The quality and production of which was aided, dramatically and *happily* by the arrival of the Polaroid camera, and its instant, self-developing black-and-white snapshots. Since its introduction a short time earlier, the Polaroid had rapidly become an essential tool among even the lowest-rung artists I knew.

While most illustrators and some syndicated-strip artists had for years posed and photographed live models, few of the comic-book guys did so. In fact, some of them actually regarded "working from photos" as a form of cheating. But the real impediments had been deadlines and the sheer number of drawings required in a typical 6 or 8 page story, as well the low pay-scale. Hiring models was simply too expensive. Added to that, the wait for, film to be developed and printed at the local camera shop or by whatever lab to which the corner drugstore farmed them out. Often to discover upon viewing the prints that one hadn't captured the right pose or other detail. The Polaroid quickly changed all that. As models, our studio-mates, spouses, pals or girlfriends were available at the right price.

So, my new, improved samples completed, I went for my initial target – someone for whom I had not previously worked: I phoned Timely Comics and requested – and was granted – an appointment with the Editor, Stan Lee!

A gifted, charming, driven fellow, Stan was already a legend in that niche business.

He looked up from my sample pages with a smile. "Nice. I really like your stuff, Tom. Let's get you started with---"

Elated, I interrupted: "Uh – excuse me, Stan. I just wanta say, I don't want to do your 'Underwear Characters…'"

He smiled affably. Back then few of us imagined that Stan, while already a respected industry-biggie, was destined to achieve deity-status as a result of his comics-progeny such as *X-men, The Incredible Hulk, Spider-Man, Captain America*, etc.

I continued: "…What I'd like to do are your romance books. To youknow get practice drawing glamorous girls and good-looking guys, so I can get out of this fucking business and into stuff that pays better."

Stan laughed. "Absolutely!" He handed me a script on-the-spot. Very satisfying, that meeting kicked off a delightful relationship with Stan Lee that lasted the several years it took for me to transition to advertising art. To the very satisfying extent that Stan so respected my artwork that, after a few gigs, he commissioned me to do several pages of heads – of gorgeous girls and good-looking young men. He then distributed copies to his other artists, as examples of what *they* should strive for. During that time, I also enjoyed illustrating stories for a few of his action-adventure characters, among them *Leopard Girl*, and *Boot-Camp Brady*. Meanwhile, I handled assignments for Ziff-Davis, DC, Avon and others. During that period, I occasionally, and tentatively, signed my work as *Tom Sawyer*. Trying it out, really.

Concurrent with my Stan Lee period, I met Nancy Russell. We were across-the-aisle passengers on a plane bound for New York from Miami, where I had visited my vacationing parents for a few days. Blonde, perky, attractive, Nancy was a flight attendant for Colonial Airlines, mostly flying the New York-Bermuda run. In those less gender-sensitive times the job-title, then 100% female, was "stewardess." Or less-formally, "stew," or, plural-and-even-less respectfully, "stewardii." Yes, she later confided, typical of that period, in auditioning for the job she'd had to stand on a desk, pull up her skirts and show her legs.

It was the winter of 1953-54, and we began dating. We hung out with my artist friends in Manhattan, and with her airline pals, mostly near LaGuardia Airport in Jackson Heights. She shared an apartment in that area with a pair of flight attendants, but soon moved into my place on 70th Street. Did we fall 'madly' in love? Hardly. We had laughs, some mutual tastes, plus a pleasant, non-argumentative level of comfort with each other. Though for me, maintaining the latter required my ignoring annoyances. Tics and issues that didn't seem to matter because it was clearly a temporary relationship. Among these, her excessive vanity, and a singular lack of shared interest in the arts, books, and intellectual stimulation.

A sign or two?

You could say so…

From this distance, boggling that I *chose* to not regard them in that way. Certainly, sadly, telling about me.

I'm sure there were many things I did, or was, about which Nancy kept silent. Unaware at the time, we suffered from the same not-uncommon – and singularly unhealthy – syndrome. We were both, essentially, cases of near-classic confrontation-avoidance. Incapable of expressing our true emotions. Especially, anger, about which we were in near-terminal denial. This was also fairly easy for me because of the refuge provided by my continuing, near-obsessive focus on my career goals. *Proving* to myself and my father that – go fuck yourself, Pop – I was a winner.

Despite all this, however – and I suppose, predictably – things between Nancy and me gradually began to evolve. Sadly unaware, I realized later, we found ourselves drifting into another of those – sigh – "I suppose we might as well get married" relationships.

Visiting, and meeting, Nancy's mother and recently-acquired stepfather introduced me to another unfamiliar world – that of an old-monied, New England WASP family. They lived in an elegant house on a hill in Troy, New York, complete with live-in servants and a uniformed chauffeur.

Nancy's similarities to her mother should have served as a warning.

On our first day there, her mother, self-involved, clearly from a lower economic echelon, proudly showed us – flaunted, really – her luxuriously-appointed private bathroom and her shoe-closet, which contained floor-to-ceiling shelves lined with more than 100 pairs of pricey women's shoes and slippers. Nancy proudly pointed out the flashy new top-of-the-line Oldsmobile convertible in the driveway, explaining that it had been her mother's final demand as a condition of her marrying the aging, locally prominent physician/surgeon. A pleasant, gentle fellow, that first evening, I was introduced to his three grown children. The oldest, a son, was mid-thirties, married, though he showed up alone. The middle child, a daughter, was in her late twenties, rather stiff. The younger son, a recent Princeton graduate who, I was told by Nancy had majored in Theology, not because he was religious, but because it was the easiest degree available. None were very interesting, nor stimulating.

Thanks to the advance briefing from Nancy, I was expecting them to be snobs, but unprepared for the level of it. During a, for me, awkward supper, they did little to conceal their contempt for their widowed father's new mate. Even less to hide their bitter resentment that, as in a cliché movie-plot, she would cost them significantly when it was time to carve up his estate.

I learned later that night, they'd already begun those divisions. After the siblings departed, and the older folks had retired, Nancy surreptitiously showed me the undersides and backsides of several antique chairs, chests and other pieces. Each bore a sticker with the name of the intended heir. None were destined for her mother.

Continuing our move toward permanence, within a few months, Nancy and I leased a one-bedroom apartment in Jackson Heights, in the Borough of Queens. Near LaGuardia Airport, it was far handier to her work, more spacious and cheaper than the place in Manhattan. Consistent with the ho-hum-ness of our courtship, neither of us desired a big, or even medium-sized wedding, nor the fuss that went with them. It was also still the era when airlines required that flight attendants be single, and Nancy wanted to keep our marriage secret so she could hold on to her job. So we made a plan. Her idea, really, though I had no objections. We carried it out several weekends later, with no announcement to friends or family. We drove down to Williamsburg, Virginia, where we married. Shortly thereafter, we flew to Chicago, where my parents approvingly welcomed Nancy into our family.

At the start, our repressed arrangement worked fairly well. Among my little but-un-complained-about irritations: her already annoying penchant for excessive baby-talk seemed to be increasing.

Of course, who the hell knew what I was doing to piss her off?

Also kept to myself were occasional guilt-pangs – and wondering – about Kiyoko…

I set up my drawing table in a corner of our bedroom. When Nancy was absent on layovers, I resumed a pleasurable habit acquired before we'd met: working late at night, all night, to the accompaniment of my favorite radio shows. Though what I failed to understand – and would continue being blind to for several years – was the slowing effect of that emotional blockage upon my development as an artist. Today, decades later, the obvious sterility of the drawings I produced back then is reflected in the cold, almost emotionless quality of my line-renderings.

Nonetheless, my drawing abilities happily continued to improve, my line-work satisfyingly showing a bit more feeling. It was also a wonderfully productive time for me, and a few months later, eager to be done with comic-books, I felt confident enough to prepare several sample-pages of advertising-comics. After vetting by Leonard Starr, and making a few tweaks per his wise suggestions, I presented them at Johnstone & Cushing. I was welcomed by Al Stenzel, the diminutive, amusing, white-handlebar-mustached Art Director. Occupying the large-windowed fifth (top) floor of an older building on the northwest corner of 58th Street and Lexington Avenue, the nine or ten drawing tables in the large main room were at that moment not in use

Al ushered me into his office, and quickly examined my samples. "Wow! Starr was right, kid. This is great!" Al immediately guided me to the executive office at the far end, overlooking 58th Street. There, he enthusiastically introduced me to Tim Johnstone and his partner, Jack Cushing. Tim, the younger of the two, seemed more outgoing. Jack, clearly a class-act was a bit more staid. I soon learned why. He was a member of the prominent and *very* old-money-wealthy New England family of that name, blood-related to the famed Cardinal Cushing of Boston. He and Tim, on-the-spot, offered me freelance space in their studio.

The arrangement: while getting started with them – basically, I would be a there-every-day, in-house guy who could handle quickie assignments for which the client hadn't specified a particular artist. And, I would also be permitted to work there on whatever outside gigs I had.

My kind of meeting – my kind of deal!

It was a great setup. At that point my eccentric work schedule had gotten old, and I was happy to adopt more regular business hours.

Within a day, I was drawing pages for the highly regarded – and relatively high-paying – edited-by-Stenzel comic-book section in *Boys' Life Magazine*, the monthly publication of The Boy Scouts of America.

Plus, starting a short time later, advertising art as well, for clients such as Tide detergent, Camel cigarettes, Ford Motor Company, and others. Sunday comics art which mostly consisted of what I came to think of as "happy people with happy problems."

The most common cast of these ads – as in TV commercials of the era – typically included your standard, super clean-cut, WASP-y consumer unit, plus their dog. I soon nicknamed them: *Mom, Dad, Junior, Sis*, and *Fido Fuck*.

The Fuck Family.

Leonard Starr had remarried and was working at his spacious apartment on Central Park West. While we maintained our close friendship, accompanying my heady, upward move in the business was the jolly opportunity to work alongside – and begin to socialize with – a new-to-me group of artists – another level of talent – or, at least, of focus. Among my J&C studio-mates – some daily, others less often – were veteran top-of-the-line craftsmen Craig Flessel, Elmer Wexler, Gill Fox, and a younger bunch which consisted of Ralston Jones, Frank Ridgeway, with the witty Dik Browne making occasional, very entertaining appearances. The latter three were "funny" cartoonists, known in the trade as "bigfoot men," while guys like myself, who drew more realistic figures, were referred to as "wrinkle-artists." All were easy-going, accessible, fun to be with. Colorful, offering the wry asides and singular attitudes that I'd become so attuned to since I'd started on West 57th Street.

Between the Johnstone & Cushing gigs and occasional ghosting of a week or two of syndicated strips such as *Flash Gordon* for Dan Barry, I was soon able to say goodbye to the standard comic-books. Truly, the only thing I missed from that period were the fun encounters and repartee with Stan Lee. Moreover, within a few months, my work was enough in-demand that I no longer had to go into Johnstone & Cushing's offices every day.

About a year into our marriage, Nancy and I began to talk about starting a family, and our one-bedroom apartment in Jackson Heights was obviously too small. So we went shopping for a house. Being first-timers, with minimal cash assets, it quickly became obvious that very desirable and attractive suburban Westchester County or, further out Connecticut, were too high-end.

So we looked the other way: west, at New Jersey. We soon found a residential tract under construction about a one-hour train ride – my pre-calculated commuting limit – to-and- from Manhattan's Penn Station. New Shrewsbury was just south of Red Bank and a few miles from the shore. It appeared to be the answer: a pleasant-looking single-story three bedroom, two bath home on a half-acre, with a two-car garage and a full basement containing a spacious, finished playroom. It was priced at the even-for-those-days affordable (and today, incredible) price of $18,990. Even better, for ex-GI's it required only $900 down! We chose our site in the planned 60 unit tract, I wrote the check, made our deal, and began the impatient, exciting wait for our house to be completed.

Meanwhile, I was never without more freelance work than I could handle, necessitating my hiring Tex Blaisdell to assist me, often not just at the drawing board. While I shot Polaroids of Nancy for my illustrations, I posed for the male figures, and when she wasn't around to snap the shutter, I depended on Tex.

One sadly memorable afternoon in September, 1956, while he was working with me at my Jackson Heights apartment we received a phone call from cartoonist Dik Browne in Connecticut.

Our mutual friend, Stan Drake, by then superbly drawing the very successful syndicated strip, *The Heart of Juliet Jones*, had just acquired a new

Corvette. In Westport earlier that day, trying it out at the wheel, with Stan beside him, his buddy, legendary comic-strip artist and fellow sports car aficionado, Alex Raymond. Dik Browne's shocking, stomach-wrenching news: coming over a rise, Alex had lost control. The car had gone airborne, they'd crashed into a tree at high speed, and Alex was killed instantly, impaled by the steering column. Stan, fortunately, had been thrown out of the car and, except for a few bruises and an ear nearly torn off, was okay.

For the rest of the day, Tex and I glumly lamented Alex Raymond's death. He was an icon, held in awe by all of us for his amazing drawing ability, which he'd demonstrated as the original artist on *Flash Gordon* and at that time on the very popular *Rip Kirby* strip. Alex allegedly knew human anatomy so well that he didn't need to use photos, but rather would draw the skeleton, add musculature and flesh, and then drapery. The result: a kind of heightened, super-dynamic, line-rendered-realism. Tex and I discussed who might step in to replace Alex on *Kirby*. There were really only two qualified successors: Starr, and another of our artist pals, the laconic Texan, John Prentice.

Within a day or two, we learned it would be Johnny. Leonard was suddenly no longer available. The reason: the head of the Chicago Tribune-New York Daily News Syndicate had been giving serious consideration to a comic-strip notion created by Leonard. On learning of Alex's death, the executive knew instantly that Starr was the logical first choice to replace him on *Kirby*, and would thus be lost – likely forever – to rival King Features Syndicate. He immediately phoned Leonard and informed him that his creation, *Mary Perkins – On Stage* was a 'go.'

An instant classic, carried in hundreds of newspapers, Leonard beautifully wrote and illustrated *On Stage* for nearly 28 years, winning along the way the National Cartoonists Society's coveted *Reuben Award*. John Prentice handled *Rip Kirby* superbly for many, many years.

At about that time, among the growing number of syndicated comic-strip artists with whom I was becoming acquainted, I was beginning to pick up on a curious, disturbing vibe. An oddly more-or-less common thread, it would be several years before I better understood it.

Within a few months, Nancy and I moved into our New Jersey home. She quit her airline job and, for a while at least, devoted her time and energies to homemaking and choosing décor. My first experience living outside of a city, I found that I truly enjoyed the privacy, the quiet and increased space afforded by suburban residential living. However, the social part left, for me, a bit of a hole. While it was easier for Nancy, especially since a number of the women were either young mothers – or like her, mother-wannabes – I had trouble finding anyone I could talk to. Especially since my interests in which brand of fertilizer or lawnmower to buy ranged from very limited-to-nonexistent. Essentially, I missed the stimulation of being around creative types. But – A.) So what else was new? And B.) I figured I'd get over it.

Moreover, several days each week I commuted to the Manhattan offices of Johnstone & Cushing where, among such people, I stayed busy drawing advertising comics. I was also picking up some interesting new clients, two of whom happened to be located in New Jersey. The Boy Scouts of America, headquartered in New Brunswick, became a major source of work. For them I illustrated Merit Badge pamphlets, camping equipment catalogues and a lot of other material. But the most creatively productive, joyous, and what would become my longest-running association, was with a man who, despite our being less than a two-hour drive from each other, I wouldn't meet face-to-face for five or six years.

Based in the southernmost part of the state, ex-journalist Harry Volk had, a few semesters earlier, come up with the idea of publishing stock artwork – high quality line-drawings of people and objects, generic, any-purpose illustrations and cartoons known in the trade as "spots" – and in Harry's case as "Clip-Art." Printed on glossy stock, costing the end-user pennies, these drawings were cut-and-pasted into advertisements, brochures, newsletters appearing all over the country, even used as artwork on packaging, on TV and displayed on billboards. For years the *Volk Clipbooks of Line Art* were ubiquitous, a presence in the art departments of virtually every non-major ad agency, house-organ and art service in the U.S.

Harry became my favorite client, both as a person and because of the

113

extraordinary creative freedom he gave me. This came about after his first few specifically described assignments of, say, a woman smiling as she clutches a fistful of paper money, or a man at the wheel of his car, grinning or worried or whatever.

From then on, once he'd seen that I could "deliver," that I understood his market, Harry would simply tell me he needed various numbers of spots for one or another of his Clipbooks, on this or that topic (*Women*, *Kids*, *Holidays*, *Sports*, *Crowds*, *Families*, etc.). I would then decide what I'd draw and, without showing him pencil sketches, I'd render them with any kind of even marginally reproducible line, from ink to pencil, charcoal or crayon, and send Harry the finished art.

I quickly became his star illustrator. I cannot come close to counting the times during the following fifteen years that I'd open a magazine or newspaper, view TV, receive a pamphlet, or pass a signboard, and see one or more of my Volk drawings. Moreover, because of the broad exposure my drawings got from his books, a *lot* more work came my way, from new clients all over the country. Though today these drawings, some of which I did almost 50 years ago, are used with far less frequency, I still see them reproduced. Some on currently marketed packaging, and even such items as kitchen-magnets. Each time I do, I am thankful anew for ASCAP and the Writers Guild (more on that, later).

During our second year in New Jersey, both Nancy and I were delighted when she became pregnant. We eagerly prepared one of the bedrooms, shopping for appropriate furniture, curtains, etc.

Nancy gave birth to our daughter, Suzy, in July, 1958. It was, as I'm sure it is for most new fathers, a special moment. Celebratory – and sobering. A few weeks later, on my parents' first visit to see their grandchild, more of the latter: I learned that my father had recently suffered a heart attack. Though it had been mild, they'd chosen not to tell us because it was during Nancy's pregnancy, and they didn't want to upset us.

My dad, then age sixty-one, confided that the doctors had assured him he'd live another 10 years. His biggest concessions – and most disappointing to him – were giving up cigarettes and finishing his morning shower under ice-cold water. He never did quit smoking, though he cut back to only lighting one at a time. He lasted 14 more years, finally succumbing to emphysema.

About the cold shower, which he claimed was what truly awakened him every day, I recall thinking each of the many times he'd mentioned it since I was a small child, that he was nuts. Except that in my forties, years after he'd died, I tried it. Damned if he wasn't right! An added benefit: ridding me of any residual morning back-stiffness. I've been doing it ever since, and each day as that icy, bracing stream engulfs my head, then the back of my neck and shoulders, I think of my dad – if not with gratitude – at least crediting him with some wisdom.

Meanwhile, over the five years since my return from Tokyo, I had periodically – and guiltily – wondered about Kiyoko – hoping again that time, and distance, and reflection had dissuaded her from taking her life.

One day a letter from Kiyoko arrived. It had been forwarded to me by our mutual friend, Tomiko who, while we were in Japan, had married a GI acquaintance, with me serving as Best Man. In Kiyoko's sadly touching note, she confessed that she now knew I was never going to return for her, that she was resigned to this, and she wished me a happy life. Though not exactly conscience-cleansing, I was profoundly thankful that at least she was alive. I debated about responding, and decided against doing so.

During this period, I ghosted several weeks of strips for Stan Drake's *The Heart of Juliet Jones*. It required my spending some very pleasurable time at Stan's home in Westport, Connecticut, where I began to get a taste of that unique community of cartoonists and illustrators, who seemed to comprise about half the population. In addition to Stan's flamboyant, entertaining presence, the area was crawling with such notables as Cartoonists Mort Walker and Dik Browne, plus bigtime illustrators Steven Dohanos, Harold von Schmidt, Noel Sickles, Albert Dorne and others. Of the latter artists, I had been admiringly clipping the work of several out of national magazines since I was a kid. Better, with Stan Drake as my "sponsor," I even lunched with some of them.

Glimpsing their proximity and lifestyle markedly pointed up my ongoing fish-out-of-water status among my New Jersey neighbors. While pleasant enough, I found it difficult to relate to most of them, their passions revolving around sales quotas, expense accounts, and their golf game.

An amusing, and for me, wonderfully astute comment on this last came before Suzy was born, during a driving/sightseeing trip Nancy and I took through the New England states. On a sunny afternoon we were walking along a jetty in Kennebunkport, Maine, where we happened on a lean, elderly, pipe-smoking gentleman standing at an easel, brush in one hand, his other thumb through the palette resting on his forearm, intently painting a harborscape on a smallish canvas. Dignified, the wide brim of his cotton hat turned down all around to shield the sun, clearly your classic "*Down Easter,*" he seemed oblivious of the few passersby, some of whom, myself included, paused to look over his shoulder.

I was impressed with his artwork: "Very nice."

This drew not a glance, but rather: "Ay-yup."

Then, after a silent beat, I tried again, figuring my next statement might lend some credence to my first remark: "I'm an artist, too. An advertising illustrator."

Eyes still glued to the canvas, continuing to paint, tight-lipped: "You from around here?"

"No. I live in New Jersey."

His deadpan response was immediate, delivered with near-theatrical timing, and again, never looking away from his work: "How unfortunate."

Which, by the time I did my gig with Stan Drake, pretty much described the way I'd come to feel about it. I decided we *had* to move to Westport.

If my work was, along with my marriage, less and less stimulating, fatherhood was both joyous and, occasionally, angst-inducing. Because I was more often working at home, I'd sometimes found myself torn between meeting a deadline and fulfilling little Suzy's need for love and attention.

About this, in delivering a job to Tim Johnstone a bit past deadline, I pleaded having been pressured by my not-quite two-year old daughter's repeated demands to sit on my lap while I was trying to work.

Tim's response was simple, wry and, for any father, *eminently* memorable: "I've got news for you, Tom. When they're seventeen they won't want to sit in your lap anymore."

While Nancy was pregnant with our second child, we found a gorgeous wooded two-acre hillside plot in Westport, on which a house was about to be built. A handsome ten-room ranch-style home, 3,000+ square feet. We loved the design, and grabbed it – happily in time to make a few minor but significant floor plan and exterior changes.

Then, in April, 1960, our daughter, Lauren, was born. My first glimpse of her in the hospital nursery was extraordinary and unforgettable. Minutes-old, she was on her stomach, tiny palms flat against the bed, elbows bent, back arched, holding her head up, *grinning* at me – and at the world in general. A definite sign, it turned out, of how she would approach her life.

SEVENTEEN
Getting It

A FEW MONTHS LATER WE DEPARTED New Jersey and moved into our new Westport home. Satisfying indeed, though admittedly, one part of my motivation in relocating was pretty superficial; Westport was a symbol that I had 'arrived.' That – along with a new Jaguar in the garage – I was finally 'showing' my dad – and yeah, myself – that I could by his standards "succeed" without a college degree, *or* a nine-to-five job.

Which is not to say I was doubt-free. At the start I had a few anxious, restless nights, laying there looking out at the dark, towering trees silhouetted against the starry sky, and wondering if I'd bitten off too big a chunk. Fortunately, all that went away quickly, helped along by the many pleasures and distractions of our new existence.

One sure sign that we had entered a different world: opening the front door to greet our first babysitter, I noted that she'd arrived in her new Cadillac.

Another, more artist-friendly contrast: back in New Jersey, though I'd long before ceased daily commuting, deliveries of my work still necessitated my schlepping it into the city. But because the Westport area was so full of graphic artists, our numbers supported an efficient daily messenger service. All we had to do was drop our work into a bin at this guy's house before 6 AM, and we could go home and get some sleep, confident that it would be delivered by 10 o'clock, and/or, new assignments would be in our hands that evening.

But perhaps tops among Westport's ongoing delights, even exceeding my expectations, were the almost daily, casual, entertaining lunches with my peers and heroes at The Pickle Barrel. An additional, exciting bonus was the evening social life, the parties and dinners with an expanding, stimulating circle of hip, intellectually curious types – among them, writers, teachers, advertising and theatre people.

During that early period in Westport, my parents journeyed from Chicago, staying with us for several days. It would be the only time they visited us in Connecticut. I remember little of it, except that as with all of our transactions then, it was rancor-free. For that matter, except for their apparent enjoyment of their grandchildren, pretty much without visible affection or emotion. Nor do I recall *any* expression of praise for, curiosity about or pleasure from my career or success, then or ever, beyond a cursory "We're proud of you."

One comment, however, does stand out. I wasn't present for it. Rather, it was conveyed to me by Nancy after they'd departed for home. It was a remark by my mother that has stayed with me, as has the memory of Nancy quoting her: "We know Tommy doesn't love us…"

One of those punch-in-the-stomach lines, the words continue to resonate with the pain and sadness I felt when Nancy repeated them that day in our living room. As with other such singular incidents, I remember where I was standing, the light, and the view from our windows.

My mother *was* right. Being a parent, I can almost feel the hurt she must have experienced as she spoke. I wished then – and now – that I *could* have felt even so much as mild affection for them. Today, as I look at their photographs, I regret that their images, and those attendant memories, don't engender more than my often-profound gratitude for that which they unintentionally bestowed on me – and sympathy. The latter because I really do not believe they enjoyed their lives – a quality mine has yielded in spades.

But, that I am unable to say I loved them will always sadden me.

As the months in Westport passed, what was slower to become the alarming part of my consciousness that it should have been was Nancy's growingly excessive drinking.

Again, unquestionably my own denial, but also a sign of our increasing personal and emotional distance, I rarely noticed it at home, and overall never discussed it. Rather, it began to work its way into my awareness when we were at parties or dining in restaurants. In the latter, Martinis were our drink of choice, and though I was essentially a one-drink guy, the routine became Nancy suggesting we order another round. My response: "Let's split one." She'd agree, I'd order one more, and she would drink most of it. And sometimes admit that she'd like to have another. I would occasionally go along with that. She was often tipsy when we headed home.

But, typical of our relationship, I never discussed it with her. Nor did I see it, as I should have, as the alarming problem it was becoming. Though I did comment on it once, in a for me memorable – and admittedly – somewhat heavy-handed, less-than-direct way.

We'd been invited to a local "funny hat" party. I don't recall the one I wore, but for Nancy, I constructed one from the kids' set of alphabet blocks, arranging them so that they spelled out 'MENTAL BLOCKS.' She didn't find it as funny as I did – it was, I later realized, one of my way too rare acts of open hostility – but she wore it anyway. Drunk when we exited the party, and still wearing it, as we drove the mile or two up the Easton Road to our house, she passed out in the passenger seat.

The truth about our relationship: by then neither of us liked the other very much, and that was diminishing daily. Sadly – or not – we continued to keep most of it repressed. Though I doubt if acting-out would have led to any improvement.

Was I tempted to wander? Yes. Westport was full of attractive women. There were several about whom I fantasized being involved. But none of them passionately so. My self-excuse for remaining faithful to Nancy was fairly lame if not laughable, but it worked for me. It started with my assumption, valid or not, that I drove the only black 1959 Jaguar XK150 convertible with red leather upholstery in Westport. Ergo, I told myself, if it was seen parked in a residential driveway other than my own, everyone in town would instantly know who I was screwing. Case closed.

A major upside of that time: my growth-curve continued, most significantly and lastingly, in the area of arriving at a kind of staggering revelation. A sudden, forehead-slap understanding of 'Stuff' – and its *true* value. Or, more accurately, its non-value.

While certainly enjoying our beautiful, spacious new home and its attendant toys, the latest hi-fidelity sound system, the Jag, household appliances, big-screen TV, custom-made suits and shirts, etc., etc., within a few months it hit me – and I mean "hit" in the most abrupt way, because it came to me in a startling, almost cosmic sense – that that was *all* they were.

Toys.

With the profound lack of meaning thus implied. Ego-gratifying? Yes. Pleasure-yielding, surely, and of course verification – of that which I'd *so* desperately needed to prove. To my father and to myself.

But in a real sense, *so what?*

On reflection, I see that it was another lesson learned via the most effective method of all – by *doing* – and, at age twenty-nine, I suddenly saw with total, deep-focus clarity that those *things* were *not* what my life was – or should be – about.

It was an exciting place to get to. And early enough in my arc for it to make a huge difference. Because I resolved that for the rest of it, from that day – it was *never again* going to be *about* money.

Instead it would be about stretching myself. About bar-raising, seeing if I could pull the next one off. Oh, sure – I became more hard-nosed and businesslike about the prices I placed on my services. But I never again – *ever* – performed work – as I had often done before – just for the financial payoff. If it didn't stretch me, or strike me as fun – or preferably – both, I wasn't interested. In later years, in the entertainment biz, on more than one occasion when I'd accepted a gig that didn't live up to those standards, I dumped it.

Which isn't to say I didn't enjoy many of the rewards and perks. I drove – and loved – that Jaguar for 18 years – until it died.

What I couldn't know for a long time was that my game-changing revelation that it was no longer about stuff was actually *way* further-reaching than that.

It was about giving myself permission to *grow*. To allow myself to *begin* functioning *not* as a draftsman, but rather as an artist. A large part of that would be the starting-from-near-zero of an entirely new learning-curve.

The subject: *Me – 101*.

Nor did I comprehend then that the key to that self-knowledge would be access to my *feelings*, so closely guarded and/or denied for much of my life.

Shut down, really, since that afternoon confrontation with my father 15 years earlier.

One of the first manifestations of all that became visible in my illustration work. I had by then achieved expertise at drawing realistic human figures. But the renderings, my line, had always been – well – sterile. Cold. Tight.

Almost abruptly, that began to change. My line work became more and more fluid. Freer. Conveying more feeling. It was an exciting, liberating experience. I began trying different instruments. New brushes. Pen points. Charcoal pencils. Even ballpoint pens and crayons. Anything that would produce a photographically reproducible mark. I eagerly searched out new surface-textures, rather than the Strathmore kid-finish drawing paper I'd used since I first learned that it was Milton Caniff's preference.

A bonus for me: the new techniques caught the interest and support of my friend/client, Harry Volk. He instructed his photographic expert to stretch himself, to make even my most marginally reproducible-as-line-art drawings work, thus telling me what tools I could best use, and which to discard.

As a result, my assignments and client-list grew, and my work took on additional challenging and satisfying dimensions.

One more indelible realization of what it was truly about, and just how different my life was – and would be – from that of my father, came on an afternoon during our first winter in Connecticut. Sitting in my studio, working as usual with the radio droning, a special broadcast began: a recording of Arthur Miller's masterpiece, *Death of a Salesman*. Though I had of course heard about the play, I'd never seen it performed, nor read the script – or seen the 1952 movie version. But within a few stunning minutes, I was transfixed. Listening to the superb Thomas Mitchell in the lead-role of Willy Loman, I put my brush aside, unable to continue working, vision blurred by my tears – tears that continued until the end.

Arthur Miller had *written* my father.

My dad *was* Willy Loman. Even to his resonant line about the importance of being 'well-liked.' Through Miller's genius, that day I saw my father in new ways, with an eerie, tragic transparency that still, as I write this, causes me to choke up.

While I identified with neither of Willy's sons – perhaps because I had no siblings, and because I had – at least physically – walked away from the problem, the play helped me imagine parts of my father's life that I'd never seen, what they had been like. It gave me fresh insights into some that I had observed or heard him rail against – such as his salesman's need to eat shit, sucking up to clients who were clearly schmucks, suffering them and other fools, and the demeaning effects that had to have inflicted on him. Obviously I was projecting. But Miller and his characters, especially Willy and his wife, and those lessons, continue to speak to me.

After that day, I began reading Freud. I also started toying with the idea of entering psychoanalysis.

Meanwhile, busy as I was with advertising assignments, and a few editorial illustrations, something re-ignited – though over a much lower flame: that old pursuit of a syndicated comic-strip. Perhaps it was my being part of the local artist-scene, and an obligation to achieve that which I continued to somewhat mindlessly insist was my end-frame.

In any case, this attempt featured a feisty female attorney in a small, male-dominated community. I wrote a month of *Portia Tanner* continuity, and set about drawing the then-requisite two weeks' worth of strips – daily and Sunday. From this distance, I think the word "dutifully" captures my by then near-diminished passion. It was almost as if I was preparing the strip at arm's length, a kind of going-through-the-motions activity.

I sent it to whoever was then in charge at the New York Daily News Syndicate. They passed, as did King Features and the others.

Significantly, I felt relieved. I had given it another try – though I still wasn't about to revisit that youthful commitment. True re-examination of that would come later.

Despite the state of Nancy's and my marriage, I was treasuring the part about being a father to our two adorable girls, Suzy and Lauren, observing and participating in their growth.

Moreover, almost daily, my enjoyment of living and working in Westport continued to be exhilarating indeed, and rarely without surprises.

One of those was provided by someone I didn't think could impress me any more than he already had. But that's what happened one afternoon as I exited The Pickle Barrel following another lunch with several of my heroes. Harold von Schmidt, the sweet-natured veteran Western illustrator, a giant talent whose work, in my judgment, surpasses Remington's, casually mentioned that "Ford" had called. Thus he would be going away again for several months. From the others' remarks I quickly and correctly surmised that Von (as we called him) was referring to legendary film Director John Ford. For as long as

I could remember, I'd been admiring the billboard and movie poster art Von had famously painted for virtually all of Ford's epic movies.

Along with Noel Sickles, Stan Drake and the others I wished him well, and as he headed for his car, I turned to them: "Months? Y'mean it takes *that* long to do those paintings?"

Stan shook his head, grinned: "You kidding? They're only part of it..." He explained that Von would be at Ford's side from pre-production to wrap, both in Hollywood and on location in Utah's Monument Valley. "Ford checks with him before every shot." Because of von Schmidt's unique, encyclopedic expertise about period Western and U.S. Cavalry gear, uniforms, harnesses and the like, Ford depended on him on as technical consultant for *all* of his productions.

Wowed doesn't come close to describing my feelings, then and now. But like so many of the extraordinary people with whom I've had the privilege of socializing, with Harold von Schmidt the real pleasure for me was getting to know his human side – and in the process, being exposed to his charm and wit and intelligence.

Another incident from my Westport period, this about a vastly premature "senior moment" I experienced at age thirty, deserves recounting if only for the comfort that readers of a certain age can take from it: on a morning in the Westport Bank I had just completed my transaction and, as I turned to head for the exit, I noticed an extremely familiar figure entering, some 60 or 70 feet away. This tall, distinguished gray-haired gentleman striding directly toward me had been in my house, in my living room, any number of times.

I *knew* him.

But I absolutely could *not* remember his name.

Unless I *immediately* changed direction, we would in a few moments pass within inches of each other. I *knew* I'd be profoundly, excruciatingly embarrassed when, as he would certainly say something on the order of: "Hi, Tom," I would have to settle for "Hey, how're things?" Or the like.

Rejecting a path-change, I rapidly paged through B-plans: 1.) I could look the other way, pretending to be absorbed by something to the side, and hope that he wouldn't recognize me, or, 2.), I could bite the bullet and behave like a grownup – I mean people forget things all the time, right? Though admittedly not the identities of people who've been in their homes as often and recently as this guy had – which was definitely within the past few days.

As we converged, I resignedly opted for 2.) and, blocking his path, I smiled and extended my hand: "Hi. Listen, I – well, I feel like a *total* schmuck. You've been in my home so often and I've totally blanked out on your---"

His handshake, disarming smile and abrupt, small laugh stopped me before I could finish. They were quickly followed by: "Hi. And don't worry, it happens all the time. I'm Harry Reasoner."

Mr. Reasoner, for those too young to recall, was then the nationally famous, universally recognizable co-host of CBS TV's *60 Minutes*, as well as a regular news commentator on that network. He had indeed often been in my house.

In addition to the lunches, there were wonderful parties – and *more* parties. For some we ventured to Manhattan, maintaining our friendships with Leonard Starr and his lovely recent bride, Betty, plus Warren and Nadine King and others. Our expanding local relationships included a few with whom we never quite became close; our association with Paul Newman and his wife, Joanne Woodward, was limited to nods, smiles and "Hi's" when, like them, we delivered our kids to or fetched them at the school bus pickup spot. There was also the exciting, remarkable Westport Playhouse, presenting such major talent as Mike Nichols and Elaine May, and even Gloria Swanson.

Another in my collection of standout-moments came one morning when I found myself chatting with a friend in his driveway. The fellow happened to be a high-level executive of one of those enormous international oil companies. Fifteen minutes earlier I had read in that day's *New York Times* that American troops, with President John Kennedy's approval, were being sent to a place called "Vietnam," allegedly because "the Commies" were trying to take over – a threat that I had from the beginning, more than a decade earlier, regarded as total, manufactured bullshit. I remembered that Vietnam had previously been French Indo-China, that the French had given up on the place, and I knew of my friend's familiarity with that part of the world. "So – why the fuck are we *really* sending soldiers over there?"

My friend's brief, quiet response, a stunning truth delivered without a moment's hesitation, has chillingly stayed with me ever since that morning in 1961: "Oil."

I threw him a "you've-gotta-be-kidding" look: "Oil? C'mon – it's what – the French – it was all about rubber plantations."

"The oil's 300 miles away, in Indonesia."

I *knew* he was right. As with virtually every war in the 20th century, oil was what it was about. Even WWII. I mean, does *anyone* believe Hitler went to North Africa to acquire sand?

While I continued to photo-pose for the males I was drawing, I'd begun to use female models – pretty ones whose closer-to-ideal proportions required less re-drawing than did Nancy's. One was a lovely young brunette named Sarah Jane, who posed for a number of illustrators in the area. She was excellent, took direction well – and with imagination.

As it happened, at about that time Stan Drake's marriage to his beautiful redhead wife, Betty Lou, was falling apart. Stan, publicly at least among his artist pals, was having an affair with Sarah Jane. Which parenthetically caused me to idly wonder if one of Stan's hang-ups might be that he was attracted to women with two first names.

Anyway, in what I had come to accept as cartoonist-style, he would occasionally share intimate details of his encounters with Sarah Jane. One example stands out. Five or six of our group were finishing another entertaining lunch at our customary round table in The Pickle Barrel, when Stan entered. En route from the door he grabbed a chair from an adjacent table and with a large grin, expansively plunked it at ours and joined us. Following our brief greetings, and a pause to ensure that he had our attention, Stan began his announcement: "Well, fellas – I just now lived out my *ultimate* fantasy…"

Again a pause, which triggered one or two amused groans and comments on the order of: "No shit, Stan. What?"

128

Beaming, Stan sat back, arms spread, palms flat on the table: "I just fucked Sarah Jane while she was wearing a garter-belt *and* bobby-socks!"

The follow-up to that came a few weeks later, when Stan broke up with Betty Lou and moved to a rental house at the beach. A short time after that, he announced – again over lunch – that he was surreptitiously leaving for Nevada to establish residence for a quicky-divorce. He asked and received from all of us the promise that, if asked, we would deny any knowledge of his whereabouts.

And, in near-sitcom fashion, the rest of it began to unfold. Within a few days, an irate, verging-on-desperate Betty Lou showed up at The Pickle Barrel while we were lunching. She stood over us, hands on hips, her white dental-assistant uniform memorably contrasting with her red hair: "All right, enough! I *know* you people know where Stanley has disappeared to. Which of you is gonna tell me?"

The deadpan responses ranged from "He's not at home?" to "I've been trying to reach him. In fact I was gonna call you." to "Beats me."

Following the last fake-mystified comment from the table, Betty Lou angrily turned and stalked out of the restaurant.

The following day I received a phone call from Dik Browne. His wife had stopped by Betty Lou's house and found the boys alone and floundering. Their mother hadn't come home the previous night, nor had she contacted them. Dik had checked with the police and local hospitals. Her whereabouts were a mystery. Stan of course was unreachable. Dik asked if Nancy and I would be willing to take in one of the boys, while Dik and his wife would take the other. We consented, and duly picked up one of them, waiting while he packed a small suitcase with clothes and personal items.

We did not learn of what happened until several days later, when Stan Drake unexpectedly appeared at The Pickle Barrel. We welcomed him back, he gathered himself, then described – with humor and irony – how this bizarre, almost incredible real-life rom-com spoof had played out.

Starting with Betty Lou's departure from our lunch-table, she had driven directly to Stan's beach-house. After ascertaining that Stan's car was still in the garage, she happened to encounter the young fellow who lived next door. From him, she managed to arm-twist his confession that he had a few mornings earlier driven Stan to JFK, where he was boarding a flight to Las Vegas. Without waiting for him to finish, Betty Lou leapt into her car, and drove directly to the airport, where she boarded the next flight to Vegas.

Later that day, at his Las Vegas motel, Stan had just finished a session at the pool, swimming and sunning himself. Grabbing his towel, he headed for his second-floor room. As he began to climb the stairs, he happened to glance at the sliding-door entry to the adjacent first-floor room – and there, behind the glass, glaring at him, arms folded, still in her white uniform, stood Betty Lou.

She had landed in Vegas and, not knowing where Stan might be staying, crossed to a payphone. Using the in-booth directory, she began calling hotels and motels in alphabetical order, asking for Stan.

While I've forgotten whatever details of their confrontation Stan shared with us over lunch, the end result was that he and Betty Lou had just flown back from Vegas. She reclaimed their sons, and a few months later they divorced. Stan married Sarah Jane. For a while.

Meanwhile, essentially, and I suppose inevitably, Nancy's and my damaged-goods-from-the-start relationship was deteriorating rapidly. Following, I now understand, its own preprogrammed downward arc.

My chief mechanism for not dealing with it – hell, for even thinking about it was (surprise) the refuge my work provided. An area where, as referenced, I was also in the middle stages of doubt-and-denial. I was still refusing to examine a growing, sort of subversive sense that overall, maybe – just maybe – this might *not* be what I wanted to do forever...

Then, one morning in my studio I received an unexpected phone call that turned out to be the catalyst for the next dramatic changes in my life.

Actually, 'dramatic' understates it – dramatically. It was, I now know, the beginning of the second half of my life.

What would be – *beyond* measurably – the *best* part!

EIGHTEEN
Another (Seemingly) Unscripted Act Begins (Though it Was Probably There All Along)

I LIFTED THE PHONE. "HI…"

The voice was vaguely familiar. "Hey, Tom…"

Then I recognized it. "…This is Al Capp, up in Boston. I've got this problem…"

Why would he be calling me…?

Capp was the legendary superstar cartoonist/nationally acclaimed humorist, creator of the phenomenally successful comic-strip, *Li'l Abner*. The influence of Al's strip had been felt for many years all over America – from his famously funny '*Schmoo*' to the annual '*Sadie Hawkins Day*' celebrations and more. Though I had met Al once or twice at cartoonist functions, we didn't "know'" each other. But having heard him on radio and on TV interviews, the distinctive, garrulous voice was unmistakable. I was totally unprepared for what followed:

"Listen, Tom – I'm in kind of a jam. One of my assistants, the guy who's been inking for me, and drawing the realistic figures – pretty girls and stuff – for the last 20-some years – he's had a stroke."

It was easy to see where this was headed, and it wasn't anyplace I wanted to go. "Gee, I'm really sorry, Al..."

"Anyway, I checked, and your name's at the top of everyone's list as a guy who can draw pretty girls. What I need is for you to come up to Boston like every other week, starting now."

"Whoa, thanks Al. I really wish I could help, but – man, I'm up to my eyeballs here..." I wasn't trying to be cute – I had more work than I could handle. *Plus*, except for, say, helping a close friend who might be in trouble, I was long since *entirely* done with "ghosting," or being *any*one's assistant. Further, the tedious prospect of splitting my time between Westport and Boston was even less appealing. Outside my studio window the trees wore that lovely green haze of new leaves that signified the end of another endless New England winter, and almost the last thing I wanted to do at that moment was leave town.

He seemed to read my mind: "Hey, look, I've got this great studio where you can bunk. It's a lovely old converted carriage-house, right at the foot of Beacon Hill. I mean we're only steps away from the Common, the Public Gardens, from Charles Street, and---"

"Thanks, Al – but the answer's no! That's not what I do anymore."

But he wouldn't let go. Another couple of refusals, and I had to resort to crass: "Look, Al, bottom line, you can't afford me."

Without hesitation: "How much?"

Shit! I did some rapid arithmetic, adding 50% to my then-weekly average, and threw the number at him, confident that I was off the hook.

"Okay. Can you be here tomorrow?"

I took the train that first time. The date: February 20, 1962. The reason I remember is that it happened to be the day that John Glenn became the first American to orbit the earth. It seemed that everyone on the train had a radio.

Capp's studio was indeed pleasant, with small-but-comfortable workspace for Al, his lettering man, his aging cartoon-character penciler, and for me. Adjacent was an adequate-sized living room with the convertible sofa on which I would bunk. Al and I hit it off with immediate chemistry, his side of which was confirmed for me a couple mornings later. With Al not yet present, his lettering guy *very* flatteringly confided that twenty minutes after my arrival, during my first trip to the bathroom, Capp had turned to the others and guffawed: "Hah! That's *me*, 30 years ago."

Al Capp turned out to be one *extraordinarily* colorful, entertaining fellow, surprising on a number of levels. As expected, majorly funny, politically aware, and commercially, brilliant. This last evidenced especially in his then-recently concocted new "Brand."

A lifelong, passionate Liberal, and fan of then-president John F. Kennedy, Al lived with his wife in Cambridge, where they socialized with Kennedys, Schlesingers and others of the Best and the Brightest. But during those "Camelot" years he had seen the lecture-circuit market for Lefties – and their speaking-fees – downsize drastically.

So Capp, ever the pragmatist, reinvented himself. He became, arbitrarily and abruptly, an articulate and of course very witty spokesperson on radio and TV for the far-Right. The Rush Limbaugh of his time, Al made it *very* clear to me that he did not believe a word of what he said in that role. Then he added, with a gleeful guffaw: "Plus – now I get three, four times the number of gigs, *and* my fees've jumped from twenty-five hundred a pop – to *ten* grand."

An important contextual point about this last: in 1962, while not superstar wages, even $2,500 for a speaking engagement wasn't considered to be chopped-liver.

The work I did on *Li'l Abner* wasn't difficult, but it was fun interacting with the characters who assisted Al, observing and being part of how the classic strip was produced. One fascinating aspect of that process: while Al was the sole writer, and sketched in the rough layouts, *all* the rest of the artwork was penciled and inked by myself and Andy, the fellow who drew the cartoony figures. *Except* for – and here's the singular part – the characters' faces and hair! Those were inked *only* by Capp – and with way-better-than-good reason. So totally distinctive, sensitive and inimitable was Al's touch that it made the strip – all of it – truly and uniquely *his*!

Unexpectedly, my time there was turning out to be a relaxed, fun interlude indeed. It was also a very pleasant, and better, *justified* vacation from Nancy. Definitely highlighted in that first week by a couple of late-evening dinner excursions with Capp, just the two of us – and the great, entertaining and stimulating conversations that went with them. A man I and many others regarded as the Mark Twain of his time, the first of these was memorably – and with undeniable wisdom – initiated by his 9PM suggestion that we go out and grab some Chinese food: "I mean hey, when you're middle-aged and Jewish and have a wooden leg, y'gotta eat a *lotta* Chinese food."

Al's famous wooden leg had been the result – at age eleven or twelve in hometown New Haven, Connecticut – of his falling off the back of a truck on which he'd apparently stolen a ride, and under the wheels of a trolley car.

Al's cartoon-assistant, Andy, provided another unusual and semi-humorous piece of theatre. Middle-aged, single, of Italian descent, somewhat silent and somber, he invariably dressed in a suit and necktie. His customary evening activity, I soon learned, was going to the dog-track and betting on the races. I got the impression that Andy, while not complaining, didn't regard his life as a fun experience. Virtually all of his sparse verbal observations and comments were dark, without joy or even pleasure. In fact, more than once he made me aware that he took some offense at my mostly pleasurable take on life.

It seemed pointless to argue.

The amusing-if-rather-depressing capper – a glimpse, actually, into his head: his life-view was uniquely, graphically reflected by the calendar he kept tacked to the upper right-hand corner of his drawing table. About the size of a half-sheet of typewriter-paper, it displayed one month at a time, divided into the usual rows of seven rectangles per week. Each evening, before departing the studio, Andy would, with a pencil, methodically, and carefully staying within the lines, darken the entire little rectangle. Thus, by the end of each month, *all* of his days had been filled in. Black.

Speaking of which, Al had a dark side as well. One that he was [in] famous for up and down the East coast. Not just a womanizer, he, along with his brother, writer Elliot Caplin, shared a major hang-up. They were compulsive fornicators. A problem which, I was soon to learn, was known in psychiatric circles as "*The Al Capp Syndrome.*"

Pretty impressive, you've got to admit – having a whole syndrome named after you. Though as I learned more, especially in that area, the initial gratification I had felt when he'd compared me to his younger self would become somewhat diminished.

Nonetheless, overall it was further evidence that Capp was, in my experience, anyway, definitely one-of-a-kind.

An interesting aspect, openly discussed at the studio: out of deference to his wife, Al rarely engaged in his sexual adventures in or near Boston. Rather, he maintained an apartment on Park Avenue in Manhattan for that purpose, staffed with a full-time butler. For procurement, he relied on the talents of a young fellow he called "Society Sam." Sam maintained a "book:" an up-to-date list of available young women, many of them models or showgirls, all gorgeous. While working in the Beacon Hill studio on days when he'd just returned from New York, Al loved to regale us with descriptions of and anecdotes about his previous-night partners, each of them salted with his wit, and punctuated with his distinctive laughter.

While I still found these tales to be somewhat squirm-inducing, listening to such stuff back in the old 57th Street studio, and more recently from Stan Drake and others, had more-or-less prepared me. The result: his tales were far less-surprising than they might have been and, given Capp's gifts of humor, his yarns *were* more entertaining. Additionally – to his credit – absent the tasteless details.

Moreover, unlike the New York guys, Al *never* described, nor even alluded to the sex he'd been having – if any – with his wife.

Prior to working with Al, I'd never visited Boston. The place turned out to be a delight. Discovering that it was a near-perfect sized walking-around town, I took immediate, touristy advantage of my free hours, enjoying the locals' accents, the city's energy, and the great restaurants.

But the town's unique visual quality was an aesthetic that I found singularly engaging. In midtown and upper Manhattan or Chicago, the streets are mostly laid out in a conventional grid-pattern, with long, straight north-south and east-west avenues. Central Boston, however, is built upon what were once narrow, frequently winding foot-pathways. Hence, the street-level vistas rarely extend in a straight line for more than a block or two before being interrupted by a building, the façade of which, instead of being seen flat-on, is almost always at an oblique, eye-intriguing angle. More than just a change of scene, and like very few other cities, between those views, and the town's many other felicitous qualities, I instantly loved it.

I was also incidentally aware that these few days away from Nancy were having a seriously buoying effect on my spirits.

Important among my initial priorities, beyond the must-strolls through the Common and the Public Gardens, were explorations of the fabled Isabella Gardner Museum, and the Boston Museum of Fine Art. I went to the latter first, where I had an encounter I shall never, *ever* forget – with *The Four Daughters of Edward Darley Boit*.

Rounding a corner in the MFA, I found myself unexpectedly face-to-face(s) with John Singer Sargent's masterpiece – and I was staggered, my eyes instantly filling with tears. Except for seeing the work of Edgar Degas, that had never happened to me before when viewing art. While somewhat familiar with Sargent's work from reproductions in books, I'd not seen any of his paintings close up, and I was not at all prepared for the impact of that one – nor all his others. But it would and did happen, again and again.

Entering the wonderful Gardner Museum a few days later through its Spanish Cloister afforded another such stunner, Sargent's magnificent, breathtaking *El Jaleo* – the Gypsy dancer.

Between those two institutions, a truly awesome collection of his work. But exquisite as those moments were, none compare even distantly to the incredible jolt I experienced toward the end of my second week in Boston.

"Hi – um – you from…around here…?" Lame. Massively. But in my instantly stunned state, all I knew for sure was that I *had* to say *something*.

Shortly after noon I had seated myself at the counter in the small, crowded Paramount Café on Charles Street, a few steps from Capp's studio. I could not have imagined it, but a minute or two later, with a turn of my head, I would experience the *luckiest* moment of my life!

A life which in that instant would be *forever* changed. Profoundly, joyously.

Actually, *neither* of the above comes *close* to describing it…

In truth, a concept that I usually reject – in *all* forms – undeniably says it best:

Magic.

Checking the restaurant menu, I was only vaguely aware that someone had sat down on my right. But – after ordering my meal, I glanced in that direction – and – literally doing a real-life double-take – looked again.

Because sitting next to me was this *incredibly* beautiful young woman with long, straight brown hair and – and this I *know* makes it seem banal – this *perfect*, W.A.S.P., pretty-girl profile that I had been drawing – idealizing really – for years, first in romance comic-books, and more recently in countless advertising illustrations.

Anything *but* banal, it was a face that until that moment I didn't think existed in real-life.

My knee-jerk, no-thought move, even as I awkwardly tried to start a conversation with her, was to thrust my left hand into my pants-pocket and slip my wedding ring off my finger.

With no control over my feelings or thoughts, on some level I *knew* in that moment that my marriage to Nancy was over.

The young woman told me she was a secretarial student at the Katherine Gibbs School. Her name: Holly McKissock. From Rowayton, Connecticut, Holly was twenty years-old.

I think I mentioned to her that I was a commercial artist. I don't recall anything else that was said. I know I did *not* tell her I was married. Also, for some reason – probably projected guilt, or more likely because I was so blown away by her presence – I did not ask for her phone number.

What I remember for sure is that exquisite face, sans makeup or styled hair. Her presence and composure which were as charming and without attitude as she was naturally drop-dead lovely. About that aura, I sensed immediately that her beauty was beyond physical. She radiated a special, *truly* remarkable quality which remained difficult to describe until, years later, the right phrase was coined: *she was comfortable in her skin.* Totally. Without vanity. Or self-consciousness in any form.

But more than that, something far deeper – an aspect of her beauty that I could only appreciate later. Among its manifestations, a natural talent at which I have come to marvel – and continue to do so. Simply stated, without trying, her *presence* makes the people around her *feel good.*

Go figure that one…

Now, after decades, when I awaken each morning and see Holly's gorgeous face beside me – this *truly* extraordinary woman – I'm reminded of how amazingly *lucky* I am.

And – I continue to wonder at the total, randomly out-of-the-blue accident of that first meeting!

Because – *think* about it – ten minutes either way, and it would *not* have happened. We would *never* have met. Thus both of our lives would have turned out differently, in ways that I cannot imagine – nor do I wish to contemplate.

But I'm getting ahead of myself…

Following lunch that day, we said goodbye, I returned to the studio, and at the end of the week, to Westport, where I was able to think of little else but that vision. I pretty much went through the motions, marking time until my next trip to Boston. There, that first noontime, I eagerly/furtively staked out The Paramount Café from the far side of Charles Street. About the only thing missing was a trench-coat, felt hat and the pretense of reading a newspaper. When Holly failed to show up, I was crushed, wondering if I would ever see her again.

The following lunch-hour, however, things brightened. I was elated to see her enter the restaurant. I went with my plan. Instead of following her inside, I stationed myself around the corner from which she'd come, where I resumed my detective number, doing my best impression of "casual" as I awaited her return.

As I did so, I was all too aware that I was forchristsake thirty-one years old, married, with two kids, a mortgage, the whole shot, and I was behaving like a fucking smitten teenager. But I just *had* to get another look, if only to prove to myself that I hadn't manufactured her in my mind.

I had not. Twenty minutes later, Holly rounded the corner, and I quickly turned so she wouldn't recognize me. Then, when she'd passed, I watched her walk away. No, she was definitely real, and, clear from those furtive glances, the rest of her was as spectacularly gorgeous as her face. Plus, she seemed even *more* unselfconscious of it than I'd remembered.

A day later, knowing fully the step I was taking was into, for me, *very* unfamiliar, dicey territory, I approached her in The Paramount, summoning as much composure and sophistication as I could muster. Along with mock surprise.

"Hey, Holly. Nice to see you."

"Oh. Hi, Tom."

"Listen, I just got back into town. I'd love to take you to dinner. Maybe tomorrow night?"

She smiled, without hesitation or unease: "Sure. That'd be great."

I'd heard the expression *my head was swimming* countless times, but that was the first occasion where truly I understood its meaning.

139

Back at Al's studio a few minutes later, following his advice on where to dine, I made a reservation for two at Locke-Ober, then regarded as the best, most elegant restaurant in Boston. The following evening, doing my best to contain my adolescent excitement, I picked Holly up at her residence.

I'm not sure if it was significant, but the moon was full. We walked, chatting and laughing nonstop, with no sense that she was after all just out of her teen years. Holly was, as I've mentioned, without airs or an "act" of any kind. She was then, and has always been, enchanting in her naturalness, without affectations in *any* direction – defensive, compensatory, you name them. Simply, uniquely – herself – the most together person in fact that I have *ever* met.

She displayed the first evidence of this perhaps three minutes after the headwaiter had seated us side-by-side at our banquette. My plan: at some opportune point during the evening, I would tell her that I was married.

Instead, as I leaned slightly forward, perusing the menu, from over my left shoulder, Holly's matter-of-fact, non-accusatory words came: "You're married, aren't you?"

To say I felt as if I'd blown it doesn't begin to describe my feelings. I turned, expecting a look of censure or, anticipatory of my response, a sign that she was about to get up and storm out. Instead, she was relaxed, her back against the cushion, apparently as nonjudgmental as she'd sounded. I was knocked out by her poise which, at the moment was way better than my own as I grinned, trying to maintain some cool: "I guess it shows… I'd planned to tell you, later, over dinner."

I waited for her to indicate that she didn't believe me, or that it was a problem. When she did neither, I continued: "I've got two daughters. My marriage – it isn't great. And – well – you – this, it's my first time…"

Holly smiled: "My girlfriends and I made bets that you were married."

I began to relax, further impressed. "Which way did you call it?"

"Oh, I figured you were, the minute we met."

An amazing young woman. Sure, maybe my wedded state was obvious, but *that* cool – at age twenty? That was but an inkling of an area in which

Holly's kept on surprising me to this day, still frequently far ahead of me in assessing what other people are *really* about.

The sparks were instantaneous. For the *first* time in my life, I was *truly* in *LOVE*. Passionately. Transported-ly. Dazzled. Before another month had passed, we were doing weekends at the Maine coast.

Driving toward one of them on a lovely spring day, I grinned: "Y'know, we're gonna get married." I glanced at Holly, beside me. She was beaming.

Less than two months later, I left Nancy, explaining that I needed to move back into Manhattan for a time, in order to sort things out. In truth, I was certain I wouldn't be returning. She was neither shocked nor argumentative. We both knew it was over. I did not inform her about Holly.

First, I had no wish to hurt Nancy by suggesting that she'd lost out to "the other woman." That, given the deteriorated state of our marriage before Holly and I had met, was emphatically *not* the case.

Selfishly ancillary to that, I wanted to head off her likely resultant poisoning of our daughters toward me and, if Holly and I did stay together, toward her as well.

Holly and I happily took up residence in a sunny duplex studio at the landmark *des Artistes* on West 67th Street. A genuinely magnificent building, it had been designed by Stanford White. Holly had completed her training at Katherine Gibbs, and was eager to find employment. I was no longer working with Capp, who at my request had found a replacement for me: first-rate illustrator Bob Lubbers.

With Nancy, I'd felt more than a little awkward during that every-other-week-in-Boston, double-life period, especially the weeks when I was back in Westport, attending the usual parties and – essentially – posing. But that time, and the build-up to my departure from Connecticut served several purposes. Some, for-me-clarifying. Others, doubt, angst and/or fear-inducing.

One of the latter: my own massive misgivings about that to which I might be exposing Holly. Because there I was, with yet another busted marriage. Was I going to become a serial-divorcee?

Adding to that was increasing concern about what to do with my professional life. Absent the comfortable certainties of my faded longtime goal-fixation, I was beginning to feel more and more nervously adrift.

So, altogether, there I was with the girl of my dreams. Did I want to subject Holly to living out her time, or even just the next few years, with a guy as cosmically fucked up as I had begun to suspect I was?

No!

This wonderful person deserved *much* better than that. Ergo, when we began living together, there were no commitments. Nor did Holly, with wisdom and instincts astoundingly beyond her age, demand – or suggest – any.

I didn't come close to fully realizing it then, but in that incredible random accident of meeting Holly, my luck, and my life, already pretty damned good, had taken the *ultimate*, dramatic, *swerving* upturn.

NINETEEN
Inward Education—
Getting Off-The-Dime—
and Other Truth-Facing

As soon as we'd settled in New York City, Holly, who'd graduated from Bradford Junior College before we'd met, set about finding herself employment. Filling in at first as a temp, she quickly obtained more interesting work, assisting the woman who managed the New York office of J. Arthur Rank Pictures, a then-prominent British film company.

Also, with her customary pragmatism, Holly headed off a potentially sticky problem. Rather than allowing our living together to become an issue with her parents, she rented a room at The Barbizon, a very respectable women's residential hotel on Lexington Avenue. An only-child like myself, the big difference was that Holly respected and loved her mother and father, who were, I would soon learn, charming people. Never, over the almost three years until we married, did she spend a single night there.

In retrospect, it seems improbable that during that entire time her parents never initiated a phone call to her room. Yet, they never questioned Holly about why they couldn't reach her there. Which tells me that they understood, at least on some level. A tribute to the kind of people they were.

One of the unexpected delights about living with Holly was that she instantly became my sole photographic model for the pretty females I drew. In doing so, she made my job so much easier, because unlike all the rest, she required no modifying or compensating re-drawing to make the women I was illustrating suitably beautiful.

Our residence at *des Artistes* being a brief sublet, we soon found a small-but-cozy furnished apartment on 54th Street, just east of First Avenue. Which meant that I was in need of a place to set up my drawing-board, and quickly.

Though Leonard Starr and I had stayed in touch, seeing each other socially from time to time, my marriage to Nancy, and geography, had created some distance in our relationship. While Leonard continued to live in Manhattan, I'd jumped from Queens to New Jersey to Connecticut. On my return to the city that disconnect happily – and abruptly – vanished. He of course was endlessly, intensely occupied, writing and illustrating his extraordinary and *very* popular comic strip. *Mary Perkins On Stage* was syndicated in hundreds of daily newspapers throughout the world. Fortuitously, Leonard also happened to be in need of new workspace, so together we leased a studio in Greenwich Village, a few steps from Fifth Avenue, on West 9th Street. The top-floor of a brownstone, with skylights and fireplaces, it was a glorious space, and a joy to be working beside him again. As always, given his presence, the rooms were also filled with gorgeous classical music and great, literate conversation.

Along with all of those plusses, however, and more and more darkly overhanging all of it was a matter that filled me with doubt and caution. As my relationship with Holly deepened, so did my growing fear that I would terminally fuck up her young life. My urgent responsibility to *not* do so was growing daily. All the more difficult to handle because I so truly wanted to spend the rest of my life with her.

The offering of an unexpected hope-ray came the afternoon Leonard and I explored the then-vacant Greenwich Village studio with an eye to renting it. Standing near a window together in the south-facing room, Leonard grinned, gesturing at the building almost directly across 9th Street: "Sid's office. Sure would be convenient..." He quickly responded to my questioning look: "Sid Levy. My shrink...?" Now he picked up on my surprise: "I guess I forgot to mention – I've been in analysis the past few months."

We moved into the studio a few days later and, further excited by the fact that Leonard praised Dr. Levy so highly, I acted on my longtime inclination in that direction. My initial exploratory session with him went well, and I eagerly signed on as one of Dr. Sidney Levy's patients.

It was a process which I now regard as the second-most key move in my life – next to initiating that lunch-counter conversation with Holly. It turned out to be a *truly* priceless, amazingly revelatory experience.

Not unlike going to school – and majoring in myself, in who the hell I *was*.

That was a topic about which, it quickly and quite stunningly became clear, I understood almost *nothing* much deeper than my name.

The truth of this is capsulized in an early exchange with Dr. Levy at the start of one of our twice-a-week sessions. As I sat and then reclined on his couch, I was already describing a social encounter I'd experienced the previous evening. The subject of it I don't recall, but it had disturbed me in some way, and I was eager to get some clarification about its meaning.

What I remember vividly was Sid's startling response. It's one that I've since learned is definitely not uncommon among such professionals, but it was, especially in that instance, entirely appropriate *and* effective!

"How did it make you feel?"

I threw him a look.

Feel?

I had *absolutely* no fucking idea of what he meant.

145

It was a start, really. First, and to my *enormous* relief, on my journey toward my realization that no, I wasn't an irredeemable head-case, and therefore would probably *not* destroy Holly's life.

Happily, reaching that part of it was relatively quick, requiring only a few months.

The longer one would eventually free me as an artist by putting me in *complete*, denial-free touch with my emotions – *and* as a result those of others – which of course is *totally* what it's about. Indeed, my years with Sid – and my debt to him – have proven far, far *beyond* priceless. Today I have not a single doubt that, had I *not* made that move, I could *never* have functioned creatively on the level(s) I've been able to enjoy.

On another sensory level, together with Leonard and his lovely wife, Betty, Holly and I quickly began what would become another unforgettable positive in our lives. We became subscribers to The Metropolitan Opera. The era of the amazing tenor, Franco Corelli, for the next several years we enjoyed the greatest, most thrilling nights in the theatre that we would ever experience. I loved everything about it – the spectacle, the passion, the emotional rush of such gorgeous music washing over me, its sheer unashamed over-the-top theatricality.

Superficially, there was the fun of dressing-up. Our tickets were for Tuesday evenings which, pre-Lincoln Center, were dress-up nights: black tie and long gowns. At one point during that era, I owned three tuxedos, and Holly had a number of floor-length evening dresses.

But it is those singular, spectacular performances and elaborate productions that I miss most of all about New York City.

Part of my postponement of moving forward with a divorce had hinged on my belief, despite zero evidence, that Nancy wanted the marriage to continue. That assumption was, I realized upon later reflection, and with Sid Levy's help, largely a product of my guilt over being the one who walked out, taking up with another woman. I'd coupled that with an even more unrealistic, ego-based notion that of course she'd want me back. Because, I figured, I was *certainly* blameless for things not working out. I mean, how could she not want *me?*

All of which conspired to help me overlook, with my usual opacity about such things, the fact that Nancy had not *once* indicated that she was saddened – or anything in that region. Nor did she ever profess any desire for me to return. Here again, my analyst, with his fortunately clearer view, was instrumental in helping me face such truths. Having listened to my reasoning (which when I think about it must have been boggling for him), he offered a brilliant – and brilliantly simple – deadpan suggestion. "Why not have Holly and Nancy come in – separately of course – for a one-on-one hour?"

Holly, without hesitation: "Sure. When?"

To my minor but no less dumb surprise, Nancy refused.

To Sid's credit as a professional, when I informed him of her response he displayed not a hint of an "*I told you so*" twinkle.

So, I explained to Nancy that I wanted a divorce. She offered no argument, and we put it into motion. Simultaneously, and with her agreement, we put the house up for sale. Within a few weeks we received an acceptable offer. Following that, we found and purchased a smaller, less-pricey but attractive home for her and our daughters on the opposite side of Westport.

Parting with the home we'd built a few years earlier, which had meant so much to me symbolically was, emotionally, relatively easy – actually, I was relieved to be rid of the expense – as I had long before lost my need for what it represented.

While I did not tell her about Holly, looking to the future, and the hope that I might limit support payments to just my children, I somewhat tentatively encouraged Nancy to meet guys, to date them. She did, though the end result would prove – well – questionable. Especially for Lauren and Suzy. The guy with whom Nancy became involved, and married soon after our divorce was, it turned out, a fellow alcoholic.

I continued my one-day-a-week visits with my daughters, and one of the first of these in their new home stands out. I was seated on the edge of the backyard sandbox, watching the girls at play, when I happened to glance past them, and the nearby trees bordering the property. The next-door neighbor had emerged from her front door to retrieve the morning paper from the stoop. She straightened, paused to check the headlines – and I saw who it was.

Though I had read that this woman was residing in Westport, I had no knowledge of where, and I quickly, excitedly gestured as I whispered to the girls: "Hey! See that lady on her doorstep?"

They looked at her, then at me, with "*So...?*" expressions. The woman went inside, closing her door.

I grinned: "Someday you're gonna tell your children that you once lived next-door to the greatest movie actress in the whole world."

It clearly wasn't all that big a deal to them, then or now, but I was knocked out. I still am.

Their neighbor was Bette Davis.

Since the divorce was finally in work, Holly and I agreed that it would be okay for me to meet her parents. We'd concocted and rehearsed a story about how we'd met, and one early summer weekend we drove to Rowayton. Despite Holly's reassurances, I was tense, full of misgivings. Me? In mid-divorce, with two children, and *eleven* years older than their gorgeous not-quite-twenty-one year-old daughter? I expected at best a *very* cool reception.

Instead, to my surprise and delight, I was warmly – enthusiastically, *genuinely* welcomed. Harriet and Allan McKissock were two of the nicest, gentlest, most charming people I had ever met. I was immediately at ease with them in their lovely home, which matched them in lack of pretension. If they had *any* doubts or hostile feelings about me, I was unable to discern them. Obviously, Holly had done one helluvva selling-job!

So began Holly's and my official courtship. Instead of my one-day-per-week visits to Suzy and Lauren in Westport, I began bringing them to Rowayton on weekends. First of course to acquaint them with Holly, and vice-versa. Though I was hardly surprised, I was knocked out that they enjoyed each other from their initial meeting.

Another less-expected pleasure: Allan and Harriet happily took on the roles of "instant" grandparents, making the girls feel genuinely welcome. There, as summer progressed, they'd frolic on the lawn, and we'd go to the beach on Long Island Sound, only a short walk from the McKissock home.

One of the more remarkable, and refreshing points that hit me about Holly, her lovely mother and father, and their relationship with each other, was the total absence of angry subtext, of ongoing issues. Those, for me, had always been synonymous with "family."

Holly's Dad, incidentally, had a truly unique profession – and expertise. For virtually his entire working-life he commuted each business day to the lower Manhattan offices of food giant Standard Brands, Inc. There, his responsibility was the blending – and maintaining the consistent flavor of – Tenderleaf Tea. This I learned was done while Allan sat at a low, round, rotating table on which were numerous cups of tea. Each had been freshly brewed from leaves supplied by a single importer or grower from somewhere in the world. Allan would sip one, judge the aroma and taste, and then turn the table to the next cup and repeat the process. After sampling all, he would decide how much of each should be used to recreate Tenderleaf's flavor.

I was genuinely impressed by his talent and also, frankly, I rather envied his ability to do the same thing over and over, without complaint or *any* outward indication of struggle or discontent.

My father and mother had been understandably concerned about my separation from Nancy. Their questions/doubts intensified when I finally informed them about the impending divorce, and then about Holly. So much so that, during a business trip to Delaware, my dad detoured to Manhattan one afternoon in an attempt to, in his view, "help." It resulted in an encounter with him which remains vividly and not at *all* pleasantly etched for me.

Over coffee in a restaurant on East 42nd Street, at length and with neither sympathy nor understanding, he reminded me of my responsibilities to my children and to Nancy. Basically and as always judgmentally, he tried to convince me of his view: "real men" don't leave their wives for another woman.

"Dad, Holly's *not* the cause. All this – between Nancy and me – things've been deteriorating for a long time. Our marriage, I mean, it was *never* all that great."

"Oh, *c'mon…*" He glanced away, then: "Okay, tell me – *what* was so bad about it?"

I was surprised and put off by his demand for specifics. But I cited several areas, including non-communication and her drinking. Then, a bit hesitant about sharing such stuff, I went for it, concluding with: "…And – well – truth is – the sex was lousy."

My father's instant, heated, contemptuous reply was another one of those indelible, what-the-light-in-the-room-looked-like moments I wish I could forget.

"Oh, come *on* – what the hell does *that* have to do with it? Your mother and I haven't had sex in twenty-five years."

I stared at him, speechless.

Shit! Not since I was a little kid?

This is *not* something *any* child wants to know about one's parents.

My unstated but unequivocal reaction, then – and now, albeit at this distance touched with *some* sadness: My god, *what* kind of putz *willingly* lives that way?

The divorce went through, and happily – for myself, anyway – Nancy quickly remarried. During my times with Suzy and Lauren, I got the impression that they weren't all that taken with their stepfather, but Holly and I urged them to make the best of it.

Holly had been enjoying her work for J. Arthur Rank, but due to a management change that gig dried up, so she took a position as secretary to a VP at Grey Advertising. We scheduled our marriage for May, 1965 and began looking for an unfurnished apartment with more space than we had on 54th Street.

Perhaps the single disappointing condition Holly placed on our future together came one evening as we drove back to Manhattan following a day in Connecticut with Lauren and Suzy.

"I – I hope it's okay with you, but – I really don't think I want to have children. I mean – you – we – we've got this family already..."

I wasn't exactly surprised. It was really *not* okay. I had been looking forward to our building our own family – *especially* because Holly was – Holly. But I totally understood her feelings, and chose to respect them without argument. "Hey, I get it. No problem, believe me..."

Regrettable, but a small enough concession...

Professionally, largely out of curiosity, I was learning more and more about how the business side of advertising worked. I was still dealing only with art services/middle-men such as Johnstone & Cushing, rather than directly with the major advertising agencies. Nonetheless, I'd become fascinated with the big agencies' approach – measuring demographics, TV viewership, print readership, and the like. I found myself questioning the how-and-why of pricing for TV time, print ads, and in my case, why some similar illustration jobs paid markedly more than others. As opposed to the "going rate" often employed in non-advertising media. Questions apparently rarely asked by my fellow illustrators. Which resulted, I suppose inevitably, in my becoming something of a pain-in-the-ass at Johnstone & Cushing, and with other clients. It eventually would alienate me from the larger arena of cartoonists and illustrators in general.

But I doubt if any of that would have happened had I not brought the topic to the attention of Dr. Levy. I'd arrived for one of my sessions at his office in a cranky state. In that morning's mail I'd received a check for some ad work I'd done, and while as usual it paid far better than the old comic-book rates, it was for an amount far smaller than I felt it deserved, especially given the wide exposure it was supposed to have. The moment I reclined on his couch, I was into it, grousing about it, and art buyers in general: "...I mean damn near none of 'em pay me what my stuff is worth."

"How does that work? You negotiate the price up front, right?"

"No. They just tell me what it's gonna pay. Or sometimes – like this one, I just take the assignment, and then I get paid whatever they decide. Like at

Johnstone & Cushing, where some ads pay fifty or a hundred bucks more – or less than others."

"So – you don't *ask* for what *you* think it's worth?"

"Nope." I explained that with one or two exceptions – Al Capp when I didn't even want the job, and a merit badge pamphlet for The Boy Scouts which they'd priced ridiculously low – I'd never done so. "Hell, I don't know any artists who do. Even the syndicated comic-strip guys. I mean, like, Leonard Starr. They send him a contract every year – and he youknow just signs it."

Sid was silent for a beat or two, which I later realized was how long it took him to un-boggle his mind. Then he spoke, delivering one of his wonderfully piercing one-line insights that would forever change how I regarded myself: "These clients, Tom – they're *not* your father."

Whoa.

To say that I took that one home with me doesn't nearly describe its resonance. A few days later, having more fully processed it, I had my first opportunity try out this fresh set of lenses. I was handed an assignment from Al Stenzel at J&C to illustrate a comic-strip style advertisement for Tide laundry detergent. The form of course was not unusual – I had drawn dozens of similar jobs. But the difference here was substantial. Instead of appearing in the Sunday color-comics section of newspapers, this one was intended as a full-page, four-color advertisement which would appear simultaneously in several slick, national women's magazines, among them *McCall's*, *Ladies Home Journal* and *Good Housekeeping*.

Al agreed that it was an entirely new venue for the comic-strip format. It immediately struck me that in those publications it would be unexpected, and therefore quite an attention-grabber – which of course is what advertising is all about. In character, as newly defined by Sid Levy, I asked Stenzel what the job would pay. Accustomed as he was to the docility, the seeming near-gratitude shown by most artists for being paid at all, Al was a bit put-off that I'd even inquired. He shrugged dismissively: "The usual – four – five hundred..." That was the standard fee for ads in the Sunday comics.

"Uh-uh, Al. For this, that's not acceptable."

He scowled. "What in hell're you talking about? That's what everybody gets."

"For newspapers. This is different."

Pissed, he said he'd take it up with management, and I returned to my drawing table. A few minutes later Al approached, deadpan-but-still-annoyed. He jerked his thumb: "Jack wants to see you." Stenzel then continued past, en route to his cubicle.

I rose and crossed to Cushing's office. He looked up, not happy: "Okay – *what* is your fucking problem?"

"Jack, look – I don't mean to be a troublemaker, but I've got friends – 'real' illustrators – like the guys at Cooper Studio – they're getting twenty-five hundred or more for advertisements in these magazines, some not even full-pages. That's what I should get for this."

"You're kidding. *Five* times our prevailing rate…?" Astonished – and offended – by such presumption, he reminded me: "Hey, pal, this is just 'comics.'"

I was appalled that he didn't understand, much less that we were even discussing it. "Wait a minute, Jack – we're talking a whole different market here. Way more upscale. And smaller, more specialized. I mean the agency that's gonna run this ad, they have to pay substantially more per pair of eyeballs in those slick magazines than they would in the Sunday comics section. And that's why the illustrators charge more…" I couldn't believe I was explaining anything so basic to this veteran of the business – a guy old enough to *be* my father. Hearing myself – well, that was a bit strange, too. "…I mean, it's the same as when advertisers have to pay higher rates to run TV spots on hit shows – or on a TV movie aimed at women – than they would, say, for a local broadcast that reaches a not-so-targeted audience."

What I omitted was even more obvious: by paying me more, Johnstone & Cushing's take would be proportionately higher.

It was my initiation, really, as a bargainer for my services. Also my first encounter with the phenomenon of the entrepreneur who, having invented a business – newspaper comic-strip ads *were* his and Johnstone's box – was reluctant to revisit any of it, to think outside of those dimensions.

Plus, me being a mere [schmuck] artist, I was about the last person Cushing expected to hear articulating any of it. His look told me that in his view, since I was a guy who spends his life at a drawing-table, I wasn't supposed to know this stuff. It pissed him off.

I waited, leaving the next move to him. After a grumpy moment or two he dismissively waved a hand: "I'll think about it."

Next day, I had the assignment – at the then-unheard-of-for- Johnstone & Cushing price I'd demanded.

Eventually I illustrated several similar advertisements – for larger fees. Thanks to Sid Levy, in becoming acquainted with who I was, I was also learning the business side of being a professional. Hey, better late than…

And – *no*, dammit, Jack Cushing *wasn't* my father. *None* of 'em were!

Consistent with our ongoing good fortune, Holly and I found a *great* apartment on the East Side at 75th Street & York Avenue. On the 18th floor, it had two bedrooms, three exposures, and a 30 foot terrace on a setback. This penthouse-like feature afforded marvelous unblocked views, from the nearby East River to the New Jersey Palisades to upper and lower Manhattan. We eagerly began to furnish our new home.

Holly's and my wedding in Rowayton was almost as gorgeous as she was, taking place on a perfect mid-May afternoon, surrounded by family – including my parents – and friends, several from my time in Tokyo. Leonard Starr was my Best Man. The following morning my bride and I flew to Paris.

A first trip to Europe for both of us, Paris was even more beautiful and exciting than we expected. As was, the following week, our stay in Nice. Memorable in every way, from never-to-be-forgotten dining at places such as Paris's *Taillevent*, on the Riviera at Eze and Beaulieau, to our tour of Versailles, and drives along the Corniches. The utter charm, beauty and aesthetic of the spots we visited, the side-trips, the spectacles.

One of those was quite unexpected. On our first morning in Paris, as we were headed out of our hotel to begin exploring the city, I approached the concierge and asked if there were any special events occurring that week in Paris. He checked a calendar, and announced that the Paris Opera, that same evening, was featuring Maria Callas, on her farewell tour, singing *Norma*. I was instantly seriously intrigued; we had passed up her final performance at the Met in New York a few weeks earlier because tickets were selling for the then-exorbitant price of nearly $200 each. I asked if he could find out about availability of seats, cautioning him that I did not want to spend a huge amount. He nodded his understanding, promised to check it out for us, and we departed for the day.

Following our thrilling and exhausting initial taste of that incredible city, Holly and I returned to the hotel late in the afternoon. Immediately on entering, I was gestured aside by the concierge. He confided that he had taken the liberty of obtaining two tickets for us, but was very apologetic about the price, assuring me that he was sure he could return them if I declined. Prepared for the worst, I listened – and damned near laughed in his face – as he explained that while the tickets' list price was $14 per seat, he had no choice but to pay an extra $2 each. Unbelievably excited and grateful, I of course reimbursed him on the spot, adding a substantial gratuity.

A few minutes later, Holly and I relaxed for a nap, elated, anticipating the evening ahead.

It was even better than we'd hoped. Ms. Callas was amazing. We'd never seen her perform before – in truth she was not my favorite soprano – and by then her voice was pretty far gone. But onstage that night, she was a living lesson in what star-quality was all about: she *owned* the house. Plus, that house, the old Paris Opera, was even more wondrous than we had expected from photos we'd seen. It was staggeringly magnificent.

A week later, on the breathtaking Riviera, we enjoyed the thrill of trackside seats at the Grand Prix of Monaco. Then, in continuing superb weather, capping our trip, Venice. There, in addition to the everywhere-we-looked visual spectacle, we attended a brilliant performance in The Doge Palace, of the Vienna Boys' Choir performing Bach's *Second St. Matthew Passion*.

The entire time was a lifelong *Keeper*.

But for me none of it came close to the most spectacular of all – this amazing young woman who had chosen to share my life. She continues to effortlessly test me intellectually. Her voice and laugh and sense of humor delight, her presence and grace awe me, as does that face I am so incredibly fortunate to see when I awaken each morning.

TWENTY
Shaking Things Up— Again

On our return from Europe, Holly and I joyously settled into our new home. Within a few months, Nancy, her husband and our daughters, Suzy and Lauren, relocated to Salem, Virginia. The downside was that we saw the girls much less often, usually flying them to New York once a month or so, for weekends with us. But their visits were fun, and in a way, the space between them provided for Holly and me a sort of time-lapse, intermittent view of their growth.

One such forward step was indelibly punctuated by a line from Suzy, then a vivacious eight or nine years-old, which was so amusing and memorable that it became part of our vocabulary. I had met her and Lauren when their flight arrived at LaGuardia, and driven them to our apartment. As they entered, Suzy's first words, excitedly blurted following her hello to Holly, were: "… And there's this girl in my class – her name's Cindy Woody – and – and she's perfect as _heck_!"

Think about it.

From the _name_ to the _description_, talk about _nailing_ it. About _resonance_ and _universality_. As a writer, I could not have _invented_ a name that more precisely summons that image, than Cindy Woody. I mean, hasn't _everyone_ – at _least_ once – had a Cindy Woody in her or his class who _was_ perfect as heck?

During the three years since returning to Manhattan, I'd made several more passes at creating a syndicated comic-strip, each separated by months and my busy advertising illustration schedule. With progressively waning enthusiasm. But, because of the freeing-up changes in my rendering technique, each one had a marginally better, envelope-pushing "look."

One strip was about an adventurous space-and-rocket-scientist. I followed that with one about a crusading newspaperman. Both were rejected by the major syndicates – and I was actually relieved. My third and final attempt, which I pretty much walked through, had a college setting, its protagonist a cutting-edge – and edgy – physicist/professor. I never got as far as trying to sell it.

It was my truth-time.

Among the many realities-not-until-then-faced were personal readings gradually accumulated, about the essential nature of this profession I'd striven for since my teens. Observations about what it did to its practitioners, the comic-strip artists I'd come to know who were successful in the business. Perceptions, and conclusions drawn that I'd either discounted or chosen to deny. Namely, that in working alongside these guys, I had almost from the beginning seen some very real negatives to their for-that-era high-paying game.

First, I had gotten the sense that they were in this velvet-lined trap, virtually all of them profoundly bored by their work, but earning so much that walking away from it was off the table. Though none actually said so (to me, anyway), it seemed that were it not for the toys and lifestyles they'd grown used to, most of them would abandon these grinds in a New York minute. For the story-strip guys especially, "endless" was the key word; they were *never* finished with a job, never experienced closure. One "story" morphed into another, on and on, with no break. I suppose the gag-a-day strip guys had it a little better – but in my view not by much.

Along with these fellows' lack of job-and-creative satisfaction were what I saw as resultant, very similar compulsive, compensatory self-destructive behavior-patterns – usually in the form of booze and/or women and/or some other more complex neuroses. I recall commenting more than once that most of them seemed to be sitting at their drawing-boards, ankle-deep in pools of their own blood.

Bottom line, I finally *accepted* what I'd known-but-denied for so long. That the very idea of spending my entire life working with the same-size sheets of drawing paper, and the same tools, over and over and over, with never a sense of finishing something and starting anew, was *not* for me.

It was a job that, bluntly put, would cause me to go out of my fucking mind.

In the same area was an even more disquieting piece of the equation – the realization that I had become as expert at my craft as I would ever be. With perhaps another 30 or 35 productive years ahead of me, the thought of continuing to do that which I'd already more-or-less mastered was dreary indeed, not one that I could possibly accept.

All of which left me – for the first time in my memory – in the truly frightening, disoriented position of being without a specific, envisionable goal.

Me. The kid who, back in Chicago, had been held up as an example, albeit self-consciously, by more than one of my friends' mothers: "See, dummy? Tommy knows what *he* wants to do with his life."

However, that scary end-frame vacuum quickly turned into a refreshing asset. It opened me to exciting possibilities I'd never before permitted myself to consider. One in particular.

At that time, the nature of my freelance advertising illustration assignments had begun to evolve. Dramatically. In ways that made excellent use of my early – as well as recent – work: telling stories in comic-strip, near-cinematic form. I was handling an increasing number of gigs which would *not* be seen in print, *never* shown to the public. Drawings intended for *very* small audiences – tiny groups of executives, actually, and filmmakers – but which, ironically, were the most lucrative artwork I *ever* produced.

Called "storyboards," they consisted of eight, to as many as sixteen – or even twenty-four small 3"x 4", or sometimes 4"x 5" drawings (called "frames") depicting the key shots of proposed TV commercials.

Even the way I got the jobs differed from the norm. I was usually summoned to the ad agency art department late in the day, or even shortly after closing time. There, the art director and often the copy writer with whom he'd collaborated, would hand me a script for a half-minute or one-minute commercial. Often, a just-finished concept they'd spent weeks creating. Frequently, it would be the kickoff idea for an entirely new ad campaign. Most of the time, my delivery deadline was the following morning, though occasionally I'd have a day or two.

The products being advertised ranged from cars to toothpaste, breakfast cereal, canned soup and the like – all of them national brands. My job: design the commercial by illustrating the script in individual frames, often detailed all the way to the wallpaper pattern or furniture-style, in a way that would *sell* the idea to the client. The completed storyboard, attractively matted, would then be presented, usually at the advertiser's home office, in hope that he/she/they would agree to go forward with the commercial – or the entire campaign concept. Rendered (at the time I began doing them) in black line, and various tones of gray, these provided by readily-obtained felt-tip markers, those that I drew were as photo-like as possible. They portrayed the actor's facial expression, body-language and or gesture as she or he was delivering the script-line at the bottom of the frame. In effect, I was directing it on paper.

Fun, challenging in the sense that I was being asked to tell – and hopefully improve upon – the copywriter's "story," my comic-strip background gave me a particular flair for the form.

Often, when I received the call, and knowing I'd be picking up an assignment, I would immediately enlist Holly's help in either posing or taking photos of me, or both. Instead of heading home that evening, she'd meet me at the studio, and we'd shoot the poses I needed. Then, usually, following dinner together in Greenwich Village, she'd head uptown.

I would work late, alone in the studio. I truly enjoyed the hurry-hurry and inside-my-head-ness of it – and I *loved* the pressure, the immediacy. I'd sometimes finish as late as 3 or 4 AM, go home with the artwork, and while I slept Holly would deliver it for me en route to her office. Within a year or two of that broadcast-transitional era, I was being asked to render them in color. Still with black line-drawing, the color-source was also felt-tipped markers. Fast, instantly dry, with a zillion available shades, that only added to the pleasure.

Another pleasurable dividend from that "Jack Cushing wasn't my father" aspect of my education occurred during that period. The Art Buyer at the then-major ad agency, Dancer, Fitzgerald & Sample, confided to me one day that he was "getting a lotta heat" from management about the prices I was billing for my storyboards.

By then, I was the highest-paid artist in that niche-market, charging $100 per frame, sometimes netting as much as $2,400 per day. Per night, actually, at the cost of my sleep.

My understanding of where he was coming from instantly kicked in: it wasn't *his* money. He was looking for an excuse. A justification.

A way to *not* be blamed.

Not missing a beat, I provided one: "Look, Dancer's got a $150 grand per year art director and a $150 grand per year copywriter who've spent weeks coming up with an ad campaign concept. Sure, you can buy cheaper storyboards – but mine *sell* the ideas to the clients out in Cincinnati – so your pricey in-house talent doesn't have to spend another 4 or 5 weeks cooking up another---" That was as far as I got. He interrupted with an upraised palm, a smile and a nod. Satisfyingly, I never had to explain it again.

One commercial to which I made a memorable contribution was for Lavoris mouthwash. On reading the script I'd just been given by the agency copywriter, I was unable/unwilling to conceal my reaction: "D'you mean this to be a – a satire?"

The subject – and arc – of the commercial was a pretty girl who had "bad breath," and was thus a social reject – *until* she discovered Lavoris, and became popular.

The copywriter's reply was a bit defensive: "No. I – we – we figured we'd do it straight. Like it's written…".

"Well – to be truthful, it feels so – youknow – corny, that it might be better to play it that way – to just – go for it …" I was making it up as I spoke. "…In fact, you could almost do it like a soap-opera spoof, with – punctuated by – oh, organ stings and…" I was on a roll: "…and instead of shooting it live-action, we could do it with – like – Roy Lichtenstein-type over-the-top comic-book panels! And – and voice-overs instead of dialogue balloons!"

"Shit. I dunno, Tom."

The copywriter flicked a brief "*are you outa your mind?*" glance at his art director, then, excitedly to me: "Tom, that is – *yeah*! Let's *do* it!"

I did the storyboard in that style, and it received an immediate, enthusiastic "Go." The finished commercial, which except for product-pictures, consisted of shots of my storyboard frames, I had titled – onscreen – "*The Trouble With Margie.*" Adding to my delight, within days of its premiere showing, it had become rather iconic. Enough so that *Tonight Show* host Johnny Carson drew big laughs from his studio audience when he referred, on-air, to a girl having "Margie's Problem." A few months later, and *very* gratifyingly, *Advertising Age* selected it as one of the best commercials of the year.

Storyboards and other assignments were phasing me out of my Johnstone & Cushing period. Happily for Tom, Jack and Al Stenzel, my place there was being taken by a brash, *very* confident and talented young guy. Neal Adams began handling the accounts I'd serviced regularly for several years, doing so excellently. Neal went on to an illustrious, really legendary career as a comics artist.

Inside my head, something *dramatic* was happening! Between the creative processes triggered by my storyboard work, and the hobby in which I'd become immersed, I was shifting my goal-gears.

I was beginning to think about an entirely new, unexpected and exciting direction for my life and career.

One which at this hindsight-point seems to have been obvious – and inevitable.

In that pre-home video age, I'd become fascinated with making home movies, shooting prodigious amounts of 8mm film footage of my daughters, Holly, and of friends during social functions.

The part that had *really* grabbed me, though, was the editing process. I found myself eagerly – almost compulsively – cutting and splicing and re-cutting until far into the night. Then, staring bleary-eyed into the tiny screen, I'd wind and rewind past this or that edit, sometimes amazed at the result. I had discovered a phenomenon I'd eventually learn was known well to people who work in the medium, wherein two disparate pieces of film joined together *can* add up to something far greater than its parts. On occasion, exponentially so. The creative possibilities were truly exciting!

But I had *absolutely* no clue about how or where to begin. Nor where I could learn the technical side of it, to enable me to move on to more sophisticated levels. Plus, I had not even the *slightest* knowledge of how I might get started professionally – though at that point such a possibility only barely occurred to me.

But – it had – *very* tentatively – crept into the remote-fantasy-part of my mind…

I began kicking the topic around with Leonard, Sid, Holly and others. I also decided to seek the advice of the two New York professional filmmakers I'd met. My questions: "How would you suggest I get from where I am to where you are?" And: "Would you recommend that I attend film production school?"

The first, a former comic-book artist I'd known from the National Cartoonists Society, had become a successful producer of commercials and designer of hip-looking film graphics. Very "Hollywood," wearing sunglasses in his darkish office, telephones clapped to both ears as he juggled simultaneous calls, Lew Sayre Schwartz opined his aside to me: "Nah, *forgeddabout* schools! All you hafta do is – learn the jargon. Come work for me, I'll teach you."

I thanked Lew and said I'd think about it.

My next brain-pickee was award-winning TV-commercial Director Barry Brown, whom I'd met recently at an ad agency. His response began with a question right back at me: "Listen, are you used to handling large sums of money? I mean, does it youknow make you uneasy or – or nervous – or throw ya?"

A bit uncertain about his seemingly off-the-wall point, I shrugged: "I'm used to being well-paid. And money – it's not really a big deal to me."

That's when Barry threw me his clincher: "Good. Because the thing you've *gotta* remember is – it's *all* funny money."

He elaborated, explaining that in his business alone, the amounts of cash advertising agencies paid for 30 seconds of film were often ridiculous. "Some filmmakers – they get all shook up by the numbers – like – it goes to their heads. A lotta the time, by way of their noses. And I mean, the Monopoly-money thing, it's like even more so out in Tinseltown…"

That observation has by the way resonated for me ever since, as I saw it demonstrated repeatedly during my years in the business. In recent times, interestingly, the phenomenon seems to have spread far beyond Hollywood, to sports stars, corporate executives, hedge fund managers and others.

While Barry conceded that I might benefit from a film course or two, he also generously offered that I was welcome to learn by working at his side. I passed on that as well. My instincts told me that I really needed to study the basics in a structured environment, uncolored – as far as possible – by a particular filmmaker's attitude or style.

Based on all that, I eagerly enrolled in a one-semester evening course at The New School for Social Research. The class, *Introduction to Film Production*, was taught by Arnold Eagle, who had been Robert Flaherty's assistant during the shooting of the latter's classic documentary, *Nanook of the North*. I found Mr. Eagle and his sessions instantly fascinating and unexpectedly rewarding as he screened, discussed and dissected with great insight, a series of short films from all over the world.

I'd neither seen nor even heard about any of them, and for me they revealed a means of artistic expression, a form, that I hadn't *ever* imagined. Few longer than 10 or 15 minutes, what I saw in those little movies startled me. Emotionally powerful and/or funny, striking in unorthodox, inventive ways, each was an intensely personal statement. Most told stories with incredible, pure, cinematic economy. I'd seen many "shorts" in movie theaters, usually accompanying a feature-length film, but they were mostly novelty, comedic franchises. *None* contained the kind of personal statements these films made.

I had long been at least vaguely aware of – and intrigued by – the sheer power, unique among *all* of the arts, that film affords the creator. Sure, a novelist can capture the reader with words, and a painter's canvas is usually framed, somewhat setting it apart. But distractions abound; noise, movement of other people in a gallery, and at home, telephones, crying babies, barking dogs and the like. In a darkened theater, however, sits a willingly semi-captive audience, feeling isolated, its attention almost *completely* under the artist's control. The filmmaker can *force* that audience to *look* at and *listen* to whatever he or she chooses!

In so many feature-length movies, I'd seen what directorial giants like Hawks, Kazan, Capra and Bergman could do, felt their impact. But few carried the concise punch of the films Mr. Eagle selected.

They opened me up to the exciting possibility that I might – for small bucks – try this abbreviated form as a *pure* creative outlet.

The whole notion grabbed me in ways I'd never experienced. I became grandly, passionately impatient to learn more about the tools of professional filmmaking, so that I could begin using them. Further, if it turned out that I *had* anything personal to say, to try expressing it in this medium which since childhood had seemed so inaccessible.

165

So hooked was I that before Eagle's course ended, I'd signed up for the following-semester of a nighttime class at NYU. There, a knowledgeable gentleman, Saul Taffet, taught what can best be described – and with *highest* compliments – as a nuts-and-bolts shop-course in filmmaking. *My* kind of learning environment, the students were divided into three-or-four-person teams. Each had at its disposal professional equipment: Arriflex 16mm camera, lights, microphones, Nagra tape recorder, an editing bench and, later, a Moviola (then, the standard editing tool).

Our class-assignments: shooting black & white negative stock, make three one-minute films.

The first, silent.

Next, with an added "wild" (non-sync) soundtrack.

Finally, with a sync-sound dialogue track. For this last we were allowed one dissolve plus a fade-in and a fade-out, and even a title. The beauty of Saul's course was that by semester-end, *each* of us would – and did – actually perform, hands-on, *every* non-lab operation used in film production at that time. From scriptwriting to storyboarding to shooting to sound recording and lighting, to editing, cutting and splicing picture and mag-track, all the way to cutting negative.

I loved *every* tactile, revelatory second of it.

TWENTY-ONE
A New Doorway

TOWARD THE END OF THE NYU COURSE, having read every book on movie production I could find, I felt ready. Stoked. I wrote and storyboarded a short film, designed so that I could shoot it myself, with no crew and, to avoid onlookers, in an isolated setting.

A simple story, it involved a single character, a lovely young woman (played by Holly – who else?), who arrives at this lonely spot to spend a few reflective days alone, inside her troubled head. There, she goes through some frightening hours, and comes out whole – or not, depending on who's looking at it.

Holly's family had the perfect such place, our every-summer destination, a tiny, charming cottage-with-a-name: *Greenestone*. Full of character and architectural touches. On a large swan-inhabited pond adjacent to the ocean at Sakonnet Point, Rhode Island, it has a feel – both house, and the surrounding area – like nowhere else in the world. So, immediately upon finishing Saul's class, Holly and I eagerly stuffed a full complement of rented film equipment into our car. Along with several thousand feet of fine-grain black & white 16mm raw stock, chosen in lieu of color because of cost and the need for more lighting, we departed Manhattan.

It was late autumn, cool, sunny, the house and beaches off-season empty. Exactly as I wanted it. I filmed, and Holly performed – beautifully – for four or five wonderful, exciting days and nights, during which I only partly followed my script. We were discovering and/or improvising a number of unplanned shots and scenes. In the house, on the beach, the adjacent meadows – massively heady, a kind of creative liberation, control and *satisfaction* I'd never before experienced.

It was a week that I can *still* taste.

Back in Manhattan, following an impatient wait for the lab to process the film, I eagerly screened a work-print of what I'd shot. Holly's on-film look and performance was smashing. While delighted that many of the exterior takes were even better than I'd hoped, it was obvious and deeply disappointing that nearly *all* of the interior footage *had* to be shit-canned.

Bummed, I viewed, and re-viewed it, hoping I was just being overcritical. But no. I had lit it dreadfully, in a painful, old-hat Hollywood-artificial way that I thought I'd avoided. I would need to reshoot almost *every* setup. On the topic of lighting, I'd clearly read the wrong books.

That phony aspect of movies, particularly the Hollywood product, had for years annoyed me. Increasingly so since I had begun learning the craft, and was viewing them with a somewhat more knowledgeable eye. In fact, at about that time it was apparently getting to at least a few others: I'd recently seen a foreign film where *some* of the lighting *seemed* more legitimately sourced. But still, I had no idea of how to light it the way I envisioned, nor where I might turn to learn how to achieve that result.

Then – talk about timing – Holly and I attended a screening for members of The Society of Illustrators, of a new Hollywood feature film that was *about* an illustrator. Filmed mostly in Manhattan and Connecticut, the cast of *Loving* included – as extras or in bit-parts – several of my artist-friends. Pleasant-but-not-great, it starred George Segal. I was stunned by the movie – but for *entirely* unexpected reasons. For the *first* time in my film-going experience, I was seeing one in which, if the main light source was a window, or a table lamp – or whatever – *that* was where the light came from!

Wow!

I quickly read the promo material the production company provided, and learned that the groundbreaking cinematographer was Gordon Willis. So it *was* possible to shoot movies that way. Still, and now *more* maddening, I had not a clue about how he did it.

Next morning, from our studio, I phoned Barry Brown. But he was out of the country, on location. I tried to reach my NYU teacher, Saul Taffet, but he was for the moment unavailable. Leonard picked up on my growing desperation: "Hey, you oughta give Steckler a call."

Of *course*! TV commercial Director Len Steckler would know! I grabbed the phone, and less than a minute into my dilemma-aria, and description of Willis's accomplishment, Len interrupted: "Easy. A white umbrella."

"White *what*?"

"Umbrella. It'll diffuse your fill on the dark side of the shot. And yeah, keep it low-ish, you'll avoid that fucking Hollywood top-of-the-head rim-light that couldn't come from anywhere close to real."

Once again it was forehead-slap time. Before I'd fully processed it, I gratefully thanked Steckler, ended the call and was on my way to the door.

A white goddam umbrella!

Stunningly uncomplicated, and readily available. *That* was the device that enabled the key light – the scene's primary light-source – to *appear* – on film – to come from where it was *supposed* to originate. It could be anything – a wall-sconce, a flashlight, a ceiling fixture. How? By placing an extra- large bulb in that device, and then providing sufficient less-intense, non-specifically sourced fill-light. This, through or reflected off of the wonderful umbrella –

and bright enough for the film-stock to "read" – make visible – the relatively unlit side of the image.

Holly and I returned to Sakonnet the following weekend, where I excitedly reshot those scenes. The difference even as I was filming them was dramatic, in concrete terms of a more authentic "look."

When I viewed the footage back at the studio several days later, it proved itself in a suitably subtle but very effective way, via its feel of being real, yielding a heightened emotion-provoking quality.

What an educational experience it was! *What* a relief…

I'd installed an editing-table adjacent to my drawing-board, and rented a Moviola. Between my then-impatiently-met illustration deadlines, I eagerly cut and re-cut my film. After several weeks, I got it as right as it was going to get. I froze it at 15 minutes, then added sound effects, titles and music.

Screening that first print of the completed *The Hiding Place* for Holly, Leonard and Betty was a thrill I shall not forget.

While I had no illusions about its worth beyond being a first-effort, it came *very* close to what I'd envisioned, and in some ways, for me, surpassed it.

I was knocked out by the medium and by this particular form, and its potential for expression. More satisfying creatively – on more levels – than *anything* I had ever tried as an artist, it fired my hunger to stretch myself further in this extraordinary venue. I had *found* my new instrument – one that could sustain and *challenge* me for the foreseeable future!

As I began screening the film for others, I had a pair of remarkable, wholly unexpected reactions. Astounding, really. They began happening with my initial showing of the film to a small "public" audience, and I thought they were aberrations. Except that it continued to happen: first, *every* time I watched it, each cut evoked in *me*, the same emotional responses I'd had as I was editing the film, the same little, or sometimes larger bang or, if you will, rush. *Every* time.

But it was the second part that I found – well, stunning comes closest to describing it.

I simply did not give a damn if the others liked it or disliked it.

Curiously, this was *not* defensive. Not about protecting myself in case of rejection. I was my own audience, and I had satisfied *myself* – coming very close to creating the film that I *wanted* to make. Despite its shortcomings, most of which I was already fully aware, I *liked* it. Ergo, praise or put-downs from others was, incredible as this may seem, virtually meaningless – of almost no interest. Sure, I was mildly pleased by compliments, and I suppose a tiny bit put off by negative remarks – though they were few.

But I really, truly did *not* care.

I realized that this was in large part a product of my liberation from an end-frame of possible financial gain: unlike the drawings I'd been cranking out for money – and for other people – since age eleven, there was virtually no commercial market for such films. Hence, there had been absolutely no excuse for producing anything that didn't please *me*.

That's when it hit me for the first time that *this* was what it is to *be* an *artist*.

While learning to *feel* my feelings had been at least the stirrings of a work in progress before I became Sid Levy's patient, *he* had accelerated-if-not-yet-finished the job of opening me up to my emotions. To *allowing* myself to become the person I'd kept bottled-up since early childhood.

Along with that, excitingly, unlike most of my work at the drawing-board, with this film the end-product was entirely of *my* choosing. Under my total control. I'd had a *delicious*, heady taste of playing god.

Directing.

That would be my role.

I promptly enrolled in an evening directing workshop taught by Robert A. Brady. There, in a 14th Street loft, under Bob's wise tutelage I began working with actors, directing scenes and, eventually entire plays. It was fun, antic, an illuminating first-glimpse into the director's job as father-figure and/or shrink for nearly everyone in his cast or company.

The actors who showed up for Brady's sessions were mostly great fun to work with. All of them were willing, talented, struggling young people trying to make it in New York Theatre, as eager to play scenes as I was to stage them.

At least one went on to a career in television: Joe Santos famously played Det. Dennis Becker in Steve Cannell's & Roy Huggins's great series, *The Rockford Files*, and later portrayed the recurring character, Angelo Garepe, in David Chase's masterpiece, *The Sopranos*.

Simultaneously screening *The Hiding Place* for my ad agency contacts, I put them on notice that I was looking to shoot TV commercial spots. I also managed to find a distributor of films for the educational market, who agreed to take it on, listing it in his catalogue – flatteringly – under *Film as Art*. While the financial returns would be negligible, it was gratifying to know that my little movie was out there, being seen.

A few weeks later, I formed a one-man-plus-answering-service-plus-insurance-policy production company, named after the summer house in Rhode Island. In between storyboard and other illustration gigs, as Greenestone Films, I began directing-and-producing commercials for Wheaties, Life Savers, New York Telephone Company and others.

To my surprise, though they were fun on a physical and social level, and experience-building craft-wise, from the beginning they were not, for me, even remotely satisfying in the ways that *The Hiding Place* had been. While several filmmakers I knew and respected, such as my friend, Len Steckler, really got off on commercials-as-an-art-form, I didn't see them that way.

Though their production used all of the same equipment employed in movies, for me they bore little resemblance to the kind of expressive vehicle with which I wanted to be stretching myself. Which is not to say that I was then or now, unable to appreciate the occasional ad-spot that is artfully pulled off.

My own clincher that it was *not* my game came – both memorably and *very* amusingly – as I screened the raw footage for my very first commercial, for major ad agency Dancer, Fitzgerald & Sample.

A simple, half-minute spot, I'd shot it myself on a gorgeous plantation some 60 miles upriver from New Orleans. I was seated in the second row of the agency's beautifully appointed screening room, between the writer and the art director, my fellow "creative team" members. In front of us were four-or-five suits – aka "account men."

The film consisted mostly of a number of takes in which the camera slowly pushed-in, past live oaks dripping with Spanish Moss, to a medium-close shot of a lovely young woman. She was seated at a table on the elegant veranda of your definitive antebellum home, about to dine.

On *Wheaties.*

The mansion I'd chosen for its cliché qualities was, incidentally, Houmas House, the one that so memorably served as the setting for the Bette Davis movie *Hush, Hush, Sweet Charlotte.*

My footage was greeted by the executives with positive-if-unenthusiastic comments.

"Nice."

"Yeah…"

"Lovely…"

Then came the final "sell"-shots. They consisted of endless takes of the same thing: tight, close-up angles of Wheaties flakes tumbling, in achingly slo-mo, out of the box and falling – fluttering really – down into the bowl.

For me it had been by far the *least* interesting part of the shoot – tediously so.

It was the account executives' reactions to that end-of- the-reel footage that *truly* surprised me. Actually, staggered describes it more aptly. I still find it *very* funny – the stuff of bang-on satire.

As the breakfast cereal fell onscreen, the business-types in the front row instantly became animated, grabbing each other's forearms, making excited, approving gestures and exclamations. The most memorable – from one of them who turned and blurted it directly at me – was, I swear: "*Wow! That* is the *greatest* pour-shot I've *ever* seen!"

My difficult-to-contain, unvoiced, dropped jaw reaction: *You've gotta be fucking kidding!*

I honestly thought he was joking.

He wasn't.

These were *grown* men, actually capable of becoming worked-up – hell, genuinely *emotional* – about shots of goddam Wheaties falling into a bowl?

What it told me, in that instant, was that I did *not* belong in that business – one in which *anybody* could take such things seriously.

Following my directing studies with Brady, I attended a few classes taught by the legendary Lee Strasberg. I confess that at least partly due to my impatience I found Brady's more to my liking.

But in fact, I believe I learned at least as much about directing from a book as I did from the workshops: Frank Capra's wonderful autobiography, *The Name Above the Title*, should be required reading – along with seeing his films – for *anyone* who wishes to make movies, especially comedies.

Incidentally, for modern filmmakers who aspire to be funny, I cannot imagine a worthwhile course of study that doesn't include repeated viewing and analysis of, besides Capra and Howard Hawks, the movies of Preston Sturges, and of course, Woody Allen.

I did continue to shoot commercials, largely because it was such a welcome change from sitting in a room drawing pictures. On several levels they *were* fun – especially the location work which took us to interesting places like Tucson, New Orleans and elsewhere. But in truth even as I was working intently, turning out these 30 second epics, I felt unsatisfied, somewhat detached, because I had so little opportunity to extend myself creatively. As referenced above, yes, we used all of the tools of cinema. But for me the resemblance ended with, say, requiring that your actor lift the glassful of product from the table to his lips in 2.8 seconds. That, for me, was *not* moviemaking.

It was – *yawn* – putting *The Fuck Family* on film.

TWENTY-TWO
Show Biz Beckons—(OK-a Bit of a Stretch, But...)

"HEY, TOM, IT'S RUSS JONES. I'm calling from L.A. listen, you're not gonna believe this – I'm producing a movie..."

He had *that* right.

"...A low-budget horror flick. It's a two-week shoot that's scheduled to roll in a month – and what it is – I want *you* to direct it."

My first "nibble" from Hollywood, though even that cornball term makes it seem far more legitimate than it really was. Totally unexpected – and even *more* improbable – describes it waaay better. First off, I mean – *me*? With all of five 30-second commercials and *The Hiding Place* under my directing-belt? *Only* someone who existed in some kind of dream-world would...

But of course, second – it *was* Russ Jones!

175

Russ was a *very* casual acquaintance who used to sometimes hang out at Leonard's and my studio, where he'd mooch space while handling an occasional comic book assignment. He worked primarily in the horror genre, my disinterest in which makes it impossible to recall any of the titles. Pleasant enough socially, vaguely a sort-of-artist/maybe-writer, he had for a few years been an oddball hanger-on in our circle. There, he was openly regarded – dismissed, really – by *everyone* I knew as a consistent-though-not-unpleasant bullshitter. But *not* on the basis of any dramatic, bombshell-type revelations that I knew about. There was just this group-acceptance that he was unable to tell the truth about *anything*.

Russ was slightly seedy-looking but not unattractive, tall, slender, with cropped blond hair, and he rarely appeared in the company of a woman. I knew little-to-nothing about his private life, and certainly among those with whom I was close, none of us cared. I'd had no contact with him, nor heard *anything* about his activities, since he'd vanished from the New York scene months earlier, shortly after I'd gotten into filmmaking.

It *was* rumored that Russ had finally departed the city because he'd conned so many people that nobody there believed him anymore.

Yet here he was, phoning on a pre-winter evening while Holly was preparing supper, all jaunty-jolly, as if we'd been in close touch.

I was plain not buying *any* of it. Least of all, given my so-limited creds, that *any*one – except maybe an outright fraud – would hire *me* to direct a theatrical film. So, with tongue jammed-into-cheek, I called his bluff: "Hey, man, that sounds great. I'd love to. Just send me a script and a – oh, $7,500 advance."

Not surprisingly, Russ explained that there was this minor problem: "The – uh – thing of it is – the money – it's still on its way. *But...*" he added quickly, "...it'll be here in a day – two at the most – and I'll forward it immediately. And the – uh – the thing about the screenplay is – it's getting a final polish. And – like the money, I'll ship it off in a few days..."

While that only bolstered my skepticism, I was further thrown by what came next; Russ was elated by what he seemed to have interpreted as my "yes."

"Anyway, that's *great*, Tom, 'cause the pressure's really on. I mean – it's gonna be a two-three week shoot, we're ready to prep, do some final casting. Oh – and set-building's already in work…"

None of which sounded any more credible than his opening remarks. I mean – no script, no money, set-construction under way, and prep about to---?

But then, damned if he didn't top himself: "Listen, our star's right here, and he's looking forward to talking to you. Rhodes Reason---"

"Who?"

"Youknow, Rex's brother. He starred in *King Kong Escapes*…?" Rhodes Reason was at the time unknown to me, as was his movie. But I knew of Rex, who had appeared in a few forgettable big-studio flicks, even playing opposite the ludicrously wretched, unwatchable-but-mystifyingly popular Joan Crawford.

The next thing I heard was this deep, theatrical baritone, clearly a guy who "played strong": "Tom, Rhodes Reason here. Great to speak to you. I'm *really* excited that we'll be working together…"

We will?

"…Russ has lined up some really terrific people. Sound stages, on Hollywood Boulevard, the whole shot."

My immediate read: either he was part of Russ's con, or a victim of it. "That's wonderful, Rhodes. I'm---"

"Listen, I'll put Russ back on."

Russ's voice came through. "So – I'll call you tomorrow or next day. Super that you're aboard. And give my best to Holly."

That ended it. Laughing, I related the details to Holly, who was as disbelieving/amused as I, and I promptly forgot about it.

A week later, another call from Russ: "Um – there've been one or two small glitches – with the script and the money…"

I was shocked. *Shocked!*

He chuckled. "Hey, you know how *that* goes…"

With Russ, I for sure knew.

177

"…But the money – it's *definitely* on the plane to L.A…"

He was *actually* using *that* line! In-fucking-credible!

"…And youknow with the production start-date looming – I mean I managed to set it back a *few* days, but I can't delay it anymore – crew and soundstage people're standing by – so can you get out here right away – like in a coupla days?"

I stifled a sigh, and the urge to hang up on him. Instead, I promised to get back to him in an hour or so.

Kicking it around with Holly, it was apparent that Russ was still blowing his customary smoke, very likely between 99 and 120 percent horseshit. But, it *was* early December, the East Coast weather was cold, and I had nothing pressing on my plate. Holly, flexible and totally supportive as always, offered that, being the slow season in the ad agency business, she'd request some time off from Grey. What the hell, we'd never been to Los Angeles together – me, not since the summer I'd graduated from high school.

Besides, hey, maybe we *could* make something happen. At the very least, I'd learn a few things about the fringe side of the movie business. Worst case, we agreed, we'd have a brief vacation in the sunshine. I called Russ and told him we were on our way.

Arriving in L.A. two days later, Holly and I rented a pleasant, inexpensive by-the-week furnished apartment on Hollywood Boulevard, a few blocks west of the landmark Mann's (formerly Grauman's) Chinese Theater. Typical of that section of Hollywood, it was a two-story, motel-like structure forming a U around a swimming pool.

The experience overall? Terrific. As anticipated, the weather was gorgeous, as was the geography, and Holly and I had laughs, fun, and acquired a few Keepers. The movie? A big part of the fun, it was similarly predictable: there was no money – *never* had been any. Also, no script, and no cast – except for Rhodes Reason. A charming, entertaining, very witty, few-illusions guy, Rhodes, was by then onto Russ's scam, which only added to the nonstop hoot-ness. *And* some surprising dividends.

My takeaway turned out to be far more valuable than I'd imagined

– *indispensable* preparation for the next chapter in my life. Not unlike an informal continuation of film school, it proved to be a kind of "out-on-the-fringe" (given that it *was* Tinseltown, I hesitate to use the term "real-world" in *any* sense) on-the-job workshop.

Among the lessons learned, observations made and conclusions reached were that Hollywood – and *especially* this non-union, under-the-hat side of it – was *indeed* a different place. But an accessible one. A world that in some ways extended to its actual, bigtime, establishment side. That facet of the business, I would eventually learn, and somewhat to my surprise, shared the seedy-side's propensity for buying into bullshitters, often paying them handsomely.

Further, the part to which I was being exposed seemed populated *entirely* by people so desperate to be in the business that they'd buy into almost *any* fantasy.

In Russ Jones's case, they definitely had one. He and this tacky part of the biz were a *perfect* match – at least up to the point where he simply could not hold his lies together any longer.

One aspect that truly, *laughably* blew me away was that because I was introduced as the Director, I was *accepted*, accorded this *automatic* respect-all-the-way-to-awe, treated as a sort of reigning authority-figure. *Nobody* questioned my credentials. Nor, in that pre-internet era, could they have checked me out if they'd cared to, except I suppose to have learned that I was not yet a member of the Director's Guild.

Among the entertaining, *so* educational scenes from those fourteen days – *all* of them without *anyone* seeing a single dollar – were the casting sessions in the soundstage offices. There, with nothing more than the *smell* of a film in the offing, sometimes with Russ present, other times not, I interviewed dozens of actors, some accompanied by their agents. They ranged from young starry-eyed kids just off the bus, to aging bimbos and even seasoned professionals – several of them semi-name character-people I'd seen on the big screen or on TV.

From the far side of the door, the sound of hammering. Carpenters were busily framing the main set, a large Swiss chalet, both interior and exterior.

Plus, location-scouting with Russ and Rhodes in the Hollywood Hills and San Fernando Valley, and laugh-filled, wine-lubricated poolside script-sessions with Rhodes. There, while soaking up winter sun in our swim trunks, we attempted to fix and add to the wretchedly inept, half-written, cliché-ridden fifty or so pages that Russ – or someone – had cobbled together.

It was a fun taste of playing *BFD*, of being deferred to for all sorts of decisions which I was daily becoming more and more certain were never going to be implemented, nor paid for.

Through it all, with consistent conviction and sincerity, Russ continued to assure me, Rhodes, the soundstage people and everyone else, that it was definitely happening.

One memorable comment about the world Holly and I were visiting came from a clearly marginal screenwriter living in the compound where we were staying. Seeing Rhodes and me seated at a table by the pool, potchkying with the screenplay one afternoon, he'd introduced himself and struck up a conversation about it, and the business. Learning that I lived in New York, he volunteered the following without-bitterness wisdom: "You wanna piece of advice about this town? Somebody gives you a check, cash it the same day – *at* the bank it was written on." I later learned – happily – that such was *certainly* not the case if one was employed in the legitimate areas of the business.

This fellow hospitably invited Holly and me for drinks one afternoon, in the second-floor apartment he shared with his wife. As we seated ourselves I noted the numerous stacks of unopened packing-boxes and cartons: "So – you've just moved in?"

"Nah, we've been here what…" He glanced at his wife. "…a coupla years?" She responded with an affirmative nod-and-shrug. It seemed to say a lot about permanence in a *very* competitive town.

Holly and I also savored weekend drives around the LA basin, soaking up the so-different look and feel of the place. Particularly memorable was Malibu, which dazzled with its mountains-meeting-the-sea vistas, immediately reminding us of one of our favorite spots in the world, the French Riviera. Topping even that fabled area, Malibu's slopes weren't overrun with houses.

Finally, on a morning just before the second week ended, Rhodes and I confronted Russ. Putting on his "sad" face, Russ confessed, nodding: "Yeah. Shit. I got confirmation an hour ago. I'm afraid the money pulled out..."

That was "it." Consistent with his style, Russ did *not* admit that the entire project was a con, that there had *never* been any money, nor anyone "behind" it. Nor did Rhodes and I accuse him. Instead, as we said our goodbyes, I actually – and sincerely – thanked Russ. For an entirely unexpected education! One that would take many months to *fully* appreciate and assimilate. Rhodes and I parted, promising to stay in touch.

Next day, Holly and I headed home smiling, amazed by the number and value and variety of lessons learned and conclusions reached in only two weeks. The key piece, the one I *knew* most certainly: I *would* be out there again, wanted more than *ever* to be part of it – albeit on a more legitimate, professional level than Russ's *Mickey Mouse* venture.

I'm aware as I write this that Russ Jones is a presence on the web, where he credits himself with pioneering the graphic novel. He claims he wrote the first one, *The Illustrated Dracula* (artwork by Al McWilliams), lettering by Ben Oda), and that he edited and wrote for the cult publication *Monster Mania*. All or some of which may be true. After our adventure in Hollywood, I never saw him again.

Back in Manhattan, I excitedly shared my tales and thoughts with Leonard and our new studio-mate, Martin Thall, a veteran comic-book artist/writer/wannabe filmmaker. "I mean it, guys. I think it might actually be possible to get a feature-film off the ground right here in New York."

To my delight, Marty and Leonard were onboard. The changing marketplace, especially the expansion of TV, was enabling the birth of more and more small, independent, low-budget non-studio product. We further agreed, given how gifted, talented and charming the three of us were, that it seemed entirely reasonable – more than that: *certain* – that we could pull it off!

They were as stoked as I was!

So, full of *"Hey-gang-let's-build-a-clubhouse!"* enthusiasm, we began kicking around ideas for an initial project. We formed a production company so that we could look "official." Complete, if it came to that – which we were sure it would – with business cards and stationery. Our name, arrived at by combining "Tom-Marty-Len:" *Tamerlane Films*. Leonard: Writer. Marty: Producer. Me: Director.

During all of this, along with some illustration and storyboard work, I continued directing/producing commercials, and enjoying it. One particularly fun shoot took Holly, Suzy, Lauren and me to Tucson for a Lifesavers spot, in which they were part of the cast.

Leonard quickly came up with a movie-concept we liked, about teenage girl runaways sent to a place for wayward girls run by a female director who was selling them for sex. It also fit the parameters we'd decided were necessary, of being relatively inexpensive, capable of being shot on mostly rural locations in New England and thus not requiring costly urban filming permits. So, with Marty's and my input, Leonard began developing a script, sandwiching it into an already endlessly labor-and-creativity intensive work schedule entailed by his hugely successful *Mary Perkins On Stage* comic-strip.

Several months after my return from Movieland, Rhodes Reason contacted me. He was coming to New York and asked if we might allow him to stay over for a few nights at our studio. Leonard and I welcomed him, and we all had a great time. Along with more than a few laughs at Rhode's acute Hollywood Actorish-ness.

Among which, he would *not* ride in my Jaguar if the convertible top was down, or a window open: his hairpiece.

But way funnier than that, one morning I happened into the main room while he was on the phone, talking, unaware of my presence. Shirtless, holding the receiver to his ear with one hand, the other at his side, phone-base dangling from his fingers, he stood before a full-length mirror, trying various muscle-flexing poses. Then, deciding he needed to appraise a more distant view of himself, he turned, walked a few steps further from the mirror. Where he was startled – shocked describes it better – as the phone-base's short cord-to-the-wall reached its limit, yanking it and the receiver from his grip.

I tried but could not come close to stifling my laughter.

In those days the long cords so common in California had not yet come into vogue in the East.

Rhodes was our guest on several very entertaining occasions, and we became warm friends. He, too, had happily lost contact with Russ Jones.

While the screenplay was in work, Marty and I began identifying as many locally-based independent film producers as we could – people we'd contact once the screenplay was nearer completion. There weren't many, but we refused to let it discourage us.

Along with that, I decided it was time to address a few unfinished parts of my hopefully soon-to-be-over illustrating career.

I was still a member of the National Cartoonists Society, and the Society of Illustrators. My longtime belief that I was virtually the only guy in town who refused to accept "the going rate" had been steadily reinforced. There was also my exasperation each year when Starr would simply accept without negotiation, and sign the contract for his services. But I found it even more appalling that he, like most of his peers had, at the start, and similarly without complaint, signed away copyright ownership of *their* creations.

I was only vaguely aware of the protections against exploitation that were provided in other fields by organizations such as ASCAP, the Writers Guild and the Directors Guild. But on the face of it, for graphic artists to form some sort of union seemed to me the obvious, no-brainer way to go. So, given that what we then had most in common was that our stuff was printed, I contacted the lithographers' union and invited them to try to organize our groups. The union people eagerly accepted.

I informed the NCS president of what I was up to, and he loved the idea. Thus, following dinner at the next monthly meeting a week later, with his blessing, and flanked by a pair of union executives, I stood, and addressed the attendees. My preface to introducing them was not especially diplomatic, but – and this is hardly an excuse – it *was* from the heart: "Look, I'm gonna share with you something that's been pissing me off for more than a decade – and I hope that a lot of you feel the same way. Bottom line, every time one of us accepts less money than our work is worth, or lets himself be screwed out of his rights, it hurts not only that individual, but the rest of us as well. How? Because it perpetuates the belief that I see evidence of with damned near everyone to whom I sell my artwork, that we're basically regarded as a bunch of schmucks. That we can all be easily taken advantage of – bought for cheap…"

As I spoke, I searched their faces, looking for some spark of recognition, some indication that they too might have experienced and/or felt what I was describing.

I saw – and heard – none. Zero. Zip.

But it went further than that. What I read in many was truly startling: outright hostility.

But I continued: "…So – what we need to do is unite – in something more organized than a bunch of guys getting together for drinks – in order for us to achieve better pay, copyright protection, minimums, a pension plan and like that…" By then, the room was downright icy. Nonetheless, already recognizing that it was a waste of time – but still hoping – I went on to introduce the union guys. They gave what I felt was a solid, enthusiastic and eloquent pitch about the potential for things like reprint payments, health benefits and the like.

Again, silence. Anger, even. It was as if we were proposing that they all start having sex with their mothers.

Had I *really* expected the cartoonists to go for it? An outside chance, I figured, but it *might* open a dialogue. Instead, except for the NCS president taking me aside, thanking me and urging that I try again, there was not a single positive comment, nor *any* follow-up.

I made a similar, though less blunt presentation at a meeting of the Society of Illustrators. While not met with hostility, its members weren't interested either.

A short time later, I resigned from both organizations.

A "done with all that" gesture, satisfying, though with a touch of sadness, it lent a kind of symbolic – if not quite final – closure to an important part of my life. All these decades later, things are still the same for graphic artists. One of them, my daughter, Lauren Scheuer, is a successful illustrator/bestselling author who suffers from those accepted practices. Hell, drawings that I did all those years ago are *still* being used commercially.

Profited from.

But *not* by me.

In dramatic contrast, thanks to the more enlightened world of entertainment, and to the WGA, I continue to be paid residuals and royalties for *any* of my work that is re-seen. Not only for what I *wrote* for TV or film: in one case, from a phone pitch that earned me a co-writer credit, even though I did *not* type a single word!

But far, far better than *any* of that, early one evening as Holly and I headed out for supper, walking along 75th Street toward the setting sun, she hooked her arm in mine: "Y'know... I think I *would* like to have a baby."

I could not have been more thrilled. Or surprised, though in truth, after the girls moved to Virginia I *had* begun to sneakily hope Holly might change her mind.

That evening turned out to be *particularly* celebratory...

TWENTY-THREE
Discoveries, Partings, Some Un-expected Recognition, a *Major* Arrival—and a *Big* Decision

"Yeah, we're goin' back in a coupla weeks. Anyway, I was like, thinking it might be fun to youknow shoot a documentary…"

I almost choked on my burger. "*Fun?*" Not even close. He had me.

Over lunch in Greenwich Village, our close friend, actor Gerry Matthews had just tossed out a *totally* irresistible proposition! To shoot a film about his actress wife, Freddie Weber, returning to her middle-American roots for her 15th high school reunion.

Gerry and Freddie were a truly hip, fun couple. Extremely successful, they appeared in top nightclubs, off-Broadway shows, and a few movies. They also performed in a *lot* of commercials both on-camera and via voice-over.

187

The prospect of filming Freddie, this now-sophisticated New Yorker, revisiting her small-town and old chums in Beardstown, Illinois? For me it was an instant winner. I could almost taste the chance to candidly observe and record all of the inherent contrasts, the attitudes and conflicts old and new, as they reacted to her, and vice-versa.

Another part of its appeal was more personal: my own high school class had never held a reunion – at least one of which I was aware. Having cut nearly all of my ties to Chicago only two years after graduation, I had sometimes wondered how my friends had fared. As well as, admittedly vainly, what it might be like to reconnect and compare lives and accomplishments, especially with those who'd chosen more conventional paths, and with a few who had dissed me. Shooting/observing Freddie's reunion suggested a sort of proxy, substitute experience for me.

I excitedly enlisted a classmate from the NYU film course, Joe Shulman, who had crewed for me on several commercials, to handle sound, paying only for his expenses. Holly also loved the idea, and eagerly agreed to serve as production assistant.

As I'd done with *The Hiding Place*, we approached the project with no commercial end-frame in mind. Further, despite almost everything by then being shot in color, at my urging we chose grainy, high-speed black & white. The reasons: to obviate the time-devouring necessity of setting up lights, and because we did not want to glamorize/artificialize any of it. Further, I had always felt that it was that very quality, that visual crudeness, which my generation associated with newsreels, that would make our film come across as more "real," more believable.

So, with Gerry and me sharing costs, and with rented cameras and sound equipment, Holly, myself, Joe, Freddie and Gerry descended on Beardstown. An achingly typical Midwest river community, its population of 2,500 virtually was the same as when Freddie had been growing up there – one of those rural non-college towns that dot America. With our two 16mm Arriflexes, mics and Nagra tape-recorder, during the following four days we shot 4.5 hours of *very* candid footage.

Another freeing, truly exciting experience, making it up as we went, not knowing ahead of time what we'd get, we covered Freddie with close friends who'd never left, and a few who had, at parties, local bars, the reunion itself and, for me the best of all – talking-head interviews with her classmates, hearing about how their lives had gone, and seeing the effects as well in their voices, body-language and dress.

The weekend's climax was Memorial Day, with its inevitable town square ceremony, complete with solemn, droning speeches, flag-raising, and an incredibly Norman Rockwell-esque VFW rifle squad firing a 21-gun salute. We captured that as well as, to me, the most telling sign of the time –1969: there were more people on the speakers' podium than there were spectators. Among the latter we filmed some wonderful, silent faces that spoke onscreen far more clearly and eloquently than words.

Back in New York City, viewing our hours of footage immediately confirmed something that had hit me while we were shooting it. Aside from Freddie, not *one* of the people we'd photographed was a "city person," with the attitude, pretense and guardedness thus implied.

Instead, they were almost startling in their openness. Unafraid to reveal who they were, to *be*, if they were, ordinary, vulnerable, unsophisticated. Life, for some, had been more fortunate than for others. But *all* had given us the gift of their honesty. Even though a *few* tried in one or two instances to conceal, they weren't very good at it, so *their* truths also came through.

Overall, their sometimes painfully candid on-camera remarks about themselves and others were almost completely without guile. It was as if they'd trusted us to not make fools of them. I *knew* as I watched them again and again, that we *owed* them. We had an *obligation* to not take the admittedly tempting, all-too-easy route of turning our film into a smartass, uppity, sophisticates-looking-down-our-noses-at-the-yokels movie.

Happily, Gerry fully agreed, and that view – more than anything other than keeping it *about* Freddie going back to her reunion – is what informed our approach.

Shortly after our return from Beardstown, just as we had seriously begun editing, I received a terse, depressing phone call from my father. "Your mother is in the hospital. They think it's a brain hemorrhage…"

Holly and I immediately flew to Chicago and, less than an hour after we arrived at the hospital, my mother died. Age sixty-nine, the probable cause: the blood-thinning effect of her for-as-long-as-I-could-remember aspirin addiction.

Holly and I stayed on for her funeral, and to be with my father for a few days. He was pretty well wiped out, especially, he admitted, because though only three years older than my mother, and having had the earlier heart attack, he'd assumed he would go first.

I was singularly unmoved by my mother's death – and only mildly dismayed by my detachment. In fact, the only truly painful moment for me was at the hospital, moments after she'd expired. A nurse took me "backstage" to give me my mother's wedding and engagement rings, and I happened to glimpse, on a nearby gurney, her nude corpse. I looked away immediately, but it's an image I've never been able to erase from my memory.

Given my sense of what their marriage was like, I found the level of my father's grief a touch difficult to comprehend. Trying to ease it over those next few days was not an easy task. But the effort did bring us into marginally closer, if still edgy touch.

An eventful period in our lives, an *especially* joyous one happened a short time later. Holly became pregnant.

Our spare-time editing of the Beardstown footage continued, ending in freezing it at 18 minutes. The title we chose: *Reunion*. We began screening the film for friends and, on the off-chance that it was in any way commercial, that we might recoup at least some of our investment, we invited theatrical distributors of short films. An always-limited, and by then really diminished market, there were very few people still in that business. Even fewer based in or near New York. Nonetheless worth a shot, once each week or so, we booked the very plush Rizzoli Screening Room, on 5th Avenue just south of 57th Street.

Where, startlingly, with each viewing of the finished version, I began to absorb a major lesson about documentary filmmaking. The obvious: it needed further cutting. Though at first I wasn't sure of what. Only a growing but still misty sense of false notes. With that came the steadily intensifying wish that we might find an excuse – a justification for going back and taking another whack or two at it.

We got it one afternoon at the end of a showing at the Rizzoli, in the form of a comment from Lester Schoenfeld. The then-number-one national distributor of theatrical shorts, Lester was the best, and pretty much the last of our always slight chances. We were grateful that he'd accepted our invitation. As the room emptied, Gerry and I stood in the row just in front of Mr. Schoenfeld's. We leaned on the seatbacks, practically *in* his discouragingly deadpan face, and with naked hope on ours, I threw him our question.

"So, Lester – whaddya think?"

Memorably, the portly, balding, middle-aged veteran of the business removed the cigar from his mouth, glanced at the ash, then back at us. Still expressionless, he shrugged and, with a wave of his other hand, dispensed his wisdom:

"Talks too much. Lose three minutes."

Period.

I mean, you've gotta *love* that kind of conciseness, and how breathtakingly *on-the-money* it was. Though I'd reached essentially the same conclusion, I'd have described it differently – and not nearly as succinctly. Gerry felt it, too.

Because during those repeated viewings we'd finally recognized a truth about the documentary form – particularly the kind that *doesn't* feature pontifical talking heads. It was this: though you may start out with a particular theme or statement in mind, you had damned well better *look at* and *listen to* what you actually get on film. Because that footage, that content, will tell *you* what your movie is *really* about.

Moreover, if you try to impose something *else* onto it, the end-product will ring the '*Wrong!*' bell. That was the increasingly loud sound Gerry and I had been hearing.

Now, I realize the above is arguably a generalization, but in the case of *Reunion*, while our original intent was to make a film *about* a New York actress returning to her hometown, we had come to realize that those 4.5 hours of footage had captured something else. Something larger. Almost in sync with Lester Schoenfeld's comment, we had figured out what it was!

With Freddie as catalyst rather than central subject, the film we'd shot was in fact – on an admittedly not-very-deep plane – *actually* about a very particular – and ubiquitous – category of American small towns. The kind that lack an intellectual core – a college or university.

The kind of place that dots America's heartland. The towns that people leave, but almost *never* move *to*.

Because of what had passed in front of our cameras – and arguably due to the personal filters we'd brought with us – we had made a comment. As said, nothing profound, but what we'd seen and recorded expressed on sub-textual levels some of the myriad factors that go with that topic.

These included but were not limited to observations – spoken and visual – about belonging and not belonging, about dreams and expectations and disappointments. About most people settling, rarely happily, for what life has dealt them. While a few – intellectual misfits, mostly – need more/demand more for themselves. *They* are the ones who leave.

It was there. But by forcing it, by trying to keep it *about* Freddie, despite the fact that the film was telling us it wasn't, we had, in effect, dulled, muddied, its meaning.

In any case, Lester's words were the trigger, giving us the impetus we needed. Gerry and I went back to the Moviola and eagerly began re-cutting.

While that was in work, on March 1, 1970, Holly gave birth to our son, Wylie. I was *thrilled*. Now that my own head was straighter, I was stoked as well by the lovely prospect of experiencing fatherhood from a very different place than I'd been when Suzy and Lauren were born. Most of all because I could share it with this woman who *so* knocked me out.

By early summer, *Reunion* had become quite another film. In the end, what Freddie's presence did was give us a kind of glue – a framework for the rest of it – with Freddie playing the role of key interlocutor/catalyst. Though others who appeared onscreen had also departed Beardstown, Freddie was the central example – *the* one who had left, become celebrity-successful, and who on film drew the others out.

Not a major work of art, but a nice, satisfying little movie to have made – finally *about* what it had *wanted* to be about. Ironically, in another way, Schoenfeld's piercing insight proved almost eerie. Without time being our primary objective, it happened that his "three minutes" were exactly what we had removed.

Holly and I were preparing to leave town for our annual summer holiday/get-together with family in Little Compton, this time with Wylie as well as my daughters. In a what-the-hell gesture, I filled out an entry form for the upcoming, very prestigious New York Film Festival, and sent it off with a print of the just-revised version of *Reunion*.

The Rhode Island visit was a delight. Suzy, Lauren, and Holly's parents shared our joy over Wylie's arrival, and I had my first opportunity in some time to essentially zone-out. I took full advantage, reading, absorbing and appreciating Holly and our family.

On our return to Manhattan, I was greeted by a *truly* total surprise. Among the accumulated mail was a notice that *Reunion* had been selected for the Festival! Delighted – I had had absolutely zero expectations – our film was to be shown at Lincoln Center! It was one *helluvva* rush. That was just the start!

In addition, as the September date approached for the Festival opening, we were invited to a glittery reception at the French Consulate. There, Holly, Freddie, Gerry and I actually rubbed elbows with international star Catherine Deneuve and famed Director François Truffaut. Topping that, on the night of its screening, *Reunion* was the lead-in for Truffaut's newest feature film, *The Wild Child*.

Later, our documentary was honored at the Rochester and Edinburgh

Film Festivals. Moreover, Lester Schoenfeld picked it up for distribution. *Then*, as if it could get *any* better, within a short time it was in wide release, being shown in movie theaters across the U.S., accompanying *The Last Run*, a feature starring George C. Scott.

Nice.

No. Fucking *amazing*.

The efforts of Leonard, Marty Thall and myself on behalf of our Tamerlane Films venture had meanwhile come to very little. We'd pitched and, for maybe ten minutes believed we had secured partial financing for our movie project, even getting as far as attaching a young leading man, the very appealing Frank Converse. Then, after months of trying to nail the rest of the backing, our original money-promise had, along with our by then scattered energies, fizzled.

Part of the learning-curve, it had become increasingly apparent that despite our wanting it to be so, Manhattan was *not* the ideal place for launching theatrical films.

At about that time, Leonard and Betty bought a home in Westport and, regretfully, vacated our splendid studio. But more than that, I *knew* I would miss our always remarkable daily dialogues. Marty Thall returned to working at home.

An end to a truly gratifying several years, I leased a smaller work-space on a lower floor in the same brownstone, and continued my work there, alone.

The truth about New York being a questionable feature film market was driven memorably and conclusively home to me a short time later by an ad-exec pal. Jim Levey had grown up in Los Angeles, where his dad, Jules, had been a bigtime feature film producer. As a high-schooler he'd been on studio-arranged dates with then teen-star Elizabeth Taylor.

Jim was one of my brightest, wittiest, most colorful acquaintances. We had worked together briefly and happily early in my TV commercial period, when he and I dreamed up and sold a concept to one of his clients. A 30 second Homelite chainsaw spot, we'd had a blast shooting it on location in Louisiana.

Recently separated from his wife, Jim was temporarily bunking at my new studio. One morning I arrived early, while he was preparing to head for his Madison Avenue office.

Making conversation, I resumed grousing about my deepening movie-biz frustrations, when Jim figuratively hit me upside the head.

"Hey – c'mon, schmuck…" Grinning at the mirror, he finished adjusting his necktie, grabbed his attaché-case and crossed to the door, where he paused, turned to me: "…You *really* wanta be in that business – you've *gotta* be *in* Hollywood."

And he was gone.

Damn! Instantly, I *knew* he was right, that I needed to just – *face it*!

It *was* coming up on that time.

In just about all other ways, for me it was a *fabulous* time. Between the joy of my marriage to Holly, there were the happy bonds with my daughters, Suzy and Lauren. Plus theirs' with baby Wylie, Holly, and with her wonderful parents, Harriet and Allan, who had so warmly become the girls' surrogate grandparents. All of that capped in 1972 by the arrival of our beautiful daughter Brooke. It didn't have to get any better.

Except – selfishly – yes. Would I *ever* find those *professional* creative challenges I so *required*? Needs that were growing more intense and daunting. This last especially because, having passed my 40th birthday, there was the *very* real question of whether it was already too late to change careers.

An amusing side-benefit of Holly's pregnancy with Brooke: she had enrolled us in a one-night-per-week Lamaze Natural Childbirth class at Mount Sinai Hospital. There were about ten couples signed up, including most notably Ann Bancroft and Mel Brooks.

While there was little socializing among the highly-focused parents-to be, from them there was none. Thus, Ann and Mel's presence created a kind of suspense, at least for Holly and me. Week after week, we waited for him (or both) to do or say something funny. Or even to make conversation. Instead, they were deadly serious, attentive, silent save for polite hellos/nods to classmates, and an occasional brief, quietly personal exchange with the instructor. The minute each session ended, they were out the door and into their waiting limo on Fifth Avenue. Nor did the others in the group, whether out of shyness or a desire to remain cool, attempt to intrude on their privacy; as far as I could observe, no words were exchanged between them and any of us.

This continued for the entire run of the course. Then, following the final session, the instructor's good luck speech and the students' thank-you's, Ann turned to Holly and asked if this was our first child. Holly said it wasn't, that we had a two year-old son. With that, the four of us found ourselves seated on a sofa, Holly and Ann together in the middle, with Mel and myself on the ends, facing in, leaning forward so we wouldn't miss anything.

Holly responded to a few more questions from Ann, whose capper was: "And, did you use the Lamaze method in giving birth to to your son?"

Mel continued to listen intently, soberly as Holly answered: "No. That's one of the reasons we're here. When I was in labor with Wylie, they gave me this 'twilight' anesthetic that – well, it wasn't great. It caused me to, youknow – to slip in and out of consciousness, and – and it made the whole experience kind of unsatisfying. Especially when all of a sudden I woke up, and – there was this baby."

At which point, with classic and, I'm sure, involuntarily superb comic timing, Mel's beady eyes narrowed. His body language in full-earnest, *I've just been imparted some serious wisdom* mode, he finally spoke: "So – they really *are* little strangers…"

A man who could simply *not* be not funny.

In the summer of 1972, not long after Brooke's birth, my father became ill, and died a short time later. In addition to having lost heart with my mother's death, his lifetime of cigarette smoking had caught up with him at age seventy-five in the form of emphysema. Just as I had been struck by my lack of emotion when my mother died, I was quite unprepared for the degree of grief I felt on this occasion. In no small measure I'm sure, because it marked the finality of so much. Also, shared I suspect by most people, the disappointment of so many things – now forever – left unsaid, the issues never to be resolved.

But additionally in my case, surprising though it should *not* have been, were the waves of anger *finally* allowed to be *felt* – to be *faced*. Some of them escalating to rage that I turned against myself in one way that I will *always* regret.

Following his funeral, with Holly at my side, I faced the massively uninviting job of dealing with and disposing of his possessions, and what was left of my mother's. To begin that task required my *very* reluctant return, for the first time in years, to their apartment, located in a high-rise overlooking Lake Michigan.

There, with numerous misgivings – not all of them yet understood – I began sifting through his personal files and memorabilia. Letters. A few to his father. Several from me. I tried to read them, but quickly stopped. Then I came upon his collection of family photographs. Hundreds of photos of, or including, me.

Unexpectedly, as the memories of past times those pictures triggered came rushing back, so did my resentments. The recollections of his endless put-downs, my mother's coldness, of his and my mother's dislike of each other, and of me. Specific moments, not *one* of them positive or gratifying, most filled with angers I'd never before given myself permission to feel.

In my enraged state, I could not bear to look at another one of the photos, to be graphically reminded of so *much* that I'd suppressed. Instead, almost frantically, I stuffed all that I had seen, plus the larger remainder, into a large carton. Then, grabbing it up, I hurriedly exited the apartment and headed for the incinerator chute, into which I dumped *all* of them.

Of course, within hours I began to recognize my overreaction. The irretrievable loss. Because there *had* to have been many that, given time, I'd have been able to appreciate. It was as if, in my extreme anger, I had turned it on myself. I had *consciously* shit-canned – *burned* – my past.

Though in truth, of the handful of photos I still have of my parents, none do I view with tenderness. Or warmth. In fact, about the only thing they trigger is an occasional minor – and admittedly ironic – regret that I can never thank them for their two most lasting legacies. One, my immunity to rejection. Two, that they never imposed religion on me.

Anyway, during that time in Chicago I did *begin* to get past those deep resentments. Between Goodwill and the willingness of several of my cousins to accept some items, Holly and I managed to dispose of the apartment's furnishings, and we headed back to New York.

It was good to be done with it. Cleansing. Closure, finally, on that part of my life.

Which was soon followed by the carefully-weighed decision – with, surprise, surprise, Holly's enthusiastic and *so*-valuable support – to *go for it*. To relocate to Southern California!

Through all of this, my sessions with Dr. Levy had continued. As did my increasing level of self-knowledge. An amazing, satisfying and *so* beneficial experience, especially being able to bounce stuff off of him along the journey. In fact, as time passed, our relationship and his part in it had changed – morphing into a combination of therapist/advisor. In a very real way, I now recognize, I had assigned him – and he'd accepted – the role of substitute-father. And one helluvva job he did!

As plans for my giving Hollywood a try began to take more specific form, the feature film *Deep Throat* was released. Its box-office success and quasi-social acceptance had made it the talk of New York and Los Angeles. The movie seemed to have taken hardcore porn out of the raincoat-on-the-lap houses, reaching a much wider-audience in those more sophisticated markets. It quickly became almost mainstream, the first-ever pornographic date-flick!

Viewing it through my critical, filmmaker-eye, not surprisingly I *knew* I could make a far better, funnier one!

Not a bad fit, I thought, since a major component of my plan was to "make some noise" once I got to California. To get their attention and sell myself as a director by making a low-budget feature film – a kind of "calling-card" – what better, more current, hot-genre could there be? *Yes*! I would make my bones by shooting a *truly* funny, stylish, well-made hardcore film, one that would put *Deep Throat* to deserved shame.

It didn't take long to come up with the premise for my debut auteur effort: a classic shaggy-dog story I'd heard and loved years earlier during one of our joke-analysis-and-punch-up sessions at the 57th Street studio. A gag that continued to crack me up – about a cute, zaftig Hollywood hamburger waitress who sleeps her way to movie-stardom and, as her roles get larger, has a series of ever-broader slapstick accidents on the set – leading to the *perfect* punchline.

It struck me as a just-about-ideal framework for what I had in mind. Because the plot was contained in well-structured joke-form, it was easy to pitch verbally – and in an entertaining way! In talking it up with people both in and out of the business, I soon found a backer – one of the latter – willing to cover my ballpark budget of $50,000. I also hooked up with a writer who had some New York comedy credits. He was eager to take it on – to write the screenplay on spec, with the promise of profit (if any) participation, plus West Coast exposure.

With that, Holly and I excitedly went forward with preparations for moving to California. Major among these was an exploratory trip, to find and lease a house for our several-months hence relocation.

But before heading out, I recalled what had perhaps been my *most* important observation during our several years earlier initiation to Movie Land. Virtually *nobody* in the business, except for character actors, some agents, and a few high-ranking Suits, permitted themselves to look – nor admitted to being – older than *very* early 40ish. Ergo, I took a hard look at myself in the mirror, and noted the graying temples. Plus, reminding myself that I'd already arrived at that age – *certainly* too old to be attempting to break *into* that world. I decided I had *damned* well better begin playing by those rules, or I'd be dead-in-the-water before I got started. The next day, for the first time, I colored my hair.

My initial gesture toward what would become my way of life: *fooling 'em*, and pulling it off without causing harm to *anyone*!

Depositing Wylie and Brooke with Holly's parents in Connecticut, we flew to LA, figuring we'd give ourselves a week to find a place. We began by looking at rentals in what was then knee-jerk thought of by most New Yorkers as synonymous with L.A.: Beverly Hills. Far too expensive, we checked out Hollywood and then worked our way west, to Santa Monica. We saw nothing to our liking within our price range, though our search did yield several telling glimpses into this *very* different world.

Touring one attractive-and-vacant Hollywood Hills home, we noted the ripped carpeting and large holes punched in a couple of interior walls. Also the smell, familiar from so many New York City vestibules, but here, unusually intense; the odor of cat-piss. The real estate agent calmly replied that of course repairs would be made and the smell taken care of. The previous tenant, she explained, had lived with a large pet lion.

Deciding to widen our search, Holly and I spotted an advertisement for a reasonably-priced rental in Malibu. At that time, in early 1973, Malibu was still more a decade away from being 'discovered,' and thus evolving into the fashionable and very pricey town it is at present. Remembering our very pleasant drive to that beach community several years earlier, we figured we might as well take a look.

One was *all* we needed. The advertised home's many sun-filled windows and glass sliding doors looked out across a broad bluff-top lawn to, less than 100 feet distant, a south-facing Pacific Ocean beach. Perfect! As *heck*!

Nor was I exactly put off when, stepping out onto the patio to better savor the view, I happened to glance toward the house next door. Our about-to-be neighbor's beautiful teenage daughter was sunning herself, topless. It made me refreshingly aware that we were *definitely* not in Kansas – nor, in our summer vacation spot in Rhode Island. Back there, even bikinis *with* tops had yet to find acceptance; the local women still wore one-piece bathing suits with little skirts.

We signed a month-to-month lease, figuring that, because Malibu was so far from town, we'd use it as a temporary base while we sought a place in Beverly Hills or environs. Instead, within a few weeks of our settling in, we realized we'd lucked into Paradise.

Preparing for that preliminary visit to Los Angeles, I'd also collected from my Manhattan filmmaking friends and ad agency buddies the names of a few people in TV commercial production and/or the movie business. I met with several of them, not in search of work, but to get a sense of how things worked, maybe pick up a morsel or two of advice.

One not especially valuable but still-amusing and insightful comment came from a producer who – I thought surprisingly – asked what kind of car I drove. Not sure of his point, I mentioned my aging Jaguar. He nodded soberly: "Yeah. Well, don't expect to be noticed. The thing about LA, no matter how distinctive your car is, every day you're gonna see at least three just like it." Not an especially useful observation – unless, I suppose, you're hoping to make a certain kind of splash. But it's one that I still think of years later – and smile at – virtually every time I see some high-end, super-exotic car. Because sure enough, within a few minutes I invariably spot another – and another.

However, one that *did* strike me as a true kernel came from a guy who, like me, was hoping to make it as a director, and who had learned some things the hard way. When I informed him of my hands-on experience in a number of filmmaking areas, he quickly cautioned me. "Whoa. *Never* tell 'em you can do more than one thing. The one you *wanta* be doing. Otherwise they just figure you're not all that good at *any* of 'em."

Brilliant. Then and now.

In addition to such insights, my contacts and inquiries helped me seek out and meet with several knowledgeable, very capable non-union production people. With them, I began groundwork for the staffing of my debut movie.

Excited, having had a tantalizing glimpse – a hint, really – of what our lives might soon be like, Holly and I returned to New York and our children, and eagerly began making specific plans. Far from least, knowing that I'd need to have some ongoing income, but not wanting to shoot any more commercials, I made an arrangement with my client/friend, Harry Volk. I would continue turning out monthly batches of line illustrations for his clip-art booklets. Best of all, it was work that I could perform at home. *Secretly*. Since I intended to pass myself off in California *only* as a film director – I definitely did not want to be thought of as even having been *any*thing else. Certainly not as an illustrator-trying-to-crack-the-film-game. Therefore, as guarded about my picture-drawing as I was about my birth date, I would surreptitiously set up my drawing table in our garage.

Across the next few months we closed things down, and said our goodbyes, many of them sadly. Especially, for me, to Leonard Starr – and Sid Levy. Plus Holly's lovely parents, Harriet and Allan. Though they had to have been not at all thrilled that she and their grandchildren would be 3,000 miles away, they did not utter a single negative word about our move.

Curiously, though I suppose not surprisingly, during those final weeks in Manhattan, I found myself seeing and processing the place from a detached, no-longer-quite-part-of-it perspective. As much as I had always savored – and still love – its undeniable dynamism and color, plus such treasures as the daily *New York Times*, the opera, the galleries and museums, I was noticing some things for the first time. I guess because I was finally allowing myself to do so. Among them, how *difficult* it is to live in New York City, the amount of energy it requires, and the things residents tolerate – choose to ignore probably says it better. The 24/7 noise, the angst and angers often suppressed – just in order to exist there.

Especially, I observed it as I never had before in the faces of my fellow subway riders and pedestrians: the impression that very few could be described as "happy" people.

Basically, as had happened with my first career, and more recently with my Chicago past, I was finished with that part of my life.

I hoped.

In mid-April of 1973, we headed west. The prospect was beyond exhilarating – actually not all that scary. Made almost relaxing, anxiety-wise by a final piece of counseling from Dr. Levy. He had asked me how long I was going to give myself to become established, to be *in* the business.

I had thought about it. A lot. "Two – maybe three years."

"Not realistic…" He shook his head. "Five."

"Five? Shit that seems like – a long time…"

"For what you're trying to do…?"

It took me a few days to accept that, to see the wisdom. Its effect once I'd done so, was *very* comforting. I *did* need to give myself time. To *not* impose additional, unnecessary pressure. Further, Holly was, as always, cheering me on. Happily there was the added cushion of my father having left me $130,000.

While I was anything but certain of the outcome, as had been my way since Connecticut, this was about exploration, testing myself. About seeing, one more time, if I could pull it off.

Sid's advice, and estimate? They would prove *uncannily* precise.

TWENTY-FOUR
California—at Last...
and Another Accidental
Direction-Change

MALIBU, WITH ITS MILD, sunny, cloudless days and starry nights. The surf-sounds, glorious shore birds, passing whales and dolphins following the dramatic curve of the shoreline, and mountains rising from the sea. A quick, easy, joyous fit for me.

Unexpected by both of us, the adjustment was a touch more difficult for Holly.

Taken for granted back in Manhattan, places like Central Park and Bloomingdale's had been an easy walk/stroller-push from our apartment. But our new environment, and the need to drive everywhere – the nearest stores and shops being two miles down our rural ocean-front, sidewalk-less road – left her feeling initially semi-stranded.

However, she soon got past that and came to love it as much as I did. For our beautiful Wylie and Brooke, free to spend so much time outdoors with minimal supervision, the place was a delight.

A few early, pleasant observations about Southern California: Perhaps the sharpest contrast with New York was the absence of anger-as-a-way-of-life among the locals. I found this reflected most pointedly in the rarity of that Manhattan staple, honking car-horns. Moreover, the lives of most drivers did not seem to depend on getting to wherever "there" happened to be sooner than you. This was strikingly illustrated in the act of changing lanes. Rather than, as it was back East, a hostile competition, here it was made simple by the willingness of most drivers to let you slide across in front of them.

Of course the non-irritating weather was at least a partial contributor to this relative benign-ness. As one of the older locals volunteered: "Nice thing about this place – you can always plan a picnic."

Another comment from a native in praise of the lack of aggravation: "What I like is you can always find a parking space in the same block where you're going."

Most striking though, was – and still is – the remarkable percentage of beautiful people. I remarked to a neighbor about the astonishing number, particularly in Malibu, of drop-dead gorgeous young women. He shrugged: "Hey, look at all the wealthy old guys…"

Within two weeks after our move to California, my debut movie plans began to change. In part, actually, to *be* changed. The writer who had agreed to do the screenplay bailed out. My disappointment and frustration were real, but short-lived. Since I had come up with the premise, and knew the gag on which it was based, I figured okay, so I'll do it myself.

The script took me a few months to write. It proved to be fun – and to my delight, a lot easier than I'd expected. Not all that much of a stretch in fact from writing my comic-strip attempts, and the several comic book stories I'd done. That I was able to crank it out so quickly, I've learned since, speaks less about efficiency and talent than about my newness as a writer. Moreover, since I was working from a simple, already-extant story, rather than having to come up with an entire construct, I was simply fleshing out these beats, turning them into scenes. Plus, along the way I added a few more old gags. Later in my writing career, as I learned more about the art and craft, my bar of course rose, and my output rate would slow proportionately.

It would be a while before I'd come to fully appreciate just how much I already understood about storytelling, and how much had been accidentally learned. Paying off handsomely even at that very early stage were those many joke-analysis-and-deconstruction sessions back at the old 57th Street studio.

Moreover, I was reminded that the basis of solid story-structure is the same for humor as it is for drama. The same for short jokes or long novels. For musical comedy or for opera. They've *got* to *entertain* – and be told in a way that *holds* the audience.

Thus, as I breezed through that first film script, I found, also to my delight, that I was feeling very free, unselfconscious, and the stuff – some of it, anyway – was turning out to be genuinely funny.

Less-positive, my decision to introduce myself to Tinseltown by directing a porn movie was striking me as increasingly questionable – and quite possibly counterproductive. Possibly, hell: *Grossly*!

This was reinforced as our initially tiny circle of insider social contacts had begun to grow. I was sensing from them a *way* less than respectful vibe toward dirty movies and their makers. This was true even among the group with whom I'd shoot my film, the crew I'd begun to assemble. A number of them had worked in that area of the business, competent professionals who were nonetheless forever to be regarded as outsiders. This was confirmed for me by the very solid, knowledgeable former actor, Gary Maxwell, with whom I'd connected during our house-hunting trip, and booked as my Line Producer.

It was telling me that for them and others in the Biz, X-rated films were emphatically *not* about to become mainstream anytime soon. *Deep Throat's* success and acceptance back East notwithstanding, here in Movieland, porn was still thought of as the product of a scorned, *never*-to-be-accepted fringe community.

Further, I found it significant that not *one* of the actual players I was getting to know socially was part of that scene.

Thus, I came to understand that introducing myself to the movie business by doing such a film would be a *huge*, likely *fatal* mistake. A first-impression mark with which, *especially*, I did *not* want to chance being branded.

Secondarily, and minor by comparison, since my film was a comedy, I had concerns about the talent pool. While *Deep Throat* was the only X-rated movie I'd seen, I doubted that many, if *any*, porn performers had the acting-chops and timing I would need.

So – *oy* – my new challenge: *change* my approach. *Quickly.*

While processing that one, I finished the screenplay – or thought I had. Which was when Holly began to play still another vital and unexpected role in our lives. She read it, and demonstrated – to my surprise and delight – one more side of her that I treasure – a marvelous, instinctive, totally unpretentious literary shit-detector! Even *better*, the diplomatic skill of critiquing my writing while not destroying me in the bargain.

Meanwhile, our networking continued to widen. Quite happily contrary to dire warnings received before departing the Other Coast, these people were every bit as smart and fascinating as those we'd hung with in New York and environs. It also wasn't lost on us that nearly *all* of them were, like ourselves, transplants.

Among the most interesting of them, for example, Holly and I quickly hit it off with the bright, entertaining couple that had moved in two houses away from us. The young man was Jonathan Fast, son of famed novelist Howard Fast. His girlfriend had recently been struck by a peculiarly American form of lightning. Erica Jong, a sweet, *hamische*, hip and very witty New York/Connecticut girl, had authored a mega-selling, *very* entertaining novel, *Fear of Flying*. With it she'd achieved worldwide fame, literary acclaim, money, *and* a major movie deal. The then *very* hot film Producer, Julia Phillips (*The Sting*), had purchased her novel, planning to turn it into a major movie.

However, in Erica's view, and not unjustified, too many months had gone by, and the movie was nowhere near getting made. Nor had she received a satisfactory explanation. Thus, she had moved to California in hope of making it happen, or regaining the rights so that she might sell it elsewhere and get it produced while it was still a reasonably hot property.

As time went by battling Hollywood lawyers and agents, Erica became increasingly frustrated. Holly and I commiserated with her and Jon over meals, drinks, schmoozes and walks/talks on the road. Then, one evening at a small dinner party in our home, prompted by several glasses of wine, Erica was moved to deliver a funny, impassioned and memorable rant about her ordeal. Several of our guests were Industry-types, among them another Malibu local, Robert Hamner, a veteran screen-and-TV writer. Portly, a Buddha-like figure who exuded a kind of seen-it-all mien, Bob listened impassively as Erica animatedly and amusingly did her number. Mostly about how pissed off she was with Ms. Phillips and the business in general. Ms. Jong concluded her tirade with a wonderfully sarcastic plea:

"So – what I'd like to know is – why the hell is it that *just* because I'm the new guy in town, I *have* to get fucked?"

To which, with impeccable timing and gesture, Hamner deadpanned: "It's tradition."

Erica and the rest of us cracked up.

He was right.

Bob was also responsible, several months later, for one of the better one-line takes on how money is regarded in Hollywood. Over lunch at the 20th Century Fox Commissary, he idly tossed me a question:

"So – what is it you're lookin' to get youknow – from your new career out here?"

Not something I had tried to put into words, I thought about it for a moment, then: "I just wanta see if I can *have* one. And maybe get some creative satisfaction in the bargain. What about you? What're you after?"

Hamner grinned, waved a hand: "I wanta make five million a year. Like Aaron Spelling."

"But – d'you really *need* that much?"

"No. But in this town – it's how they keep score."

Not, by the way, something I've ever felt or perceived. But – a for sure keeper.

My screenplay – originally titled *GOSH!* but eventually to be released as *Alice Goodbody* – was finished. Having concluded that while I fully intended, via humor, nudity and visuals, to push the bad-taste envelope, there was no way I could allow it to get an X-rating. Which meant it was time to deal with a pair of accompanying realities. The first: in filming it, I would need to replace those staples of porn, the endless humping-and-pumping shots, with real production and real actors. Next – the consequence: a bigger budget. *Double* the one for which I'd secured financing.

I put on my best salesman-hat and phoned my money-guy in New York. With enthusiasm I broke the news of my plan-change. Omitting my personal Hollywood first-impression concerns, I focused on profit potential. This I bolstered with actual figures I'd gathered; with the exception of *Deep Throat*, few X-rated films made serious money, while an R-rating would give us a *far* better chance of getting broad distribution. Thus a *much* greater profit potential for him. I informed him that a copy of my *very* funny screenplay was, as I spoke, in the mail. Finally, I mentioned that I'd need an additional $50K.

I held my breath, awaiting his reaction. A few seconds later, when it came, it somehow didn't surprise. He said he wasn't interested in putting more money into it. Further, he was pulling out completely, withdrawing his original commitment as well. "And I mean it. We're done."

"Bummed" hardly describes my reaction.

"*SHIT!*"

Closer, but still not there.

So there we were, our little family, in California, with the script for my directorial debut movie ready for prep.

With *no* goddam financing.

But wait…!

There _was_ the money my father had left me…

That night, I ran the possibility past Holly. She thought it was a great idea. I wasn't all that certain I'd describe it quite that way, but it was, I confess, one of the easiest decisions I've ever made. Not a contest, really. Though I could – and did – imagine what my dad's reaction would have been, and fully understood that it was one more nose-thumber in his direction.

I also knew that financing one's own movie was regarded in the biz as a major no-no. So I swore Holly to secrecy, and to almost anyone who asked, I lied.

Tom, age 14, meets his boyhood hero, Milton Caniff, world famous comic strip artist/writer of *Terry & the Pirates* and *Steve Canyon.*

Tom's other boyhood idol, movie actress, singer, dancer, his awesomely talented, sweet, first-cousin Ruth Terry.

Tom With his mentor/best friend, famed comic strip artist/writer
Leonard Starr, creator of *Mary Perkins, On Stage,* and *Thundercats.*

The legendary Angela Lansbury, with Tom on the set of *Murder, She Wrote.*

With Jerry Orbach on location near Boston, shooting the pilot of the CBS series *The Law & Harry McGraw*.

The brilliant Mary Tyler Moore, with Tom on the set of her comedy/variety special, *How to Survive the 1970's -- and Maybe Even Bump into Happiness*.

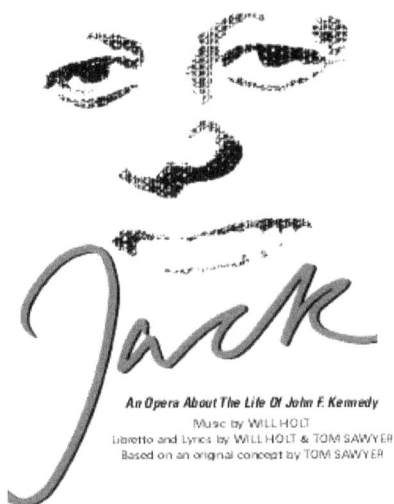

An Opera About The Life Of John F. Kennedy
Music by WILL HOLT
Libretto and Lyrics by WILL HOLT & TOM SAWYER
Based on an original concept by TOM SAWYER

Poster art for *JACK*. Designed by Dewynters, Ltd., London.

Michael Brian Dunn starring as John F. Kennedy, in the premiere of
JACK, May 7, 1993 at the Goodspeed Opera House in Connecticut.

215

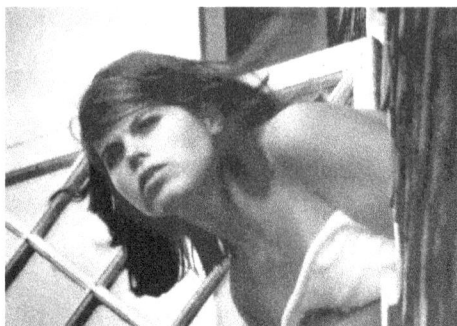

Holly Sawyer in Tom's first short film, *THE HIDING PLACE*.

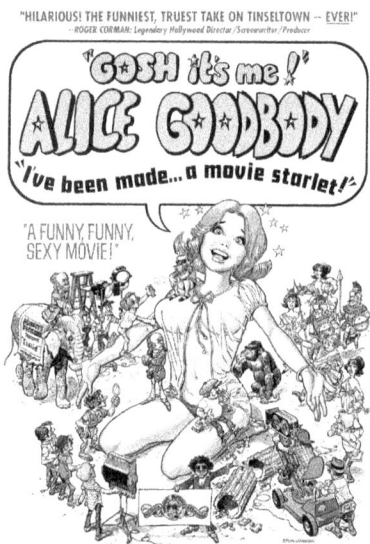

Poster for *ALICE GOODBODY*, Tom's "Hello to Hollywood" movie. Art by Bruce Steffenhagen.

Some examples of Tom Sawyer's commercial artwork

Panel from one of Stan Lee's romance comic books, 1954

Tide Laundry Detergent advertisements

A tender love story told entirely in song and musical color

ELY LANDAU presents

The Umbrellas of Cherbourg

(Les Parapluies de Cherbourg)

TWENTY-FIVE
Mark-Making—and a Bit of System-Working

TRULY EXCITED, AND ABOUT EQUALLY NERVOUS, I gave the go-signal for Gary Maxwell to finalize what he already knew was to be a low-as-possible budget, and get things rolling. On learning about my project, Maxwell had enthusiastically signed on as producer. I, just as unreservedly respecting his credentials in the indie-film area, felt entirely comfortable trusting him. It was not misplaced.

A heady time! A few days later, with Gary's help, we'd negotiated the rental of an office suite at historic old Culver City Studio, along with one of their soundstages. We began gathering a staff, casting, scouting locations, production designing, music and the like.

One of the more salutary – charming really – sides of this process, hinted at during my earlier, aborted Hollywood gig, turned out to be the number, and talent-level of the people Gary helped recruit. Hollywood, it seemed, was bursting with professional-grade, highly skilled non-union technicians and craftspeople whose favorite thing in the entire world was making movies, no matter the pay.

At Maxwell's wise suggestion, we put the word out that our film was prepping via tiny ads in the trade publications. Dozens of these folks came forward. Experienced men and women who, when not employed on a show such as mine, worked at jobs that allowed them flexibility. Driving-school instructors, baby photographers for Sears, bartending, construction and the like – occupations from which they could take temporary leave, and easily return to when the production gig ended. Shooting commercials, I'd gotten a sense that there were a number of people in New York with similar enthusiasm and expertise, but the pool of such talent in L.A. was phenomenal, and deep. They proved to be a delight to work with.

Moreover, as I later moved into the more organized, establishment levels of Hollywood, I found the same thing to be true. Oh, there were, as one encounters in any field, personality clashes. But in terms of the job itself, *only* this positive feeling. I mean, think about it – how many businesses are there where even the lowest-level people can hardly wait to show up for work every morning? No grumbling, everyone there to have a blast – and do the job well. A work-environment like very few others.

In fact, through my entire career in the entertainment business, I've continued to marvel at the rare phenomenon of virtually everyone, stage or screen – at least on the production-side – absolutely *loving* their work.

Hey, I was one of them. When it was a show or a project I didn't want to do, or individuals with whom I didn't want to work – I just said no.

As the money to finance the movie – my father's money – flowed out, I experienced more than a few restless nights, wondering – quite legitimately – if I was out of my fucking mind.

Plus, twinges of guilt about using that which my father had spent a lifetime acquiring, so imprudently and cavalierly, to make – a goddam *movie?*

But none of it stopped, nor even slowed me.

I was having too much fun.

Casting *Alice Goodbody*, and in particular, the title role, was a hoot. On one level anyway, more than a little surreal, causing me to increasingly feel as if I'd entered an alternate universe.

Forewarned in our advertisements, and by the person scheduling auditions, that the role required extensive nudity, the young women usually showed up at our office in brief, sexy outfits. My routine, after making sure at least one or two staff people were in the room with me, was to ask the actress to read a page or two of the script. Those who failed to demonstrate some acting ability and comic timing, or didn't have "the look" were quickly dismissed.

Then, similarly with a staffer present, to each who passed those tests, I would request that she remove her clothes. Now, this was not something I was accustomed to doing, especially with strangers, so there was invariably an element of comic awkwardness on my part. Less so on theirs because, as Maxwell had confided, most had worked in skin-flicks and/or porn. Whatever unease they felt, if any, tended to manifest itself in different, amusing ways as each item came off – from giggly modesty to outright 'no problem' boldness.

Among the most memorable of these was a pretty girl dressed entirely in bright red. Upon my request, she quickly put a hand to the front of her waist, apparently triggering some sort of quick-release device. Instantly, except for her shoes, *everything* she was wearing to fall to the floor.

Another young woman, presumably overcompensating, immediately leapt up onto the sofa where, twirling, she removed her blouse, tossed it aside. Then, still dancing, she stepped onto the adjacent table, stripped another item, then to a chair, where she got rid of more. Constantly moving, whirling, flinging, she performed a kind of choreographed striptease, finishing up by presenting herself directly above and in front of me on my desk, arms spread, feet wide apart, grinning, totally naked.

I was *definitely* in Hollywood. Or in *that* corner of it.

The choice of leading lady turned out to be easy.

Well, *almost*.

From about twenty candidates auditioned, it came down to two. One of them was an adorable, round, at-home-in-her-body, oopy-boopy redhead with large, gorgeous tits, a wry sense of humor, a beautiful, sweet, innocent face and smile, and a *genuine* flair for comedy. Sharon Kelly happened to be the *total* embodiment of my hamburger waitress/wannabe movie star protagonist.

Sharon wasn't sexy/seductive, but neither was the Alice I'd created. Sharon was *irresistible,* with *precisely* the same big, sweet, *innocent* smile I'd envisioned as I was writing Alice.

The other finalist was drop-dead sexy. Almost anything <u>*but*</u> Alice Goodbody.

It shouldn't have been any contest, but for a day or so it was. Until I faced what *that* was about. My ego. My vanity. She was *my* fantasy. The kind of woman who, by casting her, would be symbolic of *my* excellent taste and sophistication.

Though *certainly* not benefiting my movie.

Happily, my *good* sense kicked in, trumping self-image, and I chose Sharon Kelly as my star. One of the *best* choices I have *ever* made.

Before casting and preproduction were finished, however, *the* major hurdle remained: I still didn't know *how* to shoot the mostly-dirty jokes that were the core of my storyline – and avoid an X-rating. While the sex would be non-explicit, played for comedy rather than eroticism, that, plus a goodly amount of nudity was nonetheless known in the trade as "sexual content," virtually assuring an *X*.

I *had* to achieve that *R*. So how far could I go with the sex?

Consistent with my belief in the value of brain-picking, of "y'don't ask, y'don't get," I figured I had zero to lose by talking to the people who made those decisions. I phoned the Motion Picture Association of America, explained that I was an independent producer seeking their advice, and set up a meeting. Several days later, screenplay-in-hand and heart-on-sleeve, I faced three staff members. Two men and a young woman. I explained how badly I needed that *R* – and could they/*would* they help me?

They began tossing out suggestions – to each other. Their responses, while sympathetic to my problem, were unexpectedly, and somewhat curiously, I thought, "unofficial." As if they had no established policy for such a request. One that was offered to me by the apparently senior male was: "Look, we'd be glad to look at dailies of scenes that you feel might be questionable…"

"Well, the thing is, I don't have the kind of budget where I can afford to go back and reshoot stuff. I mean – is there some way I can get your input – your advice on *how* to shoot a scene that might questionable? So that it won't youknow…?"

They conferred for a few moments, then offered a solution: They asked me if I could leave the script with them. They would assign someone to advise me. I was greatly relieved, though still a bit unsure because of the seeming lack of nailed-down guidelines. That concern vanished the following day, when I was contacted by a young woman employee of the MPAA. She introduced herself and informed me that she had been given the job of helping make sure I shot *Alice Goodbody* in a way that would get me an R-rating.

Sure enough, bright, knowledgeable, she guided me through the script, explaining – sometimes after consulting her people – how I could or should photograph and/or frame each iffy moment so as to avoid crossing the MPAA's line.

Their solution for how I could shoot one particular scene without it being a deal-breaker still amuses the hell out of me. It provides one of the funnier insights into their logic, as well as illustrating their extraordinary, bend-over-backwards willingness to help.

The setup in question was within the film's overall story, and based on another old joke, this one involving a young woman auditioning her harmonica act for an agent. In my film, as the scene opens, she's nude, seen from the rear, her hips and tush gyrating in time with the harmonica soundtrack. The agent watches approvingly, reaches for the phone and – as the music continues, he dials Manny Spearman, the studio boss, telling Manny he's got this great act that the mogul's got to hear. He thrusts the phone toward the girl. Then, cutting to the reverse angle, the gag's visual reveal (*not* the punchline), is that she's playing the instrument on her vagina.

I fully expecting the MPAA folks to flatly reject the entire gag. Instead, after conferring on the matter, their sole proviso was that she *must* slide the harmonica *horizontally* across her pubic hair. If she moved it vertically, they told me, they'd have no choice but to give me an *X*.

In fact, being required to film it the other way somehow made the gag even funnier.

Thus, the rating problem happily solved, along with my image, and at least a shot at recovering my investment, we went forward with production. The entire shoot, in fact, was unbridled, filled-with-laughs *pleasure*. Adding to that, my daughters Suzy and Lauren were in town from their home in Virginia, and able to share some of the fun. They, plus Holly, Brooke and Wylie, appeared in various scenes.

Without doubt, Sharon Kelly's sweet, guileless presence and delivery, her superb comic timing – okay, *and* her remarkable body – made her portrayal of Alice Goodbody work. Moreover, she was an absolute delight throughout, willing, contributive, and *never* temperamental.

One of my favorite souvenirs is a photo someone shot of me, cracking up on the set. What I – and the rest of the crew – was laughing about was a scene shooting at the time. In it, one of Alice's lovers, the food-freak (each had a different comic hang-up), was – in tight close-up – dining on what appeared to be a large cherry-and-whipped-cream-topped ice cream sundae. Until the gag-reveal that underneath – as he spooned away the last of the whipped-cream – was one of Ms. Kelly's breasts. Typical of Sharon's good-natured willingness to suffer this and other indignities imposed on her by my script, she too was laughing throughout the shot. As was the crew.

After three similarly delightful, virtually glitch-free weeks of shooting, we wrapped. Maxwell and I began the post-production process, renting an editing-room at Warner Brothers. Again, his help, along with his sense of humor, knowledge and instincts, proved as they had from the start, beyond valuation.

A few days into cutting, Gary and I had been chuckling over lunch about some sound effects we'd recorded and had transferred to 35mm mag-track: a variety of fart-sounds (faked, orally) which were to be emitted by our studio-boss character, Manny Spearman. We'd been speculating that *our* farts would probably be the first-ever employed in a mass-market film. A new level of cinematic bad-taste!

A short time later, returning from lunch, we entered the corridor leading to our editing-room, and were stopped in our tracks. From the behind the closed door of the editing-room we were passing came a succession of louder, even *more* musically varied farts than ours. We glanced at each other, then at the sign on the door: *Blazing Saddles*.

Damn! We were being beaten out of our chance at a questionable First by – who else but Mel Brooks! Disappointed, Gary and I were nonetheless flattered to be in such company. The farts – his farts – would turn out to be those heard in the now-famous campfire scene of that comic milestone movie.

"Hah! Y'know, I've gotta say – most of these scenes – there's like only one way to cut 'em together…" We were in mid-editing as Gary made that observation. He chuckled: "…The way you shot 'em…"

Not at all unwelcome, nor without truth. One reason that *Alice Goodbody* had cost me only $105,000 was that I'd used my comic-strip/TV commercial background, storyboarding virtually all of it. I was thus able to avoid unnecessary setups, such as shooting masters, or other excessive footage that I wasn't going to use.

A satisfying month later, I confidently screened the final-cut work-print for the MPAA.

Alice Goodbody received its *R*, with no re-cutting. Their people had, after all, signed off on almost every problematic scene before I even began to shoot the movie. Literally so; there was a paper-trail on almost everything: written cautions, do's, don'ts and specific instructions for how I should shoot this or that sequence in order to ensure my R-rating.

By today's far looser, more grown-up conventions, the film is almost laughably tame. I still think of the end result as the cleanest dirty movie ever made. But back then they had clearly stretched their standards for me, as was testified to when I began screening it around town. More than one industry old-timer expressed shock, and occasionally resentment, that we had avoided an *X*.

Later I learned that seeking the MPAA's help upfront as I had done was apparently something that few if any filmmakers had tried before. Most studios, from the onset of the modern ratings system, had fought them over this or that ruling, or forced changes, treating the organization as an adversary.

Oh, and about my initial fear that hardcore film performers couldn't act? I was *way* wrong. Almost my entire cast came from that world, and they knew *exactly* where the jokes were, delivering them with *superb* timing and nuance. *So* importantly, understanding the need to underplay for the camera. Virtually *not* needing direction.

All told, a genuine, *hugely* satisfying creative experience. One of the *best* in my life.

TWENTY-SIX
Connecting

SIMULTANEOUSLY WITH COMPLETING MY MOVIE, came another of the many remarkable, fortuitous accidents in my life. This one with after-effects almost beyond imagining. It started when Alex & Walter, a Manhattan exercise studio specializing in gymnastics, opened a branch in Beverly Hills.

While living in New York, I had for several years been working out three times a week at a similar gym on Lexington Avenue. When we'd moved west I was a bit frustrated by the discovery that there seemed to be nothing comparable in the Los Angeles area. Thus, when I learned that this well-thought-of outfit was up and running locally, I quickly enrolled. Because in light traffic it was a 35-45 minute drive from Malibu to the corner of Wilshire and La Cienega Boulevards, rather than fight crowded rush-hour roads, I opted for their 10 AM class.

As it had been in Manhattan, in addition to the teacher, Walter, and an assistant/"spotter," class-size was limited to six people. Mine, however, consisted of only myself and two other men, one an attorney, one in advertising. They were pleasant, and I was delighted to get back into my old exercise routine. Each of us would do our tumbling, rings and parallel bar work while the others looked on, schmoozed and/or did stretches and the like.

But about two weeks into it, having learned that I was new in town, trying to establish myself in showbiz, Walter took me aside. In his heavy accent – for some reason all of these guys, including those in New York, were Russian émigrés – he urged me emphatically to switch to his 9 o'clock group. The reason: it was full of "pipple in the business." Clearly a no-brainer, without asking Walter to name names I went for it – and realized in a *hurry* that rising earlier and battling a bit of traffic was a *small* price to pay.

Make that *miniscule.*

What I could not have *dreamt* was the impact it would have on my life, the *endless* ripples that would begin there – and continue, even today.

I was welcomed a few mornings later by this affable four-member group. To say I was unprepared for the *level* of their *inside-ness* does not even remotely approach my reactions to my fellow gymnastics-classmates:

Ron Friedman was a prolific TV comedy writer among whose credits, I quickly learned, were *26 episodes* of the hit show, *Chico & The Man.*

Emmy-winning movie music arranger, conductor, composer, songwriter Ray Charles, of *The Ray Charles Singers* recording fame, wittily referred to himself as "the *deaf* Ray Charles." Ray, I soon discovered, was, like me, a graduate of Hyde Park High School.

Burt Sugarman was producer of the then *very* hot musical TV series, *Midnight Special.*

But the capper happened to be a genuine *legend*. A man whose face I'd seen on the cover of *Time Magazine*. I'd read about him in books. A seriously *BFD*, former head of CBS, James T. Aubrey was then *running* MGM Studios! Holy *shit*!

More remarkably, I, the "new kid," was *accepted*. By *all*. No-credentials-required – simply because, like them, I was *there*, in my equalizing shorts, sneakers and tee-shirt. Though I didn't realize it then, it was my introduction into a surprising, unspoken and *very* salutary Hollywood Tribal Custom. Broadly put, if you were invited to a party thrown by a Player, you were *automatically* regarded by the others present as one of *them*. It became almost as much a part of your credentials as would a screen-credit.

It meant that the other guest-Players' doors were open to you.

In a way, *exponentially* Net-Widening!

Which did *not* mean you would automatically be working for or with them. But at least it meant they would "take a meeting." Or "do lunch."

That phenomenon would play an amazingly meaningful and *vital* role in my career for years to come, a particular example of my good fortune which *still* takes my breath away.

Moreover, in and out of our 9 AM class, in addition to that core group, came and went a succession of actors, writers, directors and producers. Not least among these, beginning-Director Joel Schumacher, who went on to a truly impressive career.

All four of my initial fellow gymnasts became, to varying degrees, longtime social friends. But especially Aubrey. Remarkably and effortlessly, we happened to *click*. Distinguished, amusing, almost eerily intelligent, a lean fifty-four years old, by the time I found myself on the parallel bars with him, Jim had been a major Player for more than two decades. Yet he displayed none of the pomposity or arrogance one might expect from a guy who'd wielded such enormous executive weight for so long.

I was *not* trying to woo him – *or* the others, but within weeks we were *all* attending each other's then-frequent dinner-parties. Where I began to meet more and more people in – *really in* – the film and TV business.

Networking.

While admittedly I'd already begun that process by mixing with some locals in Malibu, this took things to a whole other plane.

Meanwhile, I continued my surreptitious, rent-paying illustration work, while also enjoying a non-paying gig directing a one-act play at the Beverly

Hills Playhouse. It starred my able, very comical Assistant Director, Michael Heit, who had also played a key acting role in my film.

But for the moment, completing *Alice Goodbody* and recovering my investment remained Job One. Upon finishing a rough-cut that satisfied, I excitedly booked a screening room at Warner Brothers and invited everyone I knew who was in the business. Which was pretty much limited to the several such acquaintances in Malibu, plus my gymnastics classmates. Because of the latter-group's status, I expected few to attend.

Instead, to my delight, *all* of them showed up. Jim Aubrey's date: the then-bigtime screen actress Barbara Eden!

Even better, they all laughed in the right places!

A few more editorial tweaks, scoring and sound-mix fixes, and I had a release-version to begin showing to prospective distributors. Of course, today, we'd be using DVD's, the web, etc. Next week, I suspect, it'll be handled in ways I can hardly imagine. But back then, seeing a new movie still meant buying a ticket at a theater, which had contracted for it with a distributor.

Just about then, another happy accident took place – a small thing that would, unpredictably, result in one *more* incredible, defining *Breakthrough Moment* in my life – actually, a Moment in several parts – which, once *it* finished playing out, would in turn would trigger many, many just as improbable others.

Holly was shopping one day in Pacific Palisades when she unexpectedly spotted a pair of way-out-of-place faces. Long a part of our back-East crowd, cartoonist Howard Post and his wife, Bobbie, had just relocated to California. Famous in the "Bigfoot World," Howie was then writing and drawing the popular – and *very* funny – daily syndicated strip, *The Dropouts*. The reason for their move: Howard's longtime friend, successful television Writer/Director/Producer Lila Garrett, had convinced him that he could have a career in Hollywood as a TV comedy writer.

So we resumed our friendship, bolstered by our mutual newcomer status, inviting each other to dinner parties and the like. The Posts were an entertaining pair, and one evening at their home, Holly and I were introduced to the woman behind their move to LA. Ms. Garrett was – *formidable*. Brassy, outspoken, New York-born, high-energy, very bright and witty, an Emmy-winner – and lifelong, outspoken Leftie. Typically, as I was beginning to perceive about most people who succeeded in Hollywood, Lila Garrett was massively, profoundly *driven*. In Lila's case, in love with the game even as she humorously bitched about it.

Lila's companion was Mort Lachman, a droll, laid-back-but-*very*-sharp guy. Mort had a gift for spontaneous, singular one-liners of the kind he'd manufactured successfully during 28 years as head-writer for legendary comedian Bob Hope. Lila and Mort, in 1976, could best be described as a real-life, female/male version of Neil Simon's *The Odd Couple*. Complete with frequent, funny/hostile zingers aimed at the other.

This was perhaps best illustrated by an exchange at one of the parties. Lila cornered Holly and me, and earnestly asked how we liked the dress she was wearing. Both of us responded enthusiastically, which Lila seemed to appreciate: "Good. Mort said he hated it."

Mort happened to hear this as he approached from behind Lila and, with superb timing, deadpanned his throwaway: "Nah. What I *said* was, it looks great on a woman your age."

Here's how *The Moment*'s kickoff came to pass.

A short time after our first social encounter, I invited them to one of my once-or-twice a week screenings of *Alice Goodbody*, I tried to salt each of these with an audience of ten-or-so of my networking-acquired friends, in hope that their communal laughter would sway whichever distributor I was romancing. When the lights came up, I was flattered to learn from both Lila and Mort that they'd genuinely enjoyed the film. But before I could even respond to their compliments, Lila emphatically – her *only* mode – added: "You should be writing for television."

Mort agreed.

"Thank you. Really. But – um – I'm a director. I only wrote the script because I had no---"

Lila cut in: "Well, you should really think about it." She and Mort departed – and that was it. End of *The Moment – Part One*.

Quickly put aside as, necessarily, I turned my attention to other attendees, particularly the distributor.

I should emphasize here that the concept of working in television in *any* capacity – but *especially* as a writer – wasn't just not on the table. Fixated as I was on *The Movies*, I had *never* considered TV even as an outside, fallback possibility! Clearly, I admit, verging on irrational, in my single-minded approach, my set of possible options – it just plain *did not exist*. As stated earlier, I'd *decided* on my goal, *saw* it. To the exclusion of *all* else. Very similar, I later understood, to my childhood fixation on becoming a comic-strip artist.

But Lila's suggestion *was* a seed…

To my relief, the screenings fairly quickly began paying off in the way I'd hoped. I soon signed with a foreign-rights rep who started selling my movie, country-by-country, thus recouping some monies, a few thousand dollars at a time. A week later, I succeeded in hooking up with a theatrical distributor. Joe Solomon, known in those circles as "*King*" of B-pictures, agreed to take on *Alice Goodbody* for domestic release. We negotiated a modest advance, to be followed by additional stipulated payments.

Now, I figured, I'd be in the black in no time.

Wrong. A few weeks and several anxiously awaited and lousy box-office reports later, I discovered that Joe was marketing the film as a steamy-sex movie. Since, because it was most assuredly *not* erotic, such a come-on would certainly piss-off exhibitors and ticket-buyers who expected that kind of flick. Which would thus kill word-of-mouth potential. While I was unable to convince Joe of this, I had gotten the ear of a young man in his employ who privately agreed with me.

After learning from this fellow that – surprise, surprise – film distribution was less than rocket science, I cancelled my contract with Joe – he was already reneging on guaranteed payments – and hired the guy. With his help, we began booking playdates ourselves.

Which led to another component of my ongoing initiation – one that was both anger-making and maddeningly helplessness-inducing.

My new associate had forewarned me about it: "Man, if you think you already know from goniffs, forgeddaboutit. I mean, the exhibitor-end of the business? It gives a whole new meaning to lying-and-cheating."

Starting, he added, with the fact that most of the major studios routinely hired people to stand outside of theaters, doing head-counts which they would then compare with that venue's box-office figures.

My expectations thus modified, while some of our exhibitors were honest, I wasn't all that dismayed by those who were not. Just *whaddya gonna do?*-pissed off.

Meanwhile, other prospects were bumping into reality. *Alice Goodbody* received a couple of reviews in 'the trades.' One, a flat-out pan from *Daily Variety,* featured a tight-assed, humorless put-down of the harmonica-gag. The reviewer described it as one of the more demeaning roles *ever* given a woman in film.

Happily, a more positive notice appeared in the *Hollywood Reporter,* whose reviewer, John Dorr, was obviously *far* deeper and more perceptive:

"…Funny…strictly low brow and broad in treatment…making the most of low budget production values…full of golly-gee dialogue and amusing movieland caricatures, directed with an unaffected simplicity, more ribald than prurient..."

There was more, along the same lines, praising the cast. All in all, I'm *still* proud of that one.

But, *Variety?* From then on it has been my pleasure to neither subscribe to, nor *ever* purchase a copy. I mean, if they couldn't take a joke, fuck 'em. Worse was their not *getting* it.

But, it became apparent within a short time that the movie studios were not exactly clamoring for my services as a film director. Disappointing, yes. Frustrating, but far from crushing. Moreover, I had been thinking about what Lila said after that screening. I began – very tentatively – to toy with the possibility of working in television.

As a stepping-stone, of course.

But still – as a…*writer?*

Invited to another party at Howard and Bobbie's, I learned that Ms. Garrett would be present. I resolved to set her straight about my preference for *running* the show – for being the *boss.*

As I would come to realize, this was the threshold of *The Moment – Part Two.* Shortly after Holly and I arrived that evening, I cornered Lila, and, reminding her of her advice, I added a challenge: "…But I mean – I'm a *director.* So – why shouldn't I direct for TV?"

"Forget it. You don't wanta *direct* television. I mean – they've gotta shoot what, seven – eight pages a day…" She sipped her wine while allowing that to sink in, following it up in her characteristic witty, dazzlingly articulate cut-to-the-chase style: "…They haven't got *time* to do anything creative. Hell, they're mostly just traffic cops, trying to keep the actors from bumping into the set…"

Then Lila, like *all* good writers, gave it her button: "…Besides – *all* those producer-credits you see at the top of every series episode? Those're *all* writers. In TV, *writers* run the show…"

While I was processing that, she added: "So – how it'll work, you'll write a few episodes, then they'll start hiring you on staff."

I actually did a real-life double-take, a la W.C. Fields (or, as I prefer to think of myself, more like Cary Grant). It was one more head-slap revelation. An earth-shift from the no-accident assumption – and truth at least in terms of then-and-still-accepted mythology – that film was 'The *Director's* Medium.'

Even as I was further digesting Lila's alien concept – one that I had *never* heard, nor read about – my lips were moving: "So – ah – okay – what would I – how would I youknow get started? As a writer?"

Lila shrugged, casually waving an upturned palm: "I've got a production deal… Y'come up with an idea, call me."

She moved off.

Leaving me with my mouth hanging open.

TWENTY-SEVEN
The Start of *Another* Surprising— and *Delicious*—Journey

As you can imagine, to say that Ms. Garrett's latest words 'got me to thinking' doesn't describe it at all. Because I had written a comedy, and since that was Lila's strong suit, *that*'s where my mind went.

One morning two weeks later, I did phone her. Her hurried, entirely in-character *Beverly Hills Lady* response: "I can't talk now. I'm on my way out to a meeting."

I was too stoked to let go. My words came in a rush – and fortunately, instinctively brief: "Lila, I just wanta give you one line."

"Okay. Quick."

"A gang-comedy on a tacky used-car lot in the Valley."

There was this two-or-three-second silence, then: "I *love* it. You'll write it, I'll produce it. Talk to you later." Followed by the *click*.

While leaving me elated, but in suspense, and with dozens of questions, *The Moment, Part Three.*

Buttoned.

I hung up the phone, went to the kitchen, and told Holly what had just taken place.

She was delighted, but... "So... What – does that mean?"

"I have no idea."

Ten days later, we learned its *stunning* meaning.

I had my first *paying* gig in Hollywood! I was writing *"Mother's Motor City,"* a comedy series pilot – for *CBS Television Network*!

My zero-perspective knee-jerk? *Way* cool. But – with a shrug: "Oh? Okay. So – *this* is how the Business works…"

Not.

It would be several years before *that* sank in. But what did *I* know? Over the following decades I became acquainted with dozens of working writers who would've *killed* for the chance to *ever* write a pilot.

Moreover, and again without my knowledge or full understanding for *years*, given the way it *does* work, by my *starting* at that level – a *Network Pilot Writer*, word *instantly* spread all over town that I was a hot new guy!

The immediate, and scary problem: could I pull it off? Except for my movie and a few TV commercials, I'd never written directly for film (or tape). A half-hour sitcom? Sure, prior to the pitch, with Lila's supervision I'd fleshed it out with a cast of characters. Along with a few one-or-two line episode-premises. But now – I had to *write* the goddam script? These people – the Network, Lila and whomever else – they all seemed to have a lot more confidence in me than I did. But with suggestions from Lila, a bit of help from Mort, and Holly cheering me on while offering her amazing insights, a few weeks – and drafts – later, I finished.

About Holly's contribution: her encouragement and *awesome* shit-detector would over the next decades, prove to be an indispensable element in *everything* I have ever been paid to write – more than 100 scripts and several novels. Even with non-paying compositions such as sensitive letters and emails, her vetting *continues* to be invaluable. *Literally*, over and over, saving me from myself…

The way the sale of *Mother's Motor City* had come about? Two Network pitch meetings, accompanied by Lila and her agent. The first a turndown, but deserving of mention because of its amusing off-the-wall-ness. Another glimpse into this very singular World I was entering.

Lila seemed a bit anxious as we arrived at NBC in Burbank. I was not, I suspect because I was without preconceptions. I didn't – or maybe hadn't *permitted* myself to – imagine a next step. Nor did I feel as if my life depended on a "yes." It was as if I was along for this ride, curious but hardly anxious, to see how things would develop.

I suppose you could say I was "cool," though my take is that I was, per usual, this observer/participant, a part of me viewing this movie – in which I was an actor – from a high corner of the room.

A lot like such things had *always* been…

The difference was that this initial pitch-meeting began to turn bizarre almost immediately after we sat down with NBC's head of Comedy Development. A pleasant-enough guy in his mid-thirties, he gave us a kind of opening-statement: "Listen, something you guys should know going in – I *hate* TV sitcoms…" Before either Lila or I could digest this, he added: "… Actually, I *despise* 'em."

All I could think of at that instant – and quite naturally – was *So – why does he have this job?*

It gets weirder.

Already slightly off-balance, Lila and I went into our act. She introduced me and, with her occasional, helpful interjections, I went on to describe our premise, and the ensemble of ongoing characters. We did it as enthusiastically and entertainingly as we could, given his declaration.

But for yet another more surreal reason, we found it difficult to maintain concentration. Or, actually, eye-contact with him – or to establish it in the first place – *or* have the sense that we even had his attention.

Because throughout our pitch – are you ready for this? – seated in his chair, he played with his Yo-Yo.

Up and down. Up and down. Sometimes watching me. Sometimes – his spinning toy.

My overall reaction: this had been one of those '*Hey, after all, this is Hollywood...*' moments. But as we left his office, the appalled Ms. Garrett was quick to assure me that it was *not* typical executive behavior. And it turned out she was right. During the rest of my career in the business, I never again encountered anything remotely similar.

Okay, *once*. A pitch-meeting years later with a Showrunner who was obviously stoned.

Which raises an incidental point. For what it may be worth, contrary to the impression in Flyover Country and beyond – in more than forty years, and having attended countless Hollywood parties, I have *never* seen anyone snort a line of coke, nor witnessed anyone using a substance stronger than booze or a joint.

Our second pitch went *way* better. The CBS Development person loved the concept and, the following day, gave us our go-ahead.

Oh – and with a new amendment. An abrupt decision that had been a long, long time cooking, and suddenly prompted by this latest change in my life. The next time Lila and I spoke, following my initial "sale" to her, and before our first pitch was scheduled, I informed her that I had decided to be billed as Tom Sawyer.

That would turn out to be one of my more lastingly valuable, impactful decisions. On more than one level. The first is obvious: it's memorable, easy to pronounce and to spell.

But there was another, *really* special, actually a touch off-the-wall, unplanned dividend. There I was, concealing my graying hair, and lying about my age as I began a new career at age forty-seven. By becoming another person, I had *no* easily traceable past!

Similarly not-anticipated, some years later the internet-age arrived, and the same held true! Sure, there are places online that list Tom _Scheuer_'s date-of-birth, and I suppose if one is sufficiently determined, everything else. But for all the years during which I needed that cover, it _worked_.

I've always felt that the name-change was good P.R. as well, in yet another way. For most of my life, when I encountered people with difficult-to-read or unpronounceable names, I've found it irritating, almost an imposition. Bad marketing. Like good ad copy, one's name should be easy to read or recite. Then, there was for me the matter of starting out in a new business, this one in particular. Close to the _last_ thing I figured I needed was to be pissing people off right from the top.

As mentioned, I'd experimented with it years before, signing some of my comic-book and illustration artwork "Tom Sawyer." But doing so while my father was alive had made me feel a bit guilty: a somehow too-obvious put-down.

Lila also felt that the name-change was a great idea.

Which it turned out to be, suddenly making my life so much easier that within a few months, with Holly's encouragement, I decided to change it legally.

And, Freud-subscribers please note: the night before it became official, I had this on-the-nose dream in which I _killed_ my father.

I found that I was truly testing myself with that _Mother's Motor City_ script, and with it came a pair of new-to-me twists. First, my initial inkling of something I would feel acutely for the next few years. The sneaky, looking-over-my-shoulder feeling that "they" were going to be _onto_ me at any moment. That it was only a matter of time until they finally figured out the _truth_: that I was this fraud, _totally_ faking it. That in trying to pass myself a writer, I _really_ didn't know what the fuck I was doing.

Second, and certainly related to the other, was my introduction to "The Wall." A phenomenon that remains even now a fixed, almost laughably so, part of my writing ritual. But laughable more on Holly's part – though she's usually stifled it – than on mine. Starting with *Mother's Motor City*, on *every* script and *every* novel I've written, at a point late in the process, this *certainty* hits me. The entirely believable, deadly-serious truth that *this* is the one that's *defeated* me, the one I'll be unable to complete.

That *this* bite is simply *not* chewable.

Though fortunately I managed to struggle past it then, and every time since – it continues to happen. And momentarily brings me down each time. Plus, in those moments, rational perspective – such as "*Oh, this again…?*" – completely eludes me.

Anyway, the characters I created and wrote for that first-ever pilot teleplay were funny and appealing, as was the overall story. My major area of self-discovery: an aversion to, and lack of a gift for, writing one-liners. Which, Lila cautioned me going in, were *required. Three* of them per page! Fortunately, Lila's significant other, Mort, helped in that area. And Holly's eye was becoming ever more important. I was in *very* good company.

Following a few changes requested by CBS, Lila Garrett delivered the final draft script for *Mother's Motor City*, and we awaited their decision about putting it into production. A week later we learned that we hadn't made the cut, and that was as far as the project ever got. But my career as a TV writer had been *very* effectively launched. With that impressive first credit, I acquired an agent, and became a proud, if humble, member of the Writers Guild of America. Moreover, in joining the WGA, I had the good sense to shave fourteen years off my age.

Tinseltown's doorways were open to me! I began writing a "spec" feature screenplay, and pitching episodes for on-air series.

TWENTY-EIGHT
The Network Widens— Getting into the Game

SUCCESSFUL SELF-DISTRIBUTION of *Alice Goodbody*, I was learning, was hindered by me being essentially a one trick operation. Unlike movie studios having the booking-leverage of additional films in the pipeline, I was trying to peddle a single film. Also, we were encountering the frequent, annoyingly questionable accounting by exhibitors, amounts shortchanged being too small or unprovable – to warrant legal action.

All that began to change when I was contacted by veteran distributor Sandy Cobe. Hearing the deal he proposed, my attention was riveted. Sandy was not only enthusiastic about releasing my film, but *further*, he promised to *immediately* recover the rest of my investment! He would set up a then still-legal limited-partnership tax shelter arrangement. I went for it. Quickly. Through Sandy, I sold *Alice Goodbody* to an anonymous group of dentists in the San Diego area. Our arrangement: all rights would revert to me ten years hence.

To my enormous relief, and pleasure, I was *done* with that part of it, my attention no longer fragmented. I had gotten my (and my father's) money's worth. Into profit, and thus able to pursue my new career without guilt or angst, but with *focus*. Though *Alice Goodbody* had launched me in not quite the direction I'd imagined, it has been among the best bets I've ever made – one that's been paying off ever since.

But despite these very positive signs, there were still seriously nagging reservations about whether the "career" appellation was really achievable.

We'd been in California for a little over four years. I was extremely thankful for my shrink's *so* prudent advice about allowing myself ample time. As I've continued to be so often grateful to him over the ensuing decades for other wisdom he imparted to me. I was barely aware then – perhaps "in denial" says it better – that I was coming up on my forty-seventh birthday. I was – at least thus far – fooling "them" and – in a *real* way, myself. Fortunately to no harm. One result of being a fool-ee: I had *zero* consciousness of there being anything special about successfully reinventing myself at that point in my life.

I mean, *why the hell not…?*

Even at this distance, my most vivid sense of its having been unusual came from the comments of others who regarded it that way. Such as my dear friend, Leonard Starr, who over and over flatteringly described it as topping his list of "gutsy moves." I can see his point – sort of. But for me, guts had very little to do with it. More, in *my* mind, like "I had no choice," it was something that was just – well – process. My natural arc.

Yet, this one *did* feel different in many ways. *Far* more exciting. *Freer.* The creative possibilities so *very* much wider than seeing another of my drawings in print, or one more TV commercial on the air. So broad, it turned out, so satisfying, so *without* an end-frame – and so much *fun* – that if I'd tried to imagine the rest of it, I could not have come close.

Over the following year or two, there would be some momentarily doubt-inducing employment-gaps, but I was learning. About the business, expressing myself, seeing so many things through fresh filters…

To place what follows in clearer perspective, television at the time that I got into it was *very* different from the medium – and the business – it is as I write this.

For starters, there were three national networks: CBS, NBC and ABC. Fox wouldn't come along for several years. Virtually all TV broadcasting via network and local stations, except for PBS, was supported by advertising revenues. Seven primetime evenings per week, half-hour comedies, one-hour dramas and made-for-TV movies were the norm. Cable did not yet exist. The internet, webcasting and such were many years in the future. Major markets such as New York City had fewer than thirteen TV channels. The smaller ones, three to five.

TV used up material *very* fast, and not many series had long runs. Which was why, each year, the networks routinely ordered numerous pilot scripts for the following season. A few of them would then be filmed or taped, screened for advertisers, and market-tested for live audiences. Their casting, the product of mostly seat-of-the-pants guesswork. Thus actor-audience chemistry, if any, was largely accidental. A small number of those produced would go on the air, usually with tentative orders of four-to-six episodes. In competition for viewers, most did not survive for even that long. They would be killed, replaced by shows from the second-tier, or sometimes newer concepts hastily ordered into production.

That was the writers' marketplace, and a dynamic one it was. But very constricted content-wise, back then only *rarely* truly creative or inventive. These limitations were largely dictated by the advertisers' and broadcasters' nearly pathological fear of offending *any* of the consumers who populated Middle America. Profanity or even street-vernacular, for instance, though they were becoming common in theatrical movies, along with of course sex, were among the major no-no's. Expressions frequently heard in network TV dialogue today – "pissed off," "asshole," "dickhead," and the like – were totally off-limits, even during the 10 PM/after-the-kiddies'-bedtime shows.

Yet, even within those bland confines, art was [very] occasionally committed. Envelopes were nudged and statements made – some occasionally sneaky so – in series such as *Barney Miller*, *All in the Family*, *M.A.S.H.*, *NYPD Blue* and a few others.

The series form – *including* those limitations, and how to do something worthwhile *despite* them – was for me, along with just seeing if I could do it on *any* level, a *very* exciting, challenging place. My kind of situation.

In addition to my new name, what I liked most about my initial taste of the Television World was the relative immediacy. Not least, of gratification and turndowns. Pitches frequently yielded yesses – and rejections – on the spot. That suspense-minimizing aspect turned out to be pretty much typical of the business. When I began working on staff for on-the-air shows, script-changes I'd write were sometimes actually *shot* on that day – and occasionally broadcast within a *week*. Another happy perk of this profession that it had in many ways chosen me.

It was many years before I became conscious of the extent to which I had taken the pace for granted. When I ventured into – and experienced the rude jolt of – the glacially slow-moving book business, my literary agent quite accurately accused me of being "patience-challenged."

TV writing was regarded then and for years after as a poor relation of writing for the movies. But in truth there are very few feature film screenplay writers who are able to sustain careers with the level of continuity that TV offers. Even among those, not many who see their work produced with any regularity. I've known – and known of – several million dollar-per-year screenwriters who almost never had their stuff shot. Money or not, that's something I would have found frustrating and worse, unsatisfying. This is particularly true since – for me anyway – most significantly the form is *so*

250

unlike writing narrative. A script, be it for film, stage or television, is never really complete on the page. It only becomes so when performed.

Moreover, there's the accepted perception that movies, with their sometimes astronomical budgets, are more carefully-written than TV. Yet, among today's major feature films, I see an astonishing number containing plot-holes that, on the most fifth-rate TV series, would have been spotted and fixed before going into production.

Within a few months of writing *Mother's Motor City*, and despite it never going beyond teleplay, other doors began to open. Opportunities to present episode ideas for on-air shows like *Chico and the Man*. I'd already been briefed that if one was asked to pitch, it was rarely going to be adversarial. Generally, it meant they *wanted* to "do business" with me. As I would learn firsthand a year or two later when I was on staff and buying scripts, they were looking for help. Often desperate for it.

Re: *Chico*, concurrent with my invitation from that series, Mort Lachman, who was by then running *All in the Family*, asked a favor. One of his writers during the Bob Hope days, Bill Larkin, who happened to be a neighbor of mine on Malibu Road, needed work, and would I do a script with him?

Delighted to comply, Bill and I came up with a story idea for *a Chico* episode. We met with the Producer and a couple of his staff writers, pitched our premise, and were given the assignment. What followed was an interesting lesson about the phenomenon of joke writing. Bill, an affable, witty guy, had obviously succeeded for many years as a gag writer, but he was unable to think in terms of a whole story, or even a complete scene. Our collaboration went like this: Bill would sit, reading a magazine while I wrote. When needed I'd ask for his help, as I did in one memorable instance: "Yo, Bill – got a 'sparkplug' joke?"

Remarkably, without hesitation, he rattled off nine or ten one-liners involving sparkplugs, several of which were very funny, and eminently usable. While I wrote the dialogue sides, he went back to his magazine until my next request. That was Bill's entire – and, given the nature of that marketplace, not inconsiderable – contribution.

Our teleplay was well-received, and we were invited to pitch anytime we had another idea. The experience had been somewhat confidence-bolstering. The characters I created, the dialogue I wrote for them and for the ongoing series characters, capturing their music, *weren't* the most difficult things I'd ever done.

But, I thought, that still could've been a fluke.

Meanwhile, I was also busy on several then non-paying-but-fascinating fronts. One was a screenplay based on a premise suggested by Michael Heit, who had been Assistant Director on, and actor in *Alice Goodbody*. Michael had proposed what I instantly saw as a hilarious idea: a comedy about a pair of schmuck window-washers who become embroiled in a mafia/CIA contract to murder a visiting Arab Sheik. We fleshed out the story, titled it *Squeegee*, and I got to work on the script.

Through a mutual friend, I met and hit it off with Bruce Lansbury, Angela's brother. Bruce was a bright, inventive, truly decent guy – a gentleman in the old-school sense – with whom I would have a long and, for this town, close relationship. Then an independent producer, Bruce and I worked together loosely over several months – on spec – coming up with pitchable sitcom series ideas. While nothing we developed during that period ever sold, we retained an abiding respect for each other. Our paths would intersect more than once.

Reyn Parke, a very bright, former New York agent, was one of the few people to whom I had an introduction when we arrived in California. Reyn and I had been brainstorming and attempting to sell a few movie and series notions. Through the exposure I received while pitching with Bruce and Reyn, I was further widening my network.

Reyn, by the way, had what I *still* regard as the definitive explanation for the presence in our part of the state of so *many* extraordinarily attractive people. His reasoning: back in the early 20th century, silent-film era, the alluring possibility of movie-stardom began to attract the most beautiful young people from all over America. They migrated to Southern California by the thousands, and while few made it in the movies, most of them stayed, selling real estate, pumping gasoline, and so on. And in doing so, they formed what Reyn wittily and aptly described as this "*Beautiful People Gene-Pool.*"

Jim Aubrey, by then an independent producer, no longer running MGM, took a liking to *Squeegee*. In trying to package it, Jim introduced me to the director he'd chosen for the project, Bill Persky.

A delightful guy, Bill lived on the beach in Malibu, several miles east of us, and we quickly became social friends. With his writing partner, Sam Denoff, Bill had been brought west from New York some years earlier by comedy icon Carl Reiner. They'd worked on Reiner's TV classic, *The Dick van Dyke Show*. It was at a party of Bill's that I first had the thrill of meeting Carl and his vivacious wife, Estelle. Ms. Reiner, who delivered the immortal line in *When Harry Met Sally*: "I'll have what she's having," was as witty as Carl. Both of them adorable, Carl was one of the sweetest, most gentle people I've known – a quality, incidentally, that infuses *all* of his work.

Again, there I was, chatting with such people, enjoying their company – being *accepted* – and being *wowed* to be in the same room with them!

All the while that "observer" part of me watching, listening. *Still* half-figuring I was this fraud who'd be found out at any moment.

Heightened a few months later when Persky chose me as a member of his writing team on a CBS TV comedy-variety special he was producing. A bit scary, I had no idea of what would be required of me, though my agent assured me it would be a breeze, that all I'd be asked to do was write "sketches." *Sketches?* But again, whatever it was, Bill had somehow decided I was equal to it, so...

That show, Mary Tyler Moore's *"How to Survive the 70's... & Maybe Even Bump Into Happiness,"* yielded a few of my all-time favorite, most-fun, proudest moments in the business.

One was exciting – and not a little intimidating. Bill immediately asked me to come up with a bit for Mary and guest star, Dick van Dyke to play together. I suggested one, and Bill reacted enthusiastically. The premise –

an entire romance-plot in maybe three minutes – without a single word of dialogue: two strangers spot each other in an office-building elevator, headed for the lobby. The plot-arc: boy meets girl, gets girl, boy loses girl, then, *just* as boy finally *gets* girl, the elevator reaches the ground floor. Both emerge – and go into the arms of their respective "others." Eyes meet, faces poignantly telling us it's the last time they'll ever see each other. Maybe.

It was, incidentally, *my* kind of punchline. Totally consistent with my own lifelong, incurable romanticism – especially on the theme of lost love. Hell, even after 40+ viewings, my eyes still tear when Ilsa and Rick part at the end of *Casablanca*, and I'm put away by *La Boheme*, *Tosca*, and anything else by Puccini.

Next, I had the thrill of seeing it being shot, performed by two of the world's greatest clowns – and *man*, did they pull it off!

It really didn't have to get much better than that. But it did. Knocked out by Mary and Dick's funny/touching performances, as they were exiting the set, I told them so, and how thrilled I'd been to be so rewarded, to have had the chance to write for them. I was flattered to the point of near speechlessness by Dick's response, with which Mary concurred: "Hey, you don't get material that good every day."

Incredible…

My education continued, as did my excitement. In the space of a few months, I wrote a *Quincy* script with Reyn Parke and, on my own, a *Wonder Woman* episode.

The *Quincy* pitch gave me my first up-close experience, albeit once-removed, with an actor-with-clout. The hit series starred the magnetic Jack Klugman as a coroner who solved murders, and the house-rule for scripts was that *all* of the clues had to come from the corpse. Writer/Producer David Shaw (*not* Angela Lansbury's stepson-David, but rather the brother of famous novelist Irwin) listened to our somewhat farfetched-but-do-able premise: a Howard Hughes-type reclusive gazillionaire is murdered by his corporate heirs – killed seven years earlier, frozen and then thawed in time to frame someone in present-time.

David reacted instantly: "Great. You've got a sale. Except – there *is* one thing. Jack's got to approve it, and the only way he's gonna do that is if I can convince him it's got some social relevance..." Off our questioning looks, David smiled and added: "So, all you need is to come up with a scene, or an overriding theme that I can sell. One that makes a statement, preferably Liberal." He suggested we think about it for a day or two, and phone him.

A problem that proved to be minor, as we were driving past the guard gate five minutes later, leaving the Universal lot, I had it. I could *see* the scene. Almost taste it, in fact, because it spoke *for* me. I ran it past Reyn, who agreed, and as soon as I got home, I dialed David.

"Okay, there's this moment in the boardroom of this giant company. Just Quincy and this guy who's murdered the Hughes-character and is now running the business. Quincy's pissed-off, accusing him of using crooked means to get the body released – so they can cremate it before the investigation is complete. Bribery, pressure on judges and congressmen, and like that. And Quincy concludes by saying: 'I mean who the hell d'you guys think you are anyway – y'think you're bigger than the government?' This executive pulls himself to his full height, and says: 'I've got news for you, Dr. Quincy. We *are* the government. We and a few other corporations like ours.' He points to the door and says: 'Now get *out!*'"

That was as far as I got. David interrupted with: "Perfect. Jack's gonna love it. I'll get back to you." Next day, we had the assignment.

Then, a funny thing happened on our way to finishing the script, which was titled *Gone But Not Forgotten.* An interview with Klugman was published in one of the trade papers, wherein he stated that *all* TV writers were hacks, unable to write anything "meaningful." Thus, he added, for next season's shows he would be checking out colleges in an effort to find quality writers.

Amused, I couldn't resist including the following for Jack's final, just-before-FADE OUT, show-ending speech:

> QUINCY
> *(Meaningful curtain-line to be provided*
> *by college-writer of Jack's choice.)*

We dropped off the teleplay, and waited. Next morning, between laughs, David Shaw informed us that the writing staff and producers were on the floor. However, probably wisely, they chose not to show the script to their leading man until they'd rewritten our button-line.

When I ran into Klugman in Malibu 30 years later and told him about it, he laughed: "Yeah. I took a lotta heat for that one." Interestingly and, I suspect, in keeping with the characteristic passion of Jack's acting performances, he didn't retract what he'd said about TV writers.

TWENTY-NINE
Discovering Some Nuggets, a Little Self-Knowledge— and a Resulting Course-Tweak

"MY ONLY NOTE – YOUR BAD GUY TALKS too much. The thing with Bad Guys, Tom – they've got tight, thin mouths and they don't say a lot – except for their aria."

Think about it – the conciseness, the awesome, nailing-it truth. I somehow doubt that that is taught at, say, the Iowa Writers' Workshop, or at other bastions of Literary Integrity. But it should be.

Instead, Bruce Lansbury, commenting on the first-draft of my *Wonder Woman* teleplay, spoke those piercingly insightful words to me. Bruce had found himself at Warner's, producing the series, and offered me a chance to write an episode. I'd grabbed it, and my matriculation continued. The highlight of this particular "class" coming in the form of that breathtakingly clear, no-frills, and *certainly* non-theory, take-it-to-the-bank lesson from Bruce.

Receiving that sort of writing advice, such priceless nuts-and-bolts knowledge, was a commonplace of my early scripting experience in TV. This is what you *should* do, and *this* is what you shouldn't – all of it supplied by the solid, zero-nonsense veteran staffers on the shows for whom I wrote scripts.

Invaluable gems, like Lansbury's, on the order of:

"Write to the Money – never have your star absent from two consecutive scenes."

"The smarter your heavy, the brighter your protagonist has to be. Dumb villains only work in comedies."

"Never dump stuff in your hero's lap. Make your good guy earn it – make 'em the engines of their own salvation."

"Limit your scenes that take place in one room to three pages – max."

But perhaps *the* most important lesson – one that applies to *any*one who writes, whether it be poetry, advertising copy, fiction or nonfiction, no matter how lofty our intentions: "*Never* forget – we are *entertainers*."

There were many more, virtually inarguable, every syllable instantly etched into my head. Were all of these people great writers? No. But they were *professionals*. Without pretension. They'd learned what *works* and what does *not*, what techniques grab and hold an audience, and those that deliver viewers to the commercial break (our mandate). This was driven home by the image of every TV writer's bogeyman: a guy in his tee-shirt, tired after another day at a job he probably hates. He's got a beer in one hand, the remote in the other. If we bore him for *one* second, we've lost him.

Talk about words that *every* writer should live by...

Rather than, as in so many fields, people jealously guarding their power and expertise, these guys were eager to pass such information along to me. They *wanted* to teach, to help. *Man*, was I delighted to absorb it!

I was being paid to *learn*. Again, the reason for their generosity: simple self-interest. The small staffs of most TV series were rarely able to write all twenty-two yearly episodes in-house. They had no choice but to employ a few freelancers like myself. Because of the Writers Guild contract, the writer could only be asked for two drafts of the story outline, and two of the teleplay. After that, it was in the staffers' court. Ergo, it was clearly to *their* benefit to hold the freelance writer's hand. To guide and nursemaid the process so that, when they had to take over and begin their final tweaks, the script wouldn't require a rewrite from page one.

The *Wonder Woman* episode was fun and, as with each of the other scripts, a stretch for me to write. And yes, part of me was continuing to furtively glance over my shoulder, more than half-certain they were going to catch on that I was faking it. Wondering why the hell it was taking them so long to figure it out. I mean – it was sure as hell obvious to *me*.

This self-doubt continued for a while, partly because I was not yet aware of how much I actually understood about the form. It was also fueled by my surprising, fluke-seeming, relatively quick acceptance as a professional. Gradually however, it did begin to sink in: maybe they *weren't* going to discover that I was a fraud! Which was very tentatively followed by the realization that during this sneaky apprenticeship, I had *learned* how to write reasonably well. Maybe not art, but craft. Though I must make it clear that getting to the place where I regarded myself as a *real* writer – whatever that implies – took a *much* longer time.

For what it's worth – arriving at that point did *not* and will *never* include taking *myself* seriously – what I will always think of as *The Ernest Hemingway Syndrome*.

Also, and amusingly *not* incidental, that teleplay, titled *Death in Disguise*, turned out to be – until *Murder, She Wrote* – residual-wise, one of my most enduring projects. Not, I'm sure, because it was so artfully-written. Rather, it was something few of us understood about the long-term appeal of that Linda Carter vehicle. *Wonder Woman* was – in the guise of just another run-and-jump adventure series – a superbly executed prime-time Tits-and-Ass Show.

Sometimes it *was* possible to sneak stuff past 'em…

In another out-of-the-blue moment – at least it seemed so to me – I was hired as part of the writing team on a Pat Boone comedy/variety special.

My most vivid memory of that gig wasn't the hoot of meeting/schmoozing guest-star George Burns, and writing a line or two for him (*certainly* no small thing). Rather, it was a moment in the office of the show's producers, a couple of very wry fellows, Bernie Rothman and Jack Wohl.

In some throwaway conversational context, the topic of comedy – and its sources – had come up. Bernie remarked on the accepted truism that with few exceptions – he gave a deferential wave at me – it seemed that funny material was almost solely conceived and written by Jews. To which I replied: "Hey, I'm three-quarters Jewish."

Bernie anxiously glanced toward the door, then at me: "Shh! Forgodsake…" Then, hushed, mock-sneaky, he confided: "…*You're* the token *goy!*"

Soon after that, Reyn Parke and I sold another *Quincy* episode premise, but we were cut off at story. A not-uncommon happening in series, and for that matter in movie development, wherein an idea that seems to work when pitched proves less-so when fleshed out into scenes and arcs. Or, sometimes, after expanding to story-outline form, it turns to be too similar to one that's already been done. Happily, I soon learned that such aborted projects were rarely counted as black marks.

Concurrently, sensing that writing wasn't really his game, Reyn enrolled in a real estate course and went on to a very successful career in that field.

Through my other networking contacts, I quite unexpectedly, and *very* happily, found the opportunity to get my personal, editorial-type rocks off, via a major TV network.

I was invited to pitch script ideas for a CBS dramatic series titled *Kaz*. An entertaining, witty lawyer show starring the wonderful comic-actor Ron Leibman, it lasted only one season. But my experience with it demonstrated that in commercial television it was and is possible for *even* a freelance writer to make a *markedly* personal statement. Albeit, as you'll see, somewhat deviously.

In *Kaz*, Leibman portrayed a former thief who became an attorney while in prison, sued, and secured his own freedom. He's hired by a prestigious law firm whose patrician boss, played by the appropriately-cast Patrick O'Neal, disdainfully regards Kaz as their low-end poster boy. He's relegated to handling pro bono cases the firm accepts in order to make them look like regular guys. Instead, Kaz's maverick independence, wit and unwillingness to play their game often created problems. Entertaining ones.

None of the story-notions I ran past Producers Sam Rolfe and Marc Merson struck the necessary sparks. But, out of the easy give-and-take fairly typical of such sessions, we began to kick around other ideas. One of them, based on a topic much in the news at that time, evolved into a premise. Kaz would defend a battered wife accused of murdering her abusive husband.

In fact, such incidents had recently resulted in the convictions of several women who had been sentenced to life in prison. Though I was only peripherally aware of it, their situations, and the issue in general were creating a wave of controversy. Some people were demanding the death-penalty, while others, asserting that these women were essentially victims themselves, were campaigning for lighter sentences. I was immediately intrigued by the subject, and how the character played by Leibman would fit in. The Showrunners supplied me with an armful of research and reportage to look at over the weekend. Based on the material – if I found it interesting – I was to go forward with a story-outline.

Next morning, to my surprise, "interesting" instantly became "involving." The stuff I read *totally* pissed me off. First, there was the clear indication in the Justice System of a pro-male/anti-female bias. Moreover, in redneck country, prosecutors' general reluctance to regard wife-beaters as criminals, not so subtly placed the onus on their victims. While the psychology positing that most of these women felt they deserved the abuse was arguably valid, they were still victims, dammit!

So, on Monday I told Marc and Sam how I'd been struck by the research and, yes, I would love to write the episode. "But on one condition. We stack it so that the killing is clearly premeditated – *not* a mid-beating act of self-defense – and she's prosecuted for first-degree murder. And then Kaz wins the woman's acquittal. Because the message I want to send to – youknow – these women – but *especially* to the pricks who beat them – is 'watch it pal, because your wife *can* kill you for that – *and* get away with it.'"

I kind of held my breath, entirely aware that while using movies as such a platform was fairly common even then, except for *Quincy*, I knew it was rare in series TV. This, comparably, was *far* more overt, as well as intended to please me rather than the show's star. Happily, as demonstrated by the series work of Oliver Stone, Aaron Sorkin, Dick Wolf and others, that of course has changed. But in running it past Sam and Marc I more than half-expected they'd tell me, the lowly, presumptuous freelancer, to fuck off.

Instead, I still treasure their reactions, which came with no hesitation: "Great!" Better, Marc quickly added: "Yeah! And we just won't tell CBS about it."

They didn't. Writing the episode was very satisfying, the production was extremely effective, and its broadcast generated thousands of pieces of enthusiastic mail from women, and from advocacy groups, several of which requested copies of the script. While its actual effect on the problem is unknowable, and likely negligible-to-none, it did teach me a heartening, valuable lesson. As fiction writers we can at least *try* to make a difference via the mass-media – and, sometimes there are even people who aren't afraid to help us do so.

At about this time, to my pleasurable surprise, the colorful Dick Brooks, from my *Pacific Stars & Stripes* days, re-entered my orbit. Dick had decided to move to California. Actually, it was his second re-appearance. Following Tokyo, we'd lost touch for a few years – until one startling moment in the 1960's when he surfaced in the Grand Ballroom of Manhattan's Plaza Hotel, in *very* unexpected company.

The occasion was the *New York Daily News-Chicago Tribune Syndicate* Cocktail Party, held annually during *Newspaper Week*. An afternoon affair, it was attended by probably three thousand of New York's hippest and most beautiful, as well as by a few more ordinary types who, like myself, were somehow connected enough to be invited. Crowded cheek-by-jowl in the well of this large, elegant room were just about every celebrity in the city that day. All the top Broadway performers, visiting movie stars, big-time authors, cartoonists, columnists – luminaries on the order of Captain Eddie Rickenbacker – you name them, were present. So, as one can imagine, it took someone *seriously* major to attract any special attention.

Into the midst of this scene, just such an individual made his entrance – and absolutely stopped conversation. All six thousand eyes turned to the entry doors at the side of the ballroom, staring at one of the three people who had just arrived – the fabled head of 20th Century Fox, Darryl F. Zanuck, cigar in hand, doing what for him was his effortless impression of *The Guy Who Owned The Place*.

On one of his arms was his knockout bimbo-of-the-moment.

On the other, to my boggled astonishment: my irrepressible friend, Dick Brooks.

Quickly cornering Dick, I was delighted – and *very* impressed – to learn he'd become Fox's Director of Publicity. We reconnected, and I continued to see him and his witty wife, Judy, socially in Manhattan – right up until Holly and I moved to Malibu. During that time, Zanuck retired and Dick became a successful freelance film publicist.

There in California, Brooks phoned us one day to announce that he was in Los Angeles, getting himself situated before bringing his family out from New York. Holly and I immediately invited him to our home, and that evening over dinner our always entertaining friend told us a captivating story. It was about two rather remarkable guys he was getting to know. They owned the motel on Sunset Boulevard at which he was staying.

These innkeepers, learning Brooks was in 'the business,' had made the assumption that he was *the* Richard Brooks, the Academy Award-winning film director/writer. Before Dick could deny it, the pair eagerly confided that they had a story that would make a terrific movie.

Now that part, in Tinseltown, is hardly unusual – *any*body within 100 miles of LA has several such properties, frequently in the form of completed screenplays that they just happen to have on their person. Today in fact, it often seems that, across the US nearly everyone *else* has at least one. Most of course are terrible.

But, as Dick related it to Holly and me, the hilarious yarn these fellows shared with him sounded, if true, like it had *genuine* possibilities. Sufficiently that, once they got into it, Dick had quickly opted to allow them to continue believing he'd been the director/screenwriter of such memorable films as *Elmer Gantry* and *Cat on a Hot Tin Roof.* Moreover, Brooks, who was not a writer (except for PR blurbs), gleefully confided to us that he'd told them of this 'bigtime' screenwriter he wanted to bring on board. Me.

Fascinated by Dick's telling of their outrageous story, though sharing with him some doubts about its veracity, I figured what the hell, and agreed to play his game. Several days later, he and I met with these fellows at the hotel, with a tape recorder running as we listened to their colorful, almost two-hour account of their adventure. I was blown away.

The pair, both in their forties, were smalltime, not-all-that-successful East Coast con artists who, down to their last few dollars, had come up with a goofy-but-brilliant idea for what proved to be one of the *great* scams. A scheme in which they were *handed* – for *no* cash and little risk – *ownership* of choice Manhattan and Miami Beach real estate – worth more than *$30 million* – at *1973 prices*! Today of course the figure would be exponentially higher. Among the properties, New York City's then-third largest hotel, the *Taft*!

A nice additional touch: even their names sounded like the creations of first-rate comedy writers: Federbush and Mason. *Plus* the fact that neither were astute enough to check out Dick's identity, nor my credits, said a *lot* about *their* smarts. As well as those of the system-gamers, devious bean-counters and tycoons *they* so easily scammed, all of them hoist by their own greedy petards. *All* of it admittedly much easier to get away with back in that pre-internet era.

Even better, research confirmed that their story was *true*!

In short, a couple of affable schleps who beat the system, their feat oddly never fully chronicled in *The New York Times*, *The Wall Street Journal* or, for that matter, by *anyone*. It struck me then – and still does – as a *wonderful* hook.

My attorney, Skip Brittenham, drew up a contract whereby Federbush and Mason would grant us, for no upfront money, the screen rights to their story. It also specified that the pair would see not a penny until a movie was produced, and then only a tiny percentage. As Skip handed me the agreement, he grinned: "These guys'll have to be out of their goddam minds to sign this."

They signed.

I wrote a brief treatment, into which I injected some badly-needed jeopardy (in real-life they'd gotten away with it *far* too easily), and began shopping *The Great Urban Renewal Caper* among my still-limited contacts. Though the property never went beyond that, it was definitely not a waste of my time. It opened some new doors for me, generating the interest of a few more players who asked to see my other projects.

Meanwhile, Dick Brooks settled in Beverly Hills, where, after moving Judy and their kids west, he engineered a PR stunt that's worth recounting as one of those only-in-Hollywood happenings.

Dick wangled a freelance publicity assignment from Fox, to get the word out about their hot new, just released feature, *The Omen*. Handed $4,000 to spend any way he saw fit, including hanging onto any or all of it for his fee, Dick regarded it as a major opportunity to trumpet his arrival in town, so he got 'creative.'

Aware that the symbol of three numeral sixes would become vitally associated with the movie, Brooks opted to stage an *event*. His plan, concocted with his customary brio, was to spend the *entire* $4000 on a skywriter who would place three gigantic vapor-sixes in the sky above Los Angeles.

Seduced by his own enthusiasm, Dick never questioned his *certainty* that local TV stations would eagerly cover it as a news story, thus providing many thousands of dollars' worth of free advertising. Exuberant, he booked the flyer to do the deed at an opportune midday moment for local coverage. 45 minutes before it was to happen, he confidently, excitedly began to alert each of the TV news outlets about his Big Show.

But, instead of the 'Wow!' reactions he'd expected, to Dick's dismay – followed quickly by despair – the broadcasters were unanimously, massively uninterested.

Unable to fathom their lack of vision, but desperate to cut his losses, Dick frantically attempted to cancel the skywriter. But it was too late. The plane was in the air, the deal done. So, a short time later he glumly watched the huge white-smoky numerals appear in the cloudless blue. Within a few minutes, he saw them dissipate on the wind – along with Fox's money, and his dream of a major self-promotional score.

Except that, yes, this *was* Hollywood. And – at least one person noticed them.

As it turned out, The Right One.

A man in Beverly Hills exited his home and, about to climb into his car, for no reason in particular glanced skyward *just* as, thousands of feet above, the third 6 was being formed. This man was instantly, *truly* impressed.

Largely because he happened to be Richard Donner, the director of *The Omen*. Rushing back into his house, Donner excitedly phoned a top executive at Fox, lavishing praise on him and the company for their *brilliant* publicity gag.

Next day, Fox awarded Brooks a $2,500 bonus. It was pure Dick Brooks, and *pure* La-La Land.

Not long after I'd co-written the *Chico and The Man* script with Bill Larkin, I had the joy of experiencing another incredible example of such *unique-to-Tinseltown* serendipity. One which all these years later continues to resonate.

One evening in February, 1978, Holly and I had viewed the latest episode of *All in the Family* and found it even more impressive than the high level usually maintained by the show. It was a funny/touching piece about Archie's brother coming back into his life, and their baggage-laden relationship. Archie had, for a number of typically biased, judgmental, Bunker-esque reasons, disapproved of him for years. Far beyond unacceptable to Archie, the brother had married and divorced several times. But Archie's major issue, which emerged gradually, was a deeply personal, long-felt resentment. Their late father had owned a prized pocket-watch that Archie coveted, believed he deserved, and fully expected to inherit. Instead, confirming Archie's belief that their Dad unfairly favored his other son, nearing his death he'd bestowed the watch on the brother.

In the episode's lovely button-scene, the brother presents the timepiece to a surprised Archie, explaining that he's about to return to St. Louis, where he'll undergo major heart surgery, which he may not survive. The brother exits and, cutting to black on a close-up of the speechless, emotionally conflicted Archie, it was comedy at its very best.

I phoned Mort Lachman the following morning, enthusiastically praising him, Director Paul Bogart and Writers Larry Rhine and Mel Tolkien for the show. Mort's generous response, after thanking me: "Hey, come up with another 'brother' story, and give me a call."

So, several days later I rang him up with a brief pitch: "His brother survives the surgery, and invites Archie to St. Louis to be Best Man at his wedding. And when Archie arrives, he discovers the bride-to-be is this sexy seventeen year-old Candy-Striper who'd nursed his brother back to health."

Mort's instantaneous response was even shorter: "Nice. Lemme put my assistant on so you can dictate it to him."

That was my entire contribution to the script for *The Return of Archie's Brother*, which aired the following season. I was paid WGA scale for the story, onscreen credit for which I shared with Bob Schiller and Bob Weiskopf (aka: '*The Two Bobs*'). They wrote the excellent teleplay, again beautifully directed by Paul Bogart.

Though I did not put a *single* word on paper, thanks again to the Writers Guild, I have over the years been paid thousands of dollars more in residuals for that essentially one-line idea.

I mean, you've *gotta* love a business that rewards creativity in that way…

This anecdote, aside from its validation of belonging to a union, especially one as wonderful as the WGA, also contains a lesson about the essence of a good pitch: if you're doing it right, the listener involuntarily begins writing the story in his or her head. As in this case, because most of us 'know' Archie Bunker, we instantly begin to picture, and smile at, his predictable, funny reactions to the setup.

Since those and other TV gigs were not quite yet adding up to steady employment, I continued to surreptitiously draw advertising spots for Harry Volk, though needing that revenue less and less. While I was elated by the growing number of TV scriptwriting assignments, I began to experience inward flashes of fear that, like my earlier career, this one might become easy, losing its challenges.

Was I ever *wrong*!

In no small part because I became aware – gradually – of several *very* welcome phenomena that have stayed with me. Among them: the more I write, the *more* daunting it becomes. Because the more I learn about the craft, the form, the higher my standards, the more I *demand* of myself.

Another, a pattern that started early, was 'secret' bar-raising (kept-to-myself, though often confided to Holly): choosing topics, nuances or areas in which I'd never tested myself.

I continue to be delighted that I was wrong. The better I become as a writer, the better I *know* I *must* become.

At around that time, life at home began to change somewhat, and *very* happily so. Wylie and Brooke had both been attending school for several years and, to Holly's and my delight, were thriving. We were enormously pleased for my oldest daughter, Suzy, who meanwhile, back in Virginia, graduated from Southern Seminary Junior College, with a certificate in Early Childhood Education. Simultaneously, her sister, Lauren, finished high school. Excited, as were we, both came west. Suzy, to find employment, and Lauren to enter college.

Lauren had since very early childhood demonstrated an extraordinary talent – and passion – for drawing and painting. A year earlier, during a visit to explore local colleges, we'd taken her on a tour of the UCLA campus. She had instantly fallen in love with the place, and particularly with the Art Curriculum. Both stayed with us for a short time, until finding lodging for themselves. Lauren moved into a Westwood campus dormitory, while Suzy rented an apartment near the beach in Venice, and went to work as a receptionist for a physician. She augmented that with babysitting an 8 year-old boy in the Hollywood Hills, and helping with his homework while his single mom worked evenings.

I was hugely proud and thrilled to see – up close – what lovely, together young women Nancy's and my daughters had become. But more than that, it made me newly appreciate my ongoing fatherhood experience. The exquisite pleasure of seeing and *savoring*, day-by-day, Wylie's and Brooke's development. And – as a still-breathtaking bonus – being with Holly.

A lovely time indeed. While there had been a few months during which I'd had difficulty maintaining the girls' child-support payments, I was by then feeling far more secure about my future in the entertainment business. Holly and I were enjoying an active and very stimulating social life. Thanks in no small way during that 'dinner-party' era to her culinary and hostessing gifts, her gorgeous presence and incredible genuineness. Which not incidentally included – and remarkably continues to this day – *no* makeup beyond *occasional* lipstick, and *never* a trip to a hairdresser.

We, along with Brooke and Wylie, *loved* Southern California – *and* living in Malibu. To the point where Holly and I decided it might be time to consider buying a home. We adored the place we were renting, but had been told by the landlord, going in, that he did not intend to sell – that he and his wife planned to eventually make it their permanent home. So, we began to look at other possibilities, most of them in or near Malibu. Problem was, we couldn't find anything within our price-range that we liked as much as our rental.

The clincher: that winter, Malibu suffered the heaviest rains in almost a century. It resulted in countless landslides, including several nearby. One of them caused the collapse of parts of the bluff on which our home stood, resulting in the total destruction of a house less than 300 feet from ours, and the near-loss of the one immediately nearer. But, we were delighted to note, not ours nor the lots on either side of us suffered *any* damage. A search of geological records at least partially explained why. The 'bench' upon which our house was built was part cut, and part fill. We were on cut.

So, I resolved to try convincing the owner to sell. To our very pleasant surprise, he was amenable, and we were able to negotiate an agreeable price. To Holly's and my – and our family's – enduring delight, we continue to reside in this amazing spot – the *only* place we've lived since departing New York City in 1973!

Soon, as Lila Garrett had predicted, following a few more miscellaneous teleplays, I was invited to go on staff for a TV series.

Actually, I received two offers. One was for a half-hour sitcom, the other for a one-hour drama. It proved to be another of those small-but-significant forks in my career-road – one that forced me to decide, on several levels, what I wanted from it.

Part of the mix in choosing my path was my already-cited aversion to, and admittedly limited talent for, writing jokes. But there were other reasons as well for my reluctance to pursue half-hour comedies. I had come to know, on a personal basis, a number of writers who worked pretty much exclusively in each of those forms. A few of them occasionally crossed over to the one-hour shows, but they were the exception. I'd observed some characteristics – about them, and about both types of shows – which were taking shape in my head, emerging smart-assedly (as is my nature) at about that time as '*The Tom Sawyer Theory of Series TV.*'

Essentially, and admittedly over-simplified (another of my penchant-faves), it eliminates the need for *so* many tedious '*on-the-other-hand*'s and gray-shadings. But with more than a little truth, for me it came down to the following, which made it a *lot* easier for me to decide to focus on the longer-form shows:

TV sitcom writing staffs tend to work far into the night. The staffers on one-hour dramas go home at reasonable hours, dine with their families and relate to their kids before bedtime.

There are reasons for this. For starters, TV sitcoms are mostly staffed-and-written by guilt-tormented Jews. Their guilt? While they're inarguably the source of most of the world's humor – which thus comes naturally – in my view, they're torn. There they are, making all that money, having all those laughs – without having become violinists or brain surgeons like their mothers wanted. So, I remain convinced, in a futile attempt expiate their shame, they write and rewrite until 2AM.

I did not then nor do I now believe that their shows improved markedly as a result of this, but, by denying themselves a life, it seemed to make these writers feel better.

On the other hand, most one-hour shows are written/staffed by gentiles who – unless they're Catholic – don't even understand the *concept* of guilt. I mean, you say that word to them, and they look at you blankly. So – they go home every evening and enjoy their families.

Now, I make no claim to being a stranger to guilt. Far from it. Even without any religious training, given my part-Jewish/part-Catholic heritage, I've long figured that my own relentless guilt-load has genetic roots.

Since, at that moment, I was *already* carrying more than enough for not having seen my daughters, Suzy and Lauren, grow up – I was *not* about to allow that to happen with Wylie and Brooke. So opting to go on staff at the one-hour show was an easy choice.

One I've *never* regretted.

With that decision, though I wouldn't fully appreciate it for a *long* time, I began a roll that would run for twenty years.

What fairly quickly *did* become obvious was that part of my cachet with the people on that side of the game was their confidence that I possessed this singular ability: to write funny for one-hour shows.

To be *their* in-house comedy-guy.

Hey, if that's what they wanted to believe…

As you may be inferring by now, to say that my new life was a blast is waaaay inadequate.

While, not-incidentally in contrast, going back to my previously postulated view, most of the successful comedy writers I knew professed *hatred* for the business.

Hey – wouldn't *you*, if you were involved in something that was just piling onto *your* guilt-burden?

For that first staff job, oddly, and I suppose ironically, I found myself to be one of four or five comedy writers, all of us hired on what was intended as a very, *very* lightweight *comedy*-drama about a bunch of teenage layabout surfers/musicians.

THIRTY
Additional Liberating, Self-and-Other-Type Revelations— and the Beat Does Indeed Continue

CALIFORNIA FEVER STARRED THE THEN twenty-one year-old Lorenzo Lamas, whose character ran a health-food stand in Malibu.

So ill-conceived was this turkey that it's *only* distinguishing accomplishment was that we gave Elizabeth McGovern one of her very first acting jobs. The moment we saw her, we *knew* she was truly extraordinary.

The sitcom series gig I'd been offered? Though I'm unable to recall its title, nor what it was about, be assured that it was even lamer than *Fever*, and shorter-lived.

But, lousy show or not, I found this first taste of insider-dom *really* exhilarating, both creatively and socially. It was a genuine delight to work closely, and daily, with other writers, all of whom had far more experience in the business than I, and to participate in the day-by-day of series production. Not unlike my time in Westport, lunches were a big part of the pleasure. Clever, colorful, entertaining people, the gags were sharp, fast and relentless.

One of those nothing-special midday meals turned quite unexpectedly into yet another keeper. It began when fellow-staffer/veteran gag-writer Barry Blitzer and I ventured into a Burbank sandwich shop a few blocks from our offices. We found ourselves standing at the counter just behind what seemed at first glance to be a nondescript pot-bellied type in a baseball cap, sweat-pants and soiled, too-short-to-hide-his-navel tee-shirt. This fellow was, at that moment, in his redneck-dialect, gently ragging on the elderly female customer alongside him.

Suddenly, Barry and I exchanged looks. Both of us had realized that the yokel was actually Jonathan Winters, famed comic-and-wildly-undisciplined-eccentric, playing as was his wont, one of his numerous comic character-creations. This one, a sort-of boorish, down-market everyman.

The lady had no idea of who he was, making her the ideal straight-person. Barry and I, along with the proprietor stifled our laughter until the woman, more than a bit addled, exited the store. Then Jonathan recognized Barry, who had written material for several of his shows. Barry introduced us, we chatted briefly until our sandwiches arrived, then Barry and I took them to a table, and that's when it became *truly* memorable.

Winters followed us, sat an adjacent table where, for the fifteen surreal minutes it took Barry and me to dine, he ad-libbed a five-handed Wild West saloon poker game, playing – hilariously – the entire cast: the greenhorn, the villain, the old-time cardsharp, et al. Included were dialects, near-fistfights, sounds of cards being shuffled and dealt, chips tossed into the pot, the snick of a .44 being cocked – all of it coming nonstop from Jonathan's mouth. Barry and I were almost on the floor.

During this, it became apparent, and funnier – from 'there he goes again'

274

eye-rolling glances and body language – that one of the two women lunching at a table near the window was his wife. When she finished and rose to leave, it was with the indulgent sigh of a mother to her small, unruly child: "Time to go, Jonathan…" Remaining in character, he stood and, as he was obediently backing out through the doorway, Winters was still playing to the room.

Even before Blitzer and I got back to the office, I'd had an exciting idea. My adman friend, Jim Levey, he of the deathless 'Schmuck, you've gotta be *in* Hollywood' advice, had recently followed it himself, relocating from New York. He was working with the CEO at Metromedia who, Jim had mentioned to me, was looking for a late-night, inexpensively producible piece to go up against the NBC and CBS powerhouses, *The Tonight Show*, and *The Late Show*.

The moment I reached my desk, I phoned Jim: "I've got it. A fake news show, with Jonathan Winters and a pretty girl as co-anchors, and Jonathan playing – in the film-clips of the day's gag-news stories – all the cops and little old ladies, the pols and lawyers and – and – the 'personalities' being interviewed."

Instantly onboard, Jim said he'd get back to me. Ten minutes later, he did. "How's ten tomorrow morning? The honcho wants to talk."

Again, that quick turnaround facet of the TV world that I was learning to love – which was, as they say, rapidly spoiling me rotten. Though this one took an unexpected, comically ironic twist.

Next morning, having filled in some blanks for the already enthusiastic Metromedia guy, he, Levey and I strolled through the studio's scene-docks, where we picked out elements that could be cheaply, quickly assembled to form a newsroom setting for the pilot-shoot. It was like a done deal.

Excited, I returned to my office, tracked down and phoned Jonathan Winters's manager, and enthusiastically ran the concept past him. His skeptical-to-blasé response should have given me a clue. a few minutes later he called back: "Jonathan doesn't want to do TV anymore."

End of story.

Discouraging? Not. As always, I *knew* it wasn't the last idea I would ever have.

Over and above the fun, the *California Fever* experience profited me in unexpected ways. From a veteran episodic TV writing team I'd invited in to pitch, a piece of advice: "Listen, in every episode you write, whatever the excuse – include lyrics for an original song, even if it's just youknow being performed in the background. Like in a nightclub scene, or a party, even someone listening to the radio at home or in his car. And then join ASCAP (American Society of Composers, Authors and Publishers), because on top of TV residuals for your script, you'll get music royalties."

I filed that one away – forgot it, really – for several years, until one day...

The step up to a staff-job marked a few more passages. One of them was financial. I finally gave up drawing advertising illustrations for my pal, Harry Volk – at least until the following year, when Harry was again – as always – ready to help me over a temporary dry couple of months. Essentially, I had succeeded in changing careers. Again.

But probably the most telling part of my initiation to being on staff was for me the altered self-perspective. The experience of working cheek-by-jowl on an everyday basis with other, more experienced writers was revelatory in that by the time *Fever* was cancelled, so were a lot of my self-doubts. Oh – I had no delusions about my own creative capabilities or potential being in any way gigantic, but I did come to understand that the standards I had imagined for *real* professionals were largely just that – imaginary. Fumbling, being unsure of how to handle a scene, or an entire episode, seemed to go with the territory. Basically I was beginning to gain a more realistic sense of where and on what levels I fit into the scheme. It was encouraging.

Similarly comforting/enabling was the sense that the business did not exact penalties for actually *having* some talent. At least none that I detected.

Which in turn eventually led me to a somewhat cautionary observation that I've passed along to numerous people aspiring to break into Hollywood – particularly as writers, though it applies to other areas as well: given the earlier referenced highly driven quality of people in the mass-entertainment business, wannabes should *know* that their success will be less-threatened by those with larger talents, than by those who are more motivated – individuals who simply *want* it worse than they do.

THIRTY-ONE
More Pilots—
and Special Moments

DURING MY FOUR-MONTH STAFF GIG on *California Fever* – given the show's concept it's almost impossible to believe it lasted that long – I was moved to resurrect and rework an old series idea. It was for a WWII one-hour drama concocted several years back by Reyn Parke and me. We'd never pitched it at the networks because the producers we'd run it past had felt, probably correctly, that WWII wasn't marketable at the time. But I had sensed that, with the broadcast a little more than a year earlier of the acclaimed, widely-viewed *Holocaust* miniseries, things might have changed.

Over dinner one evening, I described the project to Lila Garrett, who responded with immediate enthusiasm, and even more when, the next day,

279

I gave her the 'leave-behind' pages. *Cody's War* would take place in 1944, its primary setting a U.S. Army Forward Field Hospital housed in a battle-scarred French chateau in Normandy. Cody, the head surgeon/chest-cutter, was this romantic/heroic type with an eye-patch, his staff consisting of Americans, Brits and a few natives – of both sexes. Adjacent to the chateau was a little village with an Anthony Quinn-type mayor. His son was in the Resistance, and his zaftig daughter waited on tables in the local café. A few kilometers east there was this more-or-less static battle-line between the Americans and the Germans who, during the course of the series would occasionally – and temporarily – retake the town and the chateau.

It had a lot of *stuff* going for it. Life/death, medical, guy/girl, combat, Yanks, Brits, French, Nazis, the works. An exciting, solidly commercial concept, Lila instantly decided it was a show CBS would love. I told her of Reyn's co-creator status, and she assured me that if the show got on the air, Reyn would receive appropriate credit and a financial share – but that since he was no longer active in the business, it would be better to exclude his name at that point.

So, with Ms. Garrett and her agent, the elegant, dignified Roland Perkins at my side, we took it to CBS. When I finished my two-or-three minute pitch, which wasn't a whole lot more detailed than the above, Kim LeMasters, the guy who made the decisions, said he *really* liked the idea. But... "The thing is, we've already got a coupla World War II series in development for next season, so I'm gonna have to pass."

Before Lila and Roland could rise to leave, I asked Kim if he'd mind telling us what the other shows were about.

"Sure. One's about the Home Front, and the other's about the war in the Pacific. Youknow – against the Japanese."

Upon years-later reflection, I still don't know where in hell my next remarks came from, but again, as Lila and her agent prepared to stand, I went for it: "Listen, Kim, have you got about five minutes? Because I'd like to explain World War II to you."

Kim, who was clearly too young to have been born before the end of that war, grinned and told me to go ahead. With Lila and Roland looking at me as if I'd lost it, I began.

I began by recounting for him the comic-book editor's admonition to me about the necessity for attractive heavies. Then, I added: "Kim, that's why the war against the Japanese isn't commercial. I mean as a TV show, or even a movie, nobody cares about it – because the enemy was this bunch of unattractive little guys in crappy uniforms…"

Now you have to understand that the network – on Kim's advice – had already committed to at least $100,000 in scripts and rewrites on the topic. I could almost hear Lila groaning, but I plunged ahead. *"But –* the war against the Germans, that's another story. I mean how can you top this tall, blond, blue-eyed, gorgeous guy – in an SS uniform? This really cool combination of pure evil – and beauty. It's why shows about the Holocaust and World War II in Europe keep getting made, and pull big numbers – but you don't see a lotta blockbusters about the war in the Pacific…"

Silence.

Which I milked for a moment before adding my somewhat tasteless-but-true, almost-button: "Otherwise, how do you explain why half the Jews in New York and Beverly Hills drive Mercedes Benzes…?" There was an uneasy cough from Lila, throat-clearing by Roland, and an awkward grin from Kim that I read as 'where the hell is *this* going?'

I finished, attributing it – truthfully – to my New York shrink's response when I'd questioned him several years previously about this apparent anomaly. "It's this very common psychological phenomenon – known as 'identifying with the aggressor.' The thing is, a part of 'em would really like to dress up in one of those black SS uniforms, only that's not socially acceptable. But – driving a Mercedes…"

LeMasters laughed, which gave my companions permission to *sort of* laugh, though theirs was markedly less easy. We rose to leave, thanked Kim for his time, said our goodbyes and exited.

Less than a minute later the three of us were in the reception area. Both Lila and Roland started to speak but, knowing what they were about to say,

I tried to head them off: "Look – look, you're right. I've gotta learn to watch what I---" I was stopped by their eyes, which had shifted to something beyond my shoulder. I turned – and saw Kim, leaning out of his doorway. Smiling. He waved a hand: "Go ahead. Write it."

The moral? Once in a while speaking the truth *won't* result in your being taken outside and shot.

Just don't count on it.

My pilot teleplay was not filmed. Nor were the network's other two WW II projects greenlighted. But the script for *Cody's War*, which was helped by some passionate input from Ms. Garrett, got me a *lot* of other work. Due to my realistically limited expectations, I was not particularly disappointed that it didn't go forward as a series. But – I *had* written a show I would have watched and enjoyed, and I had done it *my* way.

An amusing fact about Mercedes Benzes and television of that era: late model automobiles had, for a long time, been routinely loaned by car manufacturers or distributors to studios producing movies and/or series TV. It's a form of product-placement – inexpensive free advertising for them, and budget-friendly for the studios. Back in the late nineteen-seventies/early eighties, on action-adventure and cop shows, just as routinely, the Bad Guy's vehicle of choice had become, almost invariably, a power-and-evil-symbolic shiny new Mercedes Benz.

Until one day it dawned on the suits at MB North America that TV was sending a not-all-that positive message: their cars were favored by murderers, mobsters, swindlers and master criminals. That's when they placed Hollywood on notice that henceforth Mercedes would provide free product *only* if the producers *guaranteed* that their cars would *not* be driven by Heavies, but rather by the Good Guys.

One afternoon, as I was finishing the *Cody's War* pilot, I experienced another first. My agent phoned to tell me he'd been contacted by a producer officed at Fox who wanted me to write a pilot!

My mind was nearly blown by the fact that I'd already gotten to that place. I mean 'a producer at Fox wants *me* to…?' Someone I don't even know? Before I could begin asking the rush of 'why me?' questions – hell, almost before I was finished gasping, he identified the producer as Lin Bolen.

"Who?"

My response seemed to surprise him, but instead of putting me down for not knowing, he patiently filled me in with some intriguing background. "Okay, Tommy, she's one of the toughest broads in the business. She used to be head of NBC's Daytime Programming. She's a legend, forgodsake. I mean – Paddy Chayevksy, when he wrote *Network*, he modeled the Faye Dunaway character after Lin. Oh, and---"

"Wow! So---"

"…and for what it's worth, she talks like a truck driver."

"So – how did she hear about *me*?"

"Damned if I know. Anyway, two o'clock tomorrow…"

Ho-ly shit!

Despite the buildup, I wasn't quite ready for the woman who greeted me the following afternoon. Or for her surroundings. Welcoming me warmly, Ms. Bolen quickly, amusedly explained the pedigree of her spacious, lavishly decorated-and-furnished suite. Occupying most of the top-floor in the two-story Stars' Dressing Room building, across from the studio commissary, it had been the domain of one-time Fox megastar Tyrone Power.

But the real attraction was Lin Bolen, one of the brightest, *sexiest* women I have *ever* met. She was pretty-though-not-gorgeous in the conventional sense, but nonetheless a knockout, irresistible, witty, profane, vibrantly alive, can't-take-your-eyes-off-her – a *Star*.

Quickly moving on to business, Lin informed me that she had this concept she'd already sold to ABC, a 90-minute pilot script-commitment. It was for a series about a stuffy Boston law firm that settles wills – the plot of which she proceeded to describe – in *remarkable* detail. Actually, though she'd only imagined it, so vivid and specific was her telling that it was more like a finished script she'd memorized. In what seemed like real-time, scene-by-scene terms, she bopped theatrically around as I watched, listened, enjoyed – finishing with: "So – what d'you think?"

I told her yes, I really liked the idea – and much of the story. "I mean, yeah! I'd love to write it for you – but I do have some suggestions…" I'd made a number of mental notes about how I felt the piece could be improved, which I then ran past her. She enthusiastically bought *all* of them, and told me to start writing.

As I headed for the parking structure, I tried to digest that one. *Another* revelation about how the business worked, it would be years before I ever asked – and learned – how this gig had happened.

But for the moment – *damn* – I was *still* fooling 'em…!

I had fun with, and was proud of the teleplay I wrote for Lin. *Higgins, Higgins & Holly* was never put into production, but she loved it, and as with my other scripts, it helped hone my skills. It also became an excellent sample.

I had the pleasure – and fun – of working with Lin a number of times. Best of all, though, we bonded, and became close friends. One evening 20-some years later, while Holly and I were dining with Lin and her late husband, Director Paul Wendkos, I asked a question that had been with me from our first meeting, but never voiced. "Lin, d'you happen to recall *how* we connected for that pilot? I mean – I was still the new kid on the block. Why *me*?"

Instantly, without having to grope for recall, Lin replied: "Oh, Marcy Carsey told me 'you've gotta work with Tom – he's the funniest writer in town.'"

I was astounded. Back then an already-successful TV series creator, Ms. Carsey eventually became famous for producing such hit series as *Roseanne*, *The Cosby Show*, *Cybill* and others. What makes the anecdote amazing – and worth repeating – is that my *sole* contact with Marcy was a meeting she'd asked for, which lasted *maybe* ten minutes. I had *never* written for her, and have *no* idea where *she'd* heard about me. But the part that *wowed* me: until Lin said it, I had not the *foggiest* knowledge that I had *ever* – in my *entire career* – been so regarded – by *any*one!

Her answer *still* stuns me, reconfirming the often weird, *entirely* out-of-one's-control ways that one can come to be perceived in Hollywood.

Once more – *ho-ly shit...*

THIRTY-TWO
Tasting—and *Savoring*—
Working "On the Lot"

IN MID-1980, I LANDED – WITH MIXED FEELINGS – my second staff-job. The most exciting part: it was my first experience of being officed at a studio. *B.J. and the Bear*, a one-hour series entering its third season, was housed at Universal. Less thrilling, but still challenging, was the show itself. Aimed primarily at children, and those with child-sized brains, *B.J.* was a comedy-drama. It was about the adventures of a guitar-strumming big-rig driver played by Greg Evigan, and his buddy, *the Bear*, a fun-loving chimp – who, as I quickly learned, was arguably the show's best actor.

    B.J., created and Executive-Produced by Glen A. Larson, had, like many series, been inspired by a successful theatrical movie. In this case, the source was *Smokey & the Bandit*, the 1977 hit starring Burt Reynolds. In hope of boosting the show's sagging ratings, NBC President Fred Silverman had decreed a number of changes for the coming year.

B.J.'s stories would no longer take place on the road somewhere in rural Middle America. Rather, they would be more cosmopolitan, with the hero based in Los Angeles, where – a la Snow White – he'd have seven co-drivers. But, Fred announced, instead of dwarfs (except, perhaps, mentally), *B.J.*'s helpers would henceforth consist of seven lady truckers. All of them were to be busty, zaftig bimbos in short-shorts and tight T-shirts, at least one of which, Silverman specified, was to be soaking wet at some point during each episode.

Not exactly the most stimulating material I'd encountered, the experience was, nonetheless, largely fun, furthering my education about writing. Also about interacting with my fellow participants in the TV series business. Including a progressively clearer perspective/take on where I stood – as in: compared to more and more of those I encountered, *maybe* I really *did* know what in hell I was doing?

Well, sort of, anyway...

From which I took increasing encouragement.

On the topic of writers' designated rankings on TV series, incidentally, a lot has changed. Back in the late 1970's and early 1980's, Producer, and Executive Producer were *very* exclusive, much-prized credits, each rarely given to more than one writer per series. Below them were Story Editors, which was the billing I received on *B.J.*, as I had on *Fever*. Then the most common staff credit, it was a more-or-less entry-level appellation. The average series usually had from two to four-or-five Story Editors, a job-description which, as I write this, has become virtually extinct.

Today, most weekly shows have that many Executive Producers, in part because such billing looks better on one's resume. Because of that value, management can sometimes leverage such labels in exchange for lower fees. Moreover, the Producer and Executive Producer tags have been further diminished, lumped/trumped among agents and on credit sheets – though not as of this time, onscreen – by the still, as of this writing, non-official term: 'Showrunner.'

One of the highlights of the *B.J.* gig was, as I would come to realize, typically, the *fun* of working 'on the lot' at a major studio. *California Fever* had been officed in a building near Warner Brothers, which was *not* the same. The pleasures of being based at a studio had been – tantalizingly – touted to me by writers I knew, but I did not expect it to be *such* a delicious and rewarding experience.

Best described as kind of [partially] grown-up campus life, it offered wonderful opportunities to hang out with one's peers. But almost as good for *this* star-struck kid was the chance to explore the numerous soundstages, the sets therein, and to wander the studio's huge, amazing back lot. That included its so-often seen New York streets, mid-America small-town, New England fishing village, etc., plus such shrine-like relics as the Bates Motel, from Hitchcock's classic, *Psycho*. It was like having a free pass, *every* day, to Magic-Land.

Additionally, the daily lunches-and-schmoozing in the commissary introduced me to one of the more comic career-challenges: successfully maintaining my lied-about age. Whenever the group conversation would turn to a topic from the past, I found that before my next comment, I had to rapidly page through its time-context and ask myself two quick questions.

Am I old enough to remember this?

Or, is it something my mother could (should) have told me about?

Another plus came from the people with whom I worked. One was Robert McCullough, a more experienced TV writer who'd been on the show the previous season, and whose scripting talent I respected. Bob's humorous 'seen it all' observations about the series – and many of the executives – were spot-on. The show also became the occasion of my hooking up with Janice Fishman, a wonderfully capable assistant with whom I continued to work – and laugh with, and depend on – each time I found myself at Universal during the next 17 years. Janice was feisty, awesomely efficient, a tough-minded, smart-mouth former New Yorker. She was fiercely independent, X-rayed through bullshit like few people I've known, had a firm fix on the location of buried bodies, and didn't mind that others knew she knew.

My involvement with *B.J.* resulted as well in a fortuitous near-miss. It afforded me the chance to *not* meet Glen Larson.

There are certain people who, from previews and other prior knowledge, we *know*, without ever encountering them, that we don't want to. Figures to whom we simply won't relate. In the Biz there have been a number of them. Glen was one.

I had been warned when I signed on about one of his compulsive traits. He did not *actively* run the show, had very little interaction with the people who did, and rarely appeared in the production offices. *But* – he was apt to summon the writers and several secretaries to his home for marathon weekend writing sessions under his guidance. This was an activity I badly did not want to become part of – first, since I didn't believe for a minute that the scripts would thus improve. Worse, because I regarded Larson as a colossally third-rate writer. I was far from alone in believing his success was due almost entirely to his prodigious ambition and superior abilities as a salesman.

But the *primary* reason, which I'd known well before I was hired, was that his home was less than a half-mile down the road from mine. I truly feared that if he *knew* I was that 'handy,' I'd be on constant call for such extracurricular nonsense.

Ergo, immediately upon hearing about his weekend conference-penchant, I stipulated to Showrunners Michael Sloan and Dick Lindheim that he *not* be told where I lived. It worked. To my relief, in the year that I was on the series, I found myself in the same room with Larson only once. For such a short time that – because I quickly exited, lest he might later recognize me on our road or in some Malibu hangout – we never actually met.

A few years later, Glen and I did have a brief face-to-face – because he wanted me to work on a new series of his at Fox. Skeptical from the moment my agent told me about it, following our talk, I was dispatched to a screening room to view the series pilot. I was to discuss it with him afterwards. The show, *Manimal*, was an abysmal concept about a guy who could morph into any kind of animal in order to fight crime. It was so achingly awful that I bailed after ten minutes and, without getting back to Larson, I simply went home. He apparently found someone else, and the show aired – incredibly – for eight episodes before being canceled.

Meanwhile, Jim Aubrey's feature-production plans for *Squeegee*, the window-washer comedy I'd written with Michael Heit, which Bill Persky was to direct, had receded into limbo. But I showed the Federbush-Mason real estate scam pages to Persky, who instantly fell in love with the project. A few days later, we pitched it to Paramount's head of movie development, Don Simpson.

Don bought the premise on the spot, and next day, Bill and I were writing a film treatment.

Damn! I was feeling more and more like I was in – a real part of – the business! Not quite yet taking anything for granted, but still…

Working with the veteran Persky was a pleasure, though as with so many Hollywood projects, our treatment was as far as it ever got. As another indicator, incidentally, of how the business has changed, in those days a treatment consisted of 25-40 pages. Today: 5-10 pages, max.

Following Paramount's pass, I tried repeatedly to peddle the story – in several variations – but despite generating serious interest several times, was unable to do so. A shame, because it remains one of the truly brilliant, funny cons.

I wrote a pair of scripts for *B.J. and the Bear* and, being on staff, enjoyed listening to freelancers' pitches, and commissioning several teleplays. Plus, following that, assisting in their development, and finally, the tweaking of second drafts, readying them for production.

Which by the way was not only pleasurable, but informative and reassuring. Particularly so because it confirmed my growing sense that, contrary to what I'd heard, there *wasn't* this huge pool of talent out there.

Also, taking more of a part than I'd had previously in the day-to-day aspects of production was exciting and continued to be educational. But, dampening the overall mood, everyone involved seemed to feel that the show was crap, and to take for granted that it was doomed.

Not at all surprisingly, the series *was* axed after the end of that season. Fred Silverman's tits-and-ass injections had failed to generate a larger audience. Again however, it had been as usual a *serious* delight for me, with a lot of laughs, many of them supplied by our co-star, the chimp. Singularly and especially on those occasions when, during some of our meetings, he was in the room with us, cavorting.

I suspect there aren't too many series writers whose experiences include *that.*

A short time after *B.J.*, I experienced still another Hollywood phenomenon up close – too close, actually: the full-of-himself super-agent, and his outsized ego. It was both enlightening and infuriatingly, unnecessarily costly.

I had met with Paul Witt and Tony Thomas, producers of the incredibly successful series, *Soap*, trying to sell them my next one-hour series premise, *The Investigators*. They had enthusiastically embraced my idea, and a pitch meeting was scheduled with Kim LeMasters at CBS. The concept centered on a Private Detective agency, which would include an ensemble cast of several PI's, a secretary, and multiple cases in work. While I did not for a moment believe it was an idea never tried before, at my agent's behest – and solid instincts – Paul and Tony had been my first targets. They suggested a few minor tweaks and, using only those with which I agreed, I amended my leave-behind pages.

Then, a day before the network meeting, Paul phoned: "Listen, Tom – about the CBS meeting, just so you know, Bill Haber's decided we're not settling for just a pilot script."

"I – I don't think I understand."

Adding to my already sinking feeling, Paul spelled it out. Their rep, the legendary co-founder of Creative Artists Agency, had determined that this was to be a yes-or-no film commitment pitch. If CBS liked the idea, they would *have* to agree not merely to the usual script deal, a risk at that time of roughly fifty-to-seventy-five K. Rather, they would have to guarantee to *shoot* the pilot as well, an additional gamble of three-to-four million dollars. At that time, fairly serious money.

I winced, then sucked it up: "Hey, I guess if you figure you've got that much muscle..." What I omitted – with full knowledge of Haber's awesome and justified reputation – as well as that of Witt-Thomas – was my fairly certain sense that, in truth, this was foolish-and-destructive arrogance. A Haber-throwing-his-weight-around conceit – and, because they were buying into it, theirs as well.

Thus, right from the top of the meeting next morning, I was trying to read Kim LeMasters, wondering if Haber has already laid it on him. To my relief, there was no such sign. He seemed, as always, comfortably ready to hear my latest pitch.

Okay – so far. Maybe Haber'll at least wait until I finish selling Kim the 'sizzle.'

While Paul and Tony did their prefatory number about how I had brought them this great concept, I noted Haber standing there adjusting his suitcoat sleeves. Then, Witt passed me the ball.

And *as* I was opening my mouth to speak, Haber, shooting his cuffs – and *me*, in my *foot* – interjected: "Oh, and we're *only* talking film commitment here."

The temperature in the room fell about 47 degrees. Kim threw him a long, silent look, then: "Jesus, Bill, even Aaron Spelling's willing to do pilot scripts."

What leapt to my mind was something my father-the-salesman had said more than once: 'You've gotta make 'em *want* the product before you tell 'em how much it'll cost.'

But no, we were talking Ego versus Smarts – and the score was clearly 0-10.

Bill Haber shook his head: "That's the deal, Kim."

Seeing Kim's expression become even harder as I launched into my number, I *knew* we were dead. This was further confirmed for me when the meeting ended with LeMasters coolly remarking that he'd have to think about it.

Two days later, I got the phone call from Paul, predictably informing me that Kim had indeed passed on the project. But Paul added an unanticipated punchline: "Look, Tony and Haber and I have been kicking this around, and – I'll be honest with you – we've agreed that this didn't work because – well – because of you."

"Me...? I don't think I---"

"What it is, you're basically, the weak link. So – what we wanta do is buy you out. We'll make you a deal wherein if we sell it, we'll---"

"Uh-uh, Paul. No goddam *way*. It's *my* concept!" Pissed off doesn't come close to describing my reaction, which I made no attempt to conceal. "...And as long as we're being honest, as far as I'm concerned the deal-breaker wasn't me, it was Haber insisting they must go to film. Jesus, you saw Kim's face when Bill laid it on him. I mean I couldn't believe you and Tony had gone along with him in the first---"

"Whoa – just a minute now. Who the hell d'you think you are to be questioning the judgment of the Premier agent in Hollywood?"

"No, Paul. I'm not *questioning*. He was *wrong*. That was a lousy choice and you know it. Anyway, I hope we can work together sometime."

Our conversation was over.

But the incident? Not quite...

Next day, via messenger, I was handed a written warning signed by Haber, telling me that I had better not pitch the project anywhere else. The reason, he spelled out: Witt-Thomas's input – though minor indeed – had effectively made them my co-authors.

I passed that one on, along with my rage, to my attorney, Roger Sherman, who promptly wrote them all a wonderful, memorable letter – copied to me – in which he led off by asking if none of them "had anything better to do than to try to fuck my client?"

In response, the following day I received a chilly-but-satisfying note –

without apology – from Haber, on behalf of himself, Paul and Tony. In it, they conceded that the property still belonged to me.

That of course was the last time I had any dealings with Witt, Thomas or Haber. In the case of the latter, especially, and though in many ways I respect his accomplishments, I have only gratitude.

A short time later, I had the pleasure of – and ego-boost from – being summoned to Manhattan to discuss writing a CBS comedy pilot for Grosso-Jacobson Productions.

My first meeting with CBS's New York suits was another of those '*me watching from a high corner of the room*' scenes. With more than a little wonder at my own chutzpah, *still* furtively regarding myself as one who hadn't *quite* made it all the way into the Club, I did my number about how, if they wanted jokes, they'd best find another writer.

Happily, and with *no* demurrers – at least none that I could hear – the CBS execs seemed more than willing to my go along with it, on my terms.

In hindsight, though, I know – and, on some levels understood then – that they *respected* such arrogance. Besides, they were already *committed*. I had just been flown coast-to-coast in First-Class (as mandated by the Writers Guild contract), limousine-ed at both ends, *and* they were quartering me in one of the best hotels in town.

In another way, however, I knew full well that I was still envelope-pushing, trying out my new muscles.

And – hey – what was the worst that could happen?

Over several days, I conferred about the show with the producers in their midtown offices, as well as over dinner and drinks with them at various New York watering-holes. Larry Jacobson was a very pleasant guy, and Sonny Grosso was a true legend, one of the great, fun, uniquely colorful characters I've *ever* had the pleasure of meeting.

Grosso had been, in his former-life, half of the team of NYPD Narcs portrayed in William Friedkin's great based-on-the-true-story movie, *The French Connection*. In it, Sonny was renamed 'Det. Buddy Russo,' and played by actor Roy Scheider, while Gene Hackman had the role of Sonny's partner, Eddie Egan, renamed 'Jimmy Doyle.' Actually, the real Sonny and Eddie played bit parts in the film.

Though Sonny had retired from the NYPD, he still packed a .357 Magnum revolver, stuffed prominently into the front-waistband of his trousers. For comfort (plus, I suspect, a bit of intimidation) when he'd sit down for meetings, he'd plunk the huge piece onto the desk or tabletop where, as you can imagine, it became this ominous presence.

Grosso and I had once met briefly in Malibu several years earlier, when an actress-friend, Patch MacKenzie, dropped by with him at our home one afternoon while Holly was out running errands. Our son, Wylie, about age eight or nine at the time, happened into the room, and I introduced them. Explaining to Wylie that he was in the presence of a famous detective, I got Sonny to display his weapon and badge. Impressed, Wylie soon exited, and we resumed chatting. Several minutes later, we realized *how* impressed.

Patch, Sonny and I became peripherally aware of, and looked up to see, at the far end of the room, a row of little boys. Wylie and four of his pals whom he'd apparently rushed out and rounded up, were standing side-by-side, silently – and clearly awed – observing our guest. Sonny good-naturedly repeated his badge-and-gun show.

Edgy, hip, a kind of classic New York Street-Italian, Sonny and Eddie Egan had notoriously been under investigation for years. They were prime suspects in the mysterious disappearance of the multi-million dollar *French Connection* heroin cache that, during the case, had vanished from the NYPD Evidence Room.

Since then, I learned from Jacobson, Sonny had, with understandable paranoia, handled all of his financial transactions in cash. But at the time of our East Coast meetings, because he was becoming an established TV and film producer, their accountants had recommended that he begin playing the game like regular people, establishing credit, bank accounts and the like.

Thus, as I arrived in Manhattan, Sonny happened to be in the process of buying his first automobile via installment payments – a new Cadillac which he was purchasing from a local dealership. Which led to a truly memorable incident.

We'd gathered for our initial meeting in Sonny's office, high up in the Time-Life Building on Sixth Avenue, and he'd just placed his gun on the desk when his secretary interrupted via the intercom. A bank officer, she announced, needed to talk to Sonny about his car loan.

Sonny put the guy on the speakerphone, and barked impatiently: "This is Grosso. Yeah…?"

The banker's monologue went something like this: "I'm looking at your credit app for the automobile purchase, Mr. Grosso, and your list of bank accounts…" The banker recited the names of three or four New York banks, and the amounts Sonny claimed were on deposit in each. The total came to more than $150,000.

"Yeah. So?"

"Mr. Grosso, we'll need those account numbers so we can---"

Sonny's totally in-character, sans-hesitation comeback line damned near put me on the floor, and *still* makes me smile: "None of your fuckin' business." Sonny jabbed at the button, ending the call.

I grinned when I learned several days later that he got his loan.

At about the same time that I began writing the script for Grosso-Jacobson, Bill Persky contacted me about my coming back to New York City a few months hence. He wanted me to be producer/head writer on a half-hour series he'd sold – also to CBS – a comedy cop show, to be shot on NY streets. Intrigued and, of course, flattered, before heading back to the West Coast, I met and discussed that one with the network people. I tentatively agreed to do the show – though with misgivings about returning to New York for what might be an extended period.

My mixed feelings came in part from a reluctance to spend a long time away from Wylie, Brooke, Holly and Malibu, as well as being put off by the aforementioned comedy-prospect of writing until wee-hours. I worried also that the geographic relocation would possibly be taking me out of Hollywood part of the game in which I felt I was finally getting established.

On the other hand, *running* a show…?

The pilot I wrote for Sonny and Larry was titled *The Television Hour*, and following – I later heard – a punch-up by a joke-specialist, the network dropped the project.

I debated the Persky/CBS deal through much of that summer, and when I received another offer – to go aboard a new CBS one-hour drama at 20th Century Fox, I grabbed it. Despite being only a story editor, rather than having the sought-after producer title I'd been promised on the New York show, I felt a lot better, staying in LA.

The series, executive produced by my friend Marc Merson and its creator, Jerry Ludwig, unexpectedly comprised *another* large chunk of my TV learning-curve.

On the face of it, the concept for *Jessica Novak* was solid – at that point, following *B.J.* and *Fever*, I wouldn't have taken the gig if I hadn't thought so. Jerry had traded on the popularity of the recent, very exciting thriller movie, *China Syndrome*. In it, Jane Fonda played a TV reporter covering a nuclear power plant meltdown. Jerry sold the network a weekly series featuring a similar female TV reporter and her two-man camera/sound crew.

It starred Helen Shaver, and though she, and Jerry's beautifully written pilot, were very effective, it quickly became apparent that the show wasn't going to last very long. The reasons?

One, a fatal glitch in the series' fundamental idea. In simple – you can't do nuclear meltdowns – or anything close – 22 times a year. But topping that – and this was new to me – a series about a reporter-protagonist who solves crimes on a weekly basis simply *does not work*.

While such characters can be, and have been, effective as feature movie one-shots – as in, besides *China Syndrome*, *All the President's Men* and others – those stories were about news people who, in the course of *doing their jobs*, uncovered criminal activity. But such goings on were an aberration, a deviation if you will, from their profession: *reporting*.

A reporter who's an *every-week detective*, a crime-solver and/or punisher of evildoers? Uh-uh. It *ain't* his mission. Audiences, no how matter forgiving, will start wondering why the hero's editor doesn't fire him, or why the cops don't tell him the investigation is not his business.

In short, viewers won't buy it because it rings so *false*, because *solving* crimes is *not* the journalist's job. *Writing* about them is. Even the real-life bad guys uncovered so notably by Woodward and Bernstein during Watergate were *then* dealt with and punished (some of them, anyway) by *law people*.

Ergo, with *Jessica Novak*, we were stuck with what I quickly learned was a predicament common to *any* weekly TV series featuring a reporter. If the show's arena is broader than soap-opera-ish people-to-people drama of the news organization itself, the lead character is doomed, *not* by the writers' choice, to devolve into an unattractive busybody.

Jessica Novak was cancelled after airing 3 or 4 episodes. Nonetheless, I had more fun, acquired some new friends, especially Jerry Ludwig, who shared a lot of my tastes in movies, reading and politics. Plus, I'd managed to remain in California.

I was learning that, as with so many other failed series, it was the concept, stupid! Thus unfixable. Which is, not incidentally, why the 'franchises' that consistently work for non-soap, *dramatic* series TV – are doctor, lawyer, cop, private detective, secret agent, rescue or fire person. Period. Reason? Because those jobs give their practitioners a *legitimate* right to interfere – *on a regular basis* – in other peoples' life-and-death problems.

It also afforded me another fascinating insight into the business, and choices made by the people in charge. It's something I continue to find remarkable: the networks *never* seem to get it. To this day, every few seasons one of them again develops and airs another reporter-who-solves-crimes series, which invariably dies within a few episodes. It's almost as if those executives of old, who learned it the hard way, decided to keep the information to themselves.

Or, could it be that – they *didn't* learn?

C'mon. No *way*.

I mean, these are bright, educated, *highly* qualified people – who wouldn't *have* those jobs unless they knew what they're doing.

Next…

THIRTY-THREE
Becoming the Hottest Guy in Town—for a Few Minutes, Anyway... And, a Couple of Ideas with Unexpected Legs

IN TRUTH, 'NEXT' TURNED OUT TO BE another major step in the continuously surprising phenomenon that had begun to sweep me along, that of being perceived in unaccountable, often mysterious ways.

It started with my phone ringing, one morning just after *Jessica Novak* had been pronounced deceased. The caller was Scott Siegler, Kim LeMasters' successor as drama series development chief at CBS: "Hey, Tom. Listen, we've got a pilot script here that – well, as is, it's dead-in-the-water. I was wondering if you might take a look at it, and let me know if you think you can fix it."

"Sure, Scott. I'd be delighted. Send it on over."

Scott had it messengered out to Malibu.

At that time, though fixing such scripts was not something I had *ever* claimed I could do, I did not wonder how or why Scott had decided to call *me*. Largely, I suppose, because of my tendency to regard pretty much *anything* that happened to me in the Biz as being the norm, beyond remarking on it to Holly, I gave it almost no thought. Until years later, actually, when, reflecting on *it* along with many other such incidents, I began to realize how *incredible* so *much* of it had been.

As said, nearly without my noticing.

The teleplay had been written by George Schenck and Frank Cardea. It – along with the series-concept – had obviously been bought by CBS because of the recent, phenomenal success of the first Indiana Jones movie, *Raiders of the Lost Ark*. Moreover, it contained a workable, solid-enough action/foreign intrigue setup. It was titled *Bring 'Em Back Alive*, which was the real-life commercial motto of famed 1930's adventurer/wild animal-trapper Frank Buck. The show was set in exotic 1939 Singapore, and peopled with colorful Far East rascals, many of whom – as in *Raiders* – were those ever-reliable Axis Bad Guys plotting WWII.

These last would be challenged by a fictitious, highly romanticized version of Mr. Buck, the classic intrepid jungle hero in pith helmet, riding breeches, boots and safari jacket. The episodes would feature tigers, chimps (again), and elephants. Rounding out the core human cast: a pretty blonde diplomatic attaché, plus an animal wrangler, and Frank's charismatic, aristocratic pal, the Sultan of Johore.

I gave it a quick read, and just as quickly saw how I could fix it. To make it funnier, faster, more hip and entertaining, the blonde spunkier, the Sultan and wrangler characters more lively, and involving them in a more audience-pleasing story. I love it when such things are so apparent – and more than that, I was excited by what I thought could be a fun show. Not deep, but something my teeth could, if not really *sink* into, at least manage a grip. A project I might even be proud of. Excited, I phoned Scott, told him so, and he was delighted. Within a few minutes my agent called to inform me that the deal – a very good one, indeed – had been struck. It included a substantial bonus if my rewrite resulted in the pilot being produced.

By the end of the week, I'd delivered my revised version of the teleplay. Scott Siegler said he was knocked out by my rewrite. A few days later I was even more elated to learn that the pilot episode was scheduled for production.

What I *never* expected was the near-instant fallout from their decision.

Next day, during another sunny afternoon in Malibu, I had an inspiration – an idea for a TV series that I found myself abruptly – and hurriedly – scribbling on a yellow legal pad. It was one of those rare, '*magic writing*' moments, as if I was taking dictation from somewhere outside of myself, racing to keep up with the words that were flooding into my head.

The whole process took about ten minutes, after which I laid my ballpoint pen on the desk, sat back to catch my breath, and then took the pad into the kitchen, where Holly was preparing supper. I asked her to read it and tell me what she thought. Several minutes later she found me pacing on the patio, and confirmed my own excitement. "I *love* it."

Less than a week later, Fox optioned *No Place to Run*.

The concept had been gestating for some time before I'd dashed off those first pages. I'd long been fascinated by Roy Huggins' remarkable hit TV series, *The Fugitive* (1963-67), which in turn owed its inspiration to Victor Hugo's *Les Miserables*. I was captivated by the dynamic that in my mind anyway, had made it work so well. Its protagonist, Dr. Richard Kimble, was not only running *from* something – he was running *to* something – not *just* to escape, but to achieve a really worthwhile *goal* – by proving *his* innocence in the murder of his wife, *and* catching the guilty party: the *One-armed Man*.

My variation on Hugo's and Huggins's notions: it was the saga of two young brothers, one teenage, the other just out of his teens, together on the run from mobsters and corrupt lawmen trying to kill them. The brothers' goal: to learn the identity of – and nail – Mr. Big, and to prove that they *hadn't* murdered their own parents.

What I could not have predicted was that this basic concept would acquire a life of its own. After Fox renewed, then allowed their second option to lapse, the rights reverted to me.

I sold the concept several years later – ironically, *again* to Fox. There, as you'll see, in yet another nothing-to-do-with-its-merits, *Only-in-La-La-Land* moment, its fate would be decided by the whim of a Major Player.

Eventually the premise evolved – with significant changes in protagonists and time-frame – into my second novel. Also featuring two young fugitives and titled *No Place to Run*, it's a thriller about what I regard as the truth behind 9/11.

The lesson learned – and relearned *so* many times: good ideas don't go away – they just have to wait for their moment(s).

Or, for *one's own.*

But – *before* I had even made that initial option deal for *No Place to Run*, before *Bring 'em Back Alive* was in the can, the *incredible*, heady wave that pilot-rewrite created for me had begun.

In fact - I would soon come to realize – from the *moment* the series pilot was greenlighted, word was out – *all over town* – that *I* had rescued the project! The buzz was augmented by CBS and Columbia Pictures Television – and along with it, *my* name became hotter and hotter!

Producers from *all* over the business were suddenly courting me to lock arms and pitch shows with them at the networks and studios! They were offering to hook me into series that, if sold, would star the likes of James Earl Jones, or football icon Joe Namath. I declined most of these projects because they struck me as less-than-intriguing, or I felt that I could contribute little or nothing to them. But the attention being paid was both hugely gratifying and *totally* unexpected.

By the time post-production was completed, things *really* gained momentum.

No small part of the show's high profile was due to its lavish, feature-film-caliber production values, under the first-rate hand of a veteran director. E.W.

Swackhammer was a guy who *knew* where the 'money scenes' were. *Bring 'em Back Alive*, which starred Bruce Boxleitner, was enthusiastically received by advertisers. CBS gave the series an instant 'go' for the coming season.

Plus, noise may also have been in part despite, or because of, the fact that ABC had on its schedule a similar, competing *Raiders*-rip-off show, *Tales of the Gold Monkey*. In any case, not only was *Bring 'Em Back Alive* one of the most talked-about-in-the-biz series of the new season, for my having saved the pilot script, and thus credited [by many] for it being picked up, I seemed to have become part of the conversation.

Perceptions...

All these years later, I *still* find it astounding.

In the brief interim before the *Bring 'Em Back Alive* series went into production, my friend, Lin Bolen asked me to do a rewrite of a pilot, titled *RSVP*, which she'd had scripted by someone else. I was happy to work with Lin again. Just as I finished *RSVP*, I was hired on the staff of *Bring 'em Back Alive*, this time as Executive Story Editor (another no-longer used credit, it was then an acronym for Head Writer). My first tasks were to hire staff-writers, commission scripts, and to write the initial regular episode teleplay. We were officed at Columbia, Schenck and Cardea running the series along with Executive Producers Larry Thompson and Jay Bernstein. One of the waaay more colorful characters I've ever encountered, Jay was wildly flamboyant, pistol-packing, a brandisher of elaborate-walking-sticks and, incidentally, Bruce Boxleitner's manager.

Bruce and the rest of the cast were fun, relatively temperament-free, and I was enjoying the work and its new challenges. Not least from the increased control afforded by my role – essentially, deciding what the *Bring 'em Back Alive* episodes should be about.

As scriptwriting and pre-production progressed, my own hot-streak continued, with additional requests for me to become part of more projects.

Enough of them were intriguing to me that on days when I had no meetings or other *Bring 'em Back Alive* responsibilities scheduled, I would be with this or that packager, pitching. Sometimes at one network in the morning and at another that same afternoon. Even, on one occasion, accompanying a different producer each time, taking *two* meetings on the *same* day with the same executive at CBS. *Despite* my cautioning both producers that such too-frequent exposure might be counterproductive for all of us.

I'm sure it was. But again, it was these guys' belief/hope that, augmenting whatever they were bringing to the table, *my* involvement – as *Superman-of-the-Moment* – might help make things happen for them. I figured I had very little to lose. Moreover, my agent assured me, since I had entered into a non-exclusive contract with Columbia, as long as I was fulfilling my duties there, I had *every* right to explore these other opportunities.

Bring 'em Back Alive began filming episodes, and things continued to go smoothly until an afternoon a few weeks into it. I was about to head for Malibu when Schenck and Cardea called me into their office. Their grave demeanor caught me off-guard. George spoke: "Tom, we've got a problem..." Off my look of curiosity, he continued: "...All these pitch meetings you're taking. That's got to stop."

"Why? I mean---?"

"We're not happy about it – and neither is the studio---"

"Hey, guys – it's no secret. And my deal here is---"

Frank joined in: "We know."

"Wait a minute. I *never* schedule anything that interferes with our show. D'you feel I'm – youknow – neglecting my work?"

"No. You're doing a great job. But we're not on the air yet – youknow with all the pressures that'll go with it."

Something about this remark didn't sit quite right, though at that moment I was unable to isolate it. "Hey, you have my word that I'll always put the show first."

George shook his head: "That's not enough."

"So – what're you telling me?"

"Basically, you'll have to revise your contract and become exclusive to the show, and to Columbia Pictures TV."

"Or...?"

"Or – you're out of here."

Frank nodded his agreement. "We hope you'll stay, but it's your call."

I digested this last for a moment, then: "I – I'll have to think about it."

"Sure. We'd like to have your answer tomorrow."

Suppressing a flare of anger, I acknowledged that I'd do so. But as I left their office and headed for my car, I knew that I needed to get past the unfocused resentment I felt, to *really* sort out my thoughts before cutting loose with any statement that might seem unjustified. *Or* bridge-burning.

I began by mentally reviewing what amounted to scorecard stats. Scott Siegler had brought me into this. He and CBS had insisted I be hired on the series, to write and oversee scripts. Scott seemed to have no difficulties about my non-exclusivity deal with Columbia.

I had set the tone for the series, and received *only* praise. We had teleplays ready to shoot, and others in the pipeline.

The network was *fully* aware that I was having pitch meetings. All of those were in the 'plus' column.

So – *why* were Frank and George and – according to them anyway, the studio – pushing this?

By the time I got home, I had acquired a clearer view which, after bouncing it off of Holly and then sleeping on it, became much sharper – and made me even angrier.

Arriving at the studio the following morning, I dialed up my calm, and went directly to George and Frank's office.

"Guys, I thought about it, and my answer is 'no.' I'm not willing to change my contract."

Following their glances at each other, I continued. "Look, you acknowledged that I haven't neglected any of my responsibilities. And I gave you my guarantee that I will not do so in the future. So – what you're actually saying – bottom-line – is that you don't believe I'll keep that promise. And I hafta tell you, that's *my* deal-breaker. There's no way I can go on working with people who don't trust me. So – as of now, I quit."

I turned and exited their office, sans regret, and not without some immediate, sweetly ironic satisfaction. That afternoon my agent called to inform me that I had just received a pilot-script assignment from Paramount.

Bring 'em Back Alive was cancelled after episode 16. While I would have liked to believe it was because of my absence, I suspect that the essential concept wasn't strong enough to sustain an audience, much less to have *two* similar shows competing. Its ABC clone, *Tales of the Gold Monkey*, was axed at season's end.

It was 1982, and I decided it was time for me to try catching up with the curve. I bought a computer. It's worthy of mention because of several marked changes it brought to my life, all of them positive, including a few that proved wildly unexpected.

I learned 'touch-typing' in high school, but I had rarely been able to compose anything longer than a brief letter on a typewriter. Typos, rewording, tweaking trial-and-error phrasing – all were simply too distracting when, in a sense, each keystroke was for me practically engraved in stone, there on that white sheet of paper. Veteran screenwriter-friend, Mort Lachman said he had the same problem. His way around it, he humorously explained, was to always compose his first-drafts on yellow paper. The color signifying its 'unofficial' status apparently freed him. I gave that routine a brief shot, but it didn't work for me, my misspellings and cross-outs continuing to interrupt my thought-flow.

In my case, I'd solved it by hand-lettering my scripts on yellow legal pads, using the same all-caps block-style I'd used in penciling dialogue balloons when laying out my long-ago comic-book pages. For my teleplays I used a ballpoint pen, often cutting x-ed out sections and scotch-taping the new material. These irregular-sized pages I would then give to a typist. Fortunately, a several doors away neighbor, Marj Larkin, did that work for me, expertly and promptly. But with computer word-processors, and features like spell-check and grammar-check, I began to sense that correcting mistakes and making changes might be far less annoying than was the case with typewriters.

I knew only a few writers who had made the switch, but beyond their enthusiasm, they were able to offer little or no knowledge of how their computers compared to or differed from others. So I began to read about the rapidly proliferating number of brands that were appearing. I checked reviews, and visited computer stores where I listened to sales pitches and asked questions. From all of that came a growing sense that a lot of the manufacturers were 'fly-by-night' operations that probably wouldn't last. Since I was anticipating longtime usage, I should choose a unit from a company that might last longer than the warranty, and still make replacement parts a few years down the line. Especially because the investment was then rather substantial: a computer and printer cost from $4K to around $5.5K. All of which made the decision fairly easy. The most solid company, thus not surprisingly the priciest computer: IBM.

My choice proved to be a near-instant boon – in several important ways. The first: as I was making the purchase at the IBM store in Beverly Hills, I asked the clerk if he could recommend someplace or someone who could teach me how to use it. He grinned and pointed to fellow a few yards distant "There's your guy." He hailed the young man, introduced us and explained that I needed help. On the spot I contracted for eight bi-weekly sessions, for which he would come to my home.

One minor downside, of which I quickly became aware before my first lesson: in that early period, script-formatting software programs did not yet exist. But on my instructor's first visit, upon my explaining the problem, he *immediately* solved it! In astonishing, dazzling fashion! Within minutes, using a then-feature of Microsoft Word called '*Style-Sheets,*' he created for me a homemade-but-totally professional TV/movie script formatter! Unsurpassed, really, until a few years ago by such software as Final Draft®.

As you can imagine, from that moment my output increased dramatically, its look impressive as hell.

That was but the beginning of the computer enabling me creatively to an extent I could *never* have imagined.

By then I was onto other things – far from least of which began unexpectedly one evening at the Shubert Theatre in West Los Angeles. The curtain had just fallen at the end of a performance of *Evita*. Applauding enthusiastically, I turned to Holly, who was as knocked out by the marvelous Rice/Weber show as I was, and I spoke words that I had *never*, until that moment, thought about. Oh, undoubtedly the topic must've crossed my mind on some unconscious, unaware-to-the-rest-of-my-head level – but the point is, I hadn't debated or otherwise considered it in words I could remember. They just – came. Surprising me even as I heard myself uttering them: "Y'know something – it's time to do this about Jack Kennedy."

Holly seemed to understand exactly what I was saying. She nodded, grinned: "You're right. Yeah…"

I quickly added: "And it's *gotta* be an opera."

Though neither she nor I could have known, with those statements I had begun a voyage of passion. Of *some* that I didn't know I had. Discoveries, and some abilities. An adventure full of swings from discouragement to fun to maddening frustration to profound joy to absolute fury and back, that would continue off and on for the next *eighteen* years. And – after a decade-long hiatus, again resume.

Driving home, Holly and I chatted briefly about the notion and, within a few miles had pretty much put it away. Things musical – except for enjoying them from the audience – were not my thing – and creatively *far* over my head.

But I was unable to quash the idea. It just kept on coming. By morning, I had a broad-stroke handle on what I wanted it to say, what it was – and wasn't – to be about. Actually, I'd awakened with a vision – a mental picture of the show, including a number of the scenes, one of them a *vivid* image of the ending. Plus the title: *JACK*.

Moreover, I *knew* that it would require the work of a major American composer. Strike that – *the* major composer. Leonard Bernstein.

I mean, if you're gonna fantasize – *go for it*!

It was unlike anything I'd *ever* experienced – an epiphany, actually. I realized even then that this *must* be what is meant by the expression 'pure inspiration.'

I saw other things that, in the then-nineteen years since John Kennedy's death I had never once considered. It was *apparent* for example, with the clarity of lightning against a night sky, that that day in November, 1963 had been far more of a dividing-line than I'd ever dreamt.

A line, incidentally that – as more time has passed – has only grown more vivid. Dividing our populace as *never* before. *Not* in positive ways.

In all honestly, I did not feel an acute sense of loss *until* that point.

So abruptly obvious in part because I found myself recounting the sorry collection of losers and fools who had followed him into the White House. With only a few exceptions, buffoons, tools/enablers of the military/industrial complex, paranoid crooks, fourth-rate actors, the works.

It was as if I'd suddenly found a new pair of eyeglasses, a fresh set of filters through which I was finally allowing myself to look at it. Processing what had happened, what we – our country – had come to in the wake of that afternoon in Dallas.

Still, as I hurriedly began to scribble notes, to at least semi-capture the rush of thoughts and ideas, I saw more forcibly than I'd noted the previous night that this medium was just – not – my – game.

Yet, I *still* couldn't *quite* bring myself to put it aside.

Not for a while, anyway…

Meanwhile, in what had by then become real life, my 'hot' streak seemed to have gained some evolutionary momentum. I was no longer quite as sought after to help pitch the concepts of others. But between the *RSVP* teleplay and the pre-sold gig for Paramount, *The Young Musketeers*, I'd been busy on the pilot-front.

A couple of not-exactly-thrilling premises, I did my best to turn them into vehicles I would have watched. Though everyone seemed pleased with my end-results, neither series was picked up for production. Nonetheless, my reputation, such as it was, not only did *not* suffer – it seemed to be morphing. My next gig marked the start of really fun cycle which included those so-

welcome elements of drama: edginess, mystery, questionable outcome…
What I came to think of as my 'rescuer' period.

Another out-of-one's-control perception thing.

It began when my agent told me to report to MGM on Monday morning, to work on a series that had already begun airing. What he did not explain was the *reason* I'd been hired – what was expected of me. Nor, oddly, did anyone else spell it out in so many words. Though within minutes of arriving at the studio, I got it.

The show's ratings were in the toilet. The original writing staff had been fired. In their place, in what would become the norm: myself and another usually more veteran writer I'd never met. Our assignment: save the series.

THIRTY-FOUR
The (Believed-to-Be) Series-Fixer—and Some Fun with Turkeys

ONTO WHAT HAD BECOME A PATTERN of unexpected career twists and swerves, often for reasons that at first I only dimly understood, executives at the TV networks imposed a new one. *They* decided – without notifying *or* asking me about it – that I had this special talent.

Without *my* ever making a single claim of *any* such ability, they concluded that I was one of a few writers in town who might salvage troubled series, shows that were failing to find an audience. For which I would be compensated lavishly. Whether or not I could pull it off.

Where or how they got this idea? Okay – it was probably another offshoot of my having 'saved' the *Bring 'em Back Alive* pilot.

313

Less explicable, for the next few seasons they ignored the fact that I was unable to save *any* of these shows, and *never* got on my case for failing. Instead, they continued throwing money in my direction, hiring me to hopefully resuscitate one dying turkey after another.

Again and again, I *believed* that I might, and I went at it, relishing each challenge. Testing myself anew, while addressing and trying to repair often alien series-premise-content. Plus wallowing in the pleasures of meeting and working with interesting, colorful writers, producers, directors, actors and staff people. It was – mostly – a *Blast*! Occasionally, one of the show's creators and/or original producers – or even a lead-actor would make himself heard, questioning or protesting a new direction being imposed on their baby. But these were few, and easily overruled by me and my writing teammate-of-the-moment-in-(attempted)-series-saving.

I realized gradually what each of these series had in common: they were flawed concepts from the get-go. Shows that should *never* have gone into production in the first place. Which was also somewhat revelatory – not to mention reassuring – in that it illustrated as I'd known that very few people in the entire industry were really *expert* at their jobs. This was stated most succinctly by the great screenwriter, William Goldman, in his landmark book, *Adventures in the Screen Trade*. There, Goldman eloquently and memorably summed up Hollywood in three words: "Nobody knows anything."

Perhaps most astonishing, not a single executive *ever* called me in or even phoned to ask me if I had any thoughts about *how* I might fix this or that show, or whether I figured I could do so at all. They just went ahead and made the deal with my agent.

Such, I guess, is the power of true belief, the resilience, regardless of validity, of 'The Word' getting out and, I suppose, of 'accepted wisdom,' or – what passes for it.

As evidenced by the feature-film-business's unwavering conviction, in the face of countless flops proving otherwise, that the more writers they throw at a feature-film script, the better it will become.

So, in the TV series world, with often tens of millions already invested, tossing another few bucks at a dying show arguably made a kind of ass-covering, corporate sense. On the order of: 'Okay – in case anyone asks, now we've given it our best, final shot…'

During that career-segment, as one of a handful of similarly anointed writers, I was put to work, consecutively, on as many as *three* different series in a *single season*. I'd be assigned to one, it would be cancelled within a month or two – or, as you'll see, occasionally much sooner. I'd quickly find myself at another studio – sometimes the following day – on another troubled show, again vainly trying to make something out of very little. I was employed as a fixer on more than half of the fifteen series for which I worked on staff.

Now, these failed – or rather, failing shows were not always badly written. Sometimes it was the leading-role casting. Occasionally, the choice of stories. But again, it seemed to me the most frequent culprit was the idea, the series-idea itself. While I enjoyed every one of the hurdles, trying hard to make them work, one of the best parts was – surprise – the education I received. Especially valuable was the refinement of my understanding about what sort of concept thrives in series TV, which ones usually don't, and which of them, as earlier-referenced, *never* work.

But surpassing that, I continued to absorb wonderful writing lessons while working alongside this or that veteran. Each imparted his expertise in the form to which I'd happily grown accustomed – those concise, totally theory-free nuggets. One of my favorites: the principle that no character important enough to interact with a key player should ever be 'thrown away.' Meaning that if we were giving an actor even the briefest screen-time opposite our star or someone prominent in the story, that presence must not be 'wasted.' We had an obligation to make him or her 'interesting.' Perhaps 'entertaining' says it better – by creating an 'edge.' Sometimes via no more than a word or two of dialogue as in, say, the most minor transaction with a bartender or bus depot ticket clerk.

This, I was taught, could be easily accomplished by employing such simple devices as giving that individual an attitude. One that hopefully requires no expository explanation, but rather colors his or her reaction – or manner –

toward the other character(s) within the scene. Attitudes such as anger at a colleague, or a spousal disagreement earlier that morning, or job insecurity or some-such. Or a 'condition,' like indigestion, a cold or an allergy. It *worked*, making my writing – and the show – better. *Every* time. Again, priceless, stick-to-the-ribs stuff that isn't taught in many schools.

Reflecting on my series-fixer time from this distance, my reputation as such does have a comic, slightly surreal aspect. As if it was assumed that they could just send me to the studio, and I would somehow *know* what to do. In a business so famous for the difficulty of separating people from their money, it seems more than a little ironic.

It also bolstered my by-then ongoing take that it is indeed a confidence game – and I *don't* mean that in a pejorative sense. Rather, that it's about people *acquiring* the confidence that you can do what you say you can do – or, as in this case, what they have *decided* you can do.

That they clung to that particular belief in me for as long as they did – in the face of mounting contrary evidence – continues to amaze – and amuse.

One of their perceptions I'd already known had solid grounding was that I *could* write 'funny' for filmed (one-hour) shows. As I went from one staff-gig to another, I came to realize it was a knack in pretty short supply among my fellow 'drama' writers.

Parenthetically, knowing where the laughs were – and how to make them pay off – seemed to be equally rare among the directors of such series. Often, during the week of prep for an upcoming episode-shoot, I would find it necessary to sit with the director and go through the script page-by-page. I'd literally explain that this or that line or action was a 'joke,' *intended* to be amusing. More frequently than not, he was until that moment unaware that it was meant to be humorous.

Nor, often, did he know *how* to shoot it, to make it pay off. I would explain that he needed to let the audience *know* it was funny – to in effect give viewers permission to laugh. To do this, he must shoot this-or-that character's *reaction* to the words, or pratfall, or whatever. In most sitcoms, incidentally, the 'permission' part – or perhaps more accurately, 'instruction' to the audience – is provided by the (yawn) laugh-track.

On only one occasion did I actually come close to fixing a series. Paradoxically, it was the very first of these assignments, and when I came on board *Gavilan*, it had aired three or four episodes without finding an audience. All of the original writing staff had been fired, replaced by myself and the very experienced David Levinson. Unlike some of the others to which I was later assigned, the reasons for its non-success were not immediately obvious.

In fact, it seemed to have a lot going for it. *Gavilan* was a one-hour run-and-jump show with a simple, straightforward premise which – like so many of them – seemed on the face of it fairly serviceable. Gavilan – the former code-name for a recently retired CIA agent – was played by bankable, proven TV star Robert Urich. He had quit the Company to pursue his first passion, marine biology.

The series setup: being the decent fellow he was, during each episode Gavilan would, grudging-but-determined, leave his lab and the work he loved, and travel to this or that exotic locale. There, he would be punched in the stomach and shot at while heroically saving someone's life from – and vanquishing – Bad Guys.

Gavilan had another reason as well for resigning from the CIA, which he stated onscreen in the series pilot. "I could no longer tell the good guys from the bad guys." About that, both Urich and the show received a remarkable amount of hate-mail. It came mainly from flyover people who seemed convinced the Agency was this hotbed of flag-wrapped patriots who had saved America from the Commies and worse.

Sigh...

Airing on NBC, the show was being filmed at MGM, produced by the former partner of series-mogul Aaron Spelling, and onetime president of ABC, Leonard Goldberg.

My unforgettable first encounter with Goldberg came on day two. Having received and read his annotated copy of the teleplay being prepped for shooting later in the week, I found that I disagreed with almost all of his comments. I phoned him, requested and was granted a meeting. A few minutes later he greeted me in his office suite in the Thalberg Building. Some 4,200 Hollywood-historic, lavishly appointed square feet, it had once been the private domain of the studio's legendary boss, Louis B. Mayer.

A tall, slender, pleasant, elegant man, Len guided me into a spacious, luxurious living-room setup where we sat facing each other on eight-foot sofas separated by a long coffee table. The surrounding walls were hung with large, major – and pricey – contemporary artworks.

I declined the usual beverage offer, we made brief small-talk, and then I opened the script and launched into my remarks. These of course I kept as brief as possible in order to finish within the then-Hollywood maximum-attention-span limit of seven minutes.

Patient, attentive, silent, elbows on his knees, a glass of iced Coca-Cola hanging from his fingertips, Goldberg listened as I succinctly told him how and why I disagreed with each of his dozen or so page-notes. Finishing, I closed the teleplay: "So, Len, that's about it." I was at that point addressing the top of his head, his face having been aimed at the floor between his feet during the last half of my monologue.

A moment of silence, then, Coke still dangling, he raised his head, looked me straight in the eye and, without condescension – or much of anything else – spoke. "Tom – I've made a hundred million dollars in this business… Do it my way."

Now, I can't imagine that there are a lot of places in the world where one might hear a statement like that. I knew it was extraordinary, a keeper, even before I smiled, thanked him for his time and returned to my office.

There, reminding myself that my job was *not* to cure cancer, we did indeed go forward with the shoot – his way.

Meanwhile, ratings for the show that aired that week tanked even further than those of the previous episode.

My near-series-fixing moment came several days after our meeting. The initial, unbidden and not quite fully formed part of the solution hit me – as such things often did – during my morning shower. The rest of it, which included recognition of what I had come to think of as *The Jessica Novak Syndrome*, came together as I drove along the beach toward Culver City. The answer was almost ridiculously obvious.

On arrival at the production offices, I excitedly shared my series-fix vision with Levinson, who totally agreed. I immediately phoned Goldberg and told him I'd figured out how to make *Gavilan* a success.

"Great! C'mon over and tell me about it."

A few minutes later he eagerly welcomed David and me in his office: "Okay, Go."

"All right – look, Len, the basic premise is classic. It works. I mean, from *The 39 Steps* on through *Saboteur, North By Northwest* and others, Hitchcock made a career out of filming stories about the unwilling hero. You know, a guy who's thrust into a dire situation not of his making, who then has no choice but to extricate himself, and beat the Bad Guys in the bargain. But with *Gavilan*, that's also the hang-up." Next, the *Jessica Novak* part: "The thing is – those were movies. One-shots. They were *not* about a continuing character who *repeatedly*, every week, does that which *isn't* really his game..."

Goldberg was with me the whole way, nodding, grinning.

With Levinson enthusiastically backing me up, I continued: "But that's only part of it. Because on top of all that, we've got a hero who *every week* doesn't *want* to do what he's *doing*! He'd *much* rather be in his lab. Hell, our star even plays it that way. He's this guy who's *very* reluctantly dragged away from the work he loves best – so he can be out there taking punches and getting shot at while saving somebody's life. That's our *essential* problem. Because our primary, target audience – they're these guys in their undershirts, a beer in one hand, remote in the other. They've just come home from another day at a job *they* despise, they're looking to the TV for some escape. And the *last* thing these bozos want is to spend an hour every week watching *another* guy who hates *his* job."

I paused before adding my capper: "So – *all* we have to do is rewrite Gavilan as a man whose *favorite* thing in the whole world *isn't* marine biology – it's risking his ass to rescue all those poor schmucks. A guy who *digs* the fight, the satisfaction of beating the shit outa the heavies. A man who *hates* the kind of injustice his 'clients' are suffering – and totally *loves* what he's doing. Basically, we give him a *franchise*."

Both Levinson and I buttoned the moment with smiles and palms-up/ what-was-so-hard-about-that? shrugs. Goldberg heartily, instantly agreed with *all* of it: "Yes! Of course. I mean that's *definitely* the way---"

He was interrupted by the ringing phone, which he picked up: "Yes...?" A moment, then: "Thanks." He rang off, grinned ironically at David and me. "That was NBC. We've just been cancelled."

That was as close as I ever came to rescuing one of those puppies. But I'm glad the networks and studios continued to believe that I could, because as with most of my experience in the biz, I had one helluvva lot of laughs trying.

No small part of those kicks came from the occasional off-the-wall side-problems I was asked to solve.

One of these arose when I found myself hired to try breathing life into another loser. *High Performance*, was an *especially* badly-conceived and indifferently-cast action-adventure show. Featuring three daredevils in jumpsuits (two men and a woman), in each episode they employed elaborate stunts and high-speed chases to – guess what – rescue people from the Bad Guys. Though the series was far from unique in thinness of idea and mediocre execution, the situation into which I had walked was unusual – and amusing.

A sure sign that the show had inspired very limited confidence from the start, the network, ABC, had ordered only four episodes. On the afternoon of my arrival they had just viewed and *rejected* episode three, accusing the studio of shortchanging them on production values.

They had it right. As was typical in the series business, Warner Brothers was contractually obligated to absorb costs that exceeded the per-episode monies the network had agreed to provide. Known as the 'license fee,' such amounts were rarely enough to cover the entire expenditure. These predictable deficits were routinely *only* recouped by the studios as 'back-end' revenues, from aftermarkets such as network reruns and syndication.

The studio's gamble was that if the plug was pulled earlier than say, fifty episodes, there was usually *no* back-end. In practice, such shows commonly became tax write-offs.

In the case of *High Performance*, Warner executives, like their counterparts at ABC, had quickly sensed that the series was a dog. Thus fairly certain it would be dropped after the fourth episode (or sooner), they decided to cut *their* losses, basically by shooting it as cheaply as possible. However, with episode three it was obvious to ABC that the studio had spent far *less* than the license fee, skimping most obviously on stunts, which tended to be expensive. The network took irate exception to what had ended up onscreen. Their edict, handed down as I was about to head home for supper following my first day on the show: add $200,000 in production value, meaning: excitement.

Or *else* there would not even *be* a fourth episode – *and* they would sue Warner Brothers.

My oddball, one-of-a-kind assignment: in the next hour, write $200,000 worth of stunts. That amount, in the early 1980's, was fairly serious money, buying a *lot* more than it would today. As Writer/Producer, I would then supervise the shoot, beginning at 6 AM the following morning, on location at Indian Dunes.

Moreover, *all* of it had to be filmed and in the can by tomorrow evening, so that it could be edited into the show before its scheduled broadcast a few days hence.

This was pre-internet, so I really had nowhere to look for stunt-costs. "Okay – but – how am I gonna know what constitutes two hundred grand? I mean – is there a price-list somewhere?"

The troubled Warner Brothers suit shrugged dismissively: "Beats me. Just – you know wing it…" He shoved a script at me – the one from which they'd shot episode three. "And the minute you're finished, messenger the pages to the director."

With that, he and everyone else went home. I phoned Holly and notified her that I'd be late for dinner. I started to scan the script – and stopped.

What if I go way <u>over</u> their 'budget?'

Then it hit me that it was unlikely that *anyone* would care.

Besides, even at that early point in my career, I'd *already* been taken outside and shot several times…

Within seconds the last of my misgivings had happily morphed into a feeling of freedom. From there, as it turned out, to a kind of adventure – albeit some of it a touch sneaky. And grin-provoking.

Happily, I happened to be familiar with the frequently-used location. Indian Dunes was a high-desert spot east of Los Angeles that I'd visited while on an earlier unsalvageable series. It consisted of several miles of winding roads, a variety of terrain, wooded areas, a standing exterior set that could double as a primitive Western or South-of-the-Border town street, and an airstrip.

Following a brief perusal of the original script, which was set in some nameless Latin American country, I saw what was needed and where. Almost as quickly, I rather gleefully wrote out detailed descriptions of the gags, including some specific camera-angles.

Satisfied that I'd included almost every chase-and/or-fight stunt I could imagine, I saved the most spectacular for last. A sequence I imagined so vividly that I could damn near taste it, I very intentionally spelled it out in *far* less detail than the rest. Because I *knew* that if *anyone* but the film crew understood what I had in mind, we'd have insurance people, local police and the FAA all over us, causing unacceptable delays if not flat-out refusal to let us shoot it at all.

I did lay out general prop and cast requirements: in addition to a twin-engine executive-jet and flight crew, we would need three military Jeeps with large-caliber machine-guns on mounts. Also, a dozen combat-uniformed militia to man them, and *lots* of blank ammunition and explosive-effects. I avoided mention of any particular camera angles, limiting it to: 'Our people narrowly escape via jet-plane as it is chased down runway by local soldiers.'

Chuckling at my own mischief, as part of my secret plan I added a separate note to the camera crew: they *must* include in their on-hand equipment at least two extra-long (400 mm. minimum) telephoto/zoom lenses. I handed the pages to the by-then waiting messenger, and drove home to Malibu, already excited about the early-morning shoot.

I slept fitfully that night, stoked by visualizing that key scene. Already awake when the alarm buzzed at 4 AM, I arrived at Indian Dunes just after sunrise. Greeted to my delight by *all* of the stuff I had requested – and more, including my first close-up, on-the-job interaction with what I hadn't realized was a *very* special breed: stunt people.

That began a few minutes after I got there, with the arrival of a friendly, handsome young guy in a leather suit, who removed himself and an expensive attaché case from his yellow Mercedes roadster. Introduced as 'the stunt gaffer,' and clearly not your typical executive-type, he was nonetheless totally businesslike. Eagerly greeted and surrounded by several stunt drivers, this fellow kneeled, placed his leather attaché case on the ground, and opened it.

Now, I can't say I expected it to be full of paperwork, but I could *never* have predicted what I saw.

The case was partitioned into perhaps a dozen spotless chamois-lined sections, each snugly containing a shiny, tiny '*Hot Wheels*' toy car. He removed several and placed them on the ground. Obviously familiar with the new script-pages, with his drivers intently stooping, watching, he proceeded to carefully, graphically hand-choreograph the little cars' movements in various directions. Swerving this or that one just before it might collide with another, he showed and verbally described the on-camera moves his drivers were to make during the first of the day's stunt-sequences: "Okay, Charlie – and just before a head-on with Phil, you'll spin-out to the left here. And Phil, you'll swing to avoid him, narrowly miss Jerry, who'll do a one-eighty, then smash into the fruit-stand, and you'll throw a rollover, here…" Twenty minutes later, after conferring with the director and camera people, the chase-sequence was performed and filmed in real cars – exactly as he'd demonstrated with his toys.

As the morning continued, it got better. From rigging a tree to fall, suddenly blocking the road just ahead of a speeding truck, to collisions, corner-skids, detonations and the like, all per my script – only *better*, the entire day was an unalloyed, nonstop rush.

Including an *actual* gut-churning unplanned crash that provided a fascinating insight into stunt-people – folks who *really* get off on living right up against the edge.

The stunt: one of the cars was supposed to do a rollover. A common, relatively safe movie stunt, rollovers are generally triggered by the off-camera front wheel leaving the ground as the car is steered onto a device known as a pipe-ramp. Literally, a 25 foot length of heavy pipe angling upward, firmly supported from below, which the expertly aimed vehicle strikes at a point just inside its in-our-case right front tire. One corner of the car then gradually angles skyward, tilting it sideways until it rolls or flips over.

Instead, ours took a startling, entirely unexpected turn. The reason: our youthful, red-haired driver hit the pipe-ramp at higher-than-expected speed. So, rather than toppling sideways onto the ground, *just* as it rolled, the vehicle's forward momentum carried it up and over the pipe-ramp's end. All of us watched horrified, as it went airborne, flipped to bottom-up, out over the ravine ahead, where it pancaked onto its roof, noisily smashing it nearly flat. Fortunately nobody was in its path – only a pricey, at that moment unmanned tripod-mounted camera.

But *omygod*, the driver?

Horrified, all of us rushed toward the wreck, fearing the worst, my own irrational, guilt-prone thoughts racing: *Shit! This wouldn't've happened if I hadn't written it into the goddam script! Just* as we arrived, the helmeted, flak-jacketed driver finished extricating himself, wriggling out through what had been the windshield. Uninjured! He was helped to his feet, unsteady at first, flexing neck and shoulders while the rest of us looked on, enormously relieved.

Then he grinned hugely, his face adrenalin-flushed, slowly shook his head as he spoke words that, for me anyway, *nail* what it must take to be a stuntman:

"Man, I gotta tell ya, *that* was *way* better than sex."

The day's climax for me – though not *that* good – came in early afternoon. My 'Big Production Number' – shot *exactly* the way I'd envisioned it, was as satisfying as it was exciting.

On film, it looked like this: at the far end of the landing-strip, a Learjet begins its takeoff run directly toward zoomed-in camera #1, which is positioned at the opposite end. At that moment, gun-Jeeps roar into frame from both sides, past camera and onto the runway, racing *straight at* the oncoming airplane, machine-guns rattling. With the Jeeps roaring toward it, the jet accelerating, all of them were on a *certain* collision course. As we cut from the first camera to another at the opposite end of the strip, *behind* the plane, the zoom-lenses' compressed perspective made the jet and vehicles appear far closer than the one mile that separated them at the start. Then – at the final instant – with what appeared to be only a few feet between them, the jet leaves the ground, seemingly *inches* above the Jeeps and their frustrated crews and smoking machine-guns.

It was a great-looking, truly exciting piece of film. Even better than I'd imagined

Dangerous? Not very. Thanks to the extremely long lenses, when the Learjet lifted off there was actually well over a quarter-mile between it from the Jeeps.

I learned afterward that I'd been rightly fearful of laying out my plan in any detail. When police and fire people saw the footage, they confirmed that had they known, it would have been stopped before we'd begun.

It sure as hell made for a fun first couple of days on the show, astounding me then – as it does now – that I was being paid for that sort of play. Cutting those gags into show #3 more than mollified the network. They reversed their decision, approved and aired the episode.

A few days later, after the next one was in the can, they administered the mercy-killing *High Performance* deserved.

THIRTY-FIVE
An Interesting Bump
or Two—And Then...
The Start of a Lo-o-ong Run

Following *High Performance* were a few more such gigs, some scripts, more highs, and some challenging problems. But my ongoing absorption – and frustration – with *JACK* was growing. Reality had begun to intrude, and along with it, anger at myself for not being equal to the task.

Backing up a bit, beyond that initial vision, I still had not even a fantasy of an end-frame in which the piece might actually be produced. That possibility had truly never entered my thoughts – only the question: *could* I write this – was I capable of somehow making this statement?

It was becoming more obvious to me that I was not, that this was *way* beyond my talents. My passion for the project – for telling Jack Kennedy's story – continued to intensify. As I read book-after-book about him, so did my conviction grow that it was indeed appropriate to think of it *not* as a "musical." I was propelled more and more by the *need* to express – to *dramatize* – nearly 20 years after his death – what I was learning and realizing about his specialness, his unique place in our history. Particularly how he had so singularly inspired us in his brief time to *believe* in ourselves, in our possibilities. As I learned more – much of it not commonly known – I realized that his had been a presence which, in view of what and whom had followed, had grown in stature – and in my view continues to do so. But along with all that, my own feelings of frustration, discouragement and inadequacy increased.

About the numerous books, incidentally, I was aware from the beginning of my research of an interesting phenomenon. There had emerged, starting right after Dallas, a near-cottage-industry of writers dedicated to demeaning him. Or worse. Fascinating, it was if there was this *need* to take shots at his image and in most cases, attempt to destroy it. As time passed my curiosity – and astonishment – grew as I encountered more and more books and articles that portrayed him negatively, often with hatred. I'm still not sure what that was about. Nor, after reading a couple, did I bother with more than a few pages of any of them. They were all alike, and taught me nothing I didn't already know, mostly about their authors.

In an attempt to learn more about the workings of theatre, I enlisted my attorney's help. Roger put me in touch with various local players whose brains I picked. The more I learned about what was involved – writing the libretto and getting the music composed was only the start – the problem of finding backers, my almost total lack of knowledge of the stage and opera worlds, the more daunting it seemed.

Then, just as 1983 ended, I was pleasantly distracted when Michael Sloan contacted me. He'd sold a martial arts action-adventure series titled *The Master*, about an American Ninja and his young sidekick, and wanted me to come onboard. I did so largely because I liked Michael, and believed I might help. Bright, easygoing, wry, I'd enjoyed working with him on *B.J. and the Bear*, following which we'd become social friends. The opportunity afforded me another pricelessly entertaining up-close look at the business, this one involving a major movie character actor, and the accommodations necessary in order to work with him.

The show's setup: the Master and his younger dropout buddy sort of drifted around the country, sans franchise, vanquishing bad guys in diverse locales, including occasional encounters with an ongoing chop-socky nemesis in the form of a *real*, masked ninja – something vaguely involving The Master's convoluted backstory, which I never fully understood.

Not the most deeply-conceived vehicle ever, its production was made additionally difficult by its star. Lee Van Cleef, of Spaghetti Western fame was, pretty much 24/7, close to, or actively, falling-down drunk. Fortunately however, *not* mean-spirited. Further complicating things, Lee had 'bad knees,' so that except for sitting still, or *very* slow walking, he *always* required a stunt-double. Even for such a simple move as climbing into or out of an automobile.

About Lee's drinking, however, we quickly learned to work around it. We adjusted for instance to the almost invariable need to re-record lines he delivered in master-shots (those that included Lee *and* other actors). Careless in part, but I suspect largely vain because he wasn't *featured* in the masters, even the few times he'd get the words right, they were usually slurred. Thus requiring that most of *his* dialogue be delivered in close-ups.

For those, Lee demonstrated an amusing, *very* remarkable facility. It was something to behold as this special knack would kick in. Between the sound of the clap-sticks and the director yelling "Action," the veteran actor would somehow manage to pull himself together. Not unlike watching one of those cartoon characters whose eyes ping-pong around, with *great* concentration, Lee seemed to *will* the pupils of his boozy, slit-eyes to focus. You could almost believe you were looking into his brain as pieces of it sorted themselves out – and he would then speak his lines flawlessly. The director would yell "Cut," and presto, Lee instantly reverted to his sloshed-mode. *Very* singular.

Van Cleef's young co-star, Timothy Van Patten, was green but willing, good-humored and hip, and though the show was killed after thirteen weeks, we had a *lot* of laughs. Tim went on to a successful directing career, including some memorable work on *The Sopranos*.

Of the episodes produced before *The Master*'s plug was yanked, and though we gave them our best shots, I suspect they were a lot more fun for us than for the audience.

Almost immediately after *The Master* ended, my agent notified me that I had a meeting at Universal, about a new series that would begin broadcasting in September.

Another out-of-left-field, only to be recognized later as a *big* moment, I was to confer with one of its creators. Peter Fischer, on the basis of having read my WWII pilot script, *Cody's War*, was offering me a 'blind assignment' to write one of the first episodes for his show. Which meant that all I had to do was come up with a premise acceptable to Peter.

We exchanged brief hellos, then without telling me anything about the series – and without my asking – he sent me into an adjacent office where I could view the half-hour segment they'd shot of what would be the show's two-hour pilot. That had been all that CBS needed to convince them to put it on the broadcast schedule.

Given the stuff on TV at the time, and especially conditioned by the dreck on which I'd been working for the past few years, I really didn't expect much. But, alone in that room, within a few minutes I was convinced that *finally*, here was a show I could be – albeit with a *few* reservations – as enthusiastic about as I was for my own series concepts. *Certainly* not least because it offered something I'd never encountered before: the *really* tantalizing prospect of writing for one of the world's truly *great* actresses!

The new series, developed by Fischer and the remarkably talented William Link and Richard Levinson, was *Murder, She Wrote*.

Its star, Angela Lansbury, was – as she had been in *all* of her movies – irresistible.

After watching the footage, I rejoined Peter in his office. "Wow. Does *that* ever look like you've got a hit on your hands!"

Peter shrugged: "Maybe… Anyway, come up with a story, and you can go to work."

Pleasant, quick, a former East Coaster like myself, what struck me most tellingly about Fischer – in terms of instant impressions – was his spotlessly clean desktop. That, in contrast to my own, which – along with those of most writers I knew – has always been a colossal mess of scraps and disorganized piles that periodically reaches critical mass, requiring a half-day or more for me to clean up. Peter's had not a single sheet of paper, not a pile anywhere – and it remained that way for the seven years I worked with him.

Which is not, incidentally, a knock. A direct corollary of this clearly anal trait, I would learn, was unlike *any* other Showrunner with whom I'd been associated, Peter *always* had several scripts in the drawer, finished and ready to shoot. In series TV, this is rare to the point of nonexistence. On most shows they're constantly hanging on by their fingertips, often writing them *as* they're being shot. I later adopted Peter's example, much to the benefit of my own comfort-zone.

About that first day and my initial script assignment, I felt that I should level with Peter: "Look, I've got very limited whodunit credits – A *Quincy* and a *Mike Hammer*. So you're gonna have to hold my hand."

"No problem. Anything else?"

"Yeah. The approach – the style – what kind of stories are they gonna be?"

His tossed-off-with-a-shrug, less-than-certain response: "Oh, you know, sorta Agatha Christie puzzle mysteries."

My comeback was as spontaneous as it was honest: "Peter, I hafta tell you – when I was a kid I read a couple Christies and one or two locked-room mysteries – youknow, where they gather all the suspects in the drawing-room at the end? They bored the shit out of me, and I won't write that for you."

"Okay. What *will* you write?"

"I'll write *The Maltese Falcon*."

His *so* memorable no-hesitation reply: "That'll be fine."

What still strikes me as being so totally cool about that exchange with Peter is that he fully understood – with no discussion required – what I was saying.

Without my realizing it for years, nor I'm sure did Peter Fischer see it that way, my response would become my signal contribution to his landmark TV series. Because over the next twelve seasons we nearly *never* did the 'suspects in the drawing-room' gag. Rather, what I meant by the *Falcon* analogy – and he instantly grasped – would become the show's matrix. Like Hammett's classic, *each* episode – and certainly all that I wrote or oversaw – was a play about a bunch of really colorful, interesting characters in conflict with each other, and someone would be murdered. *That* was *Murder, She Wrote*.

Back then, however, I was far from an expert on, or connoisseur of the murder mystery form. In my teens, I'd read all, and enjoyed most, of the Sherlock Holmes stories and novels, though I rarely felt the urge to revisit them. Known in the mystery field as 'Cozies,' in such yarns, which contain almost no violence, there's usually one character who behaves badly toward the other players, and is detested by all. Then – surprise, surprise – he or she is murdered. And at the end, the sleuth assembles the surviving cast in the drawing-room or its equivalent, where she/he tediously – for me, anyway – reviews (yawn) the motives of each, and then nails the guilty party.

On the other hand, by age twenty, I'd read Dashiell Hammett's *The Maltese Falcon* six times.

It *was* something else, and Peter and I knew the difference – he unquestionably more fully than I, since he'd written – and read – a *lot* of mysteries. *Falcon* was, and remains, *the* seminal modern detective novel, the one that took the genre to an entirely different level. The first murder mystery with no clues, no (in the old-context) suspects, instead it was in a sense a drama in which murders took place. But among characters *so* fascinating in their interactions – and in that instance their obsessive drive to acquire the 'Black Bird' – that the reader almost didn't *care* who committed the murders.

Endlessly imitated since its publication in 1929, *The Maltese Falcon* has, in my view, *never* been topped, though several brilliant writers have come close, tweaking/refining the form. Mainly, Raymond Chandler, Donald Westlake and Elmore Leonard. Period. In fact, I've *too* often been struck over the years by how *many* contemporary writers imitate not *those* masters, but rather, *their* failed, third-rate mimics.

Anyway, to my delight that was the basis for *all* of the twenty-four *MSW* episodes I wrote, and for the ninety-or-so scripts by other writers, which I developed and oversaw. No small part of the pleasure I took from my own were in the ongoing challenges – many of them privately, sometimes deviously self-imposed.

Also – and incidentally – I wondered, but never asked, what specific qualities Peter had seen in *Cody's War* that made him think I could write for his series. It was certainly not a mystery story. Though as time passed and I commissioned teleplays from other writers whose sample scripts I'd read, few were mysteries, and I came to better understand what he – and I – were looking for. Qualities that go beyond, or rather, straddle genres.

One of the truly *most* fun, *most* intensely satisfying, *most* challenging periods of my life. A megahit show, over which for its last five seasons I had the most control one can have in such a collaborative art-form, along with the pleasures of working with a *great* leading-lady, a great regular cast, and with countless fascinating stars of theatre and of Hollywood. A once-in-a-lifetime virtually nonstop twelve-year rush! Including almost two of those years running a show starring Jerry Orbach!

It doesn't get a whole lot better. Yet, given that initial candid exchange with Fischer, it *easily* might never have happened.

THIRTY-SIX
Some Advice Happily Recalled—and The Idea That Wouldn't Go Away

A FEW DAYS AFTER THAT FIRST MEETING with Peter Fischer, and even *more* pumped by the chance to write for Ms. Lansbury, I sold him the premise for my first *Murder, She Wrote* episode. Titled *Broadway Malady*, the arena was the New York theatre scene, a new musical in rehearsal, and the story's focus was on a dysfunctional theatre family. The link to Jessica Fletcher was via her nephew, Grady, who was involved in the fictitious musical's production.

The mystery was based on an actual Chicago homicide that my dad had told me about when I was a kid, a yarn that had remained with me. The outline and teleplay took the longest to write of any TV episode I'd done up until then – about six weeks. Which turned out to be just about the shortest time I'd spend on *any* of the others I eventually wrote for that series. Mysteries are – complex.

Late in the same day I had turned in my final draft, I received a phone call from *MSW* staffer Bob van Scoyk. My instant assumption that there was a problem was – to my relief – quickly allayed by Bob's opening line: "Listen, everyone loves your script. Thing is, I've got a question. Y'know how you've indicated in several places that the show's in rehearsal in the background?"

"Yeah…?"

"So – d'you wanta write the lyrics, or should we get someone to---?"

Suddenly, it was light-bulb time. Before Bob had finished his query, I was remembering the several years-earlier advice I'd received from the two veteran TV writers about song lyrics and ASCAP.

"Nono. Of course – I'll write 'em! And hey – thanks for reminding me."

Another corner turned. Though its full meaning would take some time to sink in.

First, though, in about ten minutes I knocked out lyrics for several Broadway-sounding songs, mostly to be sung by women. A pastiche of the form, really – containing such sentiments as 'I can open doors for myself now, thankyouverymuch,' and similar musical theatre-song bullshit. I re-read them, then ran them by Holly, who was as amused by them as I. She even observed that it was as if she'd read them or heard them before, which was precisely what I'd intended. That they should be, as we used to jokingly say about Rodgers & Hammerstein's' Broadway shows, 'Not only original, but familiar.' I printed them out, mailed them – this was before Email – to Universal, and promptly joined ASCAP.

The *MSW* staff guys were delighted with them, and contracted with a composer who set them to music. *Broadway Malady* became the 12th show of that initial season.

Damned if those writers who'd cued me about it weren't correct! Since 1984, when that show first aired, I've earned continuous royalties from those songs – tens of thousands of dollars. In the episode, they were performed by Lorna Luft (Judy Garland's daughter) and movie-musical star Vivian Blaine. In *addition* to the thrill and pleasure of watching and hearing my words delivered by them, *and* the awesome Ms. Lansbury, also guest-starring were Robert Morse and Milton Berle!

I mean – *Wow!* It was like I was finally writing for *Stars!*

But even *better*, that brief, breakthrough introduction to lyrics-writing empowered me, gave me some confidence, the belief that I *might* do it for *JACK*. Incredibly, down the line, other written-for-TV lyrics would eventually win me an EMMY nomination.

By the time I'd begun writing for *MSW*, the show was already fully staffed. So, while I immediately got started on a second teleplay, I was free to work on other series. One such assignment turned out to be my shortest-ever gig.

I was invited to come aboard *Mike Hammer* in mid-season, not as a show-fixer, rather to replace a departing staffer. But the series was cancelled – suspended says it more accurately – four days after I signed on.

But *not* because of ratings-sag. Rather, in this largely one-of-a-kind instance, because the show's star, Stacy Keach, was suddenly unavailable – for a number of months. The reason for which was abruptly revealed.

Mr. Keach had been apprehended in England for cocaine-smuggling and possession, and sentenced to do time in the Wormwood Scrubs Prison (don'tcha *love* the name?).

When I made my deal, however, nobody in Columbia Studios Business Affairs Department informed me or my agent of the actor's even having been accused, much less his possible incarceration. Nor apparently did they confide it to their own legal department. I wasn't told when I showed up for work. Instead, they simply indicated that Stacy was 'out of town for a few days.' If more was known, nobody said so. Meanwhile, during my less-than-a-week gig, we'd busied ourselves with various post-production choices on the most-recently filmed episode. I handled the looping of a few of our absent-star's lines, using of course another actor, and made some tweaks on an upcoming script. On reflection I suppose it's possible that *nobody* knew, that Keach's, or the studio's, or the network's PR was so effective that the story had been kept out of circulation entirely.

In any case, my contract carried a guarantee of four months' employment on the show. But after we were all sent home at the end of that fourth day, Columbia paid me for four *weeks*. They justified reneging on the mid-5-figure remainder they owed me – by invoking the old standard, boilerplate out-clause: *force majeure* (AKA: 'act of god').

My instant, irate reaction was also my argument to my agent and to the Writers Guild attorneys I contacted.

"C'mon guys, no fucking way is an actor getting caught blowing coke up his nose an act of god. By me, that's the act of an asshole."

It took several months but, thanks to the persistence of the WGA attorneys, Columbia finally fulfilled their contract obligation.

In addition to writing episode scripts for *Murder, She Wrote*, and for a number of less-memorable epics, such as *Scarecrow & Mrs. King*, *Runway*, *A Walk on the Wild Side*, *Glitter* and others, as well as a few short-lived staff jobs. I also continued coming up with, and pitching series and movie concepts. Having *fun*. Often *memorable*, unexpected fun.

Another instance of which resulted from a lunch with my friend, Jim Aubrey. During one of our monthly-or-so meet-ups, invariably entertaining and informative because of his eerily intuitive take on whatever the next trend would be, we came up with yet another series idea that we both liked. I wrote a few pages for a leave-behind, and we scheduled a pitch meeting.

A few mornings later, we found ourselves in the sprawling complex at Fairfax Avenue and Beverly Boulevard known as CBS Television City. There, I was about to experience one of those unforgettable only-in-the-biz moments that I so treasure.

Jim and I arrived a bit early, and when we reached the second-floor reception area, we were told that the party we'd come to see, the new head of dramatic series development, was running late. Everything on his schedule was delayed about a half-hour. Jim shrugged and, as he crossed the few steps to a side door adjacent to the receptionist's desk, he turned his head to me. "Wanta go grab some juice?"

"You mean – at the commissary?"

His hand on the doorknob, he nodded. "Yeah."

Now, I had worked for several weeks in the bowels of this enormous facility when I'd written for that Mary Tyler Moore comedy-variety special, and I vividly remembered a couple of things about the place. One was that on the far side of that door were acres and acres of dark corridors, sound stages and dim chambers – an immense, windowless, nearly impenetrable, directionless maze.

The other was that the commissary, if one could find it at all via this labyrinth, was about three city blocks distant, at the opposite end of the building, near The Farmers' Market. Hence, my very reasonable question to Jim: "D'you know how to get there from here?"

He opened the door a few inches and, with his customary charm, devoid of ego, grinned: "I built this place."

Indeed, he had.

We found the commissary, but we failed to make the sale. In fact, we never did manage to sell that project. But I went home with another genuine Keeper.

That spring, while the kids were on school break, Holly and I had decided it was time to venture further than our yearly summer visits to Rhode Island. We took them to London and Paris, with an almost unplanned but as it turned out *very* special in-between stop in Normandy. That last-minute addition to our trip was motivated by my then-agent, Carole Bennett's enthusiastic 'must' recommendation. She and her husband, Harve, had recently visited the area, staying at a 200 year-old chateau that had been converted to an inn, which they adored. They had also loved the countryside, and their visits to the nearby WWII invasion beaches. I found the latter prospect especially appealing because D-Day and the war had been such a big deal when I was a kid.

Experiencing London for the first time was great fun, though it was then still in the era of dreadful restaurant-food. Since, thankfully, changed. But our hotel arrangements, made for us by Patty Parke, Reyn's very professional travel-agent wife – and at our request, modestly priced – proved massively disappointing. We were in a small hotel near Sloane Square, with adjacent-but-not-adjoining rooms on the second or third floor of the five-or-six story establishment. The place featured a pub – saloon says it better – at one street-level corner, the relentless smoke and other smells from which fouled our rooms. We quickly sought other accommodations, but *none* were available – not even at the town's priciest hotels. The reason: it was also spring-break time in the UK and throughout Europe, and it appeared that, like us, *everyone* from the Continent had decided to spend at least part of it visiting London.

A bit disheartening, we refused to allow it to spoil our fun. In a way, I suppose it helped. By spending as little time as possible in our rooms, we undoubtedly took in and enjoyed more of that remarkable city's sights and landmarks than if we had found more comfortable lodgings.

However, that situation had immediately triggered another alarm. What if our Paris hotel was similarly unpleasant? Especially because Holly and I so loved Paris, we didn't want the experience tainted for us or for Brooke and Wylie. Thus, my first stop next morning was at a travel agency, where I cancelled our Paris hotel reservations, and booked adjoining rooms at one of that city's most famous, and most expensive – the George V.

Several days later, we arrived in France, rented a car, and drove to our lodgings in Normandy. Carole and Harve had indeed been correct. Extremely comfortable, Chateau d'Audrieu was this lovely, elegant 18th century stone structure that bore battle scars from a number of wars, the most recent in the form of machine-gun pocks and gouges from WWII. Beyond its garden-setting, the surrounding farmland with its narrow, curving roads was charming and lovely. Additionally, we enjoyed the superb spring weather as we explored the area.

Walking Utah Beach with our kids, and visualizing what had happened there – seen so many times in newsreels and movies – was unforgettable. I could almost hear the explosions, the weapons. I found myself choked up as I tried to describe what I knew of the spot's history to Brooke and Wylie. Similarly, when we visited the cemetery atop the bluffs. But by far the most amazing, and moving, partly because I'd known almost nothing about it, was Pointe du Hoc.

Even after reading about what had occurred there, I was unprepared for its initial visual impact. A 100-foot cliff rising abruptly out of the sandy beach, then arching seaward from the adjacent, not as high, rock walls. With several concrete German fortifications still prominent at the top, it looked impenetrable. Yet, on June 6, 1944, it had been almost miraculously scaled from directly below, and captured – under intense gunfire at the height of the Allied assault – by U.S. Army Rangers! As chilling as that first look was, our visit to the bunkers at the top, on the edge of the cliff, was stunningly more so. Especially exploring their claustrophobic interior rooms, with their dramatic, wide-but-perhaps 12-inch high gun-slits. Imagining our soldiers fighting their way inside, confronting the German troops who, I'm sure, *never* thought the enemy would be able to get that close. Talk about visions that stay with us.

On a much lighter note, we enjoyed the charming villages and cafes, and a visit to the spectacular Mont-Saint-Michel. Several days later, we drove to Paris – about which it is difficult to find words.

Starting with our hotel. The George V was impossible to beat. Our rooms were large and gorgeous, and its location, near the Arc de Triomphe, was ideal. All four of us had an amazing, never-to-be-forgotten week, taking in all of the usual sites, such as the Louvre, the Opera House, the lovely parks, and the incredible Versailles Palace. But almost equally memorable were our walking expeditions along streets and through neighborhoods not usually visited by tourists. This last initially motivated by Holly's determination to find a laundromat, a facility to which nobody at the hotel was able to direct us. Schlepping pillowcases full of stuff that needed washing, the laundry we finally located was in a side-street of a working-class part of town, where no one spoke English. Because the washing machines were ancient, even the experienced Holly needed help in figuring out how to operate them. Finally, though, we got them working, and while they were doing their stuff, we took off to explore the area. Another unforgettable part of our trip, seeing a fascinating side of Paris virtually unknown to Americans.

Another singular part of our French experience: even the most modest eateries – sidewalk snack counters on the way to Mont-Saint-Michel, in Normandy villages or side-street cafes in Paris – at nearly *all* of them the food was *really* extraordinary!

Following our wonderful week in Paris, we flew home. A superb, breathtakingly *perfect* vacation trip. Brooke and Wylie, then in their teens, still refer to it with fondness.

Meanwhile, the touch of confidence I'd gained when I wrote those first song lyrics had pretty much vanished. I had become more overwhelmed and disappointed by my inability to move meaningfully forward with *JACK*. To do the idea the justice it deserved. So, figuring hey, I've given it my best, I finally, and resignedly, put the project aside. Besides, there was a lot on my plate. Lin Bolen had asked me to write another pilot for her, based on a premise she'd already sold to ABC.

"Tom, you're gonna love this. It's something that's never been done before – a 'Soap Com.'" Lin was right. Her concept: five-half-hours per week, a daytime, no-laugh-track comedy/drama with continuing story-threads.

Adding to our shared enthusiasm was, for me, the fun prospect of working again with Lin. The central arena of *Love on Trial* was to be a New York City Domestic Relations Courtroom, the stories about individual cases as well as about the judge, the lawyers, and their personal lives. The primary focus was of course, on ever-viable marital conflict. Among the fresh writing challenges that made it especially interesting were the requirements we imposed. Daily resolution of at least one thread, a weekly button for another, plus several longer-term, ongoing stories that would run from six-to-twelve weeks.

It would necessitate my writing – as part of the pilot-deal – not only five half-hour scripts comprising week #1, but also as with any show telling serialized stories, a 'Bible.' In it, I would summarize the first nine months, during which multiple plot-lines intertwined, played out, and new ones were launched.

For research, Lin and I traveled to Manhattan, where we enjoyed a highly productive brain-picking week. We spoke to helpful judges and other Family Court people, as well as spending hours in the courtroom, observing actual proceedings. Tons of fascinating material, ripe for the treatment we wanted to give it, upon returning to California, I dove into the project.

Meanwhile, *JACK* refused to go away. In fact, at about this time it returned – permanently.

One evening a little further into that summer, while Holly, Brooke and Wylie were in the East with family, Lila Garrett and I grabbed dinner together in a Malibu restaurant. It had been a while since my last one-on-one with this incredible, vital woman who several years earlier had seen in me talents I didn't know I had, and believed in me enough to give me my start in Hollywood. During our enjoyable, as-always stimulating catch-up conversation, I happened to mention *JACK* to her for the first time. Lila was immediately intrigued, and eagerly drew me out about the concept, its origins, and my vision for it. I added that I'd reluctantly shelved it. "The problem – it was just too damned big for me. Something I could never pull off."

Before those words were all the way out of my mouth, Ms. Garrett, a lifelong passionate Leftie who counted Teddy Kennedy among her personal friends, responded in typical, emphatic, Lila-style: "Oh no. *No.* You've *got* to go forward with this. It's too important!"

I tried to protest, but she shushed me: "I know *just* the person you should work with!" She excitedly continued: "He's an old friend, a composer/lyricist who recently relocated to California from Manhattan." Skeptical, I didn't ask for more information, nor did she volunteer any. She said she'd get back to me about it, and we moved on to other topics.

Next morning, barely out of the shower, I was toweling myself when the phone rang. "Are you up? It's Lila…" Knowing the lady, I suppose I should've expected it: "...I'm in my car on Malibu Road, and I've got Will Holt with me. See you in a few..." Followed by the disconnect click.

In our living room minutes later, following brief introductions, and with Lila looking on approvingly, I described for Holt what I had in mind for *JACK*. He seemed to like the project, sharing my feelings about John F. Kennedy and what he'd meant to all of us. Nor did Will have a problem with my stating that it *must* be an opera, sung-through. I quickly added: "And look, you've gotta understand that even with your qualifications as a composer, if you come on board, we write the libretto and lyrics together, but – I want Leonard Bernstein to write the music." I omitted the fact that I had not the vaguest idea of how we might eventually get the material to him. Will agreed that that arrangement worked for him. Nor did he blink at my mention of Bernstein. It was some years later before I would learn why.

Affable, intelligent, a well-educated New Englander who was about my age, Holt had collaborated on several musical comedies that, while they hadn't been 'hits,' had made it to Broadway. Which certainly made him a player in that world. Years earlier he had toured as a folk-singer with his late wife, Dolly Jonas. I was impressed also by Will's most memorable commercial success. Recorded famously by The Mommas and the Poppas in the 1960's, he had written the enduring standard, "Lemon Tree".

It felt like he was someone with whom I could work, and to Lila's delight, and mine, he was amenable. I gave Will copies of notes gathered and pages I'd written on *JACK* over the preceding three years, and we were off-and-running.

To where, for how long, and over what kind of terrain I could *never* have imagined.

THIRTY-SEVEN
Beginning to Find JFK— and Making a Difference on a Megahit

OVER SUCCEEDING WEEKS AND MONTHS, I became more and more gratified by Will's grasp of the premise, with what he was bringing to it. Moving the project forward in inventive, concrete ways, along with lyrics, he offered structural suggestions which augmented and/or helped me rethink some of my earlier notions. He came up with proposals for dramatic, theatrical touches I hadn't thought of, which in turn stimulated my own idea-generation.

I began to sense a genuine and comfortable feeling of teamwork. An exciting time, some days working on our own – in my case juggling TV scripts and staff jobs as well – then Will and I would meet to compare each other's material. We'd spend hours discussing/arguing what the show was actually about, and inherent to that, the *truly* difficult question: *who* was the *real* Jack Kennedy?

This last remained unexpectedly elusive to us – ultimately, almost maddeningly so – despite the more than 30 books on Jack and the Kennedys that Will and I, between us, read and re-read. These were the serious works, separate from the numerous volumes we'd mostly chosen to discount or ignore – those earlier-mentioned, aimed primarily at trashing him.

Some of them were about his womanizing, others focusing on – 'grasping at' says it better – almost any shortcoming, real or invented, the authors could find, and exploit. Thus missing the *point*, the larger picture of this important figure in our history, and that so-special time.

Oddly though, we came to realize that we weren't alone. The authors of the better books had faced the same problem we were encountering in finding and nailing down the *essence* of this seemingly so-familiar individual. Of their takes on JFK, to both Will and me, most felt somehow incomplete. Surface-y, rather than on-the-money-penetrating.

At about that time, in what would prove to be a *vitally* fortuitous move, I reached out to one of Jack Kennedy's real-life pals to help in our research. The colorful Michael Butler, famed producer of *HAIR*, had been a close buddy of JFK, and on learning about our show, eagerly embraced my passion and offered to help. Michael's singular, very personal anecdotes and insights became a major contribution, so importantly, to our far deeper understanding of Jack and his family relationships. Our shared admiration of the man also very happily resulted in Michael and I becoming genuine friends.

Not incidentally, it's worth mentioning that while our show was not *about* the assassination, nor making a statement that contradicted the accepted version, that event was inescapably a part of our story. Because of my earlier-referenced attitudes, from day-one I had doubts about the official story, in which Lee Harvey Oswald was the lone gunman. Or, for that matter, involved as anything more than a patsy. As our research proceeded, and without my making any particular efforts in that direction, confirming evidence, or what I regarded as such, continued to mount, making it in my view a *certainty*.

Again, while I knew I was far from alone, fascinatingly, most of the pieces were obvious, accessible, easily studied. Nothing that seemed to have been concealed. Rather, it was material that appeared to have been purposely ignored. Why? Because, if noted, if publicized, it would most *definitely* raise *very* uncomfortable questions about the veracity of the Official History.

It was during this period that Will Holt and I began to diverge. It was initially revealed when he, very tentatively at first, suggested that maybe this was really the father's story. That it should really be *about* Joseph P. Kennedy, Sr. A notion I quickly dismissed, and assumed he had.

So, Will and I tried to work around that problem, making a few missteps as we built the first of what we had agreed from the outset would be two acts. *JACK* was moving forward, both he and I still struggling to get a firm handle on our protagonist who, the more we learned, and the more we wrote, seemed – oddly – to become more mysterious. More frustratingly elusive.

What we didn't realize was that we were dancing around a true understanding of our story's core, of what it *wanted* to be. What it really *was*. Which was *somewhere* in the increasingly intriguing relationship dynamic of Jack, his older brother, Joe, and their father, the willful, wealthy Joseph P. Kennedy, Sr. It was in those areas that our input from Michael Butler really began to pay off.

What neither of us could have predicted was that it would be a few years until the full answer would reveal itself. Then, in a rather electrifying moment – *our* Jack Kennedy would actually *tell* us what he would and would not say – and with it some truths we had not encountered in *any* of the books.

As with most of my pilot scripts, *Love on Trial* did not make the cut. Disappointing-but-far-from-devastating, I was already onto – and into – other TV matters. By then I'd become social friends with Bill Link, Dick Levinson and Peter Fischer, who had sold another series, *Blacke's Magic*. They invited me come on staff, doing crossover script-editorial work for both that show, and for *Murder, She Wrote*, along with writing scripts for both. A total no-brainer decision for me, its highlights were, without a doubt, the privilege of working with these brilliant guys, being welcome on the sets for both shows, and viewing the dailies that were screened every morning. Plus, in the case of *MSW*, of having a chance to appreciate, in unedited form, Angela Lansbury's awesome presence and unique acting talents.

At that juncture, I'd written three or four teleplays for *Murder, She Wrote*, which was by then solidly entrenched as a *major* hit series. I'd begun making some additional, enduring contributions – of which I am still proud. One of my favorites came out of a comment I tossed at Fischer one day over lunch, something I'd been thinking about for some time. By then, around the office we were already referring to Jessica's hometown, our fictitious Maine community as 'The Murder-Capital of America.'

"Y'know, Peter, it strikes me as a little odd that with all these homicides in Cabot Cove, even though we don't do blood or gore, nobody ever ventures a medical opinion."

"Yeah, you're right."

"What I'm thinking – why don't we introduce a local doctor who's – I don't know – a friend of Jessica's? I mean, we don't hafta get clinical, but he can be another source of little, sorta fun-conflicts and arguments."

"Good. Do it."

Thus, in the Cabot Cove script I was outlining at the time, *Joshua Peabody Died Here – Possibly*, Ms. Fletcher's lovable curmudgeon physician-buddy, Dr. Seth Hazlitt was born, played so deliciously by William Windom.

By then, having acquired a fairly solid handle on other aspects of the show, I'd already done a bit of less-obvious series-shaping – beyond my initial *Maltese Falcon* approach.

For me, the play was *the* thing. I almost didn't care about the details of the homicide, because our main challenge was to make the method, circumstances and surrounding characters *seem* different from the last six or seven episodes.

Oh, we provided clues and suspects, so that the viewers had a *reasonably* fair chance of solving the mystery before Jessica Fletcher nailed the bad guy. That indeed was the weekly game we played with our audience. As drummed into me by Link, Levinson and Fischer, these *had* to include at least one '*play-fair clue.*' Something said, read, or seen for even a millisecond – *somewhere* in the show – which would be replayed as a flashback during our trademark *Gotcha* scene, wherein Ms. Fletcher explained to the killer – and to us – *how* she'd solved the case. *Which*, if picked up on earlier by a viewer, would enable her or him to solve the murder mystery.

Admittedly, our audience would often have needed near-impossibly-quick perception to have noticed, say, the smudge Jessica recalled seeing on a lapel. Or a word she'd heard. Or observing, as she had, that an object was out-of-its-previous-place. Sure, these clues were there in the original viewing, but in the *Gotcha* scene replay we visually magnified, lengthened the shot, or otherwise emphasized each as Jessica was explaining how this or that one had led her to the solution.

It was a fun mandate, keeping all of us on our toes, constantly second-guessing our scripts. In writing mine, as part of that little competition with the viewer, I seldom decided for sure who the murderer was until I was into Act Three. Even then, I'd often take a hard look, and calculate that the one I had chosen was too obvious. In those cases, I arbitrarily chose someone less-likely to be the guilty party, and simply backtracked through the continuity, laying in the appropriate clues, motive and signs for Jessica to reveal at the end.

Also consistent with the show's 'bloodless' approach to violence, which was *never* shown onscreen, we steered *way* clear of another dark side – sociopaths and psychopaths, as in serial killers and the like. Happily for me because, despite their popularity, I find crazy people and other such stuff tedious in the extreme since they're unfixable, their motives irrational, and not, from my perspective, attention-grabbing enough to even want to try getting inside their twisted heads.

That subject/character-type was cleaned up for me decades ago in the first *Dirty Harry* movie. Such nut-cases are not people I can, nor wish to try to relate to. Nor do I find stories about their apprehension particularly entertaining. For me, those tales are almost invariably the same: watching the policeman or PI try to get inside the psychopath's head. Even with the additional, currently fashionable cachet of forensics and attendant techno-babble, I find dreary and repetitive.

Especially (yawn) the forensics.

In *Murder, She Wrote*, we employed only three motives for the killings: money, sex or power (sometimes together). A fourth, really a non-motive, was the occasional 'victim-by-mistake.' Essentially, to avoid predictability we tried to rotate these, as we did with the murder method (gunshot, knife, poison, etc.).

But beyond my thinking of them as little dramas that must include a murder or two, and right up there with creating the Doc Hazlitt character, is perhaps my favorite meaningful influence on the show's style. It's one for which I cannot take full credit, except perhaps for my recognition that we needed to use it on a more steady basis, rather than – as had been the case from the start – on only rare occasions.

This one grew out of my almost-from-the-get-go frustration with the essential blandness of the Jessica Fletcher character, and an observation about our star. Here I was, excited to be writing for one of the world's truly superb actresses, and in a way *because* of that, at the same time frustrated. Her role: the just-happens-to-be-in-the-vicinity-of-another-weekly-murder-but-otherwise-uninvolved amateur sleuth (talk about 'willing suspension of disbelief'). Due to that lack of emotional connection, we were tapping into only a *tiny* fraction of Angela's awesome talent and dramatic range.

Early on, revisiting her movies, a certain quality she displayed became newly apparent to me. Among her memorable portrayals of deeper feelings, she played irate/pissed-off better than almost *any* actor I'd ever seen – and was enormously engaging when she did.

So – I began to contrive, in each of my scripts, and later in any that I developed or otherwise critiqued or edited, to give her at least one scene which provoked that response from her. One moment, in which she'd confront someone – usually an authority-figure such as a cop or lawyer, a suspect or muckety-muck. That figure would tell Jessica that he/she didn't have time for her interference or other nonsense, and demand that she get the hell out of his or her presence.

Instantly, and entirely in-character, Jessica would get her back up, flatly refusing to leave until she got what she'd come for. Of course, played by Angela Lansbury, the scene's energy-level jumped, and the whole show came to life as abruptly as if a bomb had detonated.

Very satisfying and entertaining. It was a technique quickly adopted by whichever of my fellow writers who hadn't already caught on. All in all a joyously creative time for me. One that helped me to realize something extraordinary that for me set writing apart from drawing pictures.

In my former medium, perhaps because I'd been so fixated for so long on just learning how to draw well, by the time I'd mastered that, and then became freer and freer in my line work, it had lost something essential. It was as if I could no longer satisfy my creative needs via that medium. But by contrast in writing I was finding that those challenges were endless. In one important way, because the 'better' I became as a writer – the more that I *knew* about it – the art and the craft – the more difficult it became. Because my standards grew higher. Thus, happily absent was that prospect I'd envisioned in my former life, of 'doing the same thing every day' from then on.

That continues. I literally *thrive* on the ongoing, deeply-felt uncertainty of whether or not I'm up to pulling off the next thing I try to write. *Will* I be able to achieve what I newly demand from myself?

Back to *Blacke's Magic*, like *Murder, She Wrote*, it was a 'light' mystery, though more flamboyant/theatrical than the latter. It featured a father & son con artist/magic act that solved murders via clever stings and the like. It starred the very capable actors Harry Morgan and Hal Linden, between whom, as sometimes happens, there was absolutely no chemistry. In terms of writing-and-tone, the show never found its footing, never quite achieved the right balance between mystery and jokey. That it lasted as long as it did, through 13 fairly indifferent episodes, was largely, I suspect, because of its Link & Levinson pedigree. I resigned a few weeks into it, partly because of the above, and my inability to help make the show work. Primarily, though, it was because I had lost patience with one or two work-mates whom I regarded as maddeningly inept. Due to their relationships with Bill, Richard and Peter, and my relatively low-rank, I felt I was left with no other choice.

As I departed *Blacke's Magic*, Peter Fischer took me aside and somewhat cryptically asked me to be sure to touch base with him before taking any other staff gigs. I promised that I would.

The mini-mystery about what Peter meant was cleared up a month later. He called and asked me if I'd like to co-produce the two-hour pilot he was writing. A *Murder, She Wrote* spinoff-series he'd just sold, it was titled *The Law & Harry McGraw*.

Exciting as *that* was, it got better: *McGraw* would star the extraordinary Jerry Orbach as the comically seedy, plodding Boston Private Investigator he'd played a number of times on *MSW*. 'The Law,' in the person of classy Attorney Ellie Maginnis, would occupy the modest office across the corridor from Harry's. Ellie would be played by one of the best actresses in the business, beautiful, statuesque, red-haired Barbara Babcock. We'd film most of the pilot on location in and around Boston, shooting their office and miscellaneous interiors on a sound-stage at Universal. If the series then got picked up, I would take on the same role. I eagerly accepted.

I was knocked out by the prospect of working closely with Jerry, with whom I was already a friend, and with Barbara. Not least by the opportunity to participate, from the outset, in shaping the show and its characters. It was then early springtime, 1987, and I happened to notice an advertisement for an incredible upcoming summer spectacle. One which would permit my family and I celebrate our latest good fortune on a truly grand scale. A performance of Verdi's *Aida* was to be staged in the ancient temple at Luxor, in Egypt! The prospect – the vision – of such a dazzling piece of theatre being presented in that so-appropriate setting, plus my longtime fantasy about visiting Egypt, damn near put me away. Without hesitating, I impulsively bought four tickets, and that evening when I got home from the studio, I shared the news with Holly and the kids. They were as almost as stoked as I was, and we began to plan our trip. Perfectly timed, we wouldn't be prepping the *McGraw* pilot until we returned.

A short time later, however, our trip suddenly evaporated. But not for negative reasons.

CBS had decided to put the *McGraw* series on the upcoming autumn schedule. That meant that I had to immediately come aboard, shoot the pilot movie, and start developing and writing the series. My 'roll' was indeed continuing, and it was a daily rush. I did manage to unload our *Aida* tickets at only a fairly reasonable loss.

All that on top of the forward steps Will Holt and I were making with *JACK*.

In addition to writing and overseeing scripts for the new show, *Murder, She Wrote* continued, providing for me a major, ongoing bonus. Angela's presence on the show – plus its hit-status, attracted as guest-stars many of the best actors in the business. Which afforded me the additional privilege – and *fun* – of writing dialogue spoken by – along with Jerry, Bill Windom and others already mentioned – such talents as Len Cariou, Anne Meara, Wayne Rogers, George Furth, Sheree North, Julie Adams, Harvey Fierstein, Patrick Macnee, Brenda Vaccaro, Arte Johnson, Mickey Rooney, Theo Bikel, Arthur Hill, Herb Edelman, Tony Lo Bianco, Michael Sarrazin and more. If that sounds like it might have been heady – it *was*. Bigtime.

Holy shit! *Me*? The Chicago Kid…?

THIRTY-EIGHT
Some *Murder, She Wrote* Trivia—an Emotional Investment— and a Different, Startling Kind of Perception

MOST PEOPLE WHO ARE INTERESTED in motion picture history are familiar with tales of casting accidents that contributed to the now-classic status of such movies as *Casablanca*, *The Maltese Falcon* and others. Those instances of 'if-so-and-so had been available, or hadn't turned down a particular role, the film would probably be forgotten today.'

It should hardly be surprising, then, that such randomness extends to TV series as well. So it was with *Murder, She Wrote*. I had learned early on that when the concept had originally been sold to CBS, Angela Lansbury was the second-choice for the Jessica Fletcher role. It was initially offered to Jean Stapleton, who had so superbly played 'Dingbat'-wife, Edith, to Carroll O'Connor's Archie Bunker on the landmark comedy series, *All In The Family*.

Ms. Stapleton declined, and while she was and is an exceptional actress, and hindsight is almost invariably 20-20, I have a difficult time picturing her as Jessica. Plus an even harder one imagining that the series, with her in the lead, would have survived more than a season or two.

Then the pitch was made to Angela Lansbury who, we all know, accepted. But perhaps the most extraordinarily fascinating part of that story I did not learn until several years into the series' run. It turned out that when Angela accepted the offer to star in the show, she did so conditionally, pending the status of a stage-show then being written for her by Andrew Lloyd Webber. Angela was slated, in a *brilliant* piece of casting, to play the lead role of silent-film star Norma Desmond in Webber's musical version of Billy Wilder's classic movie, *Sunset Boulevard*.

Lloyd Webber assured Ms. Lansbury that he had no problem with her accepting the TV offer. He explained that he was still several years away from finishing her show and was, in fact, trying to complete another which was scheduled to precede it. Given the chanciness of the medium, the odds were that the series wouldn't last even that long. So, Messrs. Fischer, Link and Levinson, plus CBS and millions of viewers got lucky. Angela signed onto *Murder, She Wrote*.

But the fortuitousness in this story doesn't stop there. Because it rebounded right back, to the enormous benefit of Andrew Lloyd Webber. While he had already written several songs for Angela to sing in *Sunset Boulevard*, the show Webber was at that time racing to finish was *Cats*. Nearing its completion some months later, it became apparent that it lacked his trademark single standout number. So – because Angie was otherwise occupied, Webber lifted a major song he'd written for her to sing in *Sunset Boulevard*, and inserted it in *Cats*. A lovely, touching, totally fitting piece that the delusional Norma Desmond would have delivered near the end, while descending the grand staircase of her decaying mansion.

In *Cats*, while it conveyed but a fraction of the contextual power it would have had in its originally intended place, it ironically became the *only* song from that show that anyone remembers.

That's right, it was the gorgeous Puccini-esque aria that would have been *far* more story-and-character-appropriate in *Sunset Boulevard*, and likely a show-stopper: *Memories*.

As *The Law & Harry McGraw* project progressed, I enjoyed some of the best, most satisfying, fun experiences I'd *ever* had in the business, starting with shooting the pilot in Boston. Both Jerry and Barbara were total delights to work with, as were the rest of our cast and crew. While we were still scouting locations, Peter Fischer had needed to return to Los Angeles for the start of the next *Murder, She Wrote* production season. Which left me in charge, along with our wonderful, super-capable veteran Line Producer, Bob O'Neill.

One of my favorite souvenirs from that shoot is a framed photo on my office wall. It shows my daughter Suzy and her then-new husband, Jeff Fischer, who lived in Boston, with Jerry Orbach and me, the day they visited on location. Another, a shot of me flanked by Jerry and actor Ron Masak, who later so memorably played Cabot Cove Sheriff Mort Metzger on *Murder, She Wrote*.

A brief anecdote that Bob O'Neill shared with me is especially memorable as a succinct illustration of The *Real* Hollywood. Especially of its sentimental side, lest anyone think that Tinseltown Suits might not have 'heart,' nor appreciate those in the trenches. This story I think epitomizes the essential warmth-and-fuzziness of the Biz.

Following Season Two of *Murder, She Wrote*, Ms. Lansbury was deservedly awarded a Golden Globe for her work on the show. The presentations took place at the Shrine Auditorium in Los Angeles. After the ceremonies ended, O'Neill, feeling justifiably proud, was crossing the lobby toward the exit when he was hailed by a fellow emerging from an aisle some distance away.

The man was Sidney Sheinberg, Lou Wasserman's second-in-command at Universal Studios. Bob paused, flattered, anticipating a congratulatory pat-on-the-back, and perhaps a few 'job-well-done' words. Moments later, having threaded his way through the crowd, Sheinberg gratifyingly clapped an arm around Bob's shoulder as they wordlessly fell into step.

Then, as they neared the door, Sid finally spoke: "Listen, Bob – next season d'you suppose you could do the show for a hundred thousand bucks less per episode?"

On our return from Boston after wrapping the pilot shoot, along with getting into my own scripts for *McGraw* episodes, plus taking pitches and assigning writers, there came another couple of special incidents. Before heading East, I had completed one of my still-favorite *Murder, She Wrote* scripts, *No Laughing Murder*. The story was basically Martin & Lewis meet Romeo & Juliet, in which a long-estranged, still-hostile former comedy duo is forced to face one another because the daughter of one is about to wed the other's son.

I'd written one of the comedy team roles for Buddy Hackett, including, gleefully, a quintessentially Hackett line that, though dicey given our show, I hoped would make the cut.

But first, there was another hurdle. Given our star's dignified, ladylike persona, and Buddy Hackett's famous penchant for off-color coarseness, it was decided that before signing him, we'd ask the studio legal people to make an unusual move. At Fischer's and my request, they contacted Hackett's Manhattan lawyer and obtained a written guarantee from Buddy that he'd behave himself around Angela, muzzle his tendency to use offensive language, and so on.

Thus it was with a degree of humorous suspense that the first day of the shoot came around, on location at a rustic restaurant in the Santa Monica Mountains above Malibu. Everyone connected to the series was still basking in the afterglow of Angie's Golden Globe Award when, with the crew setting up, and most of the cast already present, she arrived in her limo. I'd been chatting with Hackett near the entrance, and as she walked toward us, she greeted me, then recognized him and paused. "Hi, Buddy. Welcome to *Murder, She Wrote.* I think we're going to have a fun week."

Cast and crew in the vicinity held their collective breaths as they awaited the comedian's response.

"Thank you, Angela. I'm delighted to be working with you."

Despite Hackett's rather obvious eyeballing of Angela's bosom, everyone exhaled, relieved. Then, as she proceeded up the path toward the front door, Buddy, 'playing to the room,' remarked in his all-but-patented, mischievous-little-boy, side-of-his-mouth aside: "Man, those really *are* golden globes."

The following tense, slightly wince-y moment was broken when Angela's laughter gave everyone else permission to crack up.

The line I gave Buddy to deliver about Jessica Fletcher, in her presence: "Hey. I mean is this a great old broad or what?" It ended up in the show, delivered with that same sly, impish twinkle I'd imagined as I wrote it.

Watching it still makes me laugh aloud.

Yet another bonus from that teleplay, which continues to give me a glow: a day or two into production, Buddy's co-guest star, famed singer/actor Steve Lawrence, buttonholed Peter Fischer on the set: "Man, are *all* your scripts this good?" *And*, playing Steve Lawrence's about-to-marry son, in one of his earliest roles: George Clooney!

Overseeing *The Law & Harry McGraw* episodes hands-on was very close to the top of my all-time most-fun-I've-ever-had list, *and* my first experience as a Showrunner. As with *MSW*, mostly because it was a mystery, as well as Fischer's creds, we got no interference from the network about scripts. But topping it all was the pleasure of working with Jerry, Barbara and the rest of the cast, as well as the enjoyment of pushing my private envelope, turning out some of the most difficult-but-satisfying writing I'd done.

Though I didn't always agree with Fischer's approach to the show, and the scripts he wrote for it, I'm sure he didn't always love mine. What it came down to was that each of us was doing the show we, individually, wanted to see on the screen. Did the series suffer from that? I don't know, but the hitches in my experience with *McGraw* were few indeed.

One, which I think did cost us, was Peter's insistence on employing a couple of directors with whom he'd worked on other series. These guys were hacks whose talents did not, in my view, bring them up to the level of 'journeyman' or, actually, even 'competent.' Which prompted me to decide, for the first and only time in my TV career, to return to directing. I scheduled myself to shoot the final episode of year-one.

Another problem proved more lethal. Peter, I learned, had cashed in some of his *MSW* clout to kind of bludgeon CBS into putting *McGraw* on the schedule. When we didn't open to 'rave' ratings, their method of dealing with it was via a not-uncommon strategy. One in which they obliquely-but-intentionally killed the series, hopefully without terminally offending a star actor or producer. A two-part approach, it began by not spending the full, allocated promotion budget. Then, several episodes into the season, they started shuffling the broadcast schedule, changing nights and airtimes, thus confusing viewers who want to watch. The resulting inevitable further drop in ratings provided the suits a degree of 'what-else-could-we-do?' self-justification as, finally, they canceled the show.

Disappointingly, we survived on-air for not quite the entire season, it was additionally frustrating because of my plan to direct the last episode, though I regretted that far less than I did the show's demise. At 67 weeks it was by far the longest single gig I'd *ever* had – in *any* of my lives, and almost entirely pleasurable. Among those delights, unlike Jessica Fletcher's mandated emotional removal from most murder victims and/or other characters in *Murder, She Wrote*, the *McGraw* approach had been different. Our two leads' franchises, PI and lawyer, and their relationship, permitted me to sometimes inject levels of feeling for these excellent actors to play that went far beyond mere bickering.

Happily, after the series ended, Jerry and I remained friends. For years, whenever we got together it was, quite literally, with an initial, wordless, momentary tear for a show into which we'd both invested a *lot* of ourselves.

As alluded to, other peoples' perceptions of us are often surprising. The predictable parts: they're not always positive, nor instantly revealed. One such pie-in-the-face moment, wherein I startlingly discovered how someone *really* regarded me, occurred one evening during a dinner party.

Holly and I were guests of Peter and Lucille Fischer at their sumptuous Calabasas mansion, the gatepost of which – incidentally – bore a witty, memorably inscribed brass plaque: *Murder, She Bought.*

Since shortly after *MSW* began, we'd socialized with the Fischers, joked, laughed, were comfortable in each other's company at our parties and theirs, as well as dining out as a foursome. Present on this particular evening was the usual assortment of interesting Hollywood Players, including a few we'd never met. Prominent among these were the legendary Sherman brothers, Richard and Robert, who had written a string of fabulous songs for such Walt Disney movies as *Mary Poppins*, *Chitty Chitty Bang Bang* and *The Jungle Book.*

A high point of the evening was Dick accompanying himself at the piano while he sang *Supercalifragilisticexpialidocious*, and regaling us with delicious anecdotes about Disney. The other notable moment came a short time later as we were seating ourselves for dinner.

Peter was at the head of the table. I had been placed at his immediate left, with Dick Sherman beside me. On Fischer's right, across from me, was Dick's wife, Ursula. Introductions were made, and as we were settling into our chairs, Ursula conversationally asked me what I 'did' (meaning, professionally).

Before I could answer, Peter jumped in: "Oh – Tom's a scavenger."

Following 'takes' from Ursula, Dick and myself – mine, I can only describe as shock mixed with rage – I explained to her that I was a writer/ producer.

Was I 'hurt?' No. But *stunned*. Because I had *not a clue* that he thought of me in that way. With that single word this individual whose talent I had respected – and continue to respect – with whom I'd been working closely for several years, had *admitted* that he actually regarded me with contempt.

Hardly world-ending. Though it marked the abrupt, *total* cessation of our socializing, we did continue to work together. But from that instant until Fischer departed *MSW* and, satisfyingly, *all* personal contact, that knowledge had colored *every* moment of my interaction with him.

THIRTY-NINE
JACK Evolves—A Waaay-Short-Lived Rush—and The First Inkling of *Another* New Direction

"Jesus, Will – how many fucking times do I have to say it? The guy was one of the major pricks of the 20th century. I mean *nobody* is gonna care, much less pay admission to see a show about him. *JACK* is about John F. Kennedy. *Not* about his father!"

It wasn't the first such argument between Holt and myself, nor would it be the last. The issue: Will's continuing inclination to regard the story as being at its core about the father *rather* than the son, had been building almost from the start.

Now, creative conflicts – and their resolutions or at least their airing-out – were from the beginning a daily part of my life in Hollywood, usually conducted at the tops of everyone's emotions. In earlier exchanges with Holt, I'd been able to prevail. Or so I thought.

But he wouldn't let go of it. Or, as I finally came to believe, he *could* not. Because as I got to know Will, it began to strike me that in wanting to portray Jack's father as flawed-but-human, it was tied somehow to his dealings with his own father. I never learned the details of that relationship, or the truth of my impression. But to Will's credit, this particular, exasperating dispute – and his tenacity – would gradually help produce an ultimately *very* positive – and for me surprising – effect on our completed show.

Meanwhile, an over-lunch chat with Jim Aubrey one day toward the end of *McGraw*'s run turned into another of those out-of-nowhere unforgettable sequences that have dotted my landscape.

From the moment we were seated, it was clear that Jim had an agenda. His topic: the then-beginnings of cable and independent channels competing for what had been for years the dominance of the three major networks – CBS, NBC and ABC. While I was aware of the phenomenon, I hadn't given much thought to its potential fallout. But Aubrey definitely had, particularly about the ways that it would affect programming and the economics of the business. Which he immediately laid out for me.

The short-form: more channels, but the same number of eyeballs, equaled smaller per-show audiences, equaled smaller advertising revenues. While some of that loss would be made up for by viewing-fees, things were *never* again going to be the same.

Ergo, we agreed, it might be worth trying to come up with a series concept we could pitch that would be ahead of the curve – especially in terms of a dramatically smaller production-budget.

His prognosis really pushed my *What-if?* button, and before we'd finished our lunch, we'd nailed it. I'd come up with the premise for a private-eye series filmed entirely on location, thus obviating the need to rent studio sound-stages and build sets – or even pay for on-the-lot office space.

Further, in those pre-tape, pre-digital days, we'd shoot our *half*-hour episodes on 16mm film, rather than 35mm. A pair of huge savings. To further avoid standing set-construction, our detective's office would be his car. Communications? Cellular phones hadn't happened yet, but pagers were common. His would be beeped, he'd pull up at a payphone, and call this sexy-sounding woman. We'd never see, nor need to pay her beyond her voice-over fees, and she'd pass along client-contact info or anything else necessary for story-purposes. His name: Barney Moon. The show's title? What else? *Paging Barney Moon.*

Next, I excitedly added, suppose Barney's a New Yorker, and he's based – stuck, really – in the place he hates most in the *entire* world – Los Angeles? About which he'll give us endless asides-to-the-camera on the order of: "D'you *believe* this fucking place?"

Jim loved it. Then I added my last touch. "He'll need somebody to talk to. So how about he doesn't drive? And – he's got this driver – one with ongoing, funny conflict. I mean who better than a young, gorgeous Southern California bimbo. A – a sort of you know, delinquent?"

We had our concept. A more natural, simple process I had never experienced. Both of us sat there silently digesting it for a moment. Then we began kicking around names. Actors who might be cast as Barney Moon. I don't recall whether it was Jim or me, but the right name, when spoken, instantly struck both of us as *perfect*.

Tony Curtis.

Yeah. The longtime *major* movie star. My next thought: Tony Curtis is still *really* big-league. "I wonder if – how – we could---?"

Knowing Jim, I should have anticipated his instant response – or something like it – but still, I was impressed.

"I'll call him." Delivered with a grin and a shrug.

A half-hour later, at Jim's office, he made the call, introduced me, and handed me the phone. Excited, I briefly described the project to Tony. His reaction: "I love it!"

Thrilled, I went home and wrote a few presentation pages. Several days later, I picked up Tony at the Bel Air Hotel where, as it happened, he was staying while in town from his home in Hawaii. I was awed. His hair was by then almost white, but his youthful face and those incredible twinkly eyes and smile were the same. Every bit as awesome and effortlessly charming in person as he'd been when, as a teenager, I'd watched him onscreen with Marilyn Monroe and Jack Lemmon in *Some Like it Hot*. Moreover, he was dressed – without prompting from us – in instinctively appropriate character. Wearing a rumpled white-linen suit, he *was* Barney Moon! We drove to the offices of the new production company Aubrey had contacted, where we connected with Jim. With Tony beside us, we went in and pitched the series.

Next day Jim phoned with astonishing news! In an unheard-of, go-directly-to-film deal, with *no* pilot, we'd sold *Paging Barney Moon!*

Finally, my *own* show, a concept I *loved* – and it would be done *my* way. Of course, it hadn't hurt our cause that we'd walked in *with* our star, who happened to be a Hollywood icon.

The bummer arrived a few mornings later, before we'd even finalized the contracts. Over breakfast, Holly looked up from *The Los Angeles Times*: "Did you know Jim's daughter is suing him?"

Even as she handed the page to me and pointed out the item, I guessed what the problem was, felt it in my stomach – and hoped like hell I was wrong.

I wasn't. A small piece, it stated that Skye Aubrey had filed suit against her father, claiming that she had loaned him – and he'd failed to repay – the last $75K of her several years-earlier divorce settlement from *Superman* producer, Ilya Salkind. With a small child to care for, she needed the money.

I sagged. "Shit."

"What?"

"Gambling. He put his house on the market the other day." I knew of Jim's habit, and had on one occasion been present in his office when he'd bet, via a single phone call, over $100K on that week's professional football games.

Maybe it was all those movies I'd seen, but all I could think of was that I'd be in business with him – and whoever might be coming after his kneecaps – or worse – could very well regard mine or those of my family as part of the deal.

Or, less melodramatic but just as troubling, there was the possibility of legal judgments against Jim that could impact what were about to become our mutual assets. Either way, not a great time to be his partner.

So, with a *lot* of regret – because I so adored the project, plus the notion of working with Aubrey, and with Tony – but trumped by survival instincts – I phoned Jim. Though I'd already decided, I explained my fears. Mensch that he was, Jim understood completely and – with his concurrence – I contacted the production company and killed the deal. I then reached Tony in Hawaii with the news, offering the hope that we might resurrect the project at some later time.

We never did. Though I couldn't have known it at the time, sadly it was Jim's and my last 'collaboration.'

A memorable sidebar: Jim Aubrey died in 1994. One of the tribal customs in Hollywood is the Memorial Service for well-knowns such as Jim, during which friends of the deceased stand at a podium and tell entertaining anecdotes about them. We had remained friends, and I was honored to be asked to speak at Jim's memorial. I told the story about his knowing the route to the CBS Television City commissary. It was well-received by the star-studded audience, but immediately – and deservedly topped by one I'd not heard but will *never* forget because it so *nailed* that side of who Jim Aubrey was.

Told by prominent comedy-writer Stanley Ralph Ross, it was an incident that had taken place in the 1950's when Jim was running CBS in New York.

At that time, most TV series pilots were produced by advertising agencies, for – and usually financed by – their clients. Once finished, they would be shopped by salesmen to the then-three networks. One day, Jim and a salesman entered Jim's private screening room in *The Black Tower* (CBS), Aubrey buzzed the projectionist, the lights went down, and the pair began viewing the new sitcom being pitched. About four minutes into it, Jim abruptly ordered the projectionist to stop the film. The lights went up, Jim stood and turned to the sales guy: "Phil, that is the *worst* piece of shit I've ever---"

The salesman jumped in: "Oh, I know, Jim. Truth is I – I was embarrassed to bring it to---"

"Nono. We're gonna put it on the air. It's going to be a *huge* hit."

It was. *The Beverly Hillbillies* ran for nine years.

Aubrey's and my final joint project, incidentally, turned out to be a not-total loss. In another instance of good ideas not necessarily vanishing, more than 25 years later Barney Moon became the protagonist of my third novel.

A curious seemingly from nowhere computer-inspired idea-flash happened during that period. It was an era in which found myself needing to come up with a lot more story-ideas than I ever thought I'd need. It was also a time when the introduction and relentless sales-promotion of new computer-software was becoming an almost daily phenomenon. That circumstantial combination brought to mind a purchase I'd made nearly two decades earlier. More precisely, it was November 9, 1965, in a Barnes & Noble bookstore on lower Fifth Avenue in Manhattan.

On that day I had chosen to *really* begin my shot at becoming a writer and filmmaker, and the first step was to acquire some recommended books on the subject(s). Wandering through the store, I had already gathered an armful (among them, Egri's *The Art of Dramatic Writing*, Georges Polti's *The Thirty-Six Dramatic Situations,* Karel Reisz's and Gavin Millar's *The Technique of Film Editing,* and others), when I came across a curiosity in the used-book section – a small blue hardcover, published in 1928. Written by William Wallace Cook, it had an arresting title: *Plotto – The Master Book of All Plots.*

One look at *Plotto*'s quirky contents, and I *had* to have it. Unlike anything I had seen before, the book consisted of several thousand short paragraphs, numbered and categorized – each bearing, above and below, numbers of other, related paragraphs elsewhere in the book.

Each was a story segment, a piece of dramatic (or comedic) business, containing conflict on some level. The numbers linked that one to several others, each containing a scene or action either preceding or following, which carried the story in different directions. Similarly, those segments were linked to others. In theory at least, it enabled the reader to build a story continuity in treelike fashion. Fascinating.

Like so many random incidents in one's life, I had not an inkling of how *Plotto* would affect mine.

Incidentally, there's a reason the exact date stands out. November 9, 1965 happened to be the night of the Great Northeast Blackout. That evening, at 5:27 PM, all of that part of the US and Canada went dark. In Manhattan, neither taxis nor buses were moving because there was total gridlock – no traffic lights. Thousands of people became trapped in elevators and subways. It was a very bizarre scene. So, impatient to get into my new life, I walked the entire distance, schlepping my *very* heavy bundle of just-acquired books, uptown from my office on West Ninth Street to East Seventy-fifth Street, where I lugged them up 18 flights of stairs to our apartment. On occasion I've wondered at the possible symbolism of my deciding to reinvent myself – and the lights going out. But hey – that way madness lies…

Back to *Plotto*. Over the next few days I played with the linked combinations Cook had assembled, and by selecting and writing out the "keeper" plot-segments, I was impressed to see that it did indeed work. A minor distraction: many reflected dated technology references, and some, a kind of distasteful 1920's sensibility (people "of an inferior race" and such). Though it was clear that the book was an incredible accomplishment, and a useful tool, I quickly moved on to the other, more theoretical books.

Flash forward seventeen years.

I pulled *Plotto* off my shelf, thumbed through it, and made a vague connection: *Plotto* appeared to fall into a still-rather-new-to-me category – it seemed to be a *database*. It struck me that, given the computer's ability to quickly call up disparate pieces of data – and thus eliminate the necessity to leaf through printed pages, if such material were somehow put into a computer program, it might become a worthwhile tool for writers.

Some research into the history of *Plotto* revealed how it had been regarded by professional fiction writers. Its author, William Wallace Cook, who had died in 1933, had been a prolific and successful pulp-fiction writer (*Nick Carter, Frank Merriwell*, etc.), as well as contributor to such publications as *Writer's Digest*. Moreover, he had been a respected contemporary and personal friend of famed Erle Stanley Gardner (creator of *Perry Mason*) who, when *Plotto* was published, wrote the following to a mutual friend: "...*Uncle Billy has given us the Rosetta Stone...*"

It was also evident that Cook's thinking had evolved out of the scholarship and theories of Georges Polti, whose still-revered-but-almost-impenetrable 1868 book (*The Thirty-Six Dramatic Situations*) is beyond the comprehension of anyone lacking a *deep* knowledge of obscure Greek drama. But, part of a continuum, Polti had in turn drawn on earlier theories that there were only nine, or at most eleven plots.

The long out-of-print *Plotto* had become a collector's item, with even poorly preserved copies fetching more than $150 (mine had cost me $9.95).

I decided to try turning *Plotto* into a software program. The good news: it was in Public Domain. The bad: it quickly became clear that *every* word, *all* of Cook's plot segments, would have to be rewritten in more contemporary language. That alone took nearly a year. Next was the hiring of a programmer, in a field that was utterly foreign to me, and the then-drastic limitations of computers. At that time, hard-drives had only recently become universal – most had a capacity of 10 megabytes or less, and our program required 3 of them. Nonetheless, while continuing my full-time career as a TV writer/producer, I formed Ashleywilde Publishers, and in 1990 introduced *Plots Unlimited* software. It received great reviews, and immediate, eager acceptance.

Jump another 10 years and several upgrades later. Sales of *Plots Unlimited* software had all but stopped – for good reason. It was still a DOS program. In the interim, Ashleywilde had published *Plots Unlimited* in book form. By then in its fourth printing, it had become a standard reference work. My career focus had shifted from TV/film to writing novels and theater. We faced a conundrum: update *Plots Unlimited*, or drop it. Enter my son and good friend, Wylie Sawyer. A voracious reader and talented writer, he felt that it was still a valuable piece of intellectual property. Wylie volunteered to examine the program with an eye to an upgrade.

After checking it out, he very astutely recognized, and I agreed, that rather than simply converting *Plots Unlimited* to the current operating systems, we take it to an entirely different level. By rewriting *all* of the individual situations and story-fragments so that we reduced their overall specificity – and the limitations that such phrasing placed on the user's imagination – we could dramatically increase the software's usefulness and its ability to stimulate free-association and creativity. He proposed that instead of merely modifying the *Plots Unlimited* story-situations, we would throw all of them out and start over – writing thousands of new story suggestions in what would amount to almost a new language, free of gender-pronouns – free in so many other ways that they would become the textual equivalent of Rorschach-test inkblots.

A daunting proposition. But we went for it and – after a year-and-a-half of intellectually and physically exhausting work and discovery, *Storybase* was born. New from top to bottom, both evolutionary and revolutionary, poetic and profound. Like *Plots Unlimited* before it, *Storybase* remains the <u>only</u> software for fiction writers developed by a successful, working writer. Tested and retested, *Storybase* provides a one-of-a-kind approach to story-building – one that works in tandem with – and truly enables the writer's own creative impulses.

Exciting <u>and</u> satisfying...

The idea for what would eventually become my first novel came just about as spontaneously as did the *Moon* project, *JACK*, and others. It was a facility which by that time I was beginning to appreciate as one more fortunate life-pattern. Asked to pitch episode ideas for a new, not yet on-air series, I found myself back at Universal Studios. The show's co-executive producer, respected veteran Bill Sackheim, welcomed me warmly, and quickly explained that *Gideon Oliver* was to be part of an ABC 'Mystery Wheel,' rotating with two other whodunit series, each airing a ninety-minute movie every third week. The others were the already long-running *Colombo*, and the more recent *B. L. Stryker*.

Based on a character about whom I had no knowledge, created by novelist Aaron Elkins, Gideon Oliver was to be portrayed by the imposing Louis Gossett, Jr.

Sackheim explained that Oliver was a Columbia University Professor of Anthropology who solved murders. Further, Bill offered that he *had* to put me into work on a script ASAP.

"We have one in its final editorial stages just now, that we plan to shoot in the southern Utah mountains, around Moab. It'd be great for us, budget-wise, if you can come up with one we could do there simultaneously..." He added that his co-exec, Dick Wolf, was at that moment on location in Mexico, shooting show number three. "...So – we need a script from you so badly that – well, I'm *not* gonna let you out of here until we've got a story."

So, pacing around Bill's office, I asked questions about various series-and-character nuances – did Gideon drive, did he have a regular assistant, any tics or phobias? When he also started pacing, tossing out answers, I stretched out on his sofa, hands behind my head – and began articulating a what-if – without much editing – almost *as* it was forming: "Okay, there's this dig taking place in those mountains, some sort of ancient burial chamber. And Gideon Oliver's called in because there are a bunch of really old skeletons in there – maybe something he's an expert about – except one of 'em isn't old. It's got a bullet in its wing bone, say – and – and these bozos start coming out of the woodwork – and killing people – *and* going after Gideon. Because that skeleton – it's connected to the JFK Assassination – to some hidden truth about it? And Gideon's about to solve what *really* happened that day in Dallas, and---"

Which was as far as I got. "Great. I love it. Let's go with that."

Heading home a few minutes later, I began thinking about what I'd just sold. While I had thus far not a single clue, beyond my pitch, about *how* to tell the story, it excited me. The best part? A chance to deal with Jack Kennedy's murder in a fiction piece – a crime that I had never for a minute believed was the work of a single gunman. It became more intriguing when I began playing with the notion of just who the modern-day skeleton had been. *What* might he have had on whoever was behind the JFK Plot that was serious enough to get this fellow killed back in late 1963?

I suppose my short-lived PI, Barney Moon was still near my thought-surface, because by the time I got home my dead-guy had taken the form of a similarly seedy investigator. This one was on a domestic surveillance job that had taken him to Texas in November 1963, where he'd shot clandestine evidence photos of his client's adulterous wife and her cowboy lover. Several of those snapshots inadvertently contained some sort of proof that Lee Harvey Oswald had *not* acted alone. I was stoked by the possibilities, and eagerly began outlining the teleplay.

Then, a few afternoons later, I received an odd phone call from Sackheim. He seemed tentative, ill-at-ease: "So – how're you coming with the story...?"

I told him I was just getting into it, laying out the overall shape. "It feels really good..." It also felt like one of those next-shoe-about-to-drop conversations. "Is there a problem, Bill...?"

His response came after a brief, awkward silence: "Tom, the thing is, we might have to shit-can it." Then, he quickly added: "But – *if* that happens, we'll work out a different premise for you to--- Listen, before you do any more work on it, why don't you come in tomorrow first-thing, and talk me through your story – in detail? And then we'll see."

Weird. I had never before encountered such a request, not one put in that way, or even close. The following morning at the studio, a somewhat embarrassed Bill Sackheim greeted me with the news that we weren't going to do the notion I'd sold him. "ABC had some – well –problems with it. But don't worry, you'll get your story money---"

"Like – what didn't they---?"

"So – let's get going on another one. How about...?" And an hour later, with a lot of plot-suggestions from Sackheim, we'd hammered out another story which was okay, though not as intriguing to me as the first one had been.

Frustrating, I figured Bill's brief phone call the previous day had been an attempt by him to buy time in hope that he could appeal the decision to a higher-up at the network. And/or maybe at this morning's meeting, between us we might find a twist or compromise that would cause them to change their minds.

Anyway, that being a done-deal, I went home and dove into the new one, which we'd similarly designed to be shot in the Moab-area. A week later, I sent him the WGA-mandated step-outline, received only a few minor notes from Sackheim and, with his enthusiastic approval plus a reminder of its urgency, I went to script. As promised, though I had never turned in even a single page on the canceled premise, I was, per the Writers Guild contract, paid for that story outline as well. A few weeks later I sent my first draft teleplay to the studio and, after several days, received *another* peculiar phone call. This time not from Bill Sackheim, but rather from one of his associates, whom I'd met once over lunch in the commissary. A bright, personable, talented guy.

Actually, 'peculiar' really doesn't describe our phone conversation. Here's where this tale takes a whole other, way-less predictable twist. Or – put another way:

Ah, Hollywood…

This executivebegan his comments by complimenting me on my 'very nice' first draft. I thanked him, a bit wary because of a rather obvious 'there's more' inflection I was hearing. Then, following a suspicion-confirming pause: "So – tell me, how'd you happen to come up with that particular story?"

An unusual question.

"Bill and I worked it out together. Why do you ask?" I awaited his response with a sort of detached, 'what now?' curiosity.

"Well, unfortunately, there's this problem. The story's almost identical to one we recently filmed…"

Now, given the waaay-less-than-routine shenanigans I'd already experienced with this show, alarms were going off in my head even as I spoke: "Did – you and Bill discuss this? I mean what does he have to say about it?"

"We haven't talked about it…" He explained that Sackheim was now off somewhere, filming the show that would precede mine and the other one to be done in Utah. "…The thing is, your script's going to require a major rewrite." More shit-buzzers began to sound.

"Wait a minute. I turned in a very detailed step outline. I mean you could've spotted the problem at that stage. But Bill only gave me a coupla notes, and– he put me right into script. Why didn't *you* say something back then?" His retort floored me.

"I never read outlines. I like to come to the scripts fresh."

What I wanted to say was the truth: *Jesus, they're paying you what – $150K per episode, or more, and one of your key responsibilities is to make sure the scripts're working? For you to not read story outlines – especially for the reason you just gave me – that is an outrageous, totally unprofessional fucking conceit!*

But instead, following a deep breath: "So – um – what d'you have in mind?"

"I'll make some notes and get back to you in a couple of days, so you can get started on a second draft."

More buzzers. Referring to it as a revised *draft*? From his choice of words, I inferred that he had no intention of calling this what it was, a rewrite, and thus, per Writers Guild mandate, paying me for it. Instead, he apparently expected to treat what would clearly be a brand new story as if it were just a few script changes.

Again, rather than confront him, we said our goodbyes. A few minutes later, via telephone, I recounted the conversation for my agent. I explained that since *all* of this was *their* fault, I refused to change a word without knowing for certain, upfront, that I'd be paid WGA scale for such a rewrite, which was essentially an entirely new script – around $20K – over and above what I was supposed to receive for the screenplay I'd just written. So we'd best *immediately* get that part of it clarified.

I received a call back from my rep in ten minutes, informing me that I'd read him bang-on. He had zero intention of paying me. Moreover, he had stated that if I insisted on being paid, he would see to it that "I would never work at Universal again."

Pissed-off doesn't approach what I was feeling as my agent asked what I wanted to do.

My answer was immediate. "Okay. Have you got a pen or pencil handy? Because I want you to give him a message, and I need to make sure you quote me – *exactly*." I then exacted a promise that it would be delivered word-for-word. "All right. Here it is: *Go – fuck – yourself.*"

Transmitted as guaranteed, the fellow backed down. We never met face-to-face, nor spoke again, but per his messengered notes I drastically revised the script, and was paid accordingly. However, *Gideon Oliver* was axed before mine was filmed.

I continued to work at Universal.

I had come away from the experience a bit wiser. Far better, I had the intriguing notion that what I'd sold to Bill Sackheim at that initial meeting two months earlier was – *maybe* – the germ of a pretty good idea for a novel.

A form I'd yet to try, though it *was* getting to be that time. Tantalizingly though, even at that early thinking-about-it stage, it presented a nagging, major storytelling-dilemma. One that, with my customary optimism, I figured would quickly sort itself out inside my head.

It did not. Instead, it became increasingly – almost maddeningly – frustrating. Until one day several years hence, when quite by accident, in a head-slap moment I would see how another writer had solved a similar problem.

FORTY
An Unforgettable Journey— More Ideas That Refused to Go Away— *JACK* Comes Together— The Changing TV-scape—and One More Attempt to Breathe Emotion into *MSW*

RATHER ABRUPTLY, I BECAME AWARE that another Holiday Time was looming. Things in the Biz would as usual grow seasonally quiet, and remain so until a week or two into the New Year. So, with Holly's enthusiastic support, we decided to take advantage of Wylie and Brooke's school-break, and celebrate our extraordinary good fortune by going ahead with the trip we'd had to postpone. We would *finally* visit Egypt!

Cognizant of the less-than-enthusiastic Middle East attitudes toward

377

Americans even then, in the late eighties, before the first Gulf War, it was nowhere near the open hostility so often – and justifiably – displayed today. But after asking questions and doing some research we ascertained that there was little to no threat of danger to us in Egypt, or in Israel, so we proceeded, excitedly, to plan our trip. We signed onto a ten-day Egypt-tour which would climax with a boat voyage of some 300+ miles down the Nile River, from Cairo to Aswan, with numerous sightseeing stops in between. Once back in Cairo, our tour ended, we'd explore on our own for a few days, then fly to Jerusalem, where we'd hire a guide.

Prepared to be excited, I never for a moment anticipated what we were about to experience.

Arriving in Cairo, we were greeted by lovely, sunny, temperate weather, and almost immediately began our tour, guided by a witty, personable young Egyptian. There were about 20 people in our group, with several of whom we began what would evolve into long-term friendships. The huge city, with its Manhattan-like energy, and mix of modern and ancient, was a blast.

Our first surprise: we encountered virtually *no* communication problems! *Every* native we encountered was friendly, helpful, and most spoke at least some English. Our informatively guided-and-narrated tours to various neighborhoods and sites in and around the city were fascinating-to-breathtaking.

Especially of course, the visits to Giza, west of Cairo and the Nile, and its major, truly mind-boggling landmarks: the Sphinx and the Great Pyramids, the scale – and age – of which are thrilling and *stunning*. Especially when seen up-close. With knowledge of the time of their construction, almost 4,500 years earlier, the amount of labor, and inventiveness required, are *beyond* imagining. Humbling, when one considered that when Julius Caesar stood where we were, among these Pyramids, they were already over 2,400 years old.

Two aspects of the Pyramids hit me most memorably. One was observable up close, while climbing through the claustrophobic tunnel-like passageway deep inside the Great Pyramid, leading upward to the Pharaoh's burial chamber. The tunnel walls were constructed with brick-wall-like, incredibly smooth sandstone blocks weighing, we were told, about 2,500 pounds each. That was remarkable enough, given the era in which they were cut and then assembled. But *most* striking to me – to all of us, actually – was the precision. That these huge stones were so *perfectly* sculpted and then tightly fitted against each other that one could not even slip a coin into the virtually hairline crack between *any* of them!

But even *more* astonishing to me: the size – the unimaginable *immensity* – of an ego that would decide he *deserved* such a monument.

Breathtaking!

But once we began our trip along the Nile, the Pyramids and Giza proved to be but a small part of this incredible journey. Because each day, we saw another place so thrilling and awesome, so old and beautiful – Karnak, Luxor, Abu Simbel – to look at and contemplate – that it caused the hair at the back of my neck to tingle. *Far* beyond anything I could have *ever* imagined...

The *most* stunning, temptingly visible from the river as our boat tied up one morning for our tour of the adjacent Valley of the Kings was, we were told, the Temple of Queen Hatshepsut. Broad, white, two-tiered but low against the beige stone backdrop of a much higher mountain wall, even from that several mile distance it seemed anomalous. It looked modern. We were informed that it would be our second site-visit.

I immediately pointed it out to Holly, Brooke and Wylie, and again during our bus ride to The Valley of The Kings. That was, like all of the others, fascinating, though my curiosity had been so piqued by the glimpse of that temple that I found myself marking time. When we were finally back on our small bus, headed toward it, I became more excited. But nothing could equal the close-up sight of this structure as we exited our bus, and walked up-ramp to its porticoed façade. More than 2,400 years old, perfectly proportioned, it is a building that could have been designed and built last week. One that would look up-to-the-minute-contemporary in the most modern of cities.

Such was our so-memorable tour of Egypt.

Incidentally, I'd graduated some years earlier from filming silent 8mm home movies, to the newer VHS videotape. In that medium I'd shot a *lot* of *very* satisfying footage of Wylie, Brooke, Holly, her parents, our cats, and when available Suzy and Lauren. But shortly before our Middle East trip was to start, came the availability of a new, higher-resolution version: S-VHS. I immediately purchased a camera and numerous blank cassettes, eager to try it out by recording such a singular adventure.

While not a heavy-duty devotee of nostalgia, I am *so* glad I did! The footage we brought back with us – nearly broadcast-quality – was amazing, a priceless keepsake of what turned out for me to be the *ultimate* travel experience. Spectacular to the point that by the time we departed Egypt, I *knew* that no matter where on our planet I might venture, *nothing* that I would *ever* see could come close to what I'd encountered there. However famous or historic or aesthetically revered, nothing could match the daily, back-of-the-neck-tingling surprises of Egypt!

Which was partly why the following week in Israel was more than slightly anticlimactic. While it was undeniably interesting, very little remains of original temples and other historical sites, and what does still exist was, comparatively, to me, largely unimpressive.

But in sum, *what* a vacation trip! A truly indelible one-off for Holly and me, and, I hope, for our children.

Back in my real – TV, that is – life, I *finally* accepted – embraced – another truth. A large and relaxing one. The realization that I actually *had* fooled 'em.

In the process I'd learned enough that I *was* no longer faking it! The career-change – maybe not quite as I'd first envisioned it more than a decade earlier when we relocated to California – had *happened*. Much of it without my step-by-step awareness. Nor, until that moment, had I acquired enough distance and perspective to allow myself full appreciation of my extraordinary *luck*. In that category I include my having the wonderful assets of intelligence and social abilities – much of which I owe to my parents and my upbringing.

Satisfying? *Incredibly.*

Exhilarating, the roll went on. And on. Thankfully the challenges and self-doubt about pulling the next one off continued as well. But the repeated highs from giving it my best shot, and then, a few months, or sometimes only weeks later, seeing my stuff on the tube were sensations I never quite got used to. Maybe not *instant* gratification, but *damned* close.

Next, in another example of a delayed punchline, I finally sold a series pilot based on my years-earlier twist on the concept of *The Fugitive*. The buyer of this next incarnation of *No Place to Run* was, via Producer/Writer Bill Blinn (of *Brian's Song* fame), Disney Studios. Bill, a terrific, *very* talented guy had at that time a production deal at Disney.

With more than a touch of the irony that seemed as endemic to the business as the quick-satisfaction factor, Disney, with Blinn and myself attached, in turn sold the project to Fox TV. Yeah, the *same* outfit that, when I'd first imagined it years before, optioned the notion from me, and then never followed up on its development.

This time, happily, I was immediately commissioned to write a two-hour teleplay. To my delight, even before completion it became a *very* hot go-project.

Savoring the prospect of *finally* getting a series of my own into actual production, Blinn and I had chosen the director and were discussing casting and locations when, *suddenly*, it was all over.

As happens with so many properties in Hollywood, that pilot-script for *No Place to Run* ended *not* with rejection of how I'd written it, nor failure in the marketplace. Rather, it was a victim of an impersonal choice made by the Fox TV honcho and serious *BFD*, Barry Diller.

On a Monday morning, Diller showed up at his office and issued an announcement. Over the weekend, it seemed, he'd acquired true wisdom. The studio's *entire* development schedule, he had decided, was *way* too heavy with youth-oriented shows – of which ours happened to be one.

So, he abruptly killed *everything* of that nature that Fox had in the pipeline, *No Place to Run* included.

Along with the *Barney Moon*/Tony Curtis project, it would turn out to be as close as I *ever* came to having one of my own concepts/pilot scripts actually go into series production. It would however *not* be – sigh – my last maddening *go-then-no-go* experience with Mr. Diller…

Again, the script and rights to the concept reverted to me. Even better, at least once during each of the ensuing six or seven years, some packager or production company would inquire about its status and, on learning it was available, ask if they might run with it. That was the positive part.

I usually let them, though nothing came of their efforts.

But the cool thing for me was that people continued to be intrigued by it. Eventually, and of course with a *lot* of changes, I would turn it into my second novel.

I continued to write TV episodes on a freelance basis, mostly for *Murder, She Wrote*. But again, on the seems-like-a-good-idea front, my attempt at a first novel had stalled at the outline-stage, wherein I was encountering that earlier-recognized barrier, and finding it insoluble.

In laying out *The Sixteenth Man*, based loosely on the *Gideon Oliver* premise that had been axed by ABC, my present-day protagonist would be a young archaeologist, Matt Packard. He discovers, near Moab, Utah, the burial chamber full of fifteen ancient skeletons, plus the more recent one which turns out to be that of Reno PI Charlie Callan. In late 1963 Charlie discovers that he has the key to who *really* killed JFK. After which, he vanishes along with his secret.

As with my original pitch, my supposition was that Packard's find would, even today, trigger the emergence of bad guys desperate to keep buried the truth about that long-ago conspiracy. People who wouldn't hesitate to kill to maintain that secret, because in my view the *real* facts would seriously-to-fatally threaten institutions and policies still in operation. Not to mention the rewriting of a *lot* of history.

Obviously, Packard would carry the bulk of the story. Additionally, logic seemed to dictate that I write the piece in linear sequence starting in 1963 and then taking it to present-day. Except that, in doing so, I'd have *no* choice but to quickly lose the player who, not surprisingly given my soft spot for rascals, had quickly emerged as the most fun: Charlie Callan. It just didn't seem right to dump him so soon. But *how* to tell the damned story without killing him off within the first few chapters continued to elude me.

So, stymied – maybe permanently – and simultaneously beyond my eyeballs juggling other projects, including *JACK* and of course *MSW*, after struggling for several weeks, with regret but still fascinated by the challenge, I temporarily laid *The Sixteenth Man* project aside.

As Will Holt and I closed in on the end of the First Act of the *JACK* libretto, we suddenly found ourselves stopped cold. Because we had come to a moment in the narrative – a key point in Jack's life, that we *knew* we must include as a scene.

Yet *none* of the books about him gave the incident more than a sentence or two. Partly because there were no witnesses to what took place, and partly because the outcome seemed to be obvious.

The incident: Jack returns from WWII and, his brother Joe having been killed, is asked by their father to take Joe's place and go into politics.

The rest, of course, is history.

The problem we faced was triggered by what often happens in writing fiction. A character in a story will *speak* to the author, pointing out that he or she wouldn't say this or that, or behave in a way that the writer is dictating. When that happens, the author had *damned* well better listen!

In our case, the character was of course a real person, but the principle remained the same.

John F. Kennedy told *us* in emphatic terms that there was no fucking way he would have said "yes" to his father! In the process, making clear for us – really for the *first* time – the *true* spine of our story!

He was right. In reexamining the Jack Kennedy about whom we'd been writing for the past few years, given his relationship to his brother and to his father, his almost-textbook second-son-ness, there was *not a chance* that he'd have agreed.

Particularly when we factored in certain known facts. Starting with Joseph P. Kennedy, Junior having been from birth *The Anointed One* – destined to be the instrument of Senior's nose-thumbing revenge against the W.A.S.P. Establishment. Those who had so unforgivably rejected him at Harvard and beyond. To *show* them, Joe, Jr. would become the first Catholic President of the United States. The resulting *known* slights and sometimes cruelties inflicted on Jack by their father, in an effort to ensure that nothing would soil Joe, Jr. or his reputation? Those *had* to have resulted in *deep* animus on Jack's part.

Okay. But Jack *did* enter politics. He did run for that 11th Congressional District seat that Joe would have sought. Jack won, and went on to fulfill his late brother's destiny. If he'd said "No" to his father, then what – or who – turned him?

Light-bulb time: His mother, Rose!

The result gave us – in the father-son confrontation about Jack running for office – one of the most powerful, moving scenes in the show. Followed by Rose, changing his mind. A sequence in Jack's life for which there is no record, though I am convinced we got it right – *true* to who he was – and to the family dynamic. Plus, we were driven to go back through the earlier scenes, bolstering that dramatic line, discovering and emphasizing various aspects – some almost Shakespearean – that we had previously ignored or softened.

Given my passion for the project, it was – and remains – truly one of *the* creatively satisfying high-points of my entire life.

But still, I had no fantasies that anything might ever happen with the show.

We finished the lyrics for Act One and, as it happened, Leonard Bernstein was Will Holt's neighbor on West 57th Street. Now, I mean how lucky is that, how consistent with so much of my journey? Will gave him our manuscript, and expressed our hope that he'd be willing to set it to music. Unfortunately, Bernstein was by then terminally ill; he declined graciously, explaining he had more projects of his own than he would be able to complete. Disappointing, but I'd known from the top that it was a long, long shot. This great artist died less than a year later, in October 1990.

Will and I then considered the work of six or seven other composers whose music, incidentally, was submitted to us by Leonard's sister, agent Shirley Bernstein. Good as some of them were, none seemed right for our show. At which point Will offered that he'd like to have a go at it. I agreed.

While we had the general outline of Act Two, work on the libretto pretty much stopped for the next several months while Holt wrote the Act One music and I pursued my busy schedule in TV.

In TV, the mostly pleasurable work continued, including more *Murder, She Wrote* scripts. Over the succeeding years of the show, despite my 'irate-and-pissed-off' contribution, my frustration over using so little of Ms. Lansbury's dramatic range continued. I'd pitched without success several stories in which Jessica Fletcher had a personal stake in the outcome, some even minor emotional connection to a murder victim, or to the murderer. Though they would have given Angela a few deeper moments to play as an actress, Peter Fischer went along with her continuing to reject them. I argued then, and still feel, that an occasional venture into such territory would have enriched the mixture.

But the notion wouldn't go away. I kept on playing with ideas, noting that in a few of the early episodes, Fischer had explored a hint of romance for her. Those hadn't really played all that well, so the subject had pretty much been dropped. But one had always intrigued me. In the two-hour series pilot, there had been a hint or two of a tentative, near-amorous relationship building between the widowed Jessica Fletcher and Preston Giles, publisher of her first mystery novel. Played by the imposing character actor, Arthur Hill, that spark ended when Jessica, not without an emotional tug, exposed him as the murderer.

So, with the seventh season looming, I tried again: "Okay, Peter, there's this publisher who wants to lure Jessica away from the outfit she's with. So he gets Preston Giles paroled, and takes him on as his top editor. We get Arthur Hill to play him again – he's this essentially broken man, and once Jessica overcomes her anger at his having disappointed her six years ago, he begins to win some of her old trust. Except he turns out to be the chief suspect in a new murder. But Jessica finds the real killer, which opens the possibility that she and Giles might renew their relationship, only---"

"Oh, I don't know. I mean we---"

"Lemme, finish, okay? Only we can't let that happen because he's a convicted murderer---"

"So – he's *gotta* die."

"Exactly. So in the button scene, as this week's murderer is about to shoot Jessica, Giles takes the bullet to save her. The killer's grabbed by a cop, or Giles takes him down, then falls. Jessica kneels, puts a hand on Giles' forehead, or cradles his head, and as his eyes close for the last time we push in on her face, see this touch of ambivalence – and fade to black."

Maybe it was because Peter had written the pilot, but he bought it. In describing that final shot, and later writing the script, I could almost taste the moment.

Instead, in the filmed episode, titled *The Return of Preston Giles*, he's on the floor, dead, and Jessica is standing over him, displaying not a trace of readable emotion. I never asked, but always suspected it was Angela's call. *Sigh...*

Hey – excuse the pun – I gave it my best shot. As usual, it was fun trying.

That same season, I did a brief show-fixing gig on one more hopeless turkey, this one titled *Paris Metal*. The concept – something about a CIA agent who'd lost his memory or some such – was so convoluted that I never really got it straight in my head. It ended with the series' death after five weeks and my having written one teleplay, the experience distinguished in only two ways. Both of them signs of how the business was changing.

First, this near-zero-budget cable show was officed not at a studio, but rather in a shabby Studio City residence. Second, I did not receive payment for my first three weeks from the largely anonymous production company. I

warned them that if I wasn't paid everything they owed me by the following scheduled payday, I was out of there.

Apparently they didn't believe me, so when they stiffed me again, I staged a one-man strike. I refused to show up until they messengered a cashier's check to me at my home in Malibu, along with confirmation that they'd made the requisite WGA P&H payments as well. Both were delivered that afternoon.

Alarmingly, much of Will Holt's initial musical composition efforts for *JACK* felt like a rehash of Kurt Weill's *Three Penny Opera*. A somewhat touchy situation, I was, happily, not alone. Joined by Lila Garrett and a few other mutual friends who had become fans of our project, we talked it through with Will. He handled our criticisms with grace and equanimity, and made another pass.

I could hardly have been more pleased with the result. By then, thanks to his contacts in the East our show had elicited some interest from a few Broadway people, including Producer Isobel Robins Konecky, an extraordinary, witty, very alive lady, a former singer with whom Will had once toured.

In the area of long, long shots, that years-earlier post-*Evita* flash of inspiration had very gradually morphed from a what-if into a possibility that the show might not only be completed, but actually *staged*!

Amazing.

But still that last prospect remained somehow ephemeral, veiled in the gauze of semi-reality that had for me surrounded the whole thing. Even when, one afternoon in Manhattan a few months later, Holly and I found ourselves at The Musical Theatre Works on Lafayette Street. There, under Will's direction (with me, the designated noodge, looking over his shoulder), with nine singers at music stands, accompanied by two pianists, we auditioned the First Act of *JACK*.

The audience? Thanks to Isobel, notice had gone out to the town's Theatre Elite. So, as the overture began, present along with the one hundred or so personal friends and relatives we'd invited, were representatives of the three companies that pretty much *are* (or were at that time) Broadway: the Niederlanders, the Jujamsins, and the Shuberts.

Here, I must invoke another major *Who Knew...?* Because, A) while I wasn't unimpressed that these people showed up, I simply didn't think about it, nor its implications. As in: No agent? No hype? No PR? Me with no record nor experience in this field?

And, B) The Shuberts – the biggest, most prestigious outfit in that world – signed on!

Actually, half of them, in the persons of Bernie Jacobs, one of the two Shubert principals, and his wife, Betty. Bernie's partner, Gerald Schoenfeld was not, I learned later, on board. Bernie and Betty's plan: upon our completion of *JACK*, they would stage a workshop (read: bare bones) production.

Was I elated? Of course. But surprised? No. Clearly, these people saw what we had in mind. They *got* it. I mean – isn't that the way it's *supposed* to happen?

Again, as with so much in my life, I had no perspective, no history of trying and failing. Not because I hadn't experienced both, but, I see now, because failure/rejection was invariably something to be ignored, since unquestionably, whoever did the rejecting was *wrong*. I basically figured success was the natural order of things. Nice? Yes, definitely. But sort of 'Okay, next?'

I mean, hey, why *wouldn't* they want to back it? We had a wonderful show.

I was unaware until years later that having our project produced *at all* was indeed a BIG deal, a monumentally rare occurrence.

With that, we got rolling on the second Act. Because we had a tighter handle on the characters, and the central conflicts, Will's and my work went more smoothly. But *hardly* bump-less.

During the writing of *JACK*, Will and I had only two encounters with Kennedy family-members. We met his brother, then-Senator Teddy, briefly at a cocktail party in Lila Garrett's West Los Angeles apartment, where, after being told of our project, he grinned: "I hope there's a part in it for me."

The other, as *JACK* was nearing completion, involved one of their sisters, and it continues to resonate, both for its slightly surreal quality, and for a small but telling insight into their father.

Jean Kennedy Smith happened to be in LA and, learning of our show, had asked to hear the material. So it was arranged that Will would perform the completed first act for her at his home in Beverly Hills, singing all of the roles while accompanying himself at his piano.

Ms. Smith was escorted by the distinguished movie Writer/Director James Bridges, among whose most notable efforts were *Urban Cowboy*, *The China Syndrome* and *The Paper Chase*. Also present was Bridges' friend, Jack Larson. Following introductions, Ms. Smith and Bridges sat on the sofa, while Larson and I occupied side chairs at either end, mine positioned so that I could observe Ms. Smith's reactions. A veteran of this sort of auditioning, Will's presentation was remarkable, superb and very moving – I've always regretted not having recorded it.

Somewhat naively, I was looking for signs that it was similarly reaching Ms. Smith. Instead, for the entire hour, she betrayed not a single indication of either approval or its opposite. However, I began to read her almost nun-like non-reaction for what it was: an understandable guardedness, studiously non-committal. As Will finished, there was a brief, awkward moment in which her escorts seemed to defer to her. Then, keying off of her brief, perfunctory applause, James and Jack added polite, discreetly non-committal compliments: "Very nice, indeed." "Lovely."

But, as Will and I ushered them to the door, Ms. Smith paused, and unexpectedly spoke to us. "I have a number of letters our father and Jack wrote to each other while he was a student at Choate, and then in college. If you'd like, I'd be happy to let you see them."

Will and I exchanged glances and, excited – flattered really – by this first hint of more than-cursory approval, we both let her know how much we'd love to see them. Next came its offset. In a parting remark – our only clue to how she *really* felt about our treatment of the story – she added: "You know – our father was a wonderful man…" A pause, then: "…He had the gift of always making each of us believe he loved us the most."

Admittedly processing her words through my own biased filters, I was truly surprised. The first question they raised for me: Did she believe them, or were they something she *wanted* to believe?

Then, rapidly paging through what we knew, I thought about part of what she'd said: "...*each* of us..." *Whoa*! Given their baggage, there was no *way* that Jack could have so regarded their father.

But – perhaps it *had* been different with his siblings.

So, with the promise of further contact, Holt and I said our goodbyes to Ms. Smith and her companions. Next day we received a phone call from her attorney, informing us that she would be unable to make the letters available to us.

A few months later, Will and I had nearly completed the book for Act Two of *JACK*. He was also closing in on finishing the music, and I was mostly delighted with the sound he was creating, and his inventive scoring. Then, one morning I received some faxed script pages from Will. They contained a number of substantive changes Holt had made. On his own and without discussion.

I disagreed with most of them and, assuming he was running them past me for comment or suggestions, I phoned him: "Listen, Will, about those revisions, I've got some problems with 'em. I'll get back to you tomorrow with my---"

"No hurry. I already shipped it to New York."

"You *what*?"

"They're expecting the script."

I was almost speechless. Then, barely able to contain my rage: "Dammit, Will, that is *totally* unacceptable. Look, we've gotta talk. *Now*! Meet me at Izzy's in 45 minutes." I banged the phone into its cradle.

The drive into Santa Monica gave me time to sort out my thoughts, though it did *not* diminish my anger. A short time later, we sat facing each other in a booth at Izzy's Wilshire Boulevard deli, our frequent halfway meeting place. Without holding back, I let him know how I felt, concluding with: "Will, you had no fucking right to do that. I mean, partners don't pull shit like that. And I want your promise that you'll never do anything like it again."

Expressionless, he'd maintained eye-contact throughout, his only words being something about how he'd promised Isobel the script by date-certain. Now, I waited for his response – a reaction which one would assume might include a word or two of apology. Instead, he just – sat there.

It was boggling. Disorienting.

"You – *do* understand what I'm saying? Why I'm angry? You don't even tell me we're committed to send her the damned script – you just make changes on your own and send 'em off to New York without…?"

Will acknowledged my questions with a nod and/or a monosyllable. Followed by silence.

I am almost unable to convey the fury I felt. The close-to-the-edge, wanting-to-hit-him anger and frustration. Not my style, instead I waited for what seemed like a long minute or two, figuring he'd say *something*.

But his expression did not change. I rose, stared at him for a moment, and departed, stunned, my stomach knotted. As soon as I got home I contacted Ms. Robbins and informed her that Will had inadvertently sent the wrong script, and that a corrected one would reach her shortly.

Clearly, the dynamic between Will and me had changed. Dramatically and permanently. Oh, I'd had earlier hints of his passive-aggressive tendencies, but with this he'd taken it to a *very* different level. It wasn't to be our last confrontation triggered by such actions. Nor would it be the most outrageous.

Not all of my theatrical negative-experiences were due exclusively to my collaborator. One emerged during an early discussion with our producers in New York. It was my initial inkling of what I came to understand as an almost palpable – and in my view pathetic – fear on the part of Broadway musical theatre people. They are *terrified* of any material that might actually *move* an audience emotionally on a level deeper than 'Ha-ha.' This, I learned, was their comfort-zone. Anything more extreme, such as inspiring throat-lumps or bringing customers to tears seemed to be unthinkable. Frightening.

Truly, given what I already knew about the nature of 'musicals,' as well as most other American entertainments, I should not have been surprised. Any more than I was by Will's lack of support in that area, or about calling the show what it was – an opera.

The certainty of a fight over that one? Already a given. My realization that it was unwinnable took a while. But I ultimately came to see that they regarded it as *The Dreaded O-word*, not even to be *whispered*. I tried a number of arguments, on occasion pointing out that the hugely successful *Evita* had been billed (albeit in *very* small print) as "an opera about the life of Eva Peron." So why not, I urged them, call *JACK* "an opera about the life of John F. Kennedy"?

Forgeddaboutit.

The only Broadway person with any clout who conceded that it was in fact an opera and should be thus labeled, was the Shubert Organization's co-top guy, Bernie Jacobs. Later, though still a major champion of the show, Bernie permitted himself to be overruled. But I will be forever grateful to him for his support.

Nonetheless, on the win-some/lose-some chart, I knew then, and know now, that I was waaay ahead. The next entry in that scorecard's win-column: even with the music not yet completed, our show was booked to open May 7, 1993 at The Goodspeed Opera House in Connecticut!

FORTY-ONE
The Most Fun I've Ever Had with My Clothes On— and *JACK* is Staged!

Before going to work on *Paris Metal*, I had begun writing what might well have been the final *MSW* episode, ever. The series was nearing the end of its seventh highly successful season, and of Angela Lansbury's contractual commitment as well. Word was out that, given Angie's growing unhappiness with Peter Fischer's autocratic management, she was ready to walk. Meaning: the show would fold, something that – given its consistent top-ten ratings – neither Universal Studios nor CBS were about to allow. This in turn guaranteed that they'd offer Angela damned near anything if she'd continue. Which of course, this being Hollywood, ensured that she, via 'her people,' was going to drive a *very* tough bargain – perhaps more than the market could handle. The outcome was definitely in at least semi-doubt.

My season-and-possibly-series finale teleplay, guest-starring Jerry Orbach as Harry McGraw, was titled *The Skinny According to Nick Cullhane*. Because of *MSW*'s uncertain future, in the closing scene, with Harry and Jessica on the front steps of her Cabot Cove home, I gave him – with a smile as I wrote it – the perhaps too-obvious but for me irresistibly appropriate button-line. Happily, Jerry delivered it with his customary, superb wryness: "And – that's all she wrote…"

Instead – and happier still – *Murder, She Wrote* ran for another five years.

First, however, those earlier-referenced end-of-seventh-season issues at *MSW* played themselves out. Lessons, really, about the power of stardom, ego, and having a powerful and creative agent.

The stardom part: in simple, Angela demanded, quite aside from money issues, the title of co-Executive Producer, alongside Peter Fischer. Or else she would exit the show.

Fischer's just-as-non-negotiable response was that he did *not* co-executive produce.

To which the studio's – and CBS's – reactions were, quite understandably, identical. At that point they needed Ms. Lansbury worse than they needed Peter. He was out of there.

So much for the ego part. The agent part tops it.

The above arrangement was considerably *more* than okay with Fischer. The reason: going in, seven years earlier, before the first episode was written, Peter's heavyweight agent, the already-mentioned Bill Haber, had negotiated a *very* inventive deal. He 'generously' proposed to Universal a dramatic switch on the series-creator's usual share of 'back-end' profits. The then-common arrangement: he or she would, *in the unlikely* event that the new show became a long-running hit, be paid a large percentage of the monies from syndication, a movie-sale if any, etc. Because most series were cancelled long before the need for such payments, it was an inexpensive, no-brainer concession for the money-people.

This time however, Haber offered them an even more attractive deal. Peter would accept a *much* smaller-than-conventional percentage. But, for this, Haber asked for an unusual quid pro quo – one that would kick-in once the series went into a third year – in itself a way rare occurrence. From that point, over and above *any* other fees Fischer was being paid, he would receive *non-returnable* advances on his reduced piece of that maybe-never back-end. The amount: *$70,000 per episode*, such payments continuing for as long as the series was in production.

Regardless of whether or not Peter was still employed on the show.

Thus, from the beginning of *Murder, She Wrote* season three, until the end of its final season twelve, 220 episodes were produced.

For *each* of them Peter received those advances. In total, $15,400,000.

Given his departure before season eight, for *half* of those, he was not present. An amazing deal, I'm fairly certain it was one-of-a-kind.

So, with Angela as Executive Producer, plans were laid for the eighth season. She surrounded herself with family-members – her director son, Anthony, stepson David, husband/manager Peter Shaw, and her brother, my old friend Bruce – all of whom came aboard.

Moreover, my then-reading of Angela's desire to avoid *anything* that smacked of Fischer seemed to be correct. One of her first moves was to fire nearly everyone connected with Peter's regime – but especially the writers. One of the suits in Universal's Black Tower did in fact plump loudly for me to be brought on as Showrunner, but I doubt that it was even considered, given that I was one of 'Fischer's People.'

Nor, for that reason had I allowed my hopes to rise. Thus, when my association with the series ended, I was disappointed – even a bit pissed-off – but also intensely grateful. I'd enjoyed seven wonderful seasons working with Angie, Jerry and so many other actors, writers, directors and others for whom I had great respect.

Now, during those years, we had zero illusions that we were curing cancer, or producing literature. But it was a given that, like almost every other TV series, the *Murder, She Wrote* premise contained a number of very particular, unique-to-the-show quirks. Qualities that not every writer in the business necessarily 'got.' Some as simple as Jessica not driving a car, the zero-degree of gore, the almost-no violence, or other such details. Then there were the mystery techniques we employed. The truth was that in our estimation during the entire run, besides the four core writers (Fischer, Bob Swanson, Bob van Scoyk and myself) we found *maybe* four freelancers whose scripts didn't need to be rewritten from page one – or simply shit-canned.

But instead of turning to them, Angela hired, as described earlier, a pair of veteran writers who, though competent, were fundamentally unfamiliar with the series. The problem however didn't stop there. As the new season got under way, it quickly became apparent to the fans, to CBS and Universal that the situation was far worse than that.

These guys *just plain didn't get it.*

Sure, a few of their changes were salutary. Jessica Fletcher's signature manual typewriter was replaced with a computer (finally). She acquired a Manhattan apartment (in addition to her Cabot Cove home), and – likely more Angela's doing – a hipper, more stylish wardrobe. But within the first few episodes, the overall product was disastrous, their introduction of violence, bodies falling, and Uzi-armed bad guys totally *not-MSW*. In fact it was *so* unacceptable to the show's loyal core-audience that, along with declining viewership, Angela and the network began receiving numerous angry protests. Their predominant flavor: 'I-feel-betrayed-and-I'll-never-watch-your-show-again!'

So, she hastily brought back one of Fischer's two staffer-since-the-beginning Writer/Producers, Robert Swanson, who promptly contacted me about doing a script or two. Before I'd gotten started on my first one, the two veterans had been dismissed, leaving Bob as Showrunner.

For a few days, that's where it stood, or so I thought, until Bruce Lansbury phoned and invited me to lunch which, I assumed was to talk about script ideas. We met at a Valley restaurant, and Bruce promptly explained that there was a new problem – one that I'd not known about. He and Swanson had 'issues.' Bob had exited the series. "We'd like you to come back on the show…" Then Bruce added, with his commendable and characteristic candor: "Strike that – we *need* you."

Surprised and, though I didn't say it, still a bit ticked by my without-a-word dismissal at the end of the previous season, I didn't immediately say yes: "What about van Scoyk?" Bob, whose career dated back to radio writing, had been there with Swanson from the start – the only writer other than Fischer and myself who had written as many *MSW* scripts.

Bruce explained that van Scoyk's age was a problem for them. Ergo, I was next in line. The end of it, really. Bruce grinned: "Anyway, we'd rather have you."

True or not, the moment was, I have to admit, delicious. I savored it for a count or two before admitting to *my* problem – a very probable deal-breaker: "Thanks, Bruce. I'd really love to. Except there's – well – my stage show premieres next May, and I'll need to spend about six weeks in Connecticut."

He shrugged. "That's toward the end of production season. I'm sure we can work it out."

They did! Next day my agent told me we had a contract: they'd agreed to pay our asking price, with no haggling – and I could phone in my work from the East, with my fees continuing. Another part of the good news: the prospect of working closely with Bruce – sharing an office-suite as it turned out. Especially pleasurable because for years we had genuinely liked and respected each other, enjoying each other's company both professionally and socially.

More than that, I was welcomed warmly by Angela and the rest of her family.

As good as it *ever* has to be.

Except that it *did* improve. I can say without qualification that the next five years on *MSW* were *absolutely* the Best. The only experience I had in the TV biz that was even close was doing *The Law & Harry McGraw*. In both cases, as said, I would *gladly* have paid for the privilege.

Over that run – and since – I've thought more than once about Peter Fischer's dinner party-admission that he viewed me as a scavenger. Along with it, the resultant fascinating lesson in how, with a single word, we can and often do reveal who we *really* are.

I admit to having been struck by the irony that despite his low opinion of me, due in no small part to my abilities, to my role in keeping the series on the air (and in the top ten) over those five seasons, he was paid, in absentia, that *additional* nearly $8 million.

Money he *wouldn't* have received had I not taken the job.

And yes, I've wondered – once or twice – and *very* idly (as in: not *really* caring) – if *he* ever looked at it that way...

But hey, it was win-win. Happens all the time, right...?

Early in my first season as Showrunner, Angela, Bruce and I agreed that too many recent episodes had involved extensive, rather tedious backstories. So I came up with several premises that would take place mostly-to-entirely in the present and, with Bruce at my side in his sister's dressing-room/trailer outside the Cabot Cove soundstage, I ran them past Angie and her husband, Peter.

She didn't much care for any of them, and asked if I had any others.

"Gee, Angie, I really---" I stopped myself in mid-sentence because I'd had a sudden vision – a way to write a very abbreviated version of my *JFK/ Gideon Oliver* stalled novel as a *Murder, She Wrote* episode. Just as instantly, I knew it went *dramatically* counter to the kind of story we'd been trying to come up with – the reason we were in her trailer at that moment. But – in that same thought-rush I figured what the hell, I'll take advantage of that: "Actually, I do have one. Except that you probably won't like it..." I paused, waiting for her questioning, 'I'm curious' look. When I saw it, I waggishly added: "...because it's got the mother of all backstories."

Which of course hooked her, as well as Bruce and Peter. Angela grinned: "Let's hear it."

Continuing on my mini-roll, and chuckling inwardly, I delivered the second part of my tease. "Okay, let me give you the *TV Guide* logline: 'Jessica Fletcher solves The Murder of the Century – almost...'" After another brief-but-suitable pause, I admitted that the murder case was the JFK assassination. All of them loved it, and that was that – they needed no further details.

As I began outlining my story, I figured it would be cool to bring back Jerry Orbach as Harry McGraw, portraying him as a former associate of my dead 1963 PI. So I phoned him at his apartment in Manhattan to check on his availability and learned to my disappointment, but delight for Jerry, that he couldn't do it. "I just signed to co-star on *Law & Order*."

Thus, in writing the episode, titled *Dead Eye*, I created a new PI character not unlike the seedy, retro McGraw. We cast the witty *M.A.S.H.* veteran Wayne Rogers in the role, and had *such* great fun for the next five years as he played Jessica's periodically recurring, exasperating bullshitter pal, Charlie Garrett.

A joy to work with, Wayne, like Angie and Jerry, always knew *exactly* where the jokes were. He also shared my affection for con artists, confiding that like me he felt more than a little of that in himself. I was proud of *Dead Eye*, pleased with the way it turned out to be an atypical but satisfying *MSW* episode.

In April, 1993, with casting completed some weeks earlier in Manhattan, Will Holt and I headed for Connecticut, and rehearsals for the Goodspeed staging of *JACK*. It was a thrilling experience. Unreal, actually, with the show taking shape even as the first green of the season was appearing on the winter-barren rural New England trees – both seeming to blossom at about the same pace. Virtually the only negative was that I missed Holly.

One of Will's more inspired ideas truly helped to make the production seem far more lavish and elegant than anybody could have expected from its miniscule $70-80,000 workshop budget. Given our imagining of the Kennedy lifestyle as a series of parties, with high-end Boston-Washington-London settings for much of the show, Holt came up with a theatrically appropriate yet money-saving notion. The males' costumes throughout would be white-tie-and-tails, and for the women, long, pastel-colored gowns. Virtually the sole wardrobe changes, when needed, consisted of removing the men's tailcoats and substituting colored bow-ties and suspenders. This visual, dramatically satisfying approach was so effective that we would use it – with only minor variations – in both of *JACK*'s subsequent, far more expensive productions. It made for a great look.

I truly liked our cast, which was led in the role of Jack by a wonderful young tenor, Michael Brian Dunne. We had the extraordinary Broadway veteran, Rita Gardner portraying his mother, Rose, while Jackie was played by a lovely young actress/soprano, Claudia Rose Golde. The multi-talented Bill Zeffiro did a priceless comic turn as Richard Nixon. Lauren Sterling, a new, very talented young actress who played The Debutante in Act One would continue to be a passionate supporter of the show. Hers, along with that of the other players, musicians and crew members, added greatly to the communality of the affair.

With the show's look becoming more and more distinct, and my being a part of these and other often moment-to-moment adjustments and invention, the days passed in a kind of joyous blur. They were made more salutary because Will and I were mostly of the same mind about the project, our disagreements, for the moment at least, minor, as we made various last-minute tweaks. My first close experience with composers and arrangers, I was then, and continue to be in awe of people who know, and can make music.

On the topic of show-labeling, still fighting my lonely campaign to call it an opera, versus those who favored 'musical,' I enjoyed a small victory. Or at least that's the way I chose to regard it: we settled for simply calling it *JACK*.

Meanwhile, my work on *Murder, She Wrote* was light. Our 'Team Player' issue had occurred and been settled before I departed, and we were just then emerging from spring hiatus, gearing up for season nine.

Suddenly, it was May 7th. As unique as the preliminaries had been, Opening Night was another matter entirely. Friends, our children and other relatives had come to Connecticut from all over the country. A full-house audience of nearly 300. To sit among them, with Holly at my side as they reacted to our show, was an experience that remains entirely singular. To be watching them watch, feeling and sharing their responses – to savor the culmination of that eleven years earlier dream that had begun back in the Shubert Theater – was for me a ride like no other.

But *all* of it was surpassed when the performance ended. Because along with the enthusiastic applause, as the lights went up I was confronted with an almost overwhelming sight.

My purpose, from the instant I conceived it, had been to grab the audience members by the throat, and *make* them look at, and *realize*, what We *had* – and what We *lost* – that day in Dallas.

No small part of that effort – and its power – was embodied in a moment – three, actually – at the end. Following the gunshots, a line from Bobby, and another from Rose, the house went completely dark. Then, one at a time, a spot illuminates a "witness," then another, and another – each briefly describing how the event had been received/reacted to in their part of the world. That was followed by more singing, then, Curtain.

Looking around us in that moment, through my own tear-blurred eyes, I saw that most of the people in the theatre were drying theirs.

Particularly gratifying, in terms of reaching tough, seen-it-all types, there, two rows in front of me, wiping his tears, was veteran CBS newsman Morley Safer.

Next day, I spoke via telephone to our daughter Brooke, who was finishing her Berkeley junior year in France. She asked how it had gone. I still kind of squirm when I recall my reply. Not without hesitation, and with my voice cracking, I offered that the opening performance and its aftermath had caused me to compare it to other thrilling moments I'd experienced in my life.

It had come down to just one, that of seeing her being born – of my four children, the only birth I'd witnessed: "…And Brooke – I have to say, last night topped even that."

It was true. For me, the absolute, ultimate, *once* in my life reward. In a real way, I guess, what being an artist *is* all about. About as close as one can come to *knowing* he's reached people in the way he intended.

Fortunately, I think Brooke understood.

A few days later, the following satisfying comment appeared in the *New Haven Register*: "The opening of *JACK* at the Goodspeed's Norma Terris Theatre left its audience tingling..."

Our two-week run played to sold-out houses.

Was the show *exactly* what I'd envisioned? Hell no. Even on that first night, amid my emotions was the acute consciousness of the numerous rewrites and modifications I'd been imagining since we'd begun rehearsals.

Still, returning to Los Angeles and my *Murder, She Wrote* responsibilities, I was so high that I had almost no thoughts of a future for *JACK*.

Happily, however, other people *were* making plans.

FORTY-TWO
Boss-Pleasures—and *JACK* Goes Forward—and Backward— and Forward...

THE LEVEL OF GRATIFICATION – and of that so-elusive aspect of the collaborative arts, the *control* – that one can enjoy as a series Showrunner is – singular. A*wesome*.

One example: every ten days during the production season, we would shoot another episode. We had, in the budget for *each*, $130,000 that I could spend on sets.

Anything I wanted.

Another: music. We employed a 32-piece orchestra to score each show. If the story-theme was, say, Italian, I would tell the composer how much garlic I wanted to smell. I could, when I chose to do so, sit in on the recording sessions, offering comments and suggestions.

Then there was casting, as well as working with the designers, editors, the stage crew, and of course, overseeing the scripts.

One of best instances of the overall creative reach, and of the almost total fun I had with it is, I think, encapsulated by the following anecdote. I was taking pitches one morning from so-dependable Bob van Scoyk, whom I'd asked to come in with some Cabot Cove story ideas. We contracted with the actors to do five of these per season, and it was time to get another teleplay into the pipeline. Bob ran several notions past me – all that he'd prepared – and none of them, even with the usual back-and-forth, the 'okay, what if we did it this way?' – had grabbed me. After a pause, Bob spread his palms "So... Whaddya wanta do?"

About the only certainty at that moment was my need to get him into work. So, improvising, I recalled a one-line pitch on which I'd sold a *Zorro* episode nearly two years earlier. I quickly calculated that by changing the locale from Old Mexico to Maine the chances were slim-to-none that viewers would ever see the similarity. Besides, how many of *our* regulars would've even watched *Zorro*? "Okay, how about we do *Pagliacci* and *Casablanca* in Cabot Cove...?"

Off Bob's questioning look, I continued: "There's this carnival that comes to town. And it's run by a boor and his wife – she's this great-looking 40-ish lady. That's the *Pagliacci* part. The *Casablanca* part, she's Ilsa. She goes to the Sheriff's office to get the permits, and the Sheriff – he's Rick. He turns around and finds himself facing the woman who dumped him back in college 20 years ago so she could run off with the boor."

That was all the priming Bob required. "I love it." He went off and wrote it – not unexpectedly, a terrific script.

Weeks later I had the satisfaction of visiting the studio's back lot town square, which for our show had been transformed into a carnival midway, complete with rides and games and tents, a Ferris Wheel, and 200 extras, including jugglers and a sword-swallower.

All because I'd said what I said to van Scoyk.

I was playing with the Ultimate Electric Train, flat-out the absolute *best* toy a kid could ever have.

Plus, they *paid* me for it!

Moreover, it went beyond the honor and pleasure of writing for Angela, and the quality actors that her presence attracted. There was the near-unique-in-TV opportunity to write dialogue containing multi-syllable words. I continued to relish the non-interference from studio and network regarding scripts. *MSW* and *McGraw* were the *only* series I ever worked on that received *no* notes from either entity.

The reason, explained to me at the beginning by Fischer, was partly confidence in himself, Link and Levinson. But mostly it was because the genre was mystery, and thus rather complex by their standards. The suits justifiably feared that given the need for key lines to be spoken and clues to be shown, their interference might cause undue problems. In my case, having suffered their sometimes nitpicky comments on other shows, it was a welcome situation. Nor did we even have to clear our story premises with them, as was de rigueur on other series, though we did so as a courtesy, and to keep them in the loop.

Further, I continued the practice, as we had similarly done with *The Law & Harry McGraw*, regarding adlibs and lines being rewritten on the set: no changes were permitted without clearance from me. This was not as dictatorial as it sounds. An actor substituting a word or sentence with an improv might very well unknowingly eliminate or alter a clue to the central mystery, thus possibly requiring dubbing, or worse, reshooting. To her immense credit, Angela never once quarreled with this policy – nor had Jerry Orbach or Barbara Babcock on their series.

Not without the occasional minor disappointment, frustration and an annoying, antagonistic personality or an occasional fool to resist suffering – again, a *damned* nice place to be.

Within a few weeks following *JACK*'s run in Connecticut, we received exciting news. Additional backers had come on board, and our show was booked for an April, 1995 production at the University of Oklahoma. The budget was to be considerably higher, in the $350,000-$400,000 range, with the leads played by professionals, and supporting roles filled by students in the school's Musical Theater Program.

Over the ensuing months Will and I, with our usual frictions, tinkered with the show. We made several trips to the OU campus in Norman, where we began to get the feel of the place and the people with whom we'd be working. These included Producer Max Weitzenhoffer, a gentleman, and a serious player in the university's theatre school.

Casting began, and along with the good fortune of having Claudia Rose Golde, Michael Dunn and Bill Zeffiro reprising their roles as Jackie, Jack, and Nixon, we had *more* amazing luck. Awesome baritone, multiple Tony-winning Broadway Star John Cullum had, with his wife, author/former dancer Emily, become our social friends in Malibu. John, who was then co-starring in the *Northern Exposure* TV series, agreed to play Jack's father, Joseph P. Kennedy, Sr!

As our opening date grew nearer, and production continued on *MSW*, I began commuting to Norman on weekends, working with Will, our Director, Craig Belknap, our orchestrator/arranger, James Faulconer, and others.

During this time I discovered and was deeply moved by a particularly relevant chapter in Theodore H. White's superb memoir, *In Search Of History*. Titled '*Camelot*,' it is almost unbearably touching to read even today. In it, White tells of receiving a phone call from Jacqueline Kennedy several days after Dallas, urgently summoning him to Hyannis. This remarkable woman told him there was something important that she needed for him to impart to the country.

Holding the presses on the special JFK memorial edition of *LIFE Magazine*, White arrived at the Kennedy compound very late that night. There, one-on-one with him at her insistence, and to the annoyance of the Secret Service people, Ms. Kennedy confided her desperate wish to set the record straight, to not leave her late husband's memory to the 'bitter people' who wrote the history books. For the next several hours, she poured out her take on Jack, and those thousand days. Including the first-ever reference in that context to *Camelot*.

Finally, at 2AM, with Jacqueline listening at his shoulder and occasionally correcting him, White dictated the story via telephone to the editors at *Life*.

Reading White's moving account, I was instantly struck – and excited – by a vision in which we'd start our show with a twist on that scene. Jackie, alone onstage, dressed in sweater and slacks as White had described. Taking the audience into her confidence, as she had with him, she would – singing and speaking – tell *us* about this past, *so* terrible week. How vitally important she feels it is to let us know how she wants Jack to be remembered. In effect, making *her* the narrator of our show. I could *not* have imagined a more effective, more emotionally stirring device for *immediately* grabbing the audience.

Thrilled by the idea, and how *right* it seemed, I eagerly wrote it. On paper it felt even more powerful. A day or two later, on my next trip to Norman I excitedly shared it with Will: "Look, I know you're busy with rehearsals and music orchestrations, but I'd *really* appreciate it if you'd take an hour or two and – youknow – even sketchily – lay in some music. Just enough so we could both see how it would play."

Noncommittal, disdainful really, Holt accepted my pages. Virtually his sole comment was dismissive – contemptuous, really: "So – all you're doing is – what – stealing what White wrote?"

That, to my profound frustration – and anger – was the end of it as far as that production was concerned. Oh, I raised the issue repeatedly during preparation for the OU staging, but there were other more immediate disagreements, and problems.

Nor could I have dreamt that it would take another 17 years until, at my deal-breaker, foot-down insistence, Will finally consented to set it to music, mystifyingly volunteering: "Oh yeah. I've always *loved* this opening."

Sigh…

Rehearsals began, and abruptly I was doing alternating entire weeks in LA and Norman, encountering more anger-generating surprises. Tweaks and changes Will continued to make without consulting me. On the positive side, our cast, including the eager, talented and hard-working student-performers, was joined by another impressive Broadway talent. Julienne Scanlon came aboard as Rose. Again, everyone's enthusiasm for the project was infectious.

There were a few more creative differences with Will, and the increasingly and for me irritatingly slick *Broadway Musical Look* it was acquiring. Plus – my protests notwithstanding – its billing as *JACK, the Musical*. But the production did seem to be coming together, and partly offsetting such annoyances, of course, was my delight that the show was having a second incarnation.

Again, sudden-seeming, it was the morning of April 19, 1995. Our first preview performance was to begin at that evening at 7:30 PM in the school's handsome Rupel Jones Theatre.

Entering the hotel dining room for breakfast, I found guests and staff huddled around the TV, silent, stunned. On the screen were images from thirty miles away, of a smoky, flaming Oklahoma City high-rise, its façade blown away. A few minutes earlier, a terrorist's truck bomb had destroyed the Murrah Building. We later learned that the blast killed 168 people.

A dark, sad day, the producers considered canceling, then decided to go forward with the opening anyway. Late in the afternoon at the Oklahoma City airport, I met Holly as she arrived on her flight from LA. Most of her similarly unsmiling fellow passengers were either news people or FBI agents.

Later, after a touching preamble acknowledging the events in Oklahoma City, written and delivered by Michael Brian Dunn, *JACK* went on. Playing to a somber sold-out house of 750, the splendid performances by Cullum, Dunn, Golde and the others seemed to lift them out of their funk. Or at least distract them from it. Sitting in the audience, I was gratified by the reactions, by some aspects of the relative-to-Connecticut lavish production, and the comparatively full orchestrations. I was thrilled by the power of Michael Dunn's and John Cullum's *"Dad, I'm Not Joe"* duet, and by Michael's rendition of his post-election solo, *"A New America"*.

Then came the show's climax – and for me, *far* more egregious than Will's disdain for my proposed new opening, a *truly* infuriating shock.

Because of my commitments to *Murder, She Wrote*, and the resultant time-splitting between Norman and Los Angeles, I had been unable to witness a full-length rehearsal. I was thus unaware of and unprepared for what Will had done, without telling me, to the ending.

As in our original production, following the gunshots and darkness a pin-spot found Bobby, who delivered his despairing, choked-up statement: "We – believed – we could make the future better…" Followed by a line from Rose.

Next – *gone* were my three 'witnesses.'

Instead, as I watched dumbfounded and with escalating anger, Jackie emerged and walked down to the center stage footlights. There, as the final chorus ended, she delivered the achingly banal, truly awful, pathetically on-the-nose – and grossly *inappropriate* – curtain-line Will had substituted without consulting me.

"The age of violence begins."

While it had been used at the Goodspeed – and I had objected to it then – I'd conceded it to Will because it had been 'buried' – in effect, barely audible.

But here, it was just – out there. Dominant. In its full, shallow lameness. Yet another of his ongoing passive-aggressive acts.

I was fucking *outraged*!

The audience was apparently equally unready, both for the overwhelming triteness of the words, and that their utterance was intended to signify the end of the show.

There was no other signal, not even a lighting change. Only the actors standing still onstage staring out at the people in their seats. The audience's realization that it was over took an interminable, awkward 30 seconds or more. Then, cued by the actors beginning their curtain-calls, they started to applaud. Tentatively at first, it grew, and they began to rise.

I sat with my head in my hands, feeling fury, betrayal, and profound, stomach-wrenching embarrassment at even being associated with such bullshit.

Though infinitely minor in comparison to the tragedy of that morning in Oklahoma City, this downer was hugely significant in terms of my own pain.

The moment I was able to corner Will, I let him know just how fed up

I was with his behavior. He brushed off my bitter admonishments with his customary, maddening, non-reaction. Leaving me of course with the by-then understood certainty that such twisted crap from him would continue.

On the positive side, Oklahoma did yield a number of singularly satisfying memories – and relationships. One, following the last performance of our run, came during our wrap party. At the restaurant where the event was being held, a young man who was waiting tables thanked Will and me, explaining that he had been a small boy at the time of Jack Kennedy's murder, and all he'd been aware of was its effect on his parents: "It was like this light went out in their eyes. But – seeing your show, finally I understand…"

Another plus: that night we learned that *JACK* was still alive, to be done next – bigger and better – in either London or Dublin! Will and I were introduced to the Director of this future production: Choreographer Larry Fuller.

But most salutary were some new acquaintances – people with whom I feel very fortunate to have formed lasting friendships. Among the undergraduate-actors, I connected especially with our talented Bobby Kennedy-portrayer: Jeremy Kent Jackson, a particularly interesting young man, is in successful mid-career in Hollywood.

Two others, both of them awesomely brilliant: former head of the OU law school, Federal Judge Wayne Alley, and then-OU law professor, the charming, erudite Anita Hill. Anita, whose life had changed so dramatically several years earlier when she'd famously testified against Supreme Court nominee Clarence Thomas, is one of the most remarkable people I have ever known. Our dialogues were, and continue to be fascinating. Wayne is one of the very few conservatives I have ever encountered who I consider to be a genuine intellectual.

Among my treasured memories are of the three of us seated at a café, arguing politics. Well, two, actually, since I was mostly an onlooker, knocked out to be in the presence of such minds.

FORTY-THREE
Murder, He ~~Wrote~~ Committed

NEAR THE ALL-TIME TOP of my personal *WEBIT?* Experiences (*Where Else But In Tinseltown?*), is one that involved working on a daily basis with – or trying to for a while, anyway – an *actual* murderer.

A fellow script-writer – and *especially* ironic, *on* my staff at *Murder, She Wrote*.

A man who had literally *gotten away with it*. Without doing time in prison.

Admittedly weird back then, now, it seems beyond bizarre. Especially in view of the number of people in the business who knew his story – and knowingly aided him in resuming his career in TV, and continuing it for three decades – *after* stabbing his wife to death. Even more remarkable, it was *not* because he was a revenue-producing asset, an award-winner, nor even, in truth, a serious talent.

Hell, because of my own silence after learning about it – and though I ultimately refused to go on working with him – I was complicit for a while in helping to enable him.

Also, hey – with no internet available at the time to easily verify or debunk or circulate the story…

When I took over as Showrunner, the former writing staff having been dismissed, it was obvious that I'd need at least one more writer to help with edits, take pitches and write scripts. The pressure of all those responsibilities, along with casting, overseeing sets, music, film-editing, viewing dailies and other production duties, plus holding a thankfully-few needy hands, was taking its toll.

Bruce Lansbury and I had agreed to think about possible choices for this additional staffer. The solution, I assumed, was provided for me one morning when Bruce knocked on my door as he strode into my office. With his customary smile and charm he announced our new writer-hire: "Just a heads-up, Tom. I'm bringing in Larry Heath. I think he'll be able to give you some solid help."

A guy I'd not met, Bruce went on to explain that he and Larry had worked together on *Mission Impossible*. In fact, my only knowledge of Laurence Heath was the he had scripted a single episode for *MSW*. Commissioned by Bruce and produced by my predecessors as the first of that eighth season, *Murder in Milan* was – okay. It had been completed as they were coming aboard, thus escaping much of their influence. The plot and style had not deviated all that far from the show's old pattern, as would their next few scripts. Among those, I would soon learn, was a second, as yet undelivered teleplay by Larry. "Thanks, Bruce. I look forward to working with him."

Next morning, Larry showed up, and we were introduced. Though a bit guarded, I thought, he seemed affable enough, and I put him to work on fixes and notes I'd made on the next episode to be filmed. He moved into his assigned office, and immediately got into the script-changes.

My initial inkling that anything might be amiss came later that week. Larry delivered his own first-draft teleplay, and upon reading it, I was distressed on several counts. First, the basic premise. It was typical of how the series had been mismanaged by Angela & Company's initial replacements for Peter Fischer and his writing crew. *Double Jeopardy*, set in New York City, featured Hispanic gangs, a missing corpse, and a religious penitent murdered with poison spray while in the confessional. Definitely *not* the type of story that had established and sustained the show's flavor and loyal viewership over its first seven years. But, in this case one we would have to live with because of the then-shortage of suitable material in the pipeline.

Worse however, and more surprisingly considering his veteran TV scripting status, I was struck by the number of outright ineptitudes and basic "Screenwriting 101" shortcomings I found.

Ergo, during our first script-note meeting I did my usual diplomatic-best to guide Larry into how to make it at least *somewhat* more like the traditional *Murder, She Wrote* episode. Even more gently, I got into suggested changes in the weaknesses and goofs I'd found.

To say that most of my comments were not well-received fails to describe his responses. Outright hostility was a far more accurate label. While argument, sometimes heated and animated, was not unusual in that showbiz world so full of driven, passionate personalities, this was markedly different. Almost – threatening. Something I had not *ever* encountered during my TV experience. But I tried to handle it, assuming at first that he might have been "having a bad day," or something of that sort.

That reading soon proved mistaken. By a lot. In each subsequent exchange with Larry, any questioning of his work produced similarly angry reactions.

I mentioned this privately to Bruce, who dismissed it with a wave of the hand. He seemed unwilling to discuss it.

Then, at a dinner party a week or two later, I began to learn why. Triggered by a conversation among a few of the guests, about working with "difficult" characters, I mentioned my ongoing problems with this "new guy" with whom I was trying to interact. When asked, I spoke his name.

Lila Garrett's immediate response: "Leonard Heideman. I went to high school with him."

"No, I said 'Larry Heath.'"

"Same person." Then, off my questioning look, she added: "He changed his name a couple of years after he murdered his wife."

My first reaction: *she's kidding.*

Wrong.

"Yeah. He got off on one of the first 'Twinkie Defenses.'" Lila went on to explain that in 1963, Leonard Heideman had brutally assaulted and killed his wife in their kitchen, while at least one of their two young sons watched. He had stabbed her more than 40 times with a pair of scissors, including 8 to her heart.

Both Heideman and his wife had been under psychiatric care for years, including, according to Lila, medications (the "Twinkie" part). He'd been judged innocent because of insanity, remanded to a mental hospital, and, one year later, set free.

I was shocked – hell, blown away – by Lila's story. There I was, working alongside a homicidal maniac. It certainly appeared to explain his angry outbursts, *and* made them far scarier. I shared it later that evening with Holly, who was appalled. I barely slept that night, wondering among other things if Bruce Lansbury was aware of the truth about his friend. Was Angela? That one struck me as difficult to believe.

It was clarified next morning. My first stop was Bruce's office, where I began telling him what I'd heard from Lila. He stopped me almost immediately. "I know, Tom… Larry and I, we go way back. And as far as I know, he's never been in any trouble since. Look, I'd appreciate it if we could keep this between ourselves. He needs the work, and I know that if Angie were to learn about it…"

Still uneasy, I assured him I wouldn't say anything.

I didn't. Though from that moment forward, I made certain that, anytime I was in a room with Larry, there was a desk or other large piece of furniture between us.

While that made me feel more secure, it didn't resolve things. A week or so later, I was giving him notes on his next script. While a surprising number of them were basic, I did my best to come off as non-confrontationally as possible. Maybe because I'd learned the truth about him, I was imagining it, but this time, his reactions seemed truly, *frighteningly* intimidating.

To the degree that I'd had enough – of that *and* his bad writing.

After our meeting I entered Bruce's office and told him I was fed up and wanted to fire Larry. I was already prepared for his reluctance and then refusal to do so.

"Okay, Bruce, then here's the deal. I will no longer take meetings with him, or work on his scripts. He's your problem. I'm gonna hire someone I can work with."

Bruce nodded his consent. It was indeed a relief, and a few days later I brought aboard my friend and talented writer, Jerry Ludwig. He remained on the show until its cancellation in 1996. Jerry and I had a great, productive time working together. Heath continued on staff until the end. It was his final credit. In January, 2007, Laurence Heath hung himself.

I never discussed it with Angela, but as far as I know she was *never* aware of the bizarre fact that we had an actual *murderer* employed on our series.

FORTY-FOUR
More *MSW* Pleasures, an Abrupt Final Season— Plus a Life-Chapter Ending, and a Novel Discovery

ON MY FIRST DAY BACK AT UNIVERSAL, the experience in Norman was put into brilliant, witty perspective for me. Angela's husband, Peter Shaw and I were walking along the corridor of the Producer's Building when he asked how *JACK* had gone.

"It was – okay... But I guess I shouldn't complain. I mean, we *did* get standing ovations."

"At the end?"

I nodded: "Yeah."

Peter's wise, tossed-off, response is one I'll always remember: "They were getting up to leave anyway…" Then, he *really* nailed it: "The only standing ovation that counts is the one Rose gets in the middle of *Gypsy*, after belting *Everything's Coming up Roses*."

Humbling, *awesomely* on the money. A kind of reality-jolt for *anyone* in the entertainment business.

Meanwhile, back in Cabot Cove, the keepers from my *Murder, She Wrote* experience kept on coming. In 1993, I was producing an episode titled *Bloodlines*. Written by my friend, Bob Hamner, directed by the very capable Don Mischer, it took place in Virginia, and concerned racehorses.

I'm on a soundstage, sitting in a private area behind the set, between setups, with Mickey Rooney. Yeah, *that* Mickey Rooney – who was our featured guest-star. His role: racehorse trainer Matt Cleveland – who ends up as the murder victim. Mickey – with all his trademark *Andy Hardy/Babes on Broadway*-type energy, enthusiasm and animation that almost made me forget his advanced age, was playing at that moment to an audience of one: *me*. He was describing/acting out, in real time, the movie he'd been dying to get made for the last thirty or maybe forty years.

This *major* Hollywood Legend had performed opposite Judy Garland, Elizabeth Taylor and yes, Angela Lansbury in *National Velvet*! The guy I'd watched thirty feet tall as a kid, all those Saturday afternoons in Chicago – is *pitching* – to *me*!

If this comes off as if I've never quite gotten used to that idea – or others like it – it's because I never have.

So entranced/awed was I by the above spectacle that I have absolutely zero recollection of what this elderly munchkin's movie was about – though I'm sure if it had grabbed me, I'd remember.

Working with Mickey, incidentally, proved to be somewhat amusingly problematic for Angela, other cast members, the crew and, after the shoot was over, especially for the film editors. As full as ever of that old, boundless, irrepressible and not-always-disciplined vitality that had so characterized him onscreen, Rooney never delivered two takes the same way.

It's a technique that can and often does work in features. But in the rapid seven-or-eight pages per day shooting of a filmed TV series, *all* of the coverage, those shots – wide, medium and/or close – must then be edited to a precise length (in minutes and seconds). When the takes don't match, don't readily cut together, it can be crazy-making.

It was.

But hey – we're talking *The Mick*. It was a small price to pay...

One of the many ongoing pleasures for me during those years as Head Writer on the series was to work again with Bruce Lansbury. Elegant but not stuffy, Bruce was a true gentleman who, along with his role as Producer/Gatekeeper for his sister, also wrote a few scripts. One day, while I was giving him notes on one of his efforts, Bruce paid me a compliment that I still cherish. Right up there with his years-earlier priceless *Wonder Woman* advice about my bad guys talking too much. "Hey, I'm not a real writer – but you, you're an artist."

One evening at home Holly and I happened to catch the 1945 classic film, *The Picture of Dorian Gray* on TV. I was as taken by Angela's portrayal of Sybil Vane as I had been when I'd first seen it as a kid. Much more, actually – because by then, knowing her, working with her, my appreciation went so much deeper. Back then it had been that initial boyish lust for the young girl with the incredible hourglass shape, singing so plaintively – and unforgettably – *Goodbye, Little Yellow Bird.*

What struck me on this viewing was the remarkable beauty of Angela's face and her power as an actress. In particular, during a moment near the end of the movie when the vulnerable Sybil is finally, totally rejected by an icy Dorian Gray. Superbly, memorably acted by Hurd Hatfield, with heartless mean-spirited finality, Gray orders her out of his house, and his life. She is devastated, and so are we as we empathize with this young woman. She exits the room, and Gray, alone now, into himself, crosses, seats himself at his piano and begins playing.

A moment later the camera shifts to the doorway – and Angie/Sybil reappears, tentatively peeking into the room. Then, in tight close-up, her sweet innocence absolutely nailed by the tiny hat perched atop her piled hair, we see a single tear roll down her cheek. An exquisite, touching, unforgettable moment, its intensity amplified in that viewing because of my then-personal connection to this truly great actress.

Next morning after parking my car I went directly to the soundstage, where I caught up with Angela in a corridor as she headed for the set and her next scene. I quickly told her what Holly and I had watched the night before, and recounted how moved I'd been, especially by her moment in the doorway: "Angie, I have *got* to kiss that little face."

She smiled. I placed a hand on each side of her face, and kissed her cheek. My hands still there, eyes misting, I smiled also as I pulled slightly away: "Thank you, Angie."

Then, she made the moment even *more* special: "Thank *you*."

I lowered my hands and she proceeded to the set.

A memory that I truly treasure.

How 1996 became the final year for *Murder, She Wrote* was about commerce. Our time-slot, as it had been from the beginning, was 8PM Sunday, with the venerable, respected *60 Minutes* as our lead-in. But starting in 1993, *MSW* acquired its first real competition.

Airing at the same time on ABC was *Lois & Clark*, a series about Superman and Lois Lane. Aimed at an entirely different, younger audience, the contest wasn't so much for numbers of viewers as it was for – surprise, surprise – dollars. Advertising dollars. The wisdom, accepted and probably true: the younger viewers of such shows were a more desirable market. They spent more money on *stuff* than did the old farts who watched our show. Understandably alarming to the suits at CBS, *Lois & Clark*'s number of viewers had risen. While it was still only about two-thirds of *MSW*'s, ABC was able to charge more per pair-of-eyeballs to advertise on their show. Considerably more. Making the show more profitable.

Not – when you're in 2nd place in that world – a promising situation. Even when your show is approaching 'Institution' status.

Ergo, the corporate bean-counters at CBS decided our show had to go –

that in effect they had to kill it. On the other hand, *Murder, She Wrote* was still in the ratings top-ten. Which meant that if they abruptly canceled us, they risked outcry and backlash from the millions of loyal (albeit less-desirable) viewers, and the inevitable period of bad-press that would follow.

So CBS Programming Director Leslie Moonves invoked the time-tested, earlier-referenced device of shuffling the schedule, broadcasting the series on different, less-desirable nights, at non-ideal times. *MSW* was switched to Thursday evening, opposite a trendy, twenty-something sitcom. It worked to their satisfaction. A few weeks, and the ratings predictably fell to levels that would arguably justify dumping the show.

Though as often pointed out, you don't see a lot of 18-24's buying Lexus automobiles, which were in fact advertised on MSW, that demographic difference, in simple, is why this classic series wasn't renewed for a thirteenth season.

It was thus with way more than a touch of resentful glee that for our final episode, we took full advantage of the years of no Network script supervision or interference. Cooked up by myself and one of our top freelancers, Donald Ross – and written by him –*Death by Demographics* ended our twelve-year series on May 19, 1996.

In the story, a stodgy radio station acquires a new programming director. Determined to make his bones by reaching a more youthful audience, he begins scheduling shock jocks and the like. Pissing off listeners and fellow employees, he is murdered, run through with a fireplace poker.

Needless to add, we could and did celebrate a *very* satisfying run of a show that was a model of its kind. Though it promised a robust afterlife in syndication, there were a lot of less-than-thrilled campers present at our wrap-party. I was definitely one of them,

But all that notwithstanding, in my case or that of anyone in the business, to be – even *once* in a career – associated with a single such quality, hit-show, is *far* beyond fortunate.

More than that, I continue to treasure the privilege of having written for and worked with Ms. Lansbury. I know that because of the responsibility I felt to give her deservedly worthy material helped me to grow as an artist. The demands I made on myself, the more than ninety episodes I generated and produced, plus the twenty-four scripts I wrote – *all* of it – helped to make me a better storyteller/writer.

Figuring that a younger-skewing TV mystery series could still work, I quickly developed several such concepts, one of them in collaboration with Jerry Ludwig, another with Bill Link, as well as a couple of my own. But we quickly learned that the accepted marketing smarts that had brought about the end of *MSW* had similarly rendered the entire genre of 'conventional mystery' shows impossible – at that time anyway – to sell.

Also frustrating, my role in *Murder, She Wrote* had become, in the TV biz, a curious kind of type-casting curse. While treated with respect, I discovered that I had been pigeonholed as a maven of 'old fart' TV, and consequently, in the minds of buyers, unable to write anything else. Annoying, yes, but hey – it's the way things often work in the Hollywood version of the world…

I did receive a few offers, only one of which was interesting – and *that* for only a short time. I was asked to become Showrunner of a direct-for-syndication series, reviving the *Mike Hammer* franchise. This go-round would again star Stacy Keach. While hesitant for starters to work with him because of my earlier experience when he'd been sent to prison, I didn't rule it out at first. Not until I was informed that Stacy was in the habit of calling the writers into his trailer for evening rewrite sessions. That made my decision easy. I explained to the packager that A) I did not get rewritten and, B) *especially* not by actors. Nor, I added, was I willing to become involved in a show where an actor – *any* actor – had that level of clout. Even Angela Lansbury had known – and respected – those limits.

The other opportunities coming my way were even less interesting than *Hammer* – and it occurred to me that the business was telling me something to which I should listen.

While I'd enjoyed an exhilarating, surprise-filled, *incredibly* fortunate twenty years in TV, it was time for me to move on.

Was it difficult facing the reality that so *very* pleasurable a part of my life was behind me? *Damned* straight it was. I'd grown accustomed to the whirl, the blur of fun that it had been, the one-of-kind people and stimulating social interaction. Plus, the seemingly-endless opportunities to test and retest myself, the impetus to push my creativity to its limits, and the often close-to-immediate gratification. I will always be thankful for the experience, and I'll *always* miss it.

But – it *was* the past – never a country in which I've chosen to spend much time.

It is a place that, as I recognized would be the case when I began writing these pages, I've had to repeatedly force myself to revisit. Occasionally it's been with a bit of distaste, and some sadness that so much of it is behind me. But largely, I'm delighted to report, with enormous pleasure and frequent astonishment as memories return, and beget so many others.

Most of which remind me of my lifetime of *incredible* good luck.

One challenge to which I happily returned was my novel. How to write my mystery-thriller about the JFK assassination without killing off my most entertaining character near the top? That was solved for me in one of those *Ohmygod, of course*! moments in 1996, by Susan Isaacs's then-latest novel.

One of my favorite authors since her delightfully funny novel (and screenplay), *Compromising Positions*, Ms. Isaacs had just published *Lily White*. Another first-rate read, in this one Ms. Isaacs told parallel stories *taking place thirty years apart*. She accomplished this by employing a simple, hardly original but *totally* effective device. Ms. Isaacs had laid out her two yarns in alternating chapters, employing a different, distinctive typeface for each thread. *Bingo*! I saw within a few pages that she'd given me the key to keeping my 1963 Reno PI alive until the end, while still telling my archaeologist's tale in present-time. Stoked, I eagerly – and finally with *some* confidence – began outlining *The Sixteenth Man*.

FORTY-FIVE
Dublin—
and Some New Chapters

ONCE MORE, THE GOOD NEWS about *JACK*: the show *was* being staged, with a budget in this incarnation of about $1.5 million and perhaps more. In addition to Isobel Robins Konecky, who'd been with us since Connecticut, the producers now included Max Weitzenhoffer from Oklahoma, and the amiable New Yorker, Stewart F. Lane. Their plan was to take the show from Dublin to London's West End and then to Broadway.

So, late in 1996, Will Holt, myself, our new Director, Larry Fuller and the Producers journeyed across the Atlantic for casting, first to Dublin, and then to London. From those two cities we auditioned and selected a company of wonderfully gifted singer/actors, all of them Irish, Scottish or British. One exception was the lovely Monica Ernesti, a Yank based in London, whom we chose to portray Jackie. Another, as understudy for various roles, Amy Weaver, who'd appeared in our Oklahoma production while she was a student at OU. The other primary players included the excellent Maurice Clarke, Gary Raymond, Stella McKlusker, and Brian de Salvo.

In March of 1997, carried along in a continuing dreamlike, mostly euphoric fog of waaay unreality – it still feels that way even from this distance – I took up residence in Dublin. The producers provided both Will and myself with comfortable, roomy apartments in a modern condominium building overlooking a lovely, duck-and-magpie-filled public park in Ballsbridge, about a mile south of that delightful city's center. Our theatre, several blocks north of Trinity College on broad, bustling Dame Street: the lovely, ornate 130-plus year-old Olympia.

Another *exciting* time, the creative challenges – read: often painful conflicts, insanely infuriating – predictably resumed.

Following *JACK*'s Oklahoma production I'd received a promise from Holt that our previous ending for the show would be restored. But in Ireland, I found myself facing a fight about it with the producers, *and* a continuation of Will's old tricks. So, there I was in a foreign city five thousand miles from Holly, and my main ally, Bernie Jacobs, had died. I was feeling more isolated than ever in trying to defend my vision – and more determined to do so.

This is not to say the producers weren't good people, Isobel Konecky in particular. In a game that makes roulette look like a sensible investment, they did after all think enough of our show to put their money and time on the line.

But, between the old and new producers, our Broadway-savvy Director, and the coterie of New York music people with whom Will had surrounded himself, I was way outnumbered. As well as increasingly angry and disheartened.

My new opening was of course even further off the table than before.

Hardly the worst of it. During rehearsals I fought, and then resignedly watched as a wretchedly tired, seen-it-before gag supplanted the beginning we'd employed in the US. A cobbled-together mishmash with the actors already onstage, getting into costume and makeup. Bad enough, but I kept finding additional areas that needed guarding.

To their credit, the New York people displayed an understandable reluctance to tinker *too* much with material that had worked in the previous productions. But there was this relentless ongoing thrust toward making *JACK* bigger and glitzier. Distressingly, each day it more and more resembled every tired Broadway musical I had ever seen – which for me has been most of them. This included but was not limited to the staging, sets, lighting, and cliché choreography. Worst of it all, each step in that direction further minimized the show's emotional content, its power, and thus its heart.

Holly joined me in Dublin several days before we opened, which definitely gave my spirits a much-needed boost. Then, the big night arrived. April 22, 1997. Toward the others who'd made the journey from America – Holly's parents, friends from Malibu and elsewhere, a few of my cousins – I felt a mixture of gratitude, and acute, squirmy, wanting-to-hide-my-head embarrassment. Because while the presentation was professional, again I was *not* proud of what we'd put up there on the stage. Nor moved by *any* of it.

To my surprise, not *all* of the reviews were negative.

Holly and the others flew home and, following our final curtain two weeks later, the producers held a somber post-mortem in the theatre's barroom. There, it was announced that they would not be taking the show to London, and were instead pondering an alternate move. This I read, correctly as it turned out, meant that they no longer believed in the project and were cutting their losses.

The twenty minutes following our good-byes are my most vivid, poignant memory of the time in Dublin.

After the farewell hugs and thank-you's, with a sense of finality and gloom, as well as serious doubts about the show's future, if any, I exited the theatre alone. Ruminating on the preceding two months which had been *such* a mixture of emotional swings, too many of them painful lows, I walked the long mile to my apartment through a murky, appropriately oppressive misty drizzle. On the nose, perhaps, but such stuff didn't become cliché without having often been, perhaps omitting some detail, a lot like life.

But as I got closer to Ballsbridge my step, and mood, began to lighten.

It was *over*.

The bullshit. The creative anguish, and yes, the ironies, the contradictions. So damned *many* of them. Fifteen years earlier, I'd conceived this show – and here we'd been, in Dublin, Ireland, forgodsake. For its *third* production! No agents, no high-powered negotiations. On its merits alone – or what were by then left of them.

By anyone's standards a fairly big fucking deal. A remarkable ride, actually. The kind most playwrights, authors, composers and lyricists would goddam *kill* for.

So, for me to not revel in that – was I – what? Spoiled? Sure. Some, anyway. But I submit that wanting it one's own way is part of the territory. Like *all* artists I am at heart a control-nut. We *want* our visions to turn out the way *we* picture them, our passions expressed as we *feel* them, and – well, you get my drift. Short of that is – dissatisfaction, frustration, and sometimes – yes, again – rage.

Next day I flew home to Holly, Malibu, and a further, *very* welcome spirit-boost. Adding to the latter was my eager immersion in turning out my first novel – and the fresh takes the narrative form afforded, not only about storytelling.

The process of writing *The Sixteenth Man* was fascinating and, best of all, I loved the new, daily inside-my-head problems the medium presented, the more difficult, the better. The Susan Isaacs-inspired alternating chapter approach was working exactly as I hoped it would. Along with the satisfaction of forward motion and many moments of pleasure came those good-old, always reassuring doubts about my ability to bring it off. But most fascinating were in dealing with the contrasts between prose and screenplay writing, and my surprise at the attitudes I was bringing to it – many of which I didn't know I had.

I was struck then, and continue to be, by how many ways my scriptwriting background helped me – in the areas of brevity, focus and especially, a visual sense. I don't mean writing descriptions of place, or people, which because of my tastes in reading novels, I preferred to leave largely to the reader's imagination. I found that one of my biggest divergences from accepted style was imagining what my actors were doing within a scene; their gestures and body-language. In effect, directing them.

While I brought no major stylistic intentions – or pretensions – to the task, a particular convention of novel writing had baffled and irritated me for years. Now that I was entering the game, it occurred to me that here was my chance to act on it. The topic: dialogue attribution – and what I had long regarded as the rampant, mindless use of 'he said,' or worse, the redundant (following a question-mark) 'she asked,' and the like. All of which, to my mind, suggest that the characters are standing there with hands at their sides.

This, in a medium wherein critics tend to celebrate poetic, often tortured and for me, tedious descriptions of place or weather.

I was aware that many highly regarded and/or successful writers and teachers recommend such usage as a kind of epitome of simplicity, but I saw it as a kind of contradiction. Why, I'd often asked myself, would experienced, quality writers who otherwise (rightly) bust their humps to avoid using clichés and word-or-phrase repetition, surrender to these without guilt? Or, viewed another way, when does a particular phrase cease being 'economical,' and morph into laziness and formula?

Moreover, I'd wondered, would it be possible to write an entire novel without *ever* employing *any* of those phrases – *any* direct, conventional 'he said'/'she said' attribution – and yet maintain clarity for the reader? So, as I began writing *The Sixteenth Man*, I set that as another of my private, sneaky goals.

I soon learned that I was far from the first to do so, but as it turned out, the self-imposition of that demand yielded unexpected side-benefits. Among those, it definitely contributed to finding my 'voice,' as well as informing my approach overall.

In other ways, I was venturing into really alien territory. I knew almost nothing about the fiction publishing business and its arcane rules. So, to that end I began to take advantage of the writers conferences at which I was speaking. Switching roles when I wasn't teaching, I became one of the wannabes, soaking up as much as I could about finding a literary agent, book – and self – promotion, and other areas, as well as brain-picking the published novelists among my fellow presenters.

I suppose consistent with who I am, one of the industry's customs leapt at me, *immediately* pushing buttons. I found the oft-used terms, 'submit' and 'submission,' not at all to my taste.

Nonetheless, I was determined to learn the rules of this new game, in which I very much wanted to become a player.

One of the protocols was/is the agent query letter. Not something I ever encountered in the entertainment business, I was cautioned about the need to write an effective one, and that it must follow a particular form. On what turned out to be excellent advice, I purchased a wonderful paperback, *The Shortest Distance Between You and a Published Book*, by Susan Page. In it, along with guidance on a lot of other relevant topics, Ms. Page laid out a paragraph-by-paragraph matrix for such letters. I put it to immediate use, devoting an entire day to composing my first such missive. After much careful rereading and tweaking, I faxed it at 10:30 on a Sunday night to my prime target, one of New York's very highest-profile agents, the legendary Albert Zuckerman.

So effectively terrific was Page's advice that my phone rang at 7:30 the following morning: "Hello. This is Al Zuckerman. Send me your pages…" Whoa!

Then, he quickly added: "But wait. Have you read my book…?"

I told him I hadn't.

"It's *Writing the Blockbuster Novel*. Read it – then send your pages."

"Thanks, Al. I will." I did read it, and learned from him. Particularly about point-of-view, which I hadn't had to worry about very much in film and TV. In TV series especially, the house-number was simply that one did not write two scenes in a row from which the main character was absent. So, after a few relevant tweaks, I shipped my pages to Al. He responded with a few thoughtful comments and suggestions, and asked to see – when I'd finished it – the full manuscript.

Less encouraging, I sent my query letter to some twenty other agents. While the responses weren't as prompt as Zuckerman's, some asked why a writer with my credits needed to write queries. Not, I thought, an unreasonable question. Little did I know...

Several said they wanted to read some pages.

All of them passed.

Surprised rather than discouraged, I assumed that they were either being honest, feeling that they couldn't sell the book, or – more typically for me – that they were out of their minds.

Neither mattered, really, because I knew I was writing a solid, entertaining yarn. It also struck me that if I wasn't so well equipped ego-wise, this agent-seeking dance could be hurtful and disheartening in the extreme.

On an incidental but not irrelevant note, a bit of research revealed an interesting statistic: 78% of the novels sold in America are written by *twelve* people. More sobering: I regard many of those as – at best – second-or-third-rate writers. Given what I had learned over time about the commerce-side of the arts, I was way less than astonished. I have, ever since discovering those sales-figures, advised my writing students to take heart from them.

FORTY-SIX
Once Again, The New Kid on the Block—Sort of

IN AUTUMN OF 1999, I finished the umpteenth draft of *The Sixteenth Man*. Finally satisfied with the result, thanks to Holly's many, many insightful, constructive notes, I resumed the agent-query routine, my letter now containing the phrase "just completed novel."

The responses were just as desultory as they'd been the first time around, with few of them interested in looking at any of it.

Per Albert Zuckerman's request, I sent him the full manuscript, which he'd promised to read promptly. He did, and wrote to me at some length, commenting on its (for him) too-thin texture, citing his problems with its "mystery structure," especially the lack of an onstage villain (there are two, actually), admonishing me that it's a "big mistake to write a novel from the point of view of the camera." He closed with the following: "If you have the time, energy, and financial resources and are desperate to become a novelist, I'll help you."

Now, I was willing to grant that his notes, and the offer, were well-intended, but...

On another side – hello?

Did it mean *nothing* that I had for years been writing *very commercial fiction*? Telling stories that hooked, and entertained and satisfied *millions* of people, *and* was *very* well-paid for those efforts? That I just *might* know what I was doing?

Obviously, in whatever world he resided, it did not.

Re: Zuckerman's comment about writing narrative from the camera's POV, my response was: "Al, the reader *is* the camera."

Put another way – then unspoken: Deliver me – *please* – from such horseshit 'literary' conventions.

Including 'he said.'

At that point no publishing houses had rejected my novel because I hadn't even been able to find an agent to represent it. This, contrasted to my more-than-two-decades of success as a writer was telling me – *very* clearly – that I was entering yet another alternate world.

Who the fuck *were* these people?

My patience-gauge was hovering on *Empty*. The following weekend, with that question still resonating, I spotted a fascinating advertisement in the *Book Review* sections of both *The New York Times* and *The Los Angeles Times*. Featuring photographs of two smiling, attractive women, co-authors who, the copy said, had chosen to have their new novel, their third, published by iUniverse.

The ad went on to explain that iUniverse was new, unique in the business, specializing in something just as new: *Print-On-Demand*. An intriguing term I'd not heard of, I visited their website, where I became even more fascinated. Their books, trade paperbacks, were produced, one copy at-a-time, by a computer-like machine. Each copy, complete with a laminated, full-color cover, was printed and bound in about five minutes. My interest began to diminish however as I read on.

Essentially it was a vanity-publishing setup, wherein an author pays to have a book printed. Which, I had already learned, was of course a traditional *no-no* for 'real' writers. This operation was distinguished by the modest initial fee, made possible because the *on-demand* feature meant that a large-quantity print-order was not required.

Their website went on to explain that upon payment, the author's book would be designed, covers included, an ISBN number assigned, *and* the title advertised for sale online at Amazon, Barnes & Noble and other such outlets, as well as being available for bookstores to order.

Plus – and this was a biggie – they *guaranteed* that the book would be stocked by *all* of B&N's brick-and-mortar stores!

A quick web search, however, revealed some not-so-positive aspects. One catch involved non-B&N store sales. Unlike books from conventional publishers, a *POD* book, once ordered, was *not* returnable. A peculiarity of the industry, definitely a key component of retail bookstores' survival, is that books they're unable to sell can be sent back to the publisher for a full refund.

Another problem with *POD* was getting reviewed.

Still, as I turned it over in my mind, what easily outweighed those negatives was – I could get my book published in a *hurry* – *and* it would be carried in those *hundreds* of B&N mall bookstores across the country! So, unable to find a whole lot wrong with that, yet acutely aware of the stigma attached to vanity-presses, I e-mailed a query letter for *The Sixteenth Man* to iUniverse. I emphasized my background, and added a limitation/proposition intended as my *Hook*. While I was *not* willing to pay them *anything* for publishing my novel, I was offering it, along with myself as a promotable poster-boy: the professional writer who chose to go around the system.

Actually, the professional telling the business to go fuck itself describes it a whole lot better.

I hit *Send*, and twenty-five minutes later they got back to me, asking to see the manuscript.

Now – call me 'shallow,' but I have to admit I'm a pushover for that kind of attention. I sent the file off to them. While awaiting their response I tracked down and touched base with one of the authors pictured in the advertisement, learning that she felt she was being well-served by the iUniverse people. Moreover, Holly and I visited several mall Barnes & Noble stores and were impressed to observe that all were indeed carrying iUniverse titles. Even better, they were prominently displayed on racks attached to end-caps of each aisle, as well as several titles conspicuously featured on posters!

Several days later the iUniverse folks informed me that they wanted to publish my novel on my terms, that they would indeed use me as an advertisement, even offering me a higher-than-normal royalty. They further assured me that my book would definitely be featured in all those Barnes & Noble stores.

Done! My novel would be published, and for sale, in two months – *and* I didn't have to pay a 15% commission to an agent. I couldn't find a lot to complain about.

Very satisfied, I quickly followed up on advice I'd received from published authors I knew who'd impressed upon me the need to obtain blurbs for the front and back covers. I could not have been more flattered by the quotes given me by mystery luminaries Dick Lochte, Bill Link, Gerry Petievich and Jerry Ludwig. Not pleased with the cover design iUniverse sent for my approval, I sketched a rough concept and sent it to my daughter-the-illustrator, Lauren Scheuer, who quickly did a wonderful job on the finished art.

In keeping with that I'd learned about the vital necessity for *BSP* (*Blatant Self-Promotion*). A need that becomes obvious with a visit to your local bookstore, with the thousands of book titles therein vying for attention. Thus, I hired prominent book publicist Milton Kahn.

My happy belief that I'd beaten the system, however, went into quick and infuriating turnaround.

During the period between making my deal, and *The Sixteenth Man*'s release, a major setback occurred – one which I was powerless to change. Presumably because of the effectiveness of iUniverse's ad campaign (the one that had caught my attention), Barnes & Noble management saw a major problem developing. They were faced with the prospect of having to stock hundred and hundreds of iUniverse titles, many if not most of which would be of less than professional-quality writing.

So, they abruptly withdrew from their commitment, refusing to market _any_ iUniverse books in their stores.

Shitshitshitshit!

My protests were futile on several counts. The first: our contract did not include that retailing commitment. While I could arguably have sued that, verbal or not, it was binding, there were too many potential downsides – from countersuits to legal expenses to cancellation and more. I was already out-of-pocket for publicity. Adding to that, *all* of the personnel at iUniverse with whom I'd been dealing, from the CEO on down, were suddenly replaced. *None* of the new people were made aware of their predecessors' plans to promote my novel and my credentials. So they did nothing. Which included ignoring my attempts to inform them of the basis for my deal in the first place.

The book came out, and Milt Kahn promptly got me booked on a number of radio and TV shows, in *The N.Y. Post*, as well as placing prominent mention in Liz Smith's nationally syndicated newspaper column, and elsewhere.

I managed to get a few excellent reviews online and in publications such as *Ellery Queen Magazine*, plus appearing on my friend Connie Martinson's wonderful TV book show. Between Milt and myself, we kept the new iUniverse people apprised of our publicity moves. Finally they *did* take the cue, planting a fairly major story about me and my novel in *The Wall Street Journal*.

I was, if only partway, into the Book Life. With Milt's intuitive and inventive promotion, and me hawking the novel at conferences and the like, the results were, for *POD*, then-record-but-still-desultory sales of about 3,000 copies.

Further, my almost-movie deal for *The Sixteenth Man* reconfirmed my long-held belief that in Hollywood especially, life doesn't imitate art – it mimics satire.

Sara Altshul, a producer who'd been shopping my treatment informed me that she had both good-and-bad news from Barry Diller. Uh-huh – the Barry Diller who'd opted to drop my *No Place to Run* series on the eve of shooting the pilot. Diller was then heading up USA TV movies. The upside: he *loved* my book and wanted to put it into script development immediately.

"Except…" Sara continued: "He – uh – doesn't want it to be about the JFK assassination."

Sigh…

I mean, it's hard to invent that kind of stuff – or to describe it without people saying something on the order of: "Get *out*!" Which was just about all that I could muster.

Ms. Altshul and I quickly 'took a meeting' with one of Diller's 'people,' during which the offer was confirmed, as was their refusal of our plea to consider doing the story as-written.

Then, two days later, before I'd chosen which way to go, and though I was leaning emphatically toward "No!" the decision was made for me. Another phenomenon imposed itself, this one not all that different from what had happened with my publisher. Diller and everyone under his command departed USA TV. As frequently happens in The Biz, lest the new people become – *yech* – tainted by the previous regime's projects, *all* of those were summarily dumped.

Though I still missed the immediacy, the antic social fun of series television – as I always will – I found that I was enjoying writing books. Especially the attendant pleasure of, in the case of fiction, living with my characters longer and more intimately, developing them more fully, and immersing myself in a project for months – or years. The opportunity – without any need to be furtive – to make a personal statement or two.

I also liked the freedom to choose, to write what I felt like writing. Thus, for a change of pace from the thriller I'd just completed, I elected to try a non-fiction piece.

For about ten years I had been teaching writing, evenings at UCLA Extension, occasionally guest-teaching at other colleges, and as a presenter at various writers conferences across the country. To hundreds of grateful, nugget-hungry wannabes I had been passing along the many great, practical, 100% literary-theory-free, *this-is-the-way-you-do-it* lessons I'd learned in TV. For many of these conversational talks I'd worn a microphone attached to a pocket tape-recorder. I'd had the tapes transcribed, and had accumulated about 350 pages, a lot of it repetitious, of course. Nonetheless they appeared to be readily workable into manuscript form. So, along with adding some new stuff, I began to rewrite/edit that material into what would become *Fiction Writing Demystified*.

Since self-publishing of non-fiction did not seem to carry a stigma, and since we'd done it before with the book-version of *Plots Unlimited*, Holly and I decided to issue it under our own imprint, *Ashleywilde*. It was nicely-received, selected as a *Writer's Digest Book Club* Alternate, it received rave-comments from such big-name authors as Linda Fairstein and Jerry B. Jenkins. *FWD* was also chosen as required reading for a number of fiction writing courses, and along with both digital and audio versions continues to do well in the marketplace.

On the *JACK* front, interest from New York Theatre people continued. A backers' reading was scheduled, which was exciting in another way. A book titled *The Kennedy Tapes* had been published. I quickly read it, and an aspect of the meetings about the Cuban Missile Crisis had instantly, excitingly told me that we *must* include a version of it in the show. Not unlike the *Dad, I'm Not Joe* number, this was *so* revealing of Jack Kennedy's character that it was *essential*. As was its dramatic value. When I told Will about it, he agreed. From the tape-transcriptions, it practically wrote itself in song. There, in a roomful of Generals, Admirals and others commenting on how many troops, vessels and airstrikes would be required, Jack Kennedy seemed startlingly inside his own head. In fact, he was commenting in a kind of operatic counterpoint:

"What does he (Khrushchev) *want?*"

"What does he *really* mean?"

"*Why* is he doing this...?"

I wrote it, and Will set it to music in time for our New York reading. Again, I requested that Will do the same with my opening. As usual, that was infuriatingly ignored.

The Missile Crisis scene played very well, however, a solid addition to our show. But the reading failed to attract investors. That, I figured, was that for *JACK.*

Until, some months later, I received from Will a newly revised draft of the libretto. Significantly changed, with scenes cut and replaced, I promptly got back to him with my comments. Disagreeing with all of his changes, and judging them not worth tweaking, I made it clear that I approved of *none* of what he was proposing.

At which point he informed me that the changes were *not* a proposal. That it was in fact the new script, which he'd been reworking with several of his New York associates.

My rage is difficult to describe. As was his utter, twisted arrogance! Put another way, I was as close to 'speechless' as I have ever come. Had he been in the room with me, within physical reach rather than on the phone from New York, I might well have become violent.

When I got past my mercifully brief silence, I laid it out for him, succinctly and with finality. I reminded him that the show could *not* be staged or performed in *any* way without both of our signatures. I also pointed out that when I took him on as my partner/collaborator – it was with *him* – *not* with two or three other people to be named at a later time. "...And *finally,* Will, the *only* way this show is *ever* going to happen again is if *both* you *and*

I sign off on *every* word, and *every* note of music. *Both of us!*" I hung up the phone.

That's where things remained for more than a decade. To the point, actually, of my declining a pair of offers for the show to be produced – one at a college and the other a small regional theatre. The show's only other signs of life during that period: an Original Cast audio recording of the script as it had been performed in Connecticut, produced by Bill Zeffiro, our original Richard Nixon. Also, a reading of that version, at Colby College in Maine, organized and staged by Ms. Lauren Sterling, who like Zeffiro had been an enthusiastic member of our Goodspeed cast. Will performed the role of Joseph P. Kennedy, Sr. It was at that performance that I had my first contact with him since I'd ended our phone conversation some six or seven years earlier.

One of *very* few areas of agreement: despite its shortcomings, that initial Goodspeed version remained the best of them – the most faithful to what we'd envisioned.

Because I'd so enjoyed writing *The Sixteenth Man*, and felt that I had much more to learn about the genre, I decided my next project would be another thriller novel. I chose for my story-spine my long-ago TV series concept/pilot movie about two young brother-fugitives: *No Place to Run*. A vehicle that continued to fascinate me, it was however instantly obvious that its dated, overused Organized Crime Bad Guys theme could stand some freshening. Moreover, I sensed that the stakes needed to be ratcheted dramatically upward.

Moreover, I became excited by the realization that if I raised them in a particular way, I might be able to use this yarn as I had very satisfyingly with *The Sixteenth Man*. In that case, to air out my view of what and who was *really* behind the JFK Assassination.

This time about what I believed was behind an event that, *as it was* happening, not surprisingly registered for me in ways quite different than it did for many others.

9/11.

FORTY-SEVEN
Finding Myself Still Out-of-Step (and Shocked—*Shocked!*)

Thus, having – for the purposes of my novel – the beginnings of the higher stakes I was looking for, including a vision of a few manageable-level heavies, I went to work on *No Place to Run*. But *not* before adding one more challenge: I decided that instead of two young brothers as fugitives, as had been the setup in my original series concept and pilot teleplay, the older sibling would be a 24 year-old woman. The choice was only partly commercial: I wanted to see if I could write such a character, get into her head in a believable, convincing way.

The book was in-progress when the *9/11 Commission Report* was published. I purchased a copy the first day it was available and, not unpredictably, it refuted *nothing* of what I posited in my story. Instead, *all* of the red flags I had encountered in my research were either ignored by the Commission or, rather lamely and unsatisfactorily, explained away.

The many other unresolved issues and doubts about the actual events of that day, and the months preceding them, remain. As does the media's slavish cooperation with the government's calculated rewriting of history. As I write this years later, the entire event is still open to *very* reasonable, non-nutcase question from those of us who might choose to ask.

As with what I posited in *The Sixteenth Man* about the truth of Dallas, I feel certain that, at least in its essentials, I got this one right as well.

My passionate hope for *No Place to Run?* That in addition to entertaining, it might '*reach*' a few people – hell, I'd settle for six or seven – and make them *think*.

About what our nation has become and what, by *very* outside chance, it might be – *if* we were to try – and *if* there's still time…

No Place to Run was published in 2009 by a small house, Sterling & Ross. It received some excellent reviews, and I was honored to be invited to become a part of a web group, *Patriots Question 9/11*. It was extremely gratifying to find myself more than just 'not alone,' but rather, in some *very* distinguished – and startlingly unexpected – company. Among them, *hundreds* of prominent Military, Intelligence, Law Enforcement Officials, Engineers, Professors, entertainment and media professionals, and others. Hardly a bunch of riff-raff Conspiracy Freaks. As a result, I appeared with several of them on a number of panels.

Getting the novel published had *begun* to teach me something that didn't quite register with me for several years. It started with the book's rejection by the top guy at a major publisher. He wrote the following to my agent: "I really like Tom's writing, but frankly, I'm offended by his premise…"

The lesson? Faced after some disappointment that *No Place to Run* failed to catch on – even as well as had *The Sixteenth Man* – it was something *key* that, when I finally accepted it, allowed a lot of other things to fall into place:

History, once it is written, becomes part of the public's 'comfort zone.'

444

Thus it is almost *never* questioned. *Even* when there are doubts from the beginning. No matter how many lies and distortions it might have contained.

Obvious – and true. Startlingly so, even now, as I read or listen to or view this or that erudite, insightful commentator arguing a cause and/or effect, while invariably omitting this or that reality. Over and over, I used to find myself mentally punching-up their arguments, wondering *why* they didn't add this or that underlying, so-clear-to-me point.

I no longer do so, because now, I understand. In fact, I sympathize with them as I sense the *extreme* challenge each must face, in creating a convincing argument without *ever* going to those deeper truths.

The ones that *must* remain unspoken.

The lies we choose to live with.

Think about it. Consider some of the examples. Dallas, Pearl Harbor, Manifest Destiny, Vietnam... The list *does* go on – and on.

In fact, it may well be true that *any* society, in order to live with itself, to continue existing, *needs* to tell itself lies, and to *believe* them. That necessity obviously and most desperately extends to the families of military people who lose their lives – or body-parts, or their sanity.

The validity of those sacrifices *must never be doubted*. At least not in public forums or media.

Aspects of that realization – of viewing things with that filter in place – extend further, helping to account for a certain susceptibility – a passionate *need*, really – on the part of *masses* of people. For myths, for magical explanations – *those*, especially – in the form of religion, and other belief-systems that are unable to withstand even the shallowest of intellectual questioning.

In any case, that's how I learned to *not* waste my time trying to change peoples' minds.

Thus, I wrote my third novel, *Cross Purposes*, with a single intention: to entertain. A satisfying and not-unchallenging venture in itself.

Accompanying that has been renewed, satisfying and *very* promising interest in *JACK*, this from New York theatre people. Especially pleasing, this has been stoked by the unflagging, ongoing love for the show from those *original* cast members, Lauren Sterling and William Zeffiro, plus a few others, including the extraordinary Michael Butler. To the point that, as I write this, there is the real, almost unspeakably exciting possibility of seeing *JACK* staged – *my* way.

The possible End-Frame is nearly beyond imagining. That Dream wherein my passion for telling the story of our last *great* leader, performed *my* way finally reaches a wide audience.

FORTY-EIGHT
Coda

THE PAST IS NOT A PLACE I NORMALLY RESIDE. Nor do I often revisit it, because in doing so, while many of the memories are wonderful, they remind me that so much of it is behind me. It was thus with some reluctance that I undertook this memoir.

But, over the course of writing it I found that I've truly enjoyed reflecting on – and for the first time fully appreciate – the overwhelming number of fortuitous turns in my life. From the often unintentional results of my parents' efforts, to the many remarkable people with whom I've been privileged to interact, to the multiple careers and attendant fun. But topping it *all*, the almost unbelievable randomness of Holly's and my chance meeting, leading in turn to so much else. Revisiting all of that has made me newly, acutely and so gratefully aware of the extraordinary good luck that has informed so much of my journey.

It's also helped me to realize that one of my most valuable gifts seems to have been a singular instinct, a knack, I suppose, for recognizing luck when it arose, and then taking advantage of it.

Yet, that fails to account for my overall, *incredibly* good fortune. The mitzvahs of physical and mental health, of literally wallowing in the delight and presence of my amazing, ever entertaining and gorgeous Holly. Her unflagging support, affection, amazing wisdom and insights, all of them gifts, I am convinced, of her being so totally together and guiltlessly comfortable with who she is. Additionally, there are our lovely, truly interesting children and their families, who are leading enjoyable, productive lives, plus our extraordinary grandchildren, beginning theirs.

Moreover, the process has enabled me to appreciate on whole new levels the many wonderful, colorful, stimulating, entertaining friends I've been so privileged to know and enjoy.

For these largely uncontrollable, enabling facets, and the certain knowledge that without them the rest would have been impossible, I feel doubly grateful.

There's another expression of gratitude I'd like to cover before closing. It's directed to Tiger, Panther, Mitty, Little Gray, Pekoe, and most recently Blackie and his sister, Misty. They are the cats who have over the past thirty-five years graced our home and our lives, sharing theirs with us, permitting us to feed, shelter, open doors and otherwise care for them.

These incredibly gentle, lovely little creatures who ask almost nothing of us have, during *every* day of their presence, made me smile. For that, plus their beauty, their unique personalities, the dialogues we've shared, I'm really unable to adequately express my appreciation. *Especially* not for those many priceless, unforgettable moments of connection, when we have peered into – and savored – each other's souls. Even more for the countless times they've lifted my spirits simply by being there in one or another effortless and invariably exquisite pose.

Dredging into so many of my memories, which begot others, and still others, has been I'm sure, far more interesting for me than for you. But I hope nonetheless that this true account of my amazingly fortunate voyage has been worth your time.

A parting suggestion: *Whenever you can, as often as you can – put yourself in luck's way.*

Speaking of which, I have sometimes wondered about my ironclad ego. About the strength it has given me from that certain knowledge that *any*one who rejected me was *WRONG. Could* the imposition of that *so* painfully-acquired asset – to which I attribute so much of the incredible life I've had – actually have been *intended* programming by my parents?

Whether or not it was, I truly wish that I could have thanked them for its immeasurable contribution to the joyous life it – and they – enabled for me...

About which only *one* thing pisses me off – and *massively* so: there's this *clock* on it...

The End

Index

Numbers in **bold** indicate photographs

Kennedy, Teddy 343, 388
King, Warren 50, 101, 104, 127
Klugman, Jack 254-256
Konecky, Isobel Robins 387, 391, 425, 426

Lachman, Mort 237-238, 242, 246, 251, 267, 308
Lansbury, Angela 2, 3, 4, **213**, 252, 254, 330, 347, 350, 353, 355-356, 358, 359, 385, 386, 393, 394, 395, 396, 397, 398, 399, 405, 413, 414, 415, 417, 418, 419-420, 422
Lansbury, Bruce 3, 252, 257-258, 395, 396-397, 398, 412, 413, 414-415, 419
Larkin, Bill 251-252, 266
Larkin, Marj 308
Larson, Glen A. 287, 290-291
Law and Harry McGraw, The 2, **214**, 352, 357, 358, 359-360, 364, 397, 405
Lawrence, Steve 359
Lee, Stan 105-106, 111
Leibman, Ron 260-261
LeMasters, Kim 280-282, 292, 293-294, 301
Levey, Jim 194-195, 275
Levinson, David 317, 319, 320
Levinson, Richard 330, 347, 348, 351, 356, 405
Levy, Dr. Sidney (Sid) 145-146, 147, 151, 152, 154, 163, 171, 198, 202, 203
Lewis, Diana 7, 9
Li'l Abner 131, 133-134
Lily White 423
Linden, Hal 351
Link, William 330, 347, 348, 351, 356, 405, 422, 436
Little Al of the FBI 45
Love on Trial 342-343, 347
Ludwig, Jerry 298, 299, 323, 415, 422, 436

MacKenzie, Patch 296
Maltese Falcon, The 28, 88-89, 331-333, 348, 355
Manimal 291
Mary Perkins – On Stage 112, 144, 182
Masak, Ron 357
Master, The 328-330
Matthews, Gerry 187-188, 189, 191, 192, 193
Maxwell, Gary 207, 225-226, 227, 230, 231
McCullough, Robert 289
McGovern, Elizabeth 273
McKissock, Allan 144, 148-149, 195, 202
McKissock, Harriet 144, 148-149, 195, 202
McKissock, Holly see Sawyer, Holly
McMahon, Bill and Rose 25-26, 28, 37, 51
McMahon, Ruthie Mae see Terry, Ruth
Merson, Marc 261, 298

www.ingramcontent.com/pod-product-compliance
Lightning Source LLC
Chambersburg PA
CBHW060321100426
42812CB00003B/847